RIGHT

MEN

ALSO BY MICHAEL BLISS

Canadian History in Documents (1966)
A Living Profit: Studies in the Social History of Canadian Business, 1883–1911 (1974)
A Canadian Millionaire: The Life and Business Times of Sir Joseph Flavelle, Bart., 1858–1939 (1978)
*Confederation: A New Nationality (1981)
The Discovery of Insulin (1982)
Banting: A Biography (1984)
*Years of Change: 1967–1985 (1986)
Northern Enterprise: Five Centuries of Canadian Business (1987)
Plague: A Story of Smallpox in Montreal (1991)

*for young adults

RIGHT HONOURABLE MEN

The Descent of Canadian Politics
from Macdonald to Mulroney

MICHAEL BLISS

A Phyllis Bruce Book
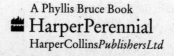
HarperPerennial
HarperCollins*PublishersLtd*

The publisher acknowledges permission to reprint the following: "W.L.M.K." from *Collected Poems of F.R. Scott* by F.R. Scott. Used by permission of the Canadian Publishers, McClelland & Stewart, Toronto. "William Lyon Mackenzie King" from *Alligator Pie* by Dennis Lee. Used by permission of Sterling Lord Associates.

First published in hardcover by HarperCollins Publishers Ltd: 1994
First HarperPerennial edition: 1995

Canadian Cataloguing in Publication Data

Bliss, Michael, 1941-
    Right honourable men : the descent of Canadian politics from Macdonald to Mulroney

1st HarperPerennial edition.
"A Phyllis Bruce book."
Includes index.
ISBN 0-00-638062-X

1. Canada – Politics and government.   2. Prime ministers – Canada.
I. Title.

FC502.B55 1995   971.05   C95-930435-5
F1033.B55 1995

---

95 96 97 98 99 ❖ HC 10 9 8 7 6 5 4 3 2 1

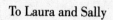

To Laura and Sally

Contents

Acknowledgements

Jack Granatstein and David Bercuson read the whole of this manuscript in an earlier form and Craig Brown read parts of it. These good friends and sharp-eyed critics suggested many improvements. The final polishing of the chapters took place in the weeks when the members of my Canadian Political Tradition seminar at the University of Toronto were helping enrich my understanding of the subject. So a special thanks to Michael Allibon, Jenny Barrett, Ed Blackburn, Kirk Brown, David Hogg, Natalie Ledgerwood, Catherine Luke, Brent McGaw, David Reble, Krista Slade, Ian Urquhart, Robert Ventresca, and Steve Williams. My summer studies in politics and peace of mind on Prince Edward Island, during which we are particularly helped by Eric and Lois Sinclair, have also been essential.

Phyllis Bruce pushed me into getting down to writing this book and then, through her wonderfully deft editing, showed me how to do it right. Jim Spence unwittingly helped by lending me a key book for thirty-three years; it has now been returned. The usual but no less heartfelt thanks to the wonderful family, Liz, Jamie, Laura, and Sally.

Michael Bliss
Springfield, P.E.I.
June, 1994

Introduction

Prime Ministers and Power

This is a book of biographical studies of Canada's most important prime ministers. I wrote it because in the last several years I have come to realize how deeply our future hinges on the quality of political leadership we can produce. Paradoxically, you will see, I believe the central task of Canadian leadership is to adjust to the limits of power in our evolving democracy.

The profiles are interpretative, analytical, sometimes anecdotal, and largely self-contained. You can dip into the book at the beginning, middle, or end. But I use the careers of prime ministers as pegs on which to hang quite a bit of more general Canadian political history and a number of arguments about the thematic evolution of Canadian politics. I hope these chapters can be read profitably by everyone from secondary school students to political science graduates, and that they will be read by all aspiring prime ministers.

Broad as I have tried to make it, my focus is necessarily limited. Many important themes and individuals are absent from these pages. Some readers will notice, for example, that the political left, as it presented itself through sixty years of the activities of the Co-operative Commonwealth Federation and New Democratic Party, hardly appears here. As Trudeau would say, tough. The CCF-NDP never attained power in national elections, and it seldom exercised the influence its adherents and court historians have claimed. Concepts of social justice and a welfare state for Canada, for example, were introduced to the national political agenda by Liberals, years before the birth of the CCF. The most important individual in creating the Canadian welfare state was not J.S. Woodsworth, but the much-maligned Mackenzie King.

These chapters do not add up to a bottom line on governing Canada. There are no quick maxims, no easy recipe for what Brian Mulroney once called "country running." It is absurd to believe that history or politics can be turned into a "science." While broad historical patterns do recur, while some factors contribute to success or failure in almost every era, the river of history is constantly changing. Each generation faces new problems, calling for new responses. Every prime minister has been unique, hence the attraction and strength of a biographical approach. The two strongest prime ministers in Canadian history were Mackenzie King and Pierre Elliott Trudeau. What did they have in common? High intelligence, an abiding faith in popular sovereignty, and the integrated personality's taste for solitude. But who can imagine Mackenzie King in buckskin, paddling his canoe through white water? Or Pierre Trudeau consulting a medium?

I subtitle these chapters "the descent of Canadian politics" for several reasons. This is a chronological presentation, organized around a descent through time, from the mid-nineteenth century to the end of the twentieth. As well, one of my main themes is the descent of power in our monarchical/parliamentary system. Sir John A. Macdonald did not like or believe in democracy and his approach to government reflected that. But democracy in the form of universal suffrage gradually came to Canada, and in our time has evolved towards new forms of direct democracy as power shifts away from politicians and backroom manipulators. The October 1992 constitutional referendum, in which Canadians told their rulers that the Charlottetown Accord was not acceptable, signalled a profound descent of power from legislatures to the people.

A more problematic connotation of "descent" is of a decline in quality. Many, perhaps most, Canadians instinctively believe that has happened in our system of government. Where are the giants of old, the Macdonalds, Lauriers, Bordens? Where are the leaders we yearn for in troubled times? Why don't better men and women go into Parliament?

I have mixed feelings about this kind of grumbling. No one who reads the profile of Brian Mulroney in chapter ten will conclude that I rank him with Canada's great prime ministers. Nor do I believe that Joe Clark or John Turner had the capacity to do a significantly better job of governing Canada during the Mulroney years. And it is probably true that Canadians have been more estranged from Parliament and the country's national political elites in recent times than in any past era. The leaders fell out of touch and we longed for better ones to govern us more wisely.

It does not necessarily follow that there has been a marked deterioration in the quality of men and women in politics. Mackenzie King was a smarter, more deft, and more successful politician than any of his predecessors. Pierre Elliott Trudeau was a man of quality by any standard, as even his opponents admitted. These pages say little about the evolving quality of Cabinet ministers or backbenchers, but my impression is that in recent years prime ministers have had better Cabinet material to work with, and better-educated, harder-working, more dedicated MPs to choose their Cabinets from, than Macdonald, Laurier, or Borden did. The quality of MPs elected in 1993, for example, was very high. I think we are attracting better, more idealistic Canadians into politics. We have trouble understanding this because we are raising our expectations of public life faster than the politicians can respond.

I also believe that Brian Mulroney and Sir John A. Macdonald had more in common than their ability to win Tory majorities. Mulroney possessed many of Macdonald's political skills and some of his personal characteristics. The Irish Canadian and the Scots Canadian spoke the same political language, thought alike on several issues, and would have swapped many a story and slapped many a back together. Had they been colleagues, Mulroney would have been an excellent minister in a Macdonald government.

But good government in the 1980s required a higher order of personal and political talents than the politics of the 1880s. The "descent" of Canadian politics since Macdonald's day has been a devolution of power from political elites towards the people, who in turn expect higher standards of performance from their leaders. The Mulroney Conservatives had not evolved. In certain crucial ways they were still locked into nineteenth-century attitudes, led by a man who was more of a throwback than a modern-day mutant. Organizations that are only as good now as they were a century ago are headed for trouble. Thus the annihilation of the Conservatives in the 1993 election.

It remains to be seen whether the new breed of politician, either the rejuvenated Liberals who took power under Jean Chrétien in 1993, or the progeny of the new populism, Preston Manning's Reformers, will give Canadians a higher quality of leadership in the twenty-first century. In the epilogue I note some of the difficult issues all politicians will have to confront. The early 1990s were a turning-point in our history, economically and socially, as well as politically, and the job of government will get much harder.

* * *

The idea of writing a book like this was on my mind for many years. In the heyday of interest in Canadian political history, the 1960s, several journalists wrote books profiling first ministers, and a series of academic lectures on prime-ministerial political ideas was published. Nothing in the way of collective biography has been written since. There is no Canadian equivalent of Richard Hofstadter's classic study, *The American Political Tradition and the Men Who Made It,* or Peter Clarke's more recent analysis of British prime ministers, *A Question of Leadership: From Gladstone to Thatcher.*

One reason why the gap did not get filled was historians' declining interest in politics. With some outstanding exceptions, those of us who write and talk about our country's past spent the better part of a quarter-century being more interested in non-political areas of Canadian life. We wrote about business and labour, the building of cities, the role of women, the contributions of ethnic minorities, the evolution of regions, the history of medicine, and many other varieties of "social" history. My own interests as a scholar reflected that eclecticism. I never thought of myself as a political historian.

But as a graduate student I was exposed to the grand tradition of Canadian political history, notably in Donald Creighton's graduate seminar at the University of Toronto in the mid-1960s. I always paid attention to Canadian politics as a citizen, and gradually found myself commenting occasionally in the media on current issues and individuals. Then the constitutional debates of 1987–1992 woke me up and reminded me that governments are our most powerful institutions.

During the five years when issues relating to the Meech Lake and Charlottetown constitutional accords were often at the top of the national agenda, I was struck repeatedly by the historical vacuum in which we talk about Canada. Canadians do not think about the historical evolution of their political and constitutional system, they do not seem to know about it, and many of them, including many intellectuals and politicians, and even historians, do not seem to care.

Whatever one felt about the specific constitutional issues of those years (I opposed both the Meech Lake and the Charlottetown Accord), it was dismaying to see the low level of knowledge and discourse about where the country has been and the leadership it has had. In October 1991 I voiced some of my concerns in a Creighton memorial lecture on the occasion of the University of Toronto history department's centennial celebrations. I entitled the lecture "Privatizing the Mind: The Sundering of Canadian History, the Sundering of Canada," and was immediately challenged by some in the audience to do something about the situation I was lamenting. So I decided to write a book about the public life of Canada, and at the same time fill the gap in prime-ministerial studies.

Is this the "history from the top down" that historians have fashionably scorned? Yes. *Right Honourable Men* is about the movement of history, politics, and power from the top down in society, as an elite-driven, deference-based British colonial system has matured into a chaotic, individualistic North American democracy. It is a study of how leadership has coped or failed to cope with the challenges posed by these and other developments. It's Canadian history from Parliament Hill.

And yes, it is a study of the "great man" in Canadian history, plus a few not-so-great men (though I neglect most of our short-term failed PMs and a couple of the full-term second-rankers). But I am not a Hegelian. I do not believe that political leaders, least of all prime ministers of Canada, are personifications of the world spirit. I do not believe that individuals alone can easily move mountains or with a snap of their fingers change the course of history. Sometimes leaders are almost powerless to hold back the tides of history; sometimes they cheerfully float with the tides, their only political principle being to take credit for the phases of the moon.

On the other hand, there is no flaw in seeing human history as the sum of individual lives, as collective biography. The interaction of humans with the situations they confront, what Creighton called the interplay of character and circumstance, is the warp and woof of all history, and the raw material of this book. Some people, of course, have much more opportunity than others to make a difference. Individual prime ministers of Canada are, like it or not, the most powerful people in the country. Their decisions will have more influence on the Canadian people's lives than any other Canadian's actions (though perhaps not as much influence as the decisions of United States presidents or other world leaders).

When Brian Mulroney decided to act as chairman/mediator for a league of first ministers around the table at the Meech Lake discussions, instead of speaking for Canada, he took actions that changed the course of recent Canadian history (though not as drastically as he hoped they would). So did Pierre Elliott Trudeau when he decided to enter politics in 1965, run for the leadership in 1968, reassume the leadership in 1979, and condemn the Meech and Charlottetown accords in 1987 and 1992. No one in the age of Gorbachev, Thatcher, or Trudeau would deny that individuals make a difference. In fact our evolving understanding that free, empowered individuals are the fundamental units of society helps explain the heavy emphasis we put on leadership in modern politics.

But the growth of assertive individualism also limits the ability of leaders to have their way, which is exactly as it should be. Who wants to live in a world where history is made by Napoleons, emperors, kings, dictators, or even conclaves of eleven white, male Canadians? This book is about finding limits to power, and forcing leaders to recognize them. At the end of my story the Prime Minister of Canada has just as much formal power as Sir John A. Macdonald ever had, but much less scope to use it. Macdonald had tremendous leeway, amounting nearly to *carte blanche*, to chart a course for the ship of state. Today the crew and the passengers are much more inclined to tell the captain where to go.

History is better at warning us where not to go than charting an exact route for the future. It shows us what can go wrong, with policies, with egos, with snap decisions. History is the enemy of the short-term perspective, which is one of the deadly occupational hazards of democratic politics. It's true that in the long term we are all dead. But our children and grandchildren inherit our country. We study the past to help us build better for their future. I don't think we did very well at either task in the present-minded, hedonistic, spendthrift years we are trying to put behind us.

But the past has made us, and we can only profit from reflecting on it. This book is very different in design and execution from Hofstadter's *The American Political Tradition*. But his introductory quotation, from the writer John Dos Passos, is an apt way to begin: "In times of change and danger when there is a quicksand of fear under men's reasoning, a sense of continuity with generations gone before can stretch like a lifeline across the scary present."

RIGHT
HONOURABLE
MEN

Whither are we drifting?

Macdonald's low point, during the Pacific Scandal

1

MACDONALD
The Prince of Canada

A hostile newspaper editor called the 1864 Charlottetown Conference on Confederation "the great Intercolonial drunk." The image nicely fits with today's popular view of John A. Macdonald as a whisky-soaked statesman, unhappy with the founding of a four-province Canada because he always had a thirst for a fifth. Macdonald's scholarly biographer, Donald Creighton, helped convey that view to our generation by concluding that Canada's prime minister in the high Victorian era was a throwback to the days of hard-drinking, hard-fighting political rogues: "'the two bottle men,' a Colonial Secretary called them, when one of the duties of the Secretary of the Treasury is said to have been to hold his hat on occasion for the convenience of the First Lord when 'clearing himself' for his speech." The Macdonald story we tell our students in history lectures is of the time he got drunk before a public debate and vomited on the platform while his opponent was speaking—only to recoup by remarking that this was just another case of a Liberal turning his stomach.

It may even have happened. Most men and most politicians drank a lot in those days, and Macdonald was a convivial fellow. The Confederation conferences were particularly convivial occasions. As Brian Mulroney told reporters in 1990, when he was comparing his tactics with the Meech Lake Accord to the methods of the Fathers of Confederation, "the boys ... spent a long time in places other than the library, eh?" George Brown, Macdonald's Liberal opponent and normally a much more sober politician, has left a famous description of the socializing at Charlottetown, which culminated in a four o'clock luncheon party aboard the Canadian delegation's steamer, the *Queen Victoria*:

> The members were entertained at luncheon in princely style. Cartier and I made eloquent speeches—of course—and whether as the result of our eloquence or of the goodness of our champagne, the ice became completely broken, the tongues of the delegates wagged merrily, and the banns of matrimony between all the Provinces of BNA having been formally proclaimed and all manner of persons duly warned there and then to speak or forever after to hold their tongues—no man appeared to forbid the banns and the union was thereupon formally completed and proclaimed!

Of course they had a harder fight than that to get the Confederation scheme accomplished, and Macdonald's drinking habits didn't help. In the last stages, as delegates prepared to gather in London, England, for a final conference, the Canadian government's appearance was delayed for weeks, in part, according to the *Globe*, because Macdonald was drinking too much back in Ottawa to attend to the nation's business. It is not known exactly why, during the London conference, he fell asleep in his hotel room one night with the candle burning, and was lucky to escape from the resulting fire with his life.

Historians know that the whole Confederation movement was a lucky escapade for the men who made it. Without any advance mandate these colonial politicians cooked up a plan of union, sold it to one another, got it through the Canadian legislature without any reference to the people, and rushed vague assenting resolutions through the New Brunswick and Nova Scotia legislatures during a Fenian scare from south of the border. The people of New Brunswick initially rejected the Confederation scheme in an 1865 election, but the pro-Confederation politicians connived with the British government to force a second vote the next year, and sent down large amounts of what Macdonald called "the needful," i.e., cash, to help sway opinion. Nova Scotians felt particularly railroaded by their politicians, and in the first Dominion election, in 1867, elected one supporter of Confederation and eighteen opponents—a kind of Bloc Nova

Scotia—dedicated to getting the province out of Canada. Macdonald had to pacify Nova Scotia with larger subsidies and a Cabinet position for the leading secessionist, Joseph Howe.

Sir John A. was Prime Minister of Canada from 1867 to 1874 and from 1878 until his death in office in 1891. During those years this master manipulator on the Canadian stage, "The Wizard of the North," heaped fifth, sixth, and seventh provinces onto the original four, juggled regional and racial and religious interests, drew the world's longest railway out of Canadian financiers' hats, played a tariff card that turned from a joker into the ace of spades, and held the whole rickety contraption together with smoke, mirrors, and hidden wires.

Macdonald's enemies and most of his supporters knew about the Tories' fine silk threads of patronage, contracts, and party discipline. Macdonald's governments rewarded friends and punished opponents. The Prime Minister and his lieutenants blatantly used all forms of patronage to support their power and build their party. "As soon as Toronto returns Conservative members it will get Conservative appointments," he told his friends there, "but not before." He installed favouritism as a central feature of the unwritten part of the Canadian constitution. Senatorships, janitorships, and all sorts of jobs in between went to loyal party men. Contracts were given only to the "friends" of the government, and, in return, they gave campaign funds to the party. Some of these funds were used in elections to buy votes (the going cash rate was about $10, the equivalent of about $200 in today's currency). Government patronage and party funds supported Conservative newspapers, such as the Montreal *Gazette*, and the Toronto *Mail* and *Empire*. The adoption of a protective tariff or "National Policy" cemented a powerful and grateful block of manufacturers to the party. At election time the Canadian Pacific Railway, built with generous government help, turned itself into "the Conservative party on wheels," supplying money and many good Conservative voters (while sending Liberals up the line to repair track).

As Macdonald grew old in power, becoming something of a national institution, opinion was about equally divided on whether his scheming and manipulation had been noble or cynical. To his admirers, including most of his biographers, the end of building a strong country with a strong national government that could keep a lid on the cacophony of interest groups justified all the means Macdonald used, and supports the judgement of him as a great statesman. "Macdonald (when not drunk) is a really powerful man," an astute British governor observed during the Confederation movement. Better John A. drunk than George Brown sober, Macdonald himself once quipped.

The more critical view was best expressed by the president of the University of Toronto, Sir Daniel Wilson, who wrote that Canada's first prime minister was

> a clever, most unprincipled party leader [who] had developed a system of political corruption that has demoralized the country. Its evils will long survive him.... nevertheless he had undoubtedly a fascinating power of conciliation, which, superadded to his unscrupulous use of patronage, and systematic bribery in every form, has enabled him to play off province against province and hold his own against every enemy but the invincible last antagonist.

This dim view of Macdonald had not prevented Wilson and the university from awarding him an honorary degree. Professors, too, sometimes had flexible principles.

*   *   *

Macdonald was born in Scotland in 1815 and brought to the Kingston area of Upper Canada with his family in 1820. His father was a shopkeeper and miller. The boy became a lawyer and from an early age learned the art of getting ahead in government. In his first surviving letter, written in 1836, Macdonald thanks a friend in high places "for the hint respecting the clerkship of the peace." If it becomes vacant, he adds, "I shall call upon you to exert your kind endeavours on my behalf."

Broadening his ambition, Macdonald became a Kingston alderman in 1843. The next year he was elected to the legislature of the Province of Canada, running as a practical man interested in developing the resources of the young country. He had no use for the Conservative hard-liners of the 1840s, who were fighting to the end against responsible government. The old Tory "Family Compact" clique, he wrote, "with little ability, no political principle, and no strength from numbers, contrive by their union and active bigotry to ... make us and our whole party stink in the nostrils of all liberal minded people."

He called himself a "liberal Conservative," a "progressive conservative," and aimed to broaden the base of the party by bringing in all men willing to work for the progress of the united province. Many Upper Canadian Tories, and many English-speaking Protestants in Lower Canada, for that matter, were instinctively hostile to the motives and aspirations of the province's substantial French-speaking Roman Catholic population, but Macdonald was happy to collaborate with them. An 1856 letter to a Montreal journalist contains one of his most important statements of principle:

No man in his senses can suppose that this country can for a century to come be governed by a totally unfrenchified Govt. If a Lower Canadian Britisher desires to conquer, he must "stoop to conquer." He must make friends with the French; without sacrificing the status of his race or lineage, he must respect their nationality. Treat them as a nation and they will act as a free people generally do—generously. Call them a faction, and they become factious.... So long as the French have 20 votes they will be a power, & must be conciliated.

Even after he first became a minister, briefly in 1847–48, politics only took up part of Macdonald's time. He devoted at least as much of his energies, perhaps more, to getting on in life. He was an active land speculator and company promoter, very much in favour of railway building, foreign investment, immigration, and other practical steps to increase the wealth of the developing province. He fell in love with a cousin on a trip back to Scotland and brought her to Canada, where they were married in 1843 and settled down to make a home and family. But Isabella Clark Macdonald suffered from one of the strange Victorian illnesses, something like chronic fatigue syndrome in our time, had a miserable life in Canada, and died in 1857. Macdonald had been a dutiful husband, although he had decided to stay in politics, and his law practice and private business affairs were given the least priority. At the end of long, troubled days, he often turned to bottled relief.

Upper and Lower Canada were united into a single province, Canada, in 1841, and later in that decade Reformers succeeded in pressuring Great Britain to grant responsible government to Canada and its other North American colonies. Then the Reformers stagnated and gradually disintegrated. In 1854 Macdonald was one of the architects of a new political alliance: of Conservatives with Reformers from Upper Canada to create the Liberal-Conservative Party; and of Liberal-Conservatives with the majority bloc of French-Canadian representatives from Lower Canada, the conservative or Bleu group. That administration evolved into his post-1857 partnership with George-Étienne Cartier as co-premiers of the still-dualistic Province of Canada. When the Macdonald–Cartier alliance seemed to have reached the end of the road in the badly deadlocked legislature of the early 1860s—no government could sustain even a "drinking majority," people said—Macdonald and company entered another expansive coalition, with George Brown, the fiery editor of the Toronto *Globe* and leader of the Upper Canadian Reformers/Liberals, to push for Confederation.

By then John A. was known to be a slick operator and a survivor. Brown had once described Macdonald's path as being studded with the grave-stones of his slaughtered colleagues. One of the opponents of Confederation accurately predicted that the coalition opened a yawning grave for Brown himself, "the noblest victim of them all." By the time the Dominion of Canada was born in 1867, George Brown was, indeed, out of the coalition and out of office. Sir John Macdonald, KCB, stood alone atop the greasy pole as prime minister (no more co-premiers), and the only one of the Fathers of Confederation with a knighthood. Even Cartier's nose was out of joint.

*   *   *

In reality Macdonald was much more thoroughly conservative and British than the image of a moderate pragmatist allows. We cannot understand his view of Confederation and his image of Canada without appreciating the depth and consistency of his conservatism. By the end of his life he had become a somewhat rigid, possibly reactionary Victorian.

The Scottish-born immigrant was British to the core. One much-quoted Macdonald comment about "overwashed Englishmen, utterly ignorant of the country and full of crotchets as all Englishmen are" was not so much a Canadian nationalist's point of view as a Scotsman's attitude. The Kingston area of Upper Canada was populated by recent emigrants from the British Isles and by families of United Empire Loyalists, refugees from the birth of the United States. They were living and working together on British soil.

As a young militiaman Macdonald had borne arms in 1837–38 rebels and Yankees. He never came to know the United States well. spent very little time there—a few trips to Georgia for his first wife health, a few months in Washington during difficult diplomatic negotiations, possibly some youthful wandering over the line as a minstrel. He usually took his summer holidays in Canada. His longer trips, for business and pleasure, were home to Britain. Despite the cost in money and time of transatlantic travel, Macdonald made the voyage regularly all of his life. If he had ever left politics, he would probably have retired to England, as did his friend George Stephen, the financier of the CPR.

Macdonald was an avid reader of British history, British fiction, British magazines, and British political writing. He met most of the leading British politicians of his time, was often entertained in their country houses, felt thoroughly at home in their company—and, in fact, was often mistaken for Benjamin Disraeli, to whom he had a strong physical resemblance. Not surprisingly, he disliked American politicians' speaking styles; he disliked most aspects of the American constitution; he even disliked American spelling. Although he served for nineteen years as Prime Minister of Canada, Macdonald met only one President of the United States, Ulysses S. Grant, and only on a couple of perfunctory social occasions while Macdonald was in Washington as part of a British delegation.

He was intensely proud of his lifelong commitment to the British monarchy and Canada's ties to the motherland. In that first 1844 election, in which he presented himself as a practical man, Macdonald also promised to "resist to the utmost any attempt (from whatever quarter it may come) which may tend to weaken that union." In 1867 he wanted to name the new country the "Kingdom of Canada," and often regretted that the British balked for fear of offending the Americans ("Dominion" was the compromise word). During his 1867 audience with Queen Victoria, Macdonald expressed to her Canada's resolve to dwell "under the sovereignty of your Majesty and your family for ever." In later years he opposed all talk of Canada ever becoming independent from Britain, suggesting instead that Canada would evolve as an "auxiliary kingdom" in the British Empire.

As prime minister, Macdonald spent years of his life worrying about American incursions into areas of Canadian jurisdiction. If the Yankees were not trying to get access to the Atlantic fisheries, then they were fishing in troubled waters in the rebellious Red River colony. They bought

they have designs on the whole of Canada's north-
n railroads reduce the west to a U.S. hinterland
be built? Would U.S. manufacturers dump products
prices, destroying Canada's infant manufacturing
ke of political genius it was to call a policy of tariff
protection a "National" Policy. Who could oppose a National Policy without appearing to be a little disloyal?

Macdonald always suspected that his opponents were at least a little
disloyal. He had been prepared to fight the Yankee-loving rebels in 1837
and he stood on guard for Canada for the rest of his life—never more
than in his last campaign, in 1891, when he concluded that the Laurier
Liberals, who were advocating unrestricted reciprocity or free trade with
the United States, were complicit with American annexationists. Macdonald turned that election into a referendum on loyalty and Canada's future:

> As for myself, my course is clear. A British subject I was born—a
> British subject I will die. With my utmost effort, with my latest breath,
> will I oppose the "veiled treason" which attempts by sordid means
> and mercenary proffers to lure our people from their allegiance.

Some said the old scoundrel was wrapping himself in the flag as a last
resort. Though he certainly understood the political benefits of raising
the loyalty cry, all the evidence indicates that he also believed every word
he uttered. On the loyalty issue, Macdonald's principles and his political
interests coincided.

Macdonald was no democrat. He and most of the other Fathers of
Confederation identified democracy with American republicanism, rule
by the ignorant masses, and breakdown. "Owing to the introduction of
universal suffrage ... mob rule had consequently supplanted legitimate
authority," said Cartier, who was even more conservative than Macdonald, of the United States during the Confederation debates, "and we
now saw the sad spectacle of a country torn by civil war, and brethren
fighting against brethren." The Fathers of Canada's Confederation were
determined not to take that route. "Not a single member of the [Que-
bec] Conference ...," Macdonald reported, "was in favour of universal
suffrage. Every one felt that in this respect the principle of the British
Constitution should be carried out, and that classes and property should
be represented as well as numbers."

Most British North American legislatures still had an upper house, analogous to the British House of Lords, whose members were appointed to represent "minority" interests. Macdonald told the Quebec Conference in 1864 that the new country's upper house, its Senate, ought to be composed of men of substance: "The rights of the minority must be protected, and the rich are always fewer in number than the poor." It happened that the Province of Canada had been experimenting with an elected upper house. Macdonald, and most of the other Fathers, preferred to revert to appointment. Upper-house elections had been expensive and the best people had not come forward. The conservatism of the Fathers was beautifully expressed in Macdonald's advice that they should follow the maxim of Upper Canada's first governor, John Graves Simcoe, which was to plant in the New World "an image and transcript of the British Constitution."

There was no room in the British constitution for the radical devices of direct democracy that a few opponents of Confederation suggested. Macdonald's sense of constitutional propriety was particularly upset by proposals that an election or some other kind of vote should be held on the Confederation scheme. "It would be unconstitutional and anti-British to have a plebiscite," he wrote a friend. "If by petitions and public meetings Parliament is satisfied that the Country do not want the measure, they will refuse to adopt it. If on the other hand Parliament sees that the country is in favour of the Federation, there is no use in an appeal to it. Submission of the complicated details to the Country is an obvious absurdity." To the legislature he argued passionately that a popular vote on the matter would be "a subversion of the first principles of British constitutional government." Only despots resorted to referenda, sometimes at bayonet point. In a free country the people's representatives made up their minds:

> Sir, we in this House are representatives of the people, and not mere delegates; and to pass such a law would be robbing ourselves of the character of representatives.... If the members of this House do not represent the country—all of its interests, classes, and communities—it never has been represented.... If we do not represent the people of Canada, we have no right to be here. But if we do represent them, we have a right to see for them, to think for them, to act for them ... and if we do not think we have this right, we are unworthy of the commission we have received from the people of Canada.

*   *   *

Macdonald had actually been something of a johnny-come-lately to the whole idea of Confederation. Right up until the last moment in 1864 he was not enthusiastic about creating a new country. He had not shared the vision of a great British North American nation that a few dreamers and poets had expounded, but had concentrated instead on trying to make the Province of Canada work properly. Unlike some of his successors, he was temperamentally too conservative to be a constitutional activist. "If there is one thing to be avoided," he declared in 1853, "it is meddling with the constitution of the country, which should not be altered till it is evident that the people are suffering from the effects of that constitution as it actually exists."

The impulse to change in the Province of Canada had come from the Reformers (some of whom were starting to call themselves Liberals; others, the more radical, had been nicknamed Clear Grits—because there was no sand in their character, only clear grit) of the old Upper Canada. They were insisting on political realignment to give fairer representation—representation by population—to their larger and faster-growing section of the province. George Brown, the Reform leader, favoured Confederation partly because there would be "rep by pop" in the House of Commons. Also because—as everyone realized—the federal principle that would underlie the scheme would mean breaking up the Province of Canada so that on local matters the two sections, to be renamed Ontario and Quebec, could go their own ways.

In sharp contrast to Brown, who was the key man in proposing the 1864 coalition that got things rolling, Macdonald stood for the status quo until he realized that change was upon him: "As leader of the Conservatives in Upper Canada, I then had the option of forming a coalition government or of handing over the administration of affairs to the Grit party for the next ten years," Macdonald explained to a follower. He climbed aboard the bandwagon, and soon led the band.

Experienced and smart, well read and better versed in constitutional law than most of his colleagues, he quickly became the chief constitutional expert of Confederation. Like most politicians in the British tradition, he did not like the idea of federations. The United Kingdom was a legislative union rather than a federation. One legislature, Parliament, under the Crown, governed all of England, Ireland, Scotland, and Wales, and the system seemed to work wonderfully. By contrast, the world's most famous experiment in federalism, the United States of America, had fallen apart and into bloody civil war. Macdonald and many of the other Fathers repeatedly said that they would have preferred to bring all of British North America together in a legislative union, like Great Britain.

They realized they could not. The French majority of Lower Canada would never accept a union that did not provide them with the capacity to maintain their own distinctiveness. Maritimers were not likely to surrender control of their local affairs to a government centred a thousand miles away in the interior of the continent. And the Reformers of Upper Canada also wanted to run their affairs without too many French and Catholic legislators standing in their way. To protect the distinctiveness of its constituent communities the union was going to have to be a federation, with two levels of government.

The proposed federation drew on both British and American experience. In the central government, the House of Commons would be based on representation by population. The appointed Senate, however, would help protect the minorities from the masses, as the House of Lords did in Britain. It would also protect regional and local interests by having equal representation from the three regions of the new country—Ontario, Quebec, and the Maritimes. Some day the west would be a fourth equal region. This protection of territorial distinctiveness vaguely mimicked the United States Senate, in which each state had equal representation.

The essence of federalism was the division of powers between the two levels of government. How much power would the provincial governments have? Macdonald was crystal-clear in explaining why they were building a federation in which the central government was clearly dominant. Consider where the Americans went wrong, he said in the Confederation debates. In their rebellion they denied the sovereignty of the mother country, and

> They declared by their Constitution that each state was a sovereignty in itself, and that all the powers incident to a sovereignty belonged to each state, except those powers which, by the Constitution, were conferred upon the General Government and Congress.
>
> Here we have adopted a different system. We have strengthened the General Government. We have given the General Legislature all the great subjects of legislation. We have conferred on them, not

only specifically and in detail, all the powers which are incident to sovereignty, but we have expressly declared that all subjects of general interest not distinctly and exclusively conferred upon the local governments and local legislatures, shall be conferred upon the General Government and Legislature.

We have thus avoided that great source of weakness which has been the cause of the disruption of the United States. We have avoided all conflict of jurisdiction and authority, and if this Constitution is carried out ... we will have in fact ... all the advantages of a legislative union under one administration, with, at the same time the guarantees for local institutions and for local laws, which are insisted upon by so many in the provinces now, I hope, to be united.

The British North America Act created what most thought was a highly centralized federal system, one in which the provinces were distinctly subordinate and secondary to the national government. Authority flowed from the Crown through the central government and then to the local governments. Macdonald called that degree of centralization a "happy medium." He had conceded the need for provincial governments, and very little more. His expectation, as he privately admitted, was that the provinces would wither away:

We have avoided exciting local prejudice against the scheme by protecting local interests, and, at the same time, have raised a strong Central Government.... If the Confederation goes on, you, if spared the ordinary age of man, will see both Local Parliaments and Governments absorbed in the General Power. This is as plain to me as if I saw it accomplished now. Of course it does not do to adopt that point of view in discussing the subject in Lower Canada.

It certainly would not do to alarm the French Canadians. Their view of the new constitution was that provincial governments would have all necessary powers to protect their language, faith, and civil law code. Some Quebecers and some Maritimers argued in the Confederation debates that the national government would not be unduly dominant, that this was not a legislative union in a federalist cloak. There is no simple generalization about the views of the Fathers of Confederation as a group because members of the group had differing and sometimes confused views. As P.B. Waite has written, "The debate in the Canadian Assembly on the 'well-understood principles of federal government' largely indicated that they were not well understood at all."

Of all the framers of Canada, George Brown was the most inconsistent. The great champion of Upper Canadians' thrust for self-government became so convinced of the unimportance of the provincial governments that he suggested they should be little more than quasi-municipal bodies. "We desire in Upper Canada that they should not be expensive, and should not take up political matters," he told the Quebec Conference. He thought the work of provincial governments would be largely clerical and routine, and he would have given them fewer powers than they finally got. But within a month of Confederation he would be complaining about Ottawa's meddling in Ontario's legitimate affairs.

Why did Brown sing for a time from Macdonald's centralist hymn book? Partly because of his own British conservatism, partly because he shared the strong sense of nationalism of the Confederation years. Brown, Macdonald, Cartier, and most of the other leaders of the Confederation movement were convinced that they were laying the foundation on which a great country would be built. Macdonald might be a latecomer to the vision, but the champagne and the whisky and the rhetoric of Confederation and his own realization of the possibility of making it all come true had made him an enthusiastic convert. His speeches resonated with images of greatness, strength, and power—"a great nation and a strong government ... a great people ... a great nationality ... one powerful and united people ... the joining of these five peoples into one nation, under one sovereign ... one people and one government, instead of five peoples and five governments ... a great country." Brown said much the same, prophesying that Confederation "will raise us from the attitude of a number of inconsiderable colonies into a great and powerful people." Local matters, petty issues, would be left to the provinces. It was the central government that would create a nation from the Atlantic to the Pacific. Contemplating such a scheme, Brown asked, "Does it not lift us above the petty politics of the past, and present to us high purposes and great interests that may well call forth all the intellectual ability and all the energy and enterprise to be found among us?"

The vision of Confederation was to create new opportunities, to broaden horizons. In discussing the sense of restlessness in the British North American provinces, the "pervasive feeling that colonial ambitions had reached a dead end," Waite quotes a Father of Confederation, Jonathan McCully, on the "farce" of local politics. "The only politics to divide parties ... [is] who shall be high constable of the parish, first footman in a Governor's hall, or master of ceremonies at a political pic-nic.... Small countries make small men." The Confederation scheme reflected the ambitions of men who would be big. "For twenty long years I have been dragging myself through the dreary waste of Colonial politics," Macdonald said in a Halifax speech immediately after the Charlottetown Conference. "I thought that there was no end, nothing worthy of ambition, but now I see something which is well worthy of all that I have suffered...."

*　　*　　*

What was the point of it all? What kind of nation did Macdonald hope to build?

The main job would be economic rather than cultural, because in Macdonald's day you could take for granted that there would never be a "Canadian" culture separate from the Old Country inheritance. Sixty per cent of Canadians were of British descent at Confederation, thirty per cent of French origin. All others, including native peoples, amounted to less than ten per cent. At elite levels there were no confused or "limited" identities. Canadians were inheritors of the rich culture of the world's most successful nation and empire. Acknowledge a few family differences between English, Irish, and Scots, add a dash of Gallic manners and *bonhomie* and the happy pluralism that Quebec contributed to the country, and go on with reading Milton and Shakespeare, Keats and Wordsworth, Dickens and (one of Macdonald's favourites) Trollope. Burke and Locke and Montesquieu for political philosophy. Perhaps some Balzac or Molière, though most often in translation. Even Cartier, who was widely read in both traditions, subscribed to more British periodicals than French—perhaps not surprising for a man who had named a daughter Reine-Victoria and talked of retiring to London.

Politically Macdonald always respected the French fact in Canada, always remembered that French Canadians had many more than twenty votes and had to be conciliated. He did not speak or read French, and there is no evidence that he believed in what today would be recognized as national biculturalism or bilingualism. Biographers have uncovered surprisingly little about his partnership with Cartier, and while they and others have argued ferociously about whether or not some kind of "compact" was sealed between English and French at Confederation, these were theoretical questions that for Macdonald were best avoided. Tolerance, political realism, and perhaps an understanding that Quebec was socially and politically the most conservative part of the country, all dictated good working relations with the French.

(But in a crisis, when he was trapped and forced into an either-or situation, Macdonald drew a line beyond which he was unwilling to go in accommodating French-Canadian interests. He sanctioned the execution of Louis Riel in 1885 in the teeth of intense agitation from Quebec. Commuting the death sentence might have been less politically costly in the long run, and could have been defended on more than political grounds. Macdonald's biographers agree that he believed Riel to have instigated a bloody rebellion and was simply unwilling to bend on the matter.)

As he had said in 1844, along with maintaining the British connection, Macdonald was interested in developing the resources and improving the physical advantages of the young country. Like Cartier and many of their colleagues, Macdonald had strong ties with the commercial community. He had certainly hoped his speculations in the 1840s and 1850s would make him rich. He and Cartier and their friends were not landed or aristocratic gentlemen, entering politics out of a sense of public duty or to preserve privilege. They were men on the make, ambitious, entrepreneurial, intent on climbing the ladder to the top rungs of power and prestige.

From the days of the Family Compact the Tory impulse was to use government as a lever for the upward mobility of those with the right connections and attitudes. In the beginning the government was everywhere. After the treaties with the natives were negotiated, the Crown owned all the land and resources in the colonies. The Crown had all the money. The Crown offered the only comfortable and lucrative jobs. The Crown's favour made or broke private enterprises. Family Compact politicians, and their Conservative successors and their Reform opponents, believed that vigorous use of the powers of the Crown was the key to the economic progress of the province and to their own personal advancement. Tories like Macdonald had no interest in limiting the scope of the Crown's activities. Unlike "country" politicians in British history, or Jacksonian Democrats in the United States, or many self-proclaimed "conservatives" today, they were not afraid of or suspicious of big government. As Gordon Stewart has argued in his brilliant book *The Origins of Canadian Politics*, the coming of responsible government meant that "court" politicians, such as the Conservatives, had simply taken control of the Crown's instruments, and would now use all those powers, all that largesse, to try to advance the general well-being.

As Prime Minister of Canada, Macdonald was never reluctant to use power. He had no qualms about governments borrowing to the limit of their credit to help finance the construction of railways and other public works. He understood the impact of taxation, primarily tariffs on imports, as an interventionist device; he used the high tariffs of the National Policy to create a partnership with a host of manufacturing firms whose survival depended on having ongoing protection supplied by a friendly government in Ottawa.

The National Policy was state paternalism leading to economic progress, the Conservatives thought. If the NP worked, they knew, there would be considerable political benefits. Even before it was implemented, paternalism's reward was the votes of citizens impressed by Macdonald's stance in the 1878 election campaign, of being prepared to act, to do something, to take responsibility for fighting unemployment and poverty in a depression. The *laissez-faire*, free-trade Liberals of that time seemed callous and insensitive by contrast. They looked like men who did not believe government should try to help people. Why give power to men who wouldn't do much with it? Canadian manufacturers were especially pleased to shelter behind government-built tariff walls, and showed their gratitude then and on many later occasions by opening their pocketbooks to Tory fundraisers.

The Canadian Pacific Railway was also created as a partnership between the state and a private company. Macdonald believed in and supported the transcontinental railway project because he felt the country was only an artificiality until it had a steel backbone. He insisted, however, that the CPR go political and back the politicians who backed it. It did, with jobs, votes, and campaign funds for Conservatives. Wherever government was active, whether helping manufacturers and railroaders, building lighthouses, dredging harbours, or building post offices, there were jobs available for the right kind of political friends.

The more areas of government activity the better, from this perspective, so long as they seemed to be vaguely useful and the taxpayers did not revolt. When Ontario's first post-Confederation premier, John Sandfield

Macdonald, went down to defeat in 1871, John A. was harshly critical of him for having been thrifty with the public finances when he was running a budgetary surplus. The Prime Minister had urged Sandfield to create more Cabinet positions in Ontario, so as to be able to give out more jobs, and thus accumulate more support. One of the first acts of the successor regime in Ontario was to expand the Cabinet.

The Crown was certainly not going to wither away in the hands of Canadian politicians. First ministers like Macdonald were almost as free to scatter favours, to buy loyalty, as monarchs of old. Gordon Stewart cites a correspondent who greeted Macdonald in 1881 as "the Prince of Canada ... [who] has friends numbered by the thousand who are most demonstrative in their joy at his being home because of the offices in his gift to bestow." Whether or not this office-seeker got his job, the Macdonald tradition helped make Canada a country in which many activities, many projects, came carrying, to use Walt Whitman's phrase, "the smells of princes' favours."*

In hindsight it could seem that Macdonald's vigorous use of the state to mould and direct the economy flowed from a coherent vision or plan of national development. Beginning with the Liberal historian and civil servant O.D. Skelton, several generations of Canadians believed that the Macdonald governments had implemented a single multi-faceted National Policy of high tariffs, western expansion, and railway construction. The NP was presented in textbooks as a kind of recipe for national development worked out by a master chef, a politician of great foresight. Macdonald's government was presented as one whose risk-taking, whose interventionism, whose commitment to the public interest, produced major benefits for successive generations of Canadians—and justified later generations of politicians in attempting similar activist policies.

The myth of one coherent National Policy was also used to legitimize the view of Sir John A. Macdonald as the heroic founding father,

* While this book was being written, I chanced to meet the Secretary of State in the Government of Canada, who is responsible for a number of grants to Canadian publishers. When I told him what I was writing, he commented, "And I'll be making it possible for you to publish it."

It happens that my publisher does not take grant money from the government, nor did I apply for or receive any financial assistance.

Canada's answer to Washington and Lincoln combined. It almost completely eclipsed the older Grit view of Macdonald the unprincipled scoundrel, who had once boasted that a government with a big majority and a big surplus could "debauch a committee of archangels," and at the least had gone on to debauch Canadians. The indictment of Macdonald was that he had entered into corrupt deals with manufacturers and railroad builders, had taxed the public to pay off his friends, and had strained the country almost beyond endurance with his procrastinating ways, his extravagance, and his favouritism. It was the politics of pelf and plunder—what Macdonald's harshest critic, Sir Richard Cartwright, regularly called "legalized robbery."

It was, in fact, the politics of self-interested paternalism. The self-interest not of personal enrichment, but of political preference and power. Macdonald was neither a scheming businessman nor a capitalist visionary in government. Recent depictions of him as a "businessman" or a "corporation lawyer" in his early years are misleading. He had no mercantile training, was not very successful in his commercial ventures, and showed no special interest or aptitude in matters of finance or economics. His two passions were the law and politics. He often served as his own attorney-general or minister of justice, but never in a finance-related or trade-related portfolio. After Confederation, except when he was in opposition, politics became his full-time profession.

Unlike George Brown, and many of the part-time politicians of their age, Macdonald had no flourishing private career or fortune. He had done so badly at his speculations and in his choice of law partners that he was in serious debt by the end of the 1860s. Wealthy Toronto friends rallied to his support. One of them, David Macpherson, wrote that "an honest Canadian Minister of State cannot support and educate a family upon his official income alone.... [John A.] relinquished the profits of his profession ... and, in the service of his country became not a richer but a poorer man." Macpherson raised at least $67,500 for a trust fund that enabled Macdonald to continue in politics. Through partners he kept his private law practice going as insurance, and in 1887 found another way of supplementing his income by agreeing to become the founding president of the Manufacturers Life Insurance Company for the then very large sum of $5,000 a year. (Many politicians lent their names, for compensation, to life insurance firms in those days. The product was a very hard sell, and the presence of familiar, trustworthy politicians on a company's board was designed to assure customers that their widows and orphans would be treated fairly. Laurier broke the tradition, declining an offer to sit on the board of Confederation Life. It gradually became customary to recruit *retired* politicians to sit on company boards and lobby on behalf of widows and orphans and all other shareholders.)

Macdonald apparently did not use public money or patronage power for his private benefit. In some areas, such as appointing judges, he was usually careful to select good men to receive the favour. But he was also unbelievably reckless in making deals to advance his political interests. His and Cartier's 1872 bargain with the Montreal capitalist Sir Hugh Allan, in which they promised Allan the presidency of the company that would build the transcontinental railway and then drew on him for more than $300,000 in campaign funds—the equivalent of perhaps $6 million at today's values—was sordid even by the looser standards of that time. When its full sordidness—"Must have another ten thousand. Will be the last time of asking" (this telegram from a prime minister who was also serving as minister of justice)—was revealed in the Pacific Scandal, Macdonald became the only Canadian prime minister who has left office under condemnation for moral turpitude (he resigned rather than suffer defeat in the House of Commons or possible dismissal by the Governor-General). By that time his intemperate drinking habits, somewhat of a public scandal since the 1860s, were also detracting from his reputation. It was not a laughing matter in Victorian Canada for the Prime Minister to appear drunk in the House and other public places, and to be periodically too sozzled to carry on public business.

After his amazing comeback only five years later, Macdonald was not caught out in any major scandal. He also eased back on his drinking, recapturing much of the dignity of his office. No one doubted that his political skulduggery in the interests of the Conservative Party continued. The Liberals were outraged by brazen collusion between the Conservatives and the protected manufacturers. It was public knowledge that before the 1883 and 1887 elections Macdonald came to Toronto and met with groups of manufacturers in the Billiard Room of the Queen's Hotel, also known as the "Red Parlour," where they pledged campaign funds on behalf of the National Policy. The Red Parlour system seemed little more than outrageously naked buying and selling of political favours. "You subsidize the manufacturers and in return the manufacturers subsidize you," Cartwright, a *laissez-faire* liberal of the old school, charged repeatedly.

The Opposition never knew how far Macdonald went in the way of cross-subsidization with the CPR. Nor have any of his biographers come to grips with the implications of the remarkable statements in George Stephen's angry July 29, 1890, letter to Macdonald, in which he reminds the Prime Minister that he has in the past decade contributed more than $1,000,000 to the Conservative Party. That is an astonishing sum by any standard, the equivalent of $15 million to $25 million in today's values. The Conservative Party must have been so flush with CPR and manufacturers' money in the 1880s that general elections were close to meaningless. If the details of the CPR's contributions to the government had ever come out—as they easily might have—this second scandal would have surely destroyed Macdonald. All that he had learned from the first Pacific Scandal was to be more sober and secretive. Above all, not to send incriminating telegrams.

*   *   *

Macdonald often spelled out his political beliefs, but never offered visionary statements about his development policies. There is no evidence that he worked to the recipe of a single National Policy—in his day the term always and only referred to the tariff—or that he foresaw the course the country's growth would eventually take. He wanted to protect industries, he wanted to build a transcontinental railway, he wanted to people the west, though in 1865 he said it might well remain a wasteland for fifty years. Textbooks and even the Creighton biography to the contrary, there is no primary documentation that Macdonald calculated on these policies creating an industrial east shipping manufactured goods west on the railway, to an agricultural west shipping grain east for export to world markets. He just hoped his policies would create jobs and opportunities and prosperity. When they did not (the late 1880s were hard years in many regions of the country, including the west) he had nothing to fall back on but procrastination and delay—winning the nickname "Old Tomorrow"—and wrapping himself in the flag to stay in power. Maybe something would turn up.

Macdonald did not have enough foresight to head off the unrest in Western Canada that led to the Northwest Rebellion of 1885. In fact, he was not able to head off resistance to his political system by most of the provincial governments. As early as 1868 he saw trouble coming with the provinces, but was confident he could manage it. He wrote a friend:

I fully concur with you as to the apprehension that a conflict may, ere long, arise between the Dominion and the "States Rights" people. We must meet it however as best we may. By a firm yet patient course, I think the Dominion must win in the long run. The powers of the General Government are so much greater than those of the United States, in its relations with the local Governments, that the central power must win....

My own opinion is that the General Government or Parliament should pay no more regard to the status or position of the Local Governments than they would to the prospects of the ruling party in the corporation of Quebec or Montreal....

Nova Scotia and New Brunswick were already clamouring for better terms from Ottawa. By the 1870s Ontario, where Oliver Mowat was building a Grit dynasty, was vigorously reasserting Upper Canada's old desire to go its own way, to govern itself. Manitoba fought Macdonald's railway policy. In 1886 Quebec elected a Liberal provincial government, headed by Honoré Mercier, which was determined to make Quebec City the capital of the French in Canada.

The provinces used legislation, threats of secession, court challenges, and interprovincial alliances to push against the national straitjacket Macdonald tried to tie on them. The old man's greatest victory, in his eyes, came in the bitter 1885 fight to get a franchise bill through Parliament, finally establishing the central government's control of voters' lists in national elections. Far better that appointees of your administration should draw up the lists and determine the franchise than the agents of provincial governments controlled by the Liberals. The Macdonald Conservatives were anxious to resist the move towards universal suffrage that was under way at the provincial level, and they still restricted the vote to property-owners. In 1887, when Mercier called some of his colleagues together for the first interprovincial conference and the conspirators called for constitutional changes to reduce the central government's powers, Macdonald simply ignored them.

But he lost more often than he won, particularly in the courts, where by the mid-1880s the doctrine of sovereign provincial governments had become well established. "Provincial autonomy" was becoming something of a sacred cow, at least in the eyes of almost all provincial politicians and most Liberals. His most serious defeat, Macdonald realized by the end of the 1880s, was his inability to stop Ontario and Quebec from expanding northwards and unbalancing the federation: "If you will look at the map and see the enormous extent of country proposed to be added to the two provinces," he wrote in 1887, "you will see what vast preponderance it gives them over the other provinces in the Dominion. History will repeat itself and posterity will find out that the evils that exist in other federations from the preponderance of one or more members will again happen. It is our duty as founders of a nation to look far into the future...."

Macdonald would compromise many of his principles, but was seldom willing to give an inch to the provinces. He stood firm on the nationalist principles of Confederation against provincial politicians whose aims, he felt, were not so much to strengthen Canada as to undermine it. "Sir," he said in Parliament during a debate on his disallowance of one of Ontario's more offensive statutes, "we are not half a dozen provinces. We are one great Dominion."

The problem in the later years was that nothing seemed to stem a tide of sectional alienation, provincial power-seeking, and cultural tensions engulfing the Dominion. The easy hopes of the Fathers of Confederation for a strong and prosperous and great nation were becoming a nightmare of uneven economic growth, emigration to the United States, and bitter religious and cultural conflicts over schooling and language. Many observers thought Canada was nearing the brink of dissolution by the late 1880s. Only the old chieftain was holding it together. And his system, deeply committed as it was to nation-building, reeked with the stench of casual, slapdash administration of the nation's business by a barely competent, patronage-ridden gang of politicos. By the early 1890s, major scandals involving federal contracts and waste were exposing the Tories' patronage and toll-gating system for everyone to see. Under the microscope, Macdonald's handiwork sometimes crawled with maggots.

But Sir John A. pulled off one final act of political wizardry in winning that 1891 election on the Tory loyalty cry. In June 1891 he died, before the full impact of this round of scandal hit home. In a way, he got out just in time.

*   *   *

He was greatly mourned. Longevity alone—almost forty years as the dominant figure in Canadian politics—created a powerful identification between the man and the country (as it would later for Laurier and Trudeau, but not Mackenzie King). More than that, even his critics acknowledged that Macdonald had been a powerful force in the building of a big country, however fragile, that was still intact. No one doubted that Sir John A., unlike some of his Liberal opponents, believed that Canada should and could become a great nation. The Liberal leader, Wilfrid Laurier, set the tone for the tributes to Macdonald in telling the House that his loss "overwhelms this parliament as if indeed one of the institutions of the land had given way."

Macdonald was mourned, too, because of personal qualities that set him several notches above the other politicians of his generation—his wit, his charm, his tolerance, his affection for Parliament and the other players in the political game. A Liberal MP who had been away from Parliament Hill for almost a whole session described the reception he got from leading Liberals, and from Macdonald, when he returned:

> The first man I met on coming back was Blake. He passed me with a simple nod. The next man I met was Cartwright, and his greeting was about as cold as that of Blake. Hardly had I passed these men when I met Sir John. He didn't pass me by, but grasped me by the hand, gave me a slap on the shoulder, and said, "Davy, old man, I'm glad to see you back. I hope you'll soon be yourself again and live many a day to vote against me—as you always have done!" Now ... I never gave the old man a vote in my life, but hang me if it doesn't go against my grain to follow the men who haven't a word of greeting for me, and oppose a man with a heart like Sir John's.

Macdonald's camaraderie and tolerance were partly expressions of his high political intelligence. Men in public life could not afford resentments, he said. His favourite card game was "Patience"—a version of solitaire. He prided himself on being a patient man in politics: "Depend upon it, the long game is the true one. The great reason why I have always been able to beat Brown is that I have been able to look a little ahead, while he could on no occasion forego the temptation of a temporary triumph." His reaction to setbacks was beautiful: "When fortune empties her chamberpot on your head," he told a follower, "smile—and say 'we are going to have a Summer shower.'"

Tory as Macdonald was, hidebound at some times, offhand and reckless at others, he had a shrewd eye for new opportunities, new stratagems in the old game. More than a few times he annoyed his friends by giving favours to sometime enemies—who responded by becoming new friends—and making the Conservatives, as Heath MacQuarrie has put it, an "ecumenical party." Then there was his classic one-upmanship in 1872, when he rushed through legislation ostensibly legalizing trade unions and embarrassing George Brown, who was fighting a bitter strike against his newspaper's printers—and then proceeded to tell working-class voters that they should vote Conservative because he was such an experienced cabinet-maker and joiner.

Macdonald could be strikingly alert to new issues. In his 1885 franchise bill, he proposed broadening the categories of voters. He still did not favour universal manhood suffrage, but thought that single women who owned property should be given the vote as an experiment. Womankind would surely be grateful, and perhaps it was also the right thing to do.

> I am strongly of the opinion, and have been for a good many years, and I had hoped that Canada would have the honour of first placing women in the position that she is certainly eventually, after centuries of oppression, to obtain.... I had hoped that we in Canada would have had the great honour of leading in the cause of securing the complete emancipation of women, of completely establishing her equality as a human being and a member of society with man.*

He also proposed that Indians who owned property would have a vote. Neither suggestion survived debate on the bill, but the leader who did not believe in universal suffrage had shown his inclination to include people—new classes, new regional interests, native Canadians, even a new gender—in his Liberal-Conservative alliance.

Picture him musing in his office on Parliament Hill, overlooking the Ottawa River, and then writing this 1871 letter to the Premier of Ontario, John Sandfield Macdonald:

* The journalist Sir John Willison wrote in his *Reminiscences*, "because women know men better than they know themselves and better than men ever suspect, there was among women a passionate devotion to Sir John Macdonald such as no other political leader in Canada has inspired. No man of ignoble quality ever commands the devotion of women..."

My dear Sandfield:

The sight of the immense masses of timber passing my windows every morning constantly suggests to my mind the absolute necessity there is for looking at the future of this great trade. We are recklessly destroying the timber of Canada, and there is scarcely a possibility of replacing it.... What is to become of the Ottawa region generally, after the timber is cut away, one cannot foresee. It occurs to me that the subject should be looked in the face and some efforts made for the preservation of our timber. The Dominion Government, having no lands, has no direct interest in the subject, but ... I think you might make a good strike by taking this subject up vigorously.

(Vigour was not Sandfield Macdonald's strong point. His government was not interested in conservation or other new initiatives, and soon struck out.)

John A. Macdonald's known drinking problems, with binges bracketing long spells of sobriety and very hard work, meant that he was unusual among Canadian public figures in not being able fully to separate his private and public lives. His escapades, which also included losing his temper to the point of threatening fisticuffs and issuing a challenge to a duel, have created the notion of him as an anachronism or throwback in the increasingly puritanical Victorian era.

On a closer look, Macdonald appears to have been a more staid Victorian than the image allows. There were no mistresses or even rumours of affairs during his marriages. He was a loving husband and father (one son from his first marriage, a handicapped daughter from his second) and, particularly in the later years, he cut back substantially on his drinking. It would not be said that the old chieftain was an alcoholic. Not deeply religious, he nonetheless practised the forms of his faith and believed in the importance of following the proprieties. "Forms are things," he often said, and expected high standards of correctness from his secretaries. He believed that a father had a right to express strong opinions to a twenty-five-year-old son on the impropriety of marrying a Roman Catholic widow. The son, Hugh John, had enough of his father's freer spirits to go ahead anyway.

Macdonald was too jaunty and effervescent and intelligent and informed ever to be a stuffy Victorian. Some thought that his second wife, Agnes, was a social tyrant who disapproved of most non-domestic entertainments and entertained boringly at their Ottawa home, Earnscliffe. Nevertheless, it seems to have been a happy marriage of reasonably like-minded and respectful souls. Macdonald's colonial political world may have stunk of liquor and tobacco and sweat, but so did the Mother of Parliaments in Westminster. Sir John Macdonald the fighting, clawing colonial was also Macdonald the respected Canadian statesman, fully at home in the world of Victorian England, at home with ideas of elegance and propriety and the hierarchy of things. He was not a raw or democratic Canadian. Culturally he was British through and through, an old codger who fulminated at how a "mass of foreign ignorance and vice" had flooded the United States "with socialism, atheism and all the other 'isms," a Tory who believed that Canada needed to be more like the structured society of the Mother Country. "The monarchical idea should be fostered in the colonies, accompanied by some gradation of classes," he wrote to a British aristocrat in 1889. "At present, with some few exceptions, Canadians are all on one democratic level, as in the neighbouring Republic, and this fact, among others, is appealed to by the annexationists in Canada, as proving that our national sympathies are with the Americans, or should be so."

*   *   *

As he fought on, defending the Kingdom of Canada against the republicans and the annexationists and the premiers and the Liberals, there were those who considered Macdonald the indispensable man, without whom Canada would disintegrate. Creighton refers to him as, in the eyes of his supporters, "the monarch who had become so necessary that he would surely live for ever." He probably thought that way himself; the speeches of his last years, particularly the last campaign, are sometimes those of an old man heading towards a martyr's death in office. He liked to hear Tories in his audiences shout back, "You'll never die, John A."

Even scholars concerned with the structural evolution of Canadian politics place a heavy emphasis on the importance of this one person. In *The Origins of Canadian Politics*, Gordon Stewart concludes that the effect of the patronage-based party system Macdonald created was to centre everything on the single man—a leader more powerful than most princes. It was not a Conservative party that Macdonald created, but a Macdonald party. Stewart approvingly cites P.B. Waite's neat summing-up: "He had been, so to speak, the only political principle the Conservatives had."

This goes too far. Macdonald had advocated a set of principles in a Canadian Tory tradition. Many of his followers shared all or part of them. Macdonald had not gathered all the power in the party in his hands; Stewart's own studies show that he left most appointments to regional henchmen, confining most of his own direct control of constituency affairs to Ontario. It was not a Macdonald party; it was a Conservative party led by a prince and his council of loyal barons. Waite shows in his excellent biography of Sir John Thompson, *The Man from Halifax*, that after Macdonald's death the Conservatives elevated the most able of the underlings to fill the old man's role with surprising success and growing promise.

John Thompson may have been nicknamed "Sir John the Lesser," but he was growing very fast in office after taking over from the stopgap successor, Senator Sir John Abbott. Thompson was young, conscientious and smart and, on the heels of the scandals Macdonald had allowed to fester and burst, had the inestimable virtue of being known to believe that morality played a central role in politics. Under Thompson's leadership from 1892 to 1894 the government appeared to be gaining strength, in Parliament and the country, in very difficult times. But in December 1894 Thompson died suddenly at Windsor Castle after an audience with the Queen. He was only forty-nine, and in a way was more indispensable than Macdonald, because there was no one in the party fit to succeed him.

John A. had been the true founding father, not only of his country, but of the distinctively Canadian version of monarchical parliamentary politics. Macdonald's career set the genetic code for the role of Prime Minister of Canada. Most of his successors inherited strands of Macdonald's political DNA. Some mastered, others fumbled, the job of adapting the legacy to rapidly changing times. Some were more successful than Macdonald, some were more respected. None was more loved, with the possible exception of his most direct political heir, Wilfrid Laurier.

Bengough/Globe/1 September 1897

"HOME, SWEET HOME."

2

LAURIER
Aristocratic Canadian

No one in the Liberal Party expected much from Wilfrid Laurier. But no one disliked him. He was handsome, cultivated, and an unusually eloquent speaker in the often raucous House. As a Catholic Frenchman he might be able to pull in more support from Quebec. As a fluently bilingual, declared Anglophile, he might have some national appeal.

The parties were still groups of friends bound by loyalty and deference to leaders. New leaders were chosen by members of inner circles. After the Liberals were beaten by Macdonald for the third straight time in the 1887 general election, the failed leader, Edward Blake, designated Laurier as heir to the office. None of the other Liberal MPs or senators could realistically challenge Blake's judgement. Laurier became Liberal leader *faute de mieux*.

Laurier himself thought he would probably serve for only a year or two, until Blake came back or someone else could be found—someone who wanted the job; someone with enough wealth and health to give his full efforts to the task; someone whose race and religion were more acceptable to the majority of Canadians.*

---

* By today's definitions English and French Canadians, Caucasians all, are not racially distinct. In the late nineteenth century, when much finer racial distinctions

Wilfrid Laurier was forty-six years old in 1887. A graduate in law from McGill University who lived and practised in rural Quebec—he was from farming stock, a ninth-generation Canadian—he had been elected to Parliament in 1874, served briefly as a junior minister in Alexander Mackenzie's Liberal regime, and had been coasting as an opposition MP since. He had formed a close friendship with Blake, sometimes virtually acting as the leader's private secretary, which got him anointed heir apparent. Laurier knew little of Canada outside Quebec, and Canada knew little of him.

The other Liberals thought Laurier was something of a lightweight. He was indolent and bookish, more interested in salon conversation with Ottawa hostesses than in plotting strategy in smoke-filled rooms. He was often ill, probably with tuberculosis. In temperament he was gentle, retiring, fastidious, a bit of a loner, bright enough but apparently lacking in passionate or even very fixed convictions. In short, a sharp contrast to old Sir John in almost everything but intelligence. Handicapped too by his race and religion, he also seemed to lack real fighting spirit. Did Laurier hate the enemy enough? Would he go for the jugular in debate or on the hustings? Was there enough iron, enough grit, in his character?

"Laurier will never make a leader; he has not enough of the devil in him," a Liberal veteran told the young journalist John W. Dafoe. "This meant ... that he could not deliver the rough stuff," Dafoe concluded. Without a leader who could get down to the Tories' level of electioneering, the Liberals were doomed to remain pure and powerless in opposition. "I know I have not the aptitude for it," Laurier himself wrote, "and I have a sad apprehension that it must end in disaster."

There was a case for suggesting that Laurier could not produce a worse disaster than Edward Blake had. Blake, one of the best lawyers Toronto ever produced, a man who combined brilliance, idealism, and conscience in equal parts, had been indecisive, pompous, negative, and stupefyingly long-winded as leader of the Opposition since 1878. Blake was utterly unsuited to lead men, and knew it. So did the men he tried

were made, they were usually considered to be separate races and it was commonly assumed that what are now considered cultural differences were grounded in race. In these pages I sometimes slip into the usage that came so naturally to contemporaries and still echoes in most histories.

to lead. Macdonald hoped Blake would not resign as leader, for he could not imagine a weaker opponent.

In those days the Liberals were far from being the party of perpetual competence that emerged in the twentieth century. Early Liberal leaders were consistently flawed. From the mercurial and impetuous George Brown to the dull stonemason Alexander Mackenzie (acccidental prime minister for four years after the Pacific Scandal) to the Hamlet-like Blake, Ontario had generated a series of Grit chieftains who were no match for the old man and his ways. Macdonald knew Laurier only as a nice chap, a fellow MP whom he shrewdly assessed as unlikely to rock many boats. "Apart from my personal regard for you," the Prime Minister wrote in his congratulatory note when Laurier took the job, "I welcome it as postponing indefinitely Universal Suffrage which I feared was in the air."

Laurier seemed to fulfil expectations in the worst way. In 1891 he led the Liberals to yet another electoral disaster. The party's policy of unrestricted reciprocity with the United States was riddled with confusions and contradictions; some of its architects had close American ties and ambiguous loyalties. Macdonald crushed the Grits on the loyalty issue. Even Blake dissociated himself from the party's policy. Soon the grandest Liberal of all, Ontario premier Oliver Mowat, was publicly threatening to leave a party that persisted in coquetting with the Americans.

Five years later Laurier went into another campaign, having apparently squandered his single greatest asset, his strength in Quebec. By refusing to take a black-and-white stand on the need to protect the educational rights of the Catholic minority in Manitoba, Laurier had roused the Quebec Catholic Church into active opposition. Here was a French-Canadian leader who looked as though he would have a devil of a time carrying Quebec.

In fact Laurier easily carried Quebec in 1896, as well as Ontario, and much of the rest of the country. He formed a dynamic ministry and led Canada into the twentieth century, presiding over the greatest period of prosperity and growth the country had yet seen. The Liberals won four straight elections; Laurier served for fifteen years as prime minister before being beaten in 1911.

Like Macdonald in an earlier day, Laurier, too, became a national institution. He came to personify Canada and Canadians' aspirations. Also like Macdonald, he forged his party into a political machine open and shameless in its determination to reward its friends and punish its enemies. Laurier led the Liberal Party for thirty-two years, during which the two-party system reached a peak of electoral effectiveness and the foundation was laid for Liberal successes for another sixty-five years. Most important, the amiable lightweight of the 1880s envisaged and helped realize for Canada a future course that became the hallmark of its twentieth-century evolution.

*   *   *

Give those Tories, with their tradition of supporting the established order, the slightest excuse, and they would wrap themselves in the flag and cry treason. Laurier was vulnerable at several points. The political friendships of his youth had been formed in doctrinaire Rouge circles in Montreal. The Lower Canadian Rouges had originally been disciples of Louis-Joseph Papineau, the rebel of 1837. By the 1850s they had re-formed themselves as French-speaking devotees of a political liberalism that was both European and Anglo-American. The Gallic strands were tinged with some of the anti-authoritarian and anticlerical notions first unleashed during the French Revolution. Red, of course, was the colour of revolution, but Quebec's Rouges were only pale pink by European standards. Real "Reds" in Europe by this time were Communists or other violent revolutionaries, who in 1848 had managed another widespread uprising against authoritarian regimes on the continent.

Some of the Rouges still flirted with visions of annexation to the republican United States. Most opposed Confederation as being likely to drown the French fact in an English sea. Many were religious skeptics and a few were doctrinaire anticlerics. All Rouges objected to the pretensions of some of the most conservative priests in Quebec, who were claiming absolute authority for the Church to intervene in the lives of citizens, including a right to suppress, even excommunicate, Catholics corrupted by Rouge ideas.

Young Laurier flirted with the various Rouge heresies and disloyalties. At times he was anti-British, anticlerical, certainly anti-Confederation. Very occasionally in later life, events inflamed him a little in the old red way (most notably at the mass meeting in Montreal after Louis Riel's execution, when he said, "Had I been born on the banks of the Saskatchewan I would myself have shouldered a musket").

At heart, though, Laurier was moderate and conservative. He read widely in British history and politics, and by the time he went to Ottawa in 1874 he liked to define himself as a British Liberal, a student of the great tradition of Burke and Fox and Bright and Macaulay and Gladstone, politically indistinguishable from his English-Canadian friends in the Liberal Party. He never tired of praising British political institutions. The old Rouge never questioned the authority of the monarchy. As Macdonald knew, Laurier did not believe in universal suffrage or most of the other ultra-democratic practices of the Americans. Canada's British parliamentary system had given French Canadians their political liberties, he argued, and it respected their distinctiveness. Neither English nor French needed to change the system.

Laurier's trade policy, not his political ideas, got him accused of disloyalty in the 1891 election. Economic policy never greatly interested him. He knew all the orthodox liberal/Liberal arguments on behalf of free trade, and by the time he became leader he was well steeped in the view that Macdonald's National Policy had unconscionably raised the cost of living to subsidize a privileged manufacturing class. Earlier, Blake, recognizing the NP's appeal to the rich and powerful and nationalistic, had downplayed the tariff issue, becoming Tweedledum to Macdonald on what many of his followers, especially the Grits from rural Ontario, considered the most important issue of the era. Laurier decided to give the free-traders their head, and thus present a sharp alternative platform to the Conservatives.

The vision was to negotiate unlimited reciprocal tariff reductions with the United States until complete free trade was achieved, thus creating a continental economy. Some Liberals wanted to go farther, and have Canada enter into a commercial union with the United States, which would mean a common tariff against the outside world. A few, most notably the country's leading intellectual, Goldwin Smith (an Oxford historian who had established himself as a prolific sage in Toronto), had decided that Canada was an artificial creation, held together only by Macdonald's corrupt methods. At his death, they thought, it would probably fall apart into its natural destiny as part of the United States.

Macdonald had always damned the Liberals for spreading "blue ruin" pessimism about the country. Edward Blake had opposed most of Macdonald's expansionist policies—scorning British Columbia as a "sea of mountains," doubting that the prairies would be settled for generations to come, predicting that the Canadian Pacific Railway would never be able to pay for its axle grease. All of the Grits had attacked Macdonald's party-building and nation-building as systematic corruptionism. As a young Rouge, Laurier had heard much talk about Quebec having a North American future as one of the United States. None of the strains of his political apprenticeship led him to have much confidence in Canada's future.

At the least, Laurier believed, the country's economic future lay in better commercial relations with the Americans. He kept on advocating unrestricted reciprocity as a solution to hard economic times even after the 1891 defeat. "We have come to a period in the history of this young country when premature dissolution seems to be at hand," he wrote Blake at the end of that year. "What will be the outcome? How long can the present fabric last? Can it last at all?"

The conservative Ontarians Blake and Mowat finally convinced Laurier that the Liberal Party could not survive the stigma of appearing to be pro-Yankee and anti-British. In 1893 Laurier made the pragmatic decision to abandon unrestricted reciprocity, and was supported by a national policy convention, the first either party had held since Confederation. In the 1896 election he said little about free trade or even the need to lower the tariff. Word spread to manufacturers and other commercial interests that the Liberals were "safe" again on the tariff. In making his peace with the National Policy, Laurier cleansed himself of the anti-British, pro-American tar that Macdonald and company had been able to apply to its critics.

Making his peace with Roman Catholic orthodoxy was a more pressing and difficult problem. Laurier fought his first campaign, for the provincial legislature in 1871, as a fairly doctrinaire Rouge; the local priest heartily and openly disapproved of him. Many Quebec priests, men of extremely conservative, authoritarian biases, disapproved of all Liberals, in fact, as being doctrinaire "Reds." By the 1860s the world-wide Roman Catholic Church had become officially reactionary in politics, condemning doctrines of democracy, liberalism, toleration, and the separation of church and state as "errors" which would not be countenanced.

The most aggressive wing of the Quebec Church, led by Montreal's zealous archbishop Ignace Bourget, was truer to Rome than Rome itself. Bourget and his followers believed that Catholics should enter politics to combat and destroy all forms of liberalism. To these ultramontane churchmen (devoted to Rome, the city "beyond the mountains"), *bleu* was the colour of heaven; *rouge* the colour of the fires of hell. Through the 1870s the Quebec Rouges had to fight for the right to be accepted by the Church as a legitimate political party. Nicknamed "Castors" (beavers) for their zeal and industry, the ultramontanes saw no reason why priests should not take sides in politics, why there should not be one Catholic party championing the true faith.

"Political strifes are bitter enough in your province," Laurier wrote an Ontario friend in 1878, "but you have no idea of what it is with us." He wrote of "war" with the clergy, of expecting to be denounced as "Anti-Christ." He made his mark in Quebec, in part, as an eloquent opponent of Church interference in politics. A major 1877 speech on the subject, in which he denied that British liberalism, Canadian-style, had any of the menacing qualities of the old European radicalism, was a highlight in his rise to provincial and national prominence. But the Castors were unrelenting. During Laurier's 1878 battle to win a by-election in Quebec East, one of his Bleu opponents warned that Liberalism would lead to people wading knee-deep in the blood of priests. "Oh well," said a veteran Rouge. "We'll put on high boots."

As he moved into national politics, Laurier championed tolerance between Protestants and Catholics, English Canadians and French Canadians. He, Blake, Macdonald, and most other national politicians devoutly believed that religion and language should be none of Parliament's business. The Canadian federation surely worked best when local issues swirling around religious and racial minorities were handled by the provinces. Even Macdonald, the old centralizer, agreed with that. Each province could devise its own school system, for example, with provision for minority schools depending on the nature of its minorities. Ideally, Ottawa would never be troubled by such issues. The Government of Canada would get on with national development—settling the west, setting the tariff, building railroads.

Like most French Canadians, especially his Rouge colleagues, Laurier was a strong and consistent supporter of provincial autonomy, a "provincial rights" man. In 1871 he talked of Canada as "a cluster of states." In 1885 he opposed Macdonald's plan to create a uniform franchise and a national voters' list, arguing in the words of a Joe Clark still unborn that "we have not a single community in this country. We have seven different communities." Laurier believed in the strict separation of Canada's two levels of government. Ottawa was not to meddle in provincial affairs. It was an approach to federalism fully shared by most of his Ontario friends, who were the bulwark of Oliver Mowat's running battles against Macdonald's penchant for treading in his domain. In Laurier's ideal Canada, strict adherence to provincial autonomy would get federal politicians off the hook whenever religion—probably the single most divisive issue of the last ten centuries of European history—reared its head. Some of the time it did.

But neither the Canadian constitution nor churchmen left matters of schooling and religion fully in the hands of the provinces. To safeguard the schools of the English Protestants in Quebec, the Fathers of Confederation had created a constitutional role for the national government as guarantor of the existing educational rights of religious minorities. In all provinces except Quebec, Catholics were the leading religious minority. The Church was committed to advancing the cause of Catholic schooling everywhere. The Quebec ultramontanes, who tended to believe that French-Canadian Catholicism was the purest form of religion, were especially interested in separate school systems in the other provinces because many Catholic children were French. Catholic schools were more likely than Protestant or non-denominational state schools to permit education to be carried out in the French language.

As Western Canada began to take shape, conflicts over religious and educational rights could not be avoided. In the 1880s, a time of increasing racial and religious consciousness across the whole country, the fate of convicted Métis and Catholic rebel Louis Riel became a national political football. By allowing his execution to proceed Macdonald turned Riel into a martyr for zealous French-Canadian nationalists and Catholics in Quebec. In 1886 Quebecers elected an aggressively French and Catholic provincial government headed by Honoré Mercier. Mercier's posturing and policies triggered angry English and Protestant reactions in both the provinces and Ottawa. Debate about school systems and language flared across the country. Many English-speaking Protestants thought the French and Catholic facts in Canada ought to be largely confined to Quebec, assuming the differences could be tolerated at all. In 1890, during a wave of heightened concern for educational uniformity and equity, the Manitoba government abolished that province's separate schools.

Most national politicians wanted to stay clear of the Manitoba controversy. Who in his right mind would either offend the Catholic Church by supporting the Manitobans, or offend the Manitobans by coming to the defence of the Church? Regrettable business, but a matter of provincial autonomy, don't you know.

Like one of Dr. Seuss's cats, the Manitoba Schools issue kept coming back, definitively so when the courts concluded that the Catholic minority in Manitoba had a legitimate appeal to the federal government for redress under the British North America Act. After intense debate and internal division, the Conservative government of Sir Charles Tupper, the fourth prime minister since Macdonald's death in 1891, finally went into the 1896 election promising remedial legislation to accommodate the Manitoba Catholics.

Laurier shared everyone's dilemma on Manitoba. His English Protestant supporters would not countenance interference with the province's Liberal government and its school laws. The Quebec bishops insisted on remedial legislation. When the Conservatives opted for remedial action, Laurier opposed them. He argued that moderation and compromise were a better strategy for getting lasting results in Manitoba. Take the "sunny way," he advised in his most famous metaphor, drawn from Aesop's fable about the sun being more effective than the wind in separating a traveller from his coat. The windy Quebec bishops wanted rights, not sunshine or compromise, and in the 1896 election urged Quebecers to vote for candidates who supported remedial legislation.

Laurier had finessed the tariff issue only, it seemed, to be hoist on religion. "How can I be strong in Quebec?" he is said to have complained in a moment of despair. "I am an old Rouge, I have been fighting priests and bishops all my life." One of his friends answered, "I am an old Rouge too, but I am not such a damn fool as to fight bishops."

Nor was Laurier, if he could avoid it. In the Quebec campaign he and his lieutenants scrambled hard, talking out of both sides of their mouths, promising to be tougher than the Tories if the sunny ways did not work with Manitoba. Many Liberals pledged to support remedial legislation if an acceptable compromise could not be found.

By 1896 Canada was ready for a change. After Sir John Thompson had died in 1894, Mackenzie Bowell had been the incompetent head of an administration hopelessly divided on the Manitoba issue. Replacing him with old Tupper had been a bravura attempt to apply last-minute polish to a deeply tarnished organization. For their part, the Grits had been looking steadily better. They were perfectly loyal and sound on the

National Policy; they respected provincial autonomy (and were very strong in most of the provinces); Laurier promised justice to the Manitoba minority. The Liberals' Quebec campaign was adeptly managed by J. Israel Tarte, a renegade from the Conservative Party who had headed several of their past campaigns. "And I must say that we didn't win elections with prayers," he had remarked, tellingly.

Quebec Conservatives had been in disarray for several years. The possibility of electing a French Canadian to the highest office in the Dominion was powerfully appealing to Laurier's fellow French Canadians. In the teeth of opposition from some of the die-hard clerics and Castors, the Liberals carried Quebec 49 seats to 16 and held their own in the rest of the country. The eloquent Rouge leader, who had been against Confederation in 1867, had changed his colouring and beaten the last of his opponents to become prime minister.

*   *   *

Laurier proved his loyalties right away. Old free-trading Grits and anti-clerical Rouges were bypassed in the formation of his first Cabinet. Former provincial premiers—W.S. Fielding of Nova Scotia, Oliver Mowat of Ontario, and A.G. Blair of New Brunswick—were given key portfolios. Fielding's anxiously awaited first budget offered only token changes in the National Policy tariff schedules, but did include an offer of special tariff preferences—not to the United States, but to the Mother Country and to Canada's sister dominions. In one superb symbolic swoop the Liberals had renounced their Yankee sympathies and wrapped themselves in the old flag.

They also wrapped themselves in cloak upon cloak of compromise in Manitoba, as Laurier personally negotiated an arrangement with the province's Liberal government to restore a modicum of Catholic education within the public school system. When the Quebec hierarchy balked at the settlement, Laurier successfully went over their heads to the Vatican. He seemed to have solved the most divisive issue in Canadian life since Riel.

As every Canadian schoolchild knows, Prime Minister Laurier was continually faced with divisive issues—the Boer War, imperial federation, imperial defence, schools in Alberta and Saskatchewan, the naval question. There was no consensus in the country about its future, or about the future of minority rights. English versus French, Protestant versus

Catholic, imperialists versus isolationists, Laurier in the middle. He comes down to us as the great compromiser, the great Canadian conciliator, trying to bring a disunited people together. It's a familiar story, worth reflecting on in order to locate Laurier's precise contribution to Canada's evolution.

The central issue was this: how British was Canada going to be? After Confederation it was still a self-governing British colony, with no right to control its relations with other countries. In Macdonald's era it was hard to pose the question of Canada's destiny intelligibly because the infant Dominion was an unpopulated land squeezed between imperial giants. Canada could continue to be British, or it could become American. Talk of a destiny to be independent—a few brave souls occasionally raised that option—was ridiculed by Macdonald and others as little more than a front for annexationism. It was hard to imagine an independent Canada surviving in the teeth of American expansionism or developing any cultural distinctiveness. That is why Macdonald was determined to die "a British subject."

To John A. and most of English-speaking Canada, the only important question was to work out the exact role Canada would play within the greatest, most noble empire the world had ever seen. As Canada and other British dominions matured, would the Empire evolve into a worldwide federation, with some kind of central parliament where decisions would be reached on common foreign policy, defence, and trade? Would the member-states develop less formal consultative mechanisms? Would Great Britain, as the Mother Country, continue to make certain decisions for the whole family?

Laurier's predecessor and mentor as Liberal leader, Edward Blake, had been virtually alone among national politicians of his generation in speculating openly, if not always consistently, on the destiny issue. For a time in the 1870s he seemed to be a prophet of imperial federation. By the early 1890s, however, he had rejected that option. Nor would he concede the inevitability of an American future. Blake said he clung

> to the hope of a higher though more arduous destiny for the great Dominion. I look for the regeneration of my own country. I cling to the hope that—sooner or later, and rather soon than late—there may be born into the world an independent Canadian Commonwealth, nerving itself to solve, after its own fashion, the many racial and religious, moral and political, economic and material problems

which confront us; united by enduring links of kinship and sympathy, hope and aspiration with three of the leading nations of the world ... and enjoying ... bright prospects of unbroken peace and absolute security, together with the fullest freedom of trade and the widest measure of intercourse compatible with the provision of our revenue and the preservation of our autonomy....

As Prime Minister of Canada, Wilfrid Laurier took the country on the road towards that more arduous destiny. It was not an aggressive, possibly not even a deliberate course, because Laurier had a tendency to react to events rather than try to anticipate them. He found himself almost constantly under pressure from Britain and British Canadians to strengthen the imperial connection. Was Canada interested in participating in permanent imperial councils? Would Canada contribute to imperial defence? Thanks, Canada, for your generous offer of troops to help us in South Africa—an offer that had not yet been made. How will you contribute, Canada, to the naval and other defences of the Empire? How would lusty young Johnny Canuck come to the aid of a motherland that admitted it was a weary, staggering Titan?*

Laurier had something of a false start in 1897 when he went to London for Queen Victoria's Diamond Jubilee and a Colonial Conference, and seemed to get carried away with the occasion. He accepted a knighthood—he later claimed, uneasily, that he had had little choice—and indulged himself and audiences with his love of things British and with the rhetoric of the new imperialism. "It would be the proudest moment of my life if I could see a Canadian of French descent affirming the principles of freedom in the parliament of Great Britain," he said, apparently endorsing the move to tighten the Empire.

But Laurier had a classic politician's inclination to try to please audiences without actually committing himself. His speeches in 1897 and at every succeeding imperial gathering were masterpieces of ambivalence, vagueness, platitudes, and contradictions. Yes, Canada was an enthusiastic daughter

---

* The *persona* of adolescent Canada, often reflected in cartoon images, was both masculine and feminine. Fair Miss Canada vied with attractive young Janey Canuck and her hardy brother, Johnny. Today's cartoonists personify the country with the prime minister, an embattled (and usually ragged) taxpayer, or a beaver.

of the Empire. Yes, the Empire was the greatest, most noble organization in the history of the world. Yes, the Empire should be strengthened in every possible way. On the other hand, Laurier would muse, things seemed to be evolving quite satisfactorily. Existing arrangements perhaps should not be tampered with lightly. Proposed changes would have to be studied carefully. Now was not the time to make rash commitments. We must be careful not to have misunderstandings. "I express my sincere conviction that this Conference must do a great deal of good, even though no more results are obtained and reached under it than those which were reached at a previous Conference, which, though they did not amount to much in the way of concrete results, effected a great deal in opening the space for future development of the ideas which were there expressed."

When he was smoked out and forced to take a stand, Laurier would not endorse the imperialist agenda. The Canadian troops that served in the South African War at the turn of the century went as volunteers paid by the Mother Country. Canada was not formally a participant in that conflict. Later, the Dominion of Canada did not endorse Colonial Secretary Joseph Chamberlain's proposals for formal colonial contributions to imperial defence. During Laurier's prime-ministership the Dominion of Canada did not offer to build ships or otherwise contribute to the Royal Navy. It decided to build its own navy instead.

At home Laurier talked vaguely but cautiously about Canada's future. His government's stance was hesitant; there were few positive initiatives. Even the founding of a Department of External Affairs in 1909, in retrospect the government's clearest signal of the way to the future, seemed at the time little more than a housekeeping rearrangement. External Affairs was housed over a barbershop on Sparks Street, and its limited business was handled by a career civil servant.

The British found Laurier's obfuscations and procrastinations endlessly confusing and frustrating. They, and many English-Canadian imperialists, thought his "foreign" race made Laurier a lukewarm imperialist. When the impatient imperialist Joseph Chamberlain was reminded that at least Laurier was a gentleman, he responded, "I would rather do business with a cad who knows his own mind."

His biographers agree that Laurier probably did know his own mind, deep down. He expected Canada to evolve towards independence. In a private letter to a French-Canadian colleague written in 1892 he had spelled out attitudes that he adhered to consistently as prime minister:

The colonial tie has become an obstacle to the development of the country; it stifles initiative, it subordinates all our aspirations to the consideration of the interests of the metropolis. But believe me, the hour has not yet come, although it cannot be, I think, very far off.

If there were only French Canadians in Confederation, I would not hesitate a single instance, but the idea is not yet ripe enough for the English population, and I contend that before commencing this change, we must have strong support from friends of both races. Without this previous condition we will put the two races in conflict—instead of hastening the change, we will put it back.

Joseph Schull subtitles his biography of Laurier *The First Canadian*. The historical quarrel here is with Macdonald biographers, who suggest that John A. was already setting a "Canadian" course and that Laurier followed in his footsteps. The Macdonaldites read a lot into a few incidents in which John A. had some freedom to manoeuvre—particularly his 1884 rebuff of mild British requests for help with a campaign in Egypt—and they do not consider how he would have reacted to the tide of emotional imperialism washing over English-speaking Canada about the time of his death. By the end of the 1890s the whole Tory party was soaked—some would say pickled—in imperialist ideas. The Conservative opposition became harsh critics of Laurier's half-measures and compromise. Their insistence that Canada take a strong, clear stand, putting loyalty on the line, became increasingly raucous and intolerant. As we see later, the Tories' next prime minister, the cautious and pragmatic Robert Borden, had no choice but to appease the imperialists at home and abroad. John A. Macdonald was so thoroughly British in his sentiments and so obsessed with loyalty—he was always an imperialist at heart—that he would have cheered on the boys in Borden's day as they sang "God Save the King" and "Rule, Britannia" in the chamber of the House during heated late-night debates and lounged about in the smoking rooms fuming about the disloyalties of the Frenchies. Imperialism in Laurier's day was ethnocultural loyalty to things British. It somewhat distorts language to call it a form of Canadian nationalism.

Laurier was so clearly holding the line against the imperialists, and his compromises on issues like troops for South Africa were so obviously compromises, that he ought not to have had to worry about criticism from his French-Canadian supporters. But critics there were. The prominent anti-imperialist Henri Bourassa was wildly unrealistic in believing that Laurier could effectively ignore the sentiments of a clear majority of the Canadian people. In the early years Laurier could dismiss Bourassa as a young man in a hurry, for by 1900 the Prime Minister was also the political master of Quebec. He had wielded the machinery of the Liberal Party and the largesse at its command, both nationally and provincially, to turn the province into as red a fortress as it had been blue in the time of Cartier. For a time the political future there looked secure and calm.

Laurier probably did not foresee how imperial questions could become entangled with the old domestic issues of schools, Roman Catholic rights, and ultimately the race question. With immense effort he had obtained religious and educational peace in Manitoba. By 1905, however, it was necessary to create constitutions for two new western provinces. Laurier found himself trapped on the issue of Catholic schools in these former territories. He may have thought his wording of the schools clauses in the autonomy bills for Alberta and Saskatchewan was a compromise in accord with past precedent, but many felt that he had given in to the Vatican in creating a new and binding right to separate schools. The outcry from English Protestant Canada cost him considerable political capital and the loss of his most prominent western minister and power broker, Clifford Sifton. Then his backpedalling and concessions in the revised legislation did still more damage to his standing with Bourassa and other Catholic activists in Quebec.

Pile religion and French and Catholic minority rights on top of the imperial issues, and the charges of some disgruntled Quebecers that Laurier was a sell-out, perhaps a traitor to his race, began to take on more credibility. And this was not just a last gasp from the coalition of bedraggled Tories and ineffectual ultramontane clergymen that Laurier had beaten in the 1890s. Henri Bourassa was more formidable, far more ideological and creative than any of Laurier's former Quebec opponents. In his speeches and pamphlets, and then his newspaper, *Le Devoir*, Bourassa was forging a new French-Canadian nationalism that would become a major strain—*double entendre* intended—in Canadian political life for most of the twentieth century.

For Bourassa, imperial issues and religious questions were connected because they were rooted in culture. A devout Catholic and a proud, passionate French Canadian, Bourassa accepted the idea that the French in Canada had a special mission to advance the Catholic faith. Attacks on the rights of the Church were attacks on the race, and perhaps vice versa. For Bourassa the notion of equal rights meant both religious and racial equality, all across the country. He became the prophet of a Canadian dualism very close to the notion Trudeau later implemented, arguing that the country had to respect its two founding peoples and their rights. Canada was not British or Protestant, with one French Catholic province. Canada was both British and French, Protestant and Catholic.

Laurier, Bourassa finally concluded, had surrendered too often to the British and Protestant majority. The last straw was the government's decision in 1908 to found a Canadian navy, with the concession that it would be integrated with the Royal Navy during wartime. Though Bourassa had begun his political career as a Laurier Liberal, by 1911 he was the leader of the Nationalist movement in Quebec dedicated to overthrowing a politician who had compromised too often.

Indeed Laurier's compromises led by 1911 to a classic rejection of the middle by the two extremes. In the election campaign that year Laurier complained eloquently of Canadians' intolerance.

> I am branded in Quebec as a traitor to the French, and in Ontario as a traitor to the English. In Quebec I am branded as a Jingo, and in Ontario as a Separatist. In Quebec I am attacked as an Imperialist, and in Ontario as an anti-Imperialist. I am neither. I am a Canadian. Canada has been an inspiration of my life. I have had before me as a pillar of fire by night and a pillar of cloud by day a policy of true Canadianism, of moderation, of conciliation. I have followed it consistently since 1896....

Wilfrid Laurier's distinctiveness lay in his principled determination to walk a political tightrope towards an independent Canada. Macdonald does not seem to have been prepared to go the same way. Certainly by Laurier's day his old party, the Conservatives, were not. Without Laurier's vision, misted over though it often was with clouds of verbal fog and contradictions, and without his conciliatory skill, Canada at the beginning of the twentieth century would surely have suffered wrenching internal disunity.

*   *   *

The twentieth century would have begun with a burst of prosperity for Canada no matter who was prime minister. In the late 1890s, international terms of trade moved in Canada's favour, the western frontier became a magnet for immigrants as North America's last great supply of free farmland, and mineral discoveries and technological change were turning the northern wilderness into a cornucopia of raw wealth. The "Laurier years" were an era of constant, sometimes spectacular economic growth. The country's apparently unlimited prospects were not lost on speechmakers. Several other Canadians claimed to have coined the phrase that Laurier popularized while campaigning in 1904:

> Canada has been modest in its history, although its history is heroic in many ways. But its history, in my estimation, is only commencing. It is commencing in this century. The nineteenth century was the century of the United States. I think we can claim that it is Canada that shall fill the twentieth century.

Towards the end of the twentieth century Canadians are inclined to wonder what went wrong, and why the century has not belonged to their country, but in the beginning the boast was credible and the cheers at the prospect were warm and loud. Laurier talked about how Canada's population would grow from six million to "soon" become "twenty-five, yes, forty millions." The young, he said in 1904, would live to see Canada have at least sixty million people. What a stunning change from Macdonald's years, when a stagnant country was losing citizens to the United States and Laurier himself predicted its premature dissolution.

What a stunning about-face for the Liberal Party. Alexander Mackenzie, Edward Blake, and the other old Grits had scorned the Tories' identification with all-out national development policies. They had attacked the National Policy as inequitable and corrupt, the CPR as another crooked deal that would bankrupt the country, western expansion as reckless and expensive. They had been free-traders and *laissez-faire* ideologues, suspicious of activist government, oriented towards agrarian and individualist values. Now the Laurier Liberals were as growth- and development-oriented, as happy to play with the levers of state power, as any of Macdonald's governments. After all, hadn't Macdonald's policies worked? Hadn't they been vindicated by events? The CPR was making money, the west was filling up, industries were prospering. Surely the message was clear: Don't sell Canada short. Have faith. Trust the future. Only believe.

The Liberals merrily juggled tariffs to try to stimulate more Canadian industries. They were pleased to support new railways to service the new west and the new north. With the tariff bringing in record revenues year after year (there were still no national income or corporation taxes), the Liberals were happy to spend lavishly on any public works that would build Canada's infrastructure. "We are entering on a new era; it is no use being afraid to spend more money," said Laurier's first Minister of Public Works, Israel Tarte. Elder Grits like Oliver Mowat were appalled; but theirs were the voices of the nineteenth century, and were soon stilled. "Lavish," of course, is a relative term: the $55.5 million the Government of Canada spent in 1900 has to be compared with the $13.7 million it had spent in 1867. In the 1990s it goes into debt a further $100 million every day.

The dawn of the new century was a time to dream great dreams and plan great projects. The Conservatives had sponsored Canada's first transcontinental railway. Laurier's Liberals would launch the second transcontinental, in partnership with the old Grand Trunk (central Canada's original trunk line, but a sulking bridesmaid after the CPR emerged). They would support other megaprojects—a Manitoba railway to Hudson Bay, huge port developments on both oceans and on Hudson Bay,* improvements to the St. Lawrence canals, possibly a Georgian Bay canal linking the Ottawa River with the upper Great Lakes. When two private entrepreneurs, William Mackenzie and Donald Mann, appeared ready to build a third transcontinental railway, and half-hearted attempts to amalgamate the transcontinental projects fell through, the Liberals saw no reason to be alarmed. The riches and potential of the country would surely support three great railroads, maybe more. The Laurier government was soon offering subsidies and bond guarantees to help Mackenzie and Mann expand their Canadian Northern system from sea to sea.

The excessive optimism and activism of the Liberal politicians led to

---

* A Governor-General, Lord Grey, visited Hudson Bay during a mild spell and called it "the Mediterranean of Canada."

wildly expensive overbuilding of Canada's railway network. The inflated system would consume billions upon billions of taxpayers' dollars and be a burden to Canada for the rest of the twentieth century. Laurier bears considerable personal responsibility for this mess because he was a reckless expansionist on railway matters. He pressured the Grand Trunk to go along with a wild scheme to build its project's eastern division across northern Quebec and Ontario. It would be a development road through wilderness. There were no surveys, no traffic estimates, instead only the naive dreams of promoters and colonizing priests and other visionaries of Canada's northern wealth. Laurier could have forced an amalgamation of the competing transcontinental projects, but did not think it was necessary. He could have said no to Mackenzie and Mann, but did not. Sixty million people could support a lot of railways.

Critics urged the government to be careful, to slow down. Laurier's own Minister of Railways, A.G. Blair, was one of the chief critics, and resigned to oppose the policy. The Prime Minister drowned the protests in a flood of Shakespearean rhetoric:

> To those who urge upon us the policy of tomorrow and tomorrow and tomorrow, to those who tell us, wait, wait, wait; to those who advise us to pause, to consider, to reflect, to calculate and to inquire, our answer is: No, this is not a time for deliberation, this is a time for action. The flood-tide is upon us that leads on to fortune; if we let it pass it may never recur again. If we let it pass, the voyage of our national life, bright as it is today, will be bound in shallows. We cannot wait because time does not wait; we cannot wait, because in these days of wonderful development, time lost is doubly lost; we cannot wait, because at this moment there is a transformation going on in the conditions of our national life which it would be a folly to ignore and a crime to overlook....

Laurier's admiring biographer O.D. Skelton, described these words as "somewhat perfervid." Read closely by those who know, as we do, the immense waste that Laurier's railway policy would generate, they stand as possibly the most irresponsible statements ever made by a Canadian national politician—and that's a tough competition. Such wild optimism contrasts strikingly with Laurier's caution in imperial matters or his finesse with school systems.

The Prime Minister was on native ground in considering matters of the law, politics, the fine points of school systems, imperial diplomacy, and the BNA Act. He was utterly out of his depth with economic and development issues. Journalist Hector Charlesworth was present on one of the rare occasions when Laurier pretended to economic expertise. After doing some homework during the summer of 1899, Laurier addressed a Liberal meeting in Paisley, Ontario, accompanied by his finance minister, W.S. Fielding.

> Sir Wilfrid thought it particularly fitting that he should address a Scottish audience in terms of dollars and cents, and genially announced his intention of making a financial address, though disclaiming that he was a man of figures. It was magnificent, but it was not war. It sounded well, but Mr. Fielding sitting at his side was driven almost to profanity in his efforts to make whispered corrections of the errors with which it bristled. The Scots listeners were frankly puzzled....
>
> After the meeting ... Sir Wilfrid ... entrusted his bag to Alexander Smith ... [a] Liberal organizer to carry to the hotel. This was Mr. Fielding's chance. "Get rid of that speech," he whispered to Smith. The organizer fell in with the suggestion and, as he crossed the picturesque bridge of Paisley, extracted the precious notes and scattered them on the bosom of the Saugeen River.... Sir Wilfrid never knew what became of the fruits of his summer's browsing among the blue books.

One fundamental assumption underlying Laurier's development policies was that they would bring major political benefits to the Liberal Party. Under Laurier's mature leadership the Liberals were determined not to be the virtuous innocents who had been cast into the wilderness after one term in the 1870s. "Remember Mackenzie's mistakes" was one of their slogans after taking power in 1896. Mackenzie's mistakes were thought to have included too little attention to using the stout glue of patronage, too few efforts to build support with the powerful interest groups in the country. Some of the *cognoscenti* sneered that he had been too principled, too honest. Laurier and his ministers would not repeat Mackenzie's mistakes.

Their tariff policy placated the organized manufacturers, neutering the traditional Conservatism of the most single-minded and best-financed occupational interest group in the country. The railway policy was aimed at creating a railway "partner" for the Liberal Party just as the CPR had been for the Conservative Party (Laurier also worked diligently to neutralize the CPR by becoming a good friend of its interests). Public works minister Tarte, whose natural habitat was political muck, frankly spelled out the strategy in a letter to Laurier: "The Conservative party kept you almost permanently in opposition by means of the big interests and through the influence of the Church. On the latter one cannot rely. We must link as solidly as possible to our chariot the secular influences, the power of capital."

Laurier's western lieutenant, Clifford Sifton, outdid even Tarte as the arch-practitioner and symbol of the new linkages. An Ontario-born Manitoban, educated as a lawyer, Sifton learned all the rough stuff of nineteenth-century electioneering in provincial politics before going on to Ottawa. As Laurier's Minister of the Interior he was both a dynamic administrator and a ruthlessly partisan Liberal. Placed in charge of the Yukon Territory during the Klondike gold rush, he turned it into a mother-lode of jobs and campaign funds for Liberals. The Liberal equivalent of Macdonald's "Must have another ten thousand" telegram during the Pacific Scandal was a British Columbia candidate's wire to Sifton during a provincial election: "Province must have 40,000 gallons." The reference was to Yukon liquor permits, sold in return for Liberal campaign contributions.

Most western farmers clung to a faith in free trade and a fear of being exploited by railroad barons and other capitalists. Clifford Sifton, the west's man in the Cabinet, became a protectionist, a good friend of the railroads, and an ostentatiously successful capitalist. He not only admired Macdonald's achievements in nation-building, he replicated all of Macdonald's methods of building and sustaining political parties. Soon the Conservative opposition targeted "Clifford $ifton" as the arch-corruptionist of the Laurier government. In his abuse of patronage and liquor permits, he had inaugurated, Sir Charles Tupper charged, a "carnival of crime."

It proved hard to expose Sifton's machinations in ways that would stand up in court, but everyone could see by his lavish lifestyle that Laurier's Minister of the Interior was personally prospering. David Hall's thorough biography of Sifton makes clear that he used the perks of office to increase his fortune. "It hardly seemed decent for a minister of the

Crown whose wealth obviously was increasing rapidly to be so ostentatious," Hall writes, and tells how Sir Richard Cartwright is said to have remarked to a young Liberal one day while watching Sifton step into his carriage,

> Young man, do you note this display of affluence on the part of a minister so new and so young? Do you note those spirited horses, that silver-mounted harness, and the magnificent chariot behind? Shall I tell you what Sir John Macdonald would have said to one of his ministers if he'd appeared thus? Sir John would have said, "My dear fellow, it is bad enough to do it, but for heaven's sake don't advertise it."

Many years later, Macdonald might have given the same advice to Brian Mulroney.

Before the days of Laurier, Canadian Liberals had used the politics of purity and of fiscal prudence and free trade to emphasize their differences from the Tories. Now the similarities between the two parties during their periods of governance were striking. Laurier and his ministers had donned the mantle of Macdonald and his gang; the old Grits were left out in the cold, with only their principles to keep them warm. Historian Frank Underhill, himself an old-fashioned Ontario Grit, often wrote scathingly of the impact of the 1896 revolution in Canadian politics:

> Under [Laurier] the Liberal party as well as the Conservative party became a party which made its appeal to all sections of the dominion and therefore ceased to stand for anything in particular. Before Laurier the party had been cursed with principles....
>
> It was not until Laurier took charge that the Liberal party acquired sophistication and felt really at ease with railway promoters, land companies and industrialists. Laurier put an end to the anti-clerical Rouge tradition. Fielding put an end to the stiff-necked Cobdenism of Cartwright. And in Sifton ... Laurier had a disciple of Alexander Hamilton who believed with all his heart in the gospel of creating prosperity by tying to the government all the private profit-seeking interests who could most effectively exploit the material resources of the country. The Laurier-Fielding-Sifton party had thus emancipated itself from its narrow English liberalism; it was now North American ... all things to all men.

The old agrarian Liberals labelled the party's new orientation, particularly its about-face on the tariff, the "Great Betrayal."

*   *   *

The Prime Minister's special contribution to the strengthening of his party came in Quebec, where he personally supervised the allocation of major patronage positions and the development of party newspapers. He made himself and his party the masters of Quebec; Quebec became the most fertile area of Liberal political strength. Laurier involved himself directly in fairly sordid details of Quebec party affairs. When his Postmaster-General, for example, tried to dismiss Arthur "Boss" Dansereau from a sinecure as postmaster of Montreal on the ground of dissipation, neglect of duty, and bad influence, Laurier pre-emptorily ordered reinstatement, "for reasons which I deem paramount, knowing the situation in Quebec perfectly." Laurier sent the offending minister, William Mulock, a draft letter of apology to be sent to Dansereau. A few months later, just before the 1900 election, Mulock received this note from the Prime Minister: "My brother, A.C. Laurier, who is our candidate for L'Assomption county, will send in his resignation as postmaster of Laurentides. I wish you to appoint in his place his son, Wilfrid Laurier."

The Prime Minister's involvement in sordid politicking normally went unnoticed. Macdonald had done much of the party-building and electioneering himself, and everyone knew it. Now there was a handy division of labour, which usefully kept the leader free from taint. Laurier was not seen to "deliver the rough stuff" openly; he was much too elegant and fastidious and dignified and preoccupied with the great affairs of the country. Political lieutenants like Tarte and Sifton held the portfolios full of pork barrels and ran the organization during elections. Increased specialization in the political system meant that the "better elements" left the sordid side of politics to the "baser sort" of their friends.*

* And even they had their limits. After he had resigned from the Cabinet, Sifton gave as one reason for not returning to it, "I should practically take the responsibility for what is euphemistically called 'political management.' ... That was a phase of the affair which I positively cannot face. It is too distasteful and life is not worth living at the price."

Later Liberal prime ministers, such as Mackenzie King and Lester Pearson, were more innocent than Laurier and more disapproving of the underside of the game. Laurier had a worldly appreciation of the necessities of politics that echoed Macdonald's understanding of human frailties. "It is always more easy to govern men if, besides appealing to their best nature, we can also show them some substantial advantage," Laurier remarked as he was in the process of manipulating a lands fund to blackmail Manitoba into accepting his schools settlement. "I do not pretend to be a moral reformer," he said when his ministry was under attack for corruption. "I wish the *Globe* would stop urging reforms," he told the leading Liberal paper's reform-minded editor in 1897; "Reforms are for Oppositions. It is the business of Governments to stay in office." Laurier once remarked that Macdonald's chief disservice to Canada was to suggest that politics was a game without rules. In power, the Liberals played by Macdonald's rules.

The Tories charged that the government had no interest in anything but staying in office. After 1901, we shall see later, Robert Borden made the Conservative Party more progressive on many issues than Laurier's Liberals. J.S. Willison, who left the *Globe* for independent journalism and finally became a Conservative, would claim that Laurier was a nearly complete conservative: "Sir Wilfrid was unmoral, not deliberately immoral. After forty-five years of age he had no sentiment nor any strong conviction on any subject.... He told me once, I think in 1902, that he was in politics for one reason only—to beat the other man."

The desire to beat the other man could, of course, generate important new initiatives. The Laurier government was not insensitive to new forces and issues bubbling to the surface of Canada's rapidly changing society. In 1900 it established a Department of Labour; the civil servant chosen to run it, Mackenzie King, made a glowing mark for himself and entered Parliament a few years later as the fair-haired boy of twentieth-century Liberalism. King initiated both the Industrial Disputes Investigation Act and the Combines Investigation Act, which were widely noticed pioneering attempts to come to grips with problems of power and conflict in industry. The Laurier government began serious regulation of the railways (which in no way inhibited reckless overbuilding). It established a Commission of Conservation to begin to take stock of the environment. Against many of its instincts it appointed a Civil Service Commission to consider responding to public concern about excessive patronage and incompetence in government. Some of Laurier's Ontario ministers hoped to go further into major experiments in public ownership. Postmaster-General Mulock, for example, wanted to take over Bell Telephone's long-distance service and run it as part of the post office.

In the 1890s the national Liberal Party had briefly been touched by early stirrings of North American populism. It had held the first real convention in Canadian history, and one of the resolutions committed the party to consulting the people on a burning issue of the day, temperance. Laurier kept the promise, holding a national plebiscite in 1898 on whether or not to prohibit the manufacture and sale of alcoholic beverages. He agreed to abide by the people's will. The prohibitionists won the plebiscite, but the government, sensing trouble, concluded that a small majority on a low turnout was not a clear expression of a Canadian consensus.

No one thought that Laurier had any taste for this or future experiments in plebiscitary democracy. Though he claimed that he was a "democrat to the hilt," he showed little evidence of interest in broadening the bases of Canadian democracy. Laurier's idea of electoral reform was not to extend the franchise to all men or to grant votes to any women, but simply to undo Macdonald's 1885 act and give control of the voters' lists back to the provinces, most of which had Liberal governments. A few years later he tried to take back federal control in areas of the country where the Conservatives had made major gains provincially. With rare candour, he told the House of Commons that the issue came down "to this, that you gentlemen on the other side of the House, do not want to go before the country on electoral lists prepared by your opponents and we, on this side of the House, do not care to go to the country on electoral lists prepared by our opponents." On economic matters, the Prime Minister was uncomfortable with ministers wishing to extend public regulation or ownership; he distrusted, he wrote, "the growing view of substituting collectivism for individualism in the relations of the Government with the people."

Normally, Laurier considered himself a champion of provincial rights. During his prime-ministership both provincial and dominion governments operated reasonably harmoniously within their legislative spheres. There was a significant flare-up in 1906, when Laurier gave in to pressure from special-interest groups based in Ontario and supported a Lord's Day Observance Bill aimed at imposing the closed Sunday across the country. Henri Bourassa led angry opposition from Quebec, where Catholics had little interest in being subjected to the dreary extremes of Protestant sabbatarianism. The government backed off, leaving enforcement of the Lord's Day Act to provincial attorneys-general.

Otherwise there were few areas of friction. Neither level of government was inclined to initiate quarrelling or confrontation. As Minister of Labour, Mackenzie King sometimes eased onto provincial territory in areas like his Royal Commission on Technical Education, without causing major resentments. Some provinces, notably Ontario, were actually urging Ottawa to help them out by spending money in areas of their jurisdiction. Laurier would not play that game. Conservative leader Robert Borden soon promised to do more for the provinces than the do-nothing Liberals.

Politics in the later Laurier years centred on the troubles of a government that seemed to be wasting, some said rotting, away. Many of Laurier's strong English-speaking ministers had resigned or retired; for the most part their replacements, unlike some of the young Quebecers Laurier was bringing along, were unimpressive. Mackenzie King was the only real sign of Liberal rejuvenation outside Quebec; he was surprised to note how often some of his fellow ministers fell sound asleep during meetings. The Borden Conservatives were toying with more creative ideas and progressive policies than the Liberals, and they were zeroing in on Liberal corruption. Between 1906 and 1908 they made "purity in politics" the theme of a prolonged parliamentary campaign against the Liberals' connection with what one MP called "women, wine, and graft." The government offered the usual denials. "I have never been in a hotel in Montreal with a woman of ill repute," said the Minister of Railways, solemnly, only to resign as a result of other allegations he could not deny. The most prestigious target, Clifford Sifton, was literally deaf to his critics.

At this stage in the evolution of the party system the most effective defence against charges of corruption was to ignore them and instead go on the attack. When Laurier said he did not pretend to be a moral reformer, he immediately went on, "but I do think that I am as good a man as Mr. Borden and as good a man as George Eulas Foster." Foster, a morally upright Conservative warhorse, was being slanged as "Foster the Forester" for his business dealings with a prominent fraternal society, the International Order Of Foresters. Not for the last time in parliamentary history, the scandal campaigns blackened MPs from both parties and increased public contempt for politics and politicians.

The Laurier years were both the zenith and the nadir of the two-party system. Parties, party patronage, and party discipline were stronger than ever before. Elections were contested ferociously. Elaborate Liberal and Conservative machines, driven by paid organizers, rumbled into battle in both provincial and federal arenas. Governments bought voter support with old-fashioned bribes (the cost of procuring a loose vote had risen to $60 to $70), and with policies aimed at turning constituents and interest groups into grateful clients. Governments doled out jobs and contracts, they subsidized railways and other companies, they poured money into public works. Foreign observers, such as the astute Frenchman André Siegfried, could not discern clear sets of ideas held by the parties or any significant differences between them. "Party spirit ... may even be a substitute for thinking," the English visitor James Bryce noted.

The last major "reform" the Laurier Liberals championed was a return to their roots as free-traders and continentalists. When the Taft administration in Washington proposed serious tariff negotiations with Canada, Ottawa responded eagerly. The Liberals were under heavy pressure from agrarian interests, whose power had grown with every acre of prairie homestead brought under cultivation, and whose resentment at the privileges of protected manufacturers and other capitalist interests knew few bounds. Unless the government offered some major initiative, it was likely to be defeated at the next election. Reciprocal trade liberalization with the Americans might be a way of pulling chestnuts from the fire and winning at least one more mandate.

If nothing else, the Canadian–American reciprocity agreement of 1911 showed that there could be fundamental differences between the political parties. As in 1891, politics polarized around the old issues of free trade versus protection, continentalism versus nationalism, north–south orientation versus the pull of the British Empire. The protected business interests rallied round the Conservative Party. So did Macdonaldian Liberals like Clifford Sifton. Laurier's loyalty to the British connection was once again in question. In Quebec, Bourassa's nationalists were using the naval issue to attack his loyalty to the French connection. Sandwiched between English-Canadian imperialists and French-Canadian isolationists, calling for a nationalism it had trouble defining, the Laurier government expired even as the country reached new heights of prosperity and growth.

*   *   *

In 1911 Laurier turned seventy. He had been Liberal Party leader for twenty-four years, prime minister for fifteen. He talked about retiring, but no one in the party thought there was a better replacement. On the surface he had aged well in power (his actual health, which had begun to worry some of his ministers, was more problematic). He had always looked and sounded like a prime minister: his flowing rhetoric—they called him "silver-tongued"—and his gracious manners seemed an appropriate twentieth-century contrast to the more homely, rougher-hewn, slapdash Macdonald. Like Macdonald, Laurier had become a professional politician, supported by a trust fund, living his whole life for the political game. Also like Macdonald, he had appeared to rise above the game to become a statesman abroad and an institution at home.

Some of the doubts about Laurier had lingered, especially in the minds of those he thwarted. Governor-General Minto claimed he was too impressionable, and didn't know his own mind. Clifford Sifton thought he was so sure of his own mind that he was impervious to reasonable arguments in another direction. Bourassa privately called him "Waffly Willie"; others called him the "great procrastinator." Perhaps the dignified Sir Wilfrid had been more forceful some years earlier, in his personal friendship with Emilie Lavergne, the wife of his law partner. Ottawa socialites paid little attention to the retiring Lady (Zoë) Laurier, and gossiped instead about the striking physical resemblance between Sir Wilfrid and young Armand Lavergne, MP.

For all the doubts, Laurier was admired and respected. He had remained a private person at heart (save for the Lavergne friendship, little has been written about his personal life, and in those days journalists respected discretion), but had always been attentive to his caucus, always had time for a few minutes' chat with a backbencher. His charm and his manners, his "sunny ways" of dealing with people, were legendary. Laurier was one of the gentle men of Canadian political life, his weapons being fine rapiers rather than blunt instruments. Some thought he would have made a good Quaker; others, noting his political skills, opined that he would have been a great cardinal. Sir John Willison reminisced that "Laurier belonged to the old Whig group of England, or to the old Court circle of France, gracious, restrained, of serene spirit and simple tastes, hating noise and swagger and loving culture and the surroundings of beauty and plenty." Laurier also loved Parliament. Perhaps more than any other Canadian prime minister, he respected the institution, enjoyed the rhythms of parliamentary life, gloried in making the greatest system of government in the world function smoothly. He never stooped to question the loyalty of His Majesty's loyal opposition.

There was an aristocratic touch to Laurier that set him apart from his countrymen. He was not a rough, adventuresome, progressive twentieth-century man like Teddy Roosevelt, his American counterpart. He was perhaps as nearly a nineteenth-century symbol of his country as Macdonald had been. Nobody ever saw Laurier in shirtsleeves; nobody ever heard him using slang. Mackenzie King recorded in his diary a conversation with Laurier in which the old man lamented most aspects of the modern age. "He disliked the motor, the telegraph, telephone, the real charm of the world had gone. He would rather have the eighteenth century."

A man most comfortable when the world did not change, he was happier to rest with the status quo than bring in reforms. His goals for the country were vague, often worked out defensively as the least evil of the alternatives the English and French were posing. Often he was at the mercy of events, a follower rather than a leader. He had no final solution to resolve conflicts between the English and French in Canada, for example. He was at his best when pleading the complexity of the job of governing Canada, and suggesting that, after all, it wasn't such a bad place. In 1909 he wrote to an Ontario Liberal who disgreed with his naval policy:

> I would ask you further to consider this point: our existence as a nation is the most anomalous that has yet existed. We are British subjects, but we are an autonomous nation; we are divided into provinces, we are divided into races, and out of these confused elements the man at the head of affairs has to sail the ship onwards, and

to do this safely it is not always the ideal policy from the point of view of pure idealism which ought to prevail, but the policy which can appeal on the whole to all sections of the community. This has been my inspiration ever since I assumed the leadership of the party and up to the present time this policy has, if it has done nothing else, given to the people these blessings which I have just mentioned: peace, harmony and prosperity.

During Laurier's prime-ministership it was mavericks like Bourassa who were trying to think through concepts of the meaning of a bi-national state. It was left to Armand Lavergne, possibly Laurier's son, to portend the future in 1907 by moving a resolution in the House of Commons that the French language should be "placed on a footing of equality with the English language in all public matters." Typically, Laurier responded by recognizing the justice in Lavergne's views, then arguing that it would not do to be pedantic in the matter, then privately ordering some token concessions to be made.

Laurier did have a vision, a vague one, of an independent Canada at some time in the future, where people of different views would live in prosperity and harmony. It was both a trite and a profound idea, a sign of his intellectual weakness and his moral and political strength. The clearer, more striking visions being proposed for Canada in those days were the flowerings of ethnicity—the imperialists' belief in a British hegemony, the French-Canadian nationalists' dream of a Catholic people quarantined from outside corruptions. For all of the breadth of his mind and character, Macdonald had maintained a fundamental loyalty to his ethnic origins—he had been the leader of British Canada, who was wise enough to get along with the leaders of the French minority. Laurier had transcended his ethnic and cultural roots. He belonged to neither ethnic group and he belonged to both of them. So Joseph Schull was right to label him "the first Canadian."

Laurier belonged to the country and to the Liberal Party. He and the party proved durable. Chubby Power wrote in his memoirs that thousands of Canadians, French and English, shed bitter tears of sorrow the night Laurier was defeated in 1911. A biased view, certainly. But the only man other than Macdonald who beat him, Sir Robert Borden, wrote privately after Laurier's death in 1919, "On the whole I think there never has been a more impressive figure in the affairs of our country." On the other hand, perhaps there was better insight in the prayer of a little girl in Nova Scotia, as told by Sir John Willison: "Now, O God, take care of yourself, for if we lose you we shall only have Laurier left to take care of us and he is not doing as well as papa expected he would do."

Borden Out-Prussians the Hun

Regina Morning Leader, September 11, 1917

Liberal criticism of Borden's drastic wartime electoral legislation

3

BORDEN
Among the Beasts of Ephesus

The battles in Europe had been raging for almost a year when Sir Robert Borden made his first wartime trip abroad in July 1915. The official purpose of his visit was consultation with the British government. Unofficially Borden had made an astonishing personal commitment to visit every wounded Canadian soldier in Britain and France. To his dismay, he found it would be virtually impossible. There were already one hundred hospitals in the British Isles alone housing wounded Canadians.

The Prime Minister did what he could. In two months he met Canadian boys in fifty-two hospitals in Britain and France, while also visiting thousands of healthy soldiers. The hospital visits were among the most unsettling and exhausting experiences of his life. He often found it hard to keep back the tears in the presence of brave men he knew were going to die. He could not sleep at night afterwards. "The memory of those visits has never faded and will endure as long as my life," he wrote in his *Memoirs*.

He had no children of his own, but he felt an intense personal bond with the young men sent into battle by the government he led. It was a bond of faith in the cause, a bond of faith that the government and the country would stand with its soldiers, stand to the end. Millions of people around the world were chilled by the message of the war poem written by the Canadian officer John McCrae, after burying a friend during the second battle of Ypres: "If ye break faith with us who die/We shall not sleep, though poppies grow/In Flanders fields."

The Prime Minister kept the faith. In 1917 he broke the Canadian political system and the unity of the country as never before, risking serious civil strife, rather than lessen support for the soldiers fighting in France. For Borden the cause was greater than the country, the duty stern and clear, the responsibility his and his alone.

*   *   *

Robert Borden was the product of a period when young Canadians were brought up to be intensely conscious of their duties as citizens and Christians. He was born in 1854 in the pastoral village of Grand Pré, overlooking the Annapolis Valley in Nova Scotia. His ancestors were English, his family Canadian for several generations. His father was a sometime farmer, his mother was strict and strong-willed. From her, from the preachers and Sunday School teachers at the Presbyterian church on the hill, from the masters who taught him his lessons in school, Borden absorbed an earnest code of duty, commitment to hard work, respect for education, and honest ambition that governed the rest of his life.

He was a bright lad but his family was not well-to-do. So by age fifteen he was earning his way as an assistant master in the local school he had attended. "A most intense appreciation of the value of time possessed me," he remembered, "and uppermost in my thoughts was the duty to utilize it to the utmost for the development of any intellectual qualities with which I was endowed." As he would not be able to afford to go to university, Borden carefully organized his days for systematic study on his own.

> I succeeded in reading a good deal of Latin and Greek, the Odes and some of the Satires of Horace were an especial delight, a little German also, and some French; I delved also into higher mathematics. To English literature I gave inadequate attention through lack of a sufficient library, but I read Milton's and Byron's and other poems, with some of Shakespeare's plays, Macaulay's *History of England*, all the works of Scott, Dickens and Thackeray, and many old numbers of English quarterlies which had been stored in the attic. To read the whole of the Old and New Testaments as well as the Apocrypha was a recognized duty which I did not neglect.

He moved from school-teaching to apprenticeship in the law, working as an articled clerk in a Halifax law office. In 1878 he was admitted to the provincial bar, having led all other candidates in his final examinations. Borden had the least formal education of all of Canada's twentieth-century prime ministers, but he was surely the best educated and most scholarly. While in office he would relax at night by reading Demosthenes or Cicero, in Greek or Latin. He was the only Anglophone Canadian prime minister before Brian Mulroney who could give a passable speech in French. He is the only Canadian prime minister who wrote his own memoirs (the others had ghost writers, sometimes by the houseful).

Borden was not much of a politician. Like his Nova Scotian predecessor, Sir John Thompson, he first devoted his life to his career in the law. He worked extremely long hours ("I was a rather prodigious worker") and became spectacularly successful, practising with the same Halifax firm that had employed both Thompson and the active Tory politician Charles Hibbert Tupper, son of Sir Charles. By the 1890s Borden was head of the firm, happily married, owner of a beautiful Halifax mansion, well on his way to becoming a man of wealth and a pillar of his community. But while the law firm had deep Tory affiliations, Borden himself had not been much of a partisan. In 1896, at age forty-one, he agreed to stand for Parliament at the urging of the Tuppers and from a sense of duty spiced with interest in a new challenge. He was one of the few outstanding new candidates the Conservatives produced in that campaign, one of fewer still who got elected in Laurier's first triumph.

Five years later, after Sir Charles Tupper had led the party through another crushing electoral defeat, the old man and his son put forward Borden's name as the best man to take over the Conservative leadership. "I have not either the experience or the qualifications which would enable me to successfully lead the party," Borden responded. "It would be an absurdity for the party and madness for me." He had not liked being in politics, had become disillusioned with the House of Commons, and had talked often of getting out. But in the decade since Macdonald's death the Conservatives had become utterly bereft of talent; Borden was about the best hope, perhaps the only hope, they had. He decided to try the job for a year; the Conservative parliamentary caucus endorsed the Tuppers' coronation of the hard-working, blunt, but somewhat colourless Maritimer.

"I like Mr. Borden very much," young Mackenzie King wrote of the new Tory leader. "I think he is a gentleman and an honorable man, and a most desirable sort of person to have in the House. He respects him-self, and others respect him...." Biographers have been less kindly, criticizing Borden for the dull earnestness of his leadership; they see him as a "mere shadow" in the presence of Laurier. Possibly, but the Conservatives could have done much worse. Physically handsome, even imposing with his shock of grey hair and his piercing eyes, Borden was smart and learned and experienced in court. He never learned to relax and smile in public, partly because he was so serious about his duties. He worried incessantly about his health, almost to the point of hypochondria, largely because he worked so hard. He had a sharp, dry sense of humour that could shade into biting sarcasm, and after many wooden performances learned to give speeches that could hold the attention of the House. No one insisted that he had to enjoy the job. After he became prime minister, when Parliament was in session Borden would leave home with the comment to his wife, Laura, "Well, Old Girl, I'm on the way up to face the wild beasts of Ephesus."*

* * *

It took Borden three general elections over a ten-year period to reach the highest office. His quandary was acute: What could he do as leader of the party of Sir John A. Macdonald at a time when Laurier seemed to have donned Macdonald's mantle, complete with pocketfuls of Macdonaldian tariffs, railways, and subsidies? Canada was enjoying a prolonged period of growth. The government was taking credit for it. In good times the bias was to assume that all its policies were working, and if the country was progressing the policies must be progressive. The Prime Minister was popular, respected by everyone, including Borden. In short, the Laurier Liberals seemed invincible, the party to whom the twentieth century was already belonging.

Borden had little inclination to attack Laurier on the imperial or racial issues that had such potential for dividing the country. Instead he probed

---

* "If after the manner of men I have fought with beasts at Ephesus, what advantageth it me, if the dead rise not? Let us eat and drink; for tomorrow we die." I Corinthians, 15: 32. The apostle is asking, in effect, "Why am I undertaking these terrible struggles if I do not receive eternal life as a reward?"

for chinks in the Liberals' armour on social questions. By North American standards they were not especially progressive. Laurier was socially a conservative, and he and most of his followers seemed increasingly satisfied with the status quo. Here was an important opening. The beginning of the new century was a time of impressive progress, with impulses to improvement breaking out everywhere, especially in the United States during the presidency of dashing, dynamic Teddy Roosevelt. Beginning with agrarian-based "Populism" in the 1890s, now with urban and upper-class "Progressivism" in the 1900s, the U.S.A. was generating wave upon wave of reform sentiment and politics.

Many Canadians shared Americans' concern with issues involving abuses of power in a rapidly changing, increasingly urban and industrial society. Huge private corporations, such as railways and banks, seemed to be exercising tremendous power without much sense of responsibility. Gas and telephone and electricity and street railway companies were growing like weeds to provide essential utility services in captive markets, but it was not always clear that their promoters' interest in private profits would match the public's interest in economical services. How could corporate power best be curbed?

The obvious answer seemed to be by the watchdog of government. But who would watch the watchdog? Crooked or incompetent politicians could sanction the worst of all abuses of power. So practically all reformers in the United States and Canada called for better government—an end to graft and corruption, more honesty and efficiency, less "professionalism" by men making a living out of being politicians, more real professionalism by civil servants, more commitment to the public interest by governors and citizens alike. This was the first of the several waves of "good government" crusading that are still breaking over the system today.

Borden, a non-politician with high ideals about public service and the need to clean up government, was temperamentally far more in tune than Laurier with reform voices. He eagerly reached outside the claustrophobic circle of the Conservative caucus for advice on public issues. Much of it came from progressive businessmen, journalists, and others who hoped to make government work more creatively to serve individual Canadians and advance the cause of nation-building. The irresponsibility of Laurier's Grand Trunk Pacific/National Transcontinental railway policy, for example, genuinely worried Borden and his friends. The Conservatives' alternative involved extending the Intercolonial Railway to the Great Lakes, nationalizing part of the CPR's northern Ontario main line, and implementing full government ownership of the whole second transcontinental system—a policy in accord with progressive interest in public ownership. Borden argued that the policy choice was between "a government-owned railway or a railway-owned government."

Borden's railway policy would have saved Canada hundreds of millions of dollars and avoided much of the ghastly mess that Laurier's policies eventually created. But in the heady optimism of 1903–04, his relative sanity was overwhelmed by Laurier's rhetoric and Canadians' lust to be on the receiving end of railway spending. Borden had trouble carrying his own followers with a policy that seemed so un-Macdonaldian, so Edward Blakean, in its caution. A prominent Montreal Conservative told him that Laurier's bold transcontinental policy would give Canada good times for at least ten years, "and after that I do not care."

Beaten by railways and prosperity in the 1904 general election, Borden doggedly clung to a two-pronged reform agenda. One strategy was the Tory campaign against "wine, women, and graft." It took up whole sessions of Parliament and succeeded in reinforcing Canadians' progressivist suspicion that most politicians were crooked. The other initiative was to put together an alternative platform reflecting the most advanced thought of the day within and without the Conservative Party.

The job of finding advanced Conservative thought was not quite so difficult by the middle of the decade, for at the provincial level voter rebellion against corrupt, entrenched Liberal governments had led to several triumphs by reform-minded Tories, notably James Whitney in Ontario and Rodmond Roblin in Manitoba. These premiers soon took their governments into bold new realms of public service by "provincializing" electricity in the one province (Ontario Hydro became the world's first publicly owned electrical distribution company), telephone service in the other. Borden was interested in similar kinds of initiatives at the national level. Why shouldn't Ottawa also expand the array of public services it offered, perhaps through its efficient post office (as the frustrated Liberal reformer William Mulock had suggested)? At the same time the national government should improve its capacity for reform by removing patronage from the public service and limiting other abuses of power by politicians.

Borden announced a striking new platform for the Conservatives in a speech at Halifax on August 20, 1907. The Halifax platform was a sweeping attempt to reposition the party of Macdonald and Tupper on the cutting edge of twentieth-century progressive politics. Some of its planks still resonate almost a century later.

1. Honest appropriation and expenditure of public moneys in the public interest.

2. *Appointment by Merit:* Appointment of public officials upon considerations of capacity and personal character and not of party service alone.

3. *Honest Elections:* More effective provisions to punish bribery and fraud at elections, to ensure thorough publicity as to expenditure by political organizations, to prevent the accumulation of campaign funds for corrupt purposes and to prohibit contributions thereto by corporations, contractors and promoters....

4. *Civil Service Reform:* A thorough and complete reformation of the laws relating to the Civil Service so that future appointments shall be made by an independent commission ... after competitive examination.

5. *Reform of the Senate:* Such reform in the mode of selecting members of the Senate as will make that Chamber a more useful and representative legislative body.

6. *Immigration:* A more careful selection of the sources from which immigration shall be sought, a more rigid inspection of immigrants ...

7. *Public Lands and Franchises for the People:* The management and development of the public domain (in which are to be included great national franchises) for the public benefit and under such conditions that a reasonable proportion of the increment of value arising therefrom shall insure to the people.

8. *Non-Partisan Management of Government Railways:* The operation and management of our government railways by an independent commission free from partisan control or influence.

9. *National Ports, Transportation and Cold Storage:* The development and improvement of our national waterways, the equipment of national ports, the improvement of transportation facilities and consequent reduction of freight rates between the place of production and the market ... and the establishment of a thorough system of cold storage.

10. *A Public Utilities Commission:* The reorganization of the present Railway Commission as a Public Utilities Commission with wider powers and more extended jurisdiction, so as to establish thorough and effective control over all corporations owning or operating public utilities....

11. *Public Telegraphs and Telephones:* The establishment, after due investigation, of a system of national telegraphs and telephones under conditions which shall be just to capital already invested in those enterprises.

12. *Improved Postal Facilities:* The improvement of existing postal facilities, especially in newly developed portions of the country, and the inauguration, after proper inquiry as to cost, of a system of free rural mail delivery....

16. *Provincial Rights:* The unimpaired maintenance of all powers of self-government which had been conferred upon the provinces of Canada under the Constitution.

Some Conservatives were uncomfortable with policies that hardly seemed conservative, and a leader who had committed the party to the platform and then told his caucus about it. Borden did not think of himself as an interest-group broker, a consensus seeker, or a slave to his party. He asked for advice from a few people he trusted, he considered it according to his best judgement, and he took his stand. If the party didn't like it, he implied, it could find another leader.

The problem was that ordinary Canadians didn't seem to care about the Halifax proposals. Borden was not so much out in front of opinion as he was detached from the concerns that could actually rouse the voter—"hard" issues of jobs and contracts, emotional questions of religion and race. The Tories lost again in 1908. Borden thought a major factor in his defeat was a scurrilous anti-Catholic pamphlet put out by over-zealous Conservative members of the Orange Order, which backfired in favour of the Liberals—that era's equivalent of the "attack ad."

*   *   *

Issues that aroused simplistic passions gradually squeezed out the presentation of progressive ideas and policies. The pressure on the Conservatives to play to their base in Anglo-Saxon Protestant Canada was very strong. It crept into the Halifax platform, for example, in point six, a call for controls on immigration. From the beginning of his leadership Borden had responded to and echoed a persistent undercurrent of alarm in Anglo-Canadian circles about the Liberals' policy of apparently welcoming immigrants of every race and culture. How could so many foreigners, from so many different cultures, be assimilated into the mainstream of Canadian life?

In their sour moods Conservatives complained about Canada being "the dumping ground for the refuse of every country in the world." The Canadian magnet was now beginning to attract people of strikingly different racial backgrounds, and many Tories believed there should at least be more selectivity in immigration policy. British Columbia, governed after 1903 by the Conservative Richard MacBride, was a hotbed of anti-Asian sentiment. Both parties responded to West Coast racism, the Laurier government with tighter controls on Chinese and Japanese immigration, the Conservatives with demands for even tighter controls.

Robert Borden was not an intolerant man by the standards of the time. He shared the conventional belief that racially based cultural differences were probably ineradicable and likely to produce constant friction, especially in the labour market. "The Conservative party stands for a white Canada and the absolute protection of white labour," he told British Columbians in the 1908 campaign.

Such sentiments did not necessarily offend the country's largest "racial" minority, its French population. French Canadians could see that massive immigration from other cultures was bound to reduce their demographic and ultimately their political clout in Canada. Borden's Quebec followers were among the first to complain about the prospect of liberal immigration swamping the French presence in the west. As renegade Liberal Henri Bourassa sharpened the tools of resurgent French-Canadian nationalism, he, too, suggested that the rights of Canada's two "founding" peoples not be diluted. Canada should not become "a land of refuge for the scum of all nations," he argued. Here was an interesting and unusual convergence, a common ground for conservative-minded English Canadians and French Canadians, in taking steps to protect their common heritage.

There was no such basis for co-operation when the call of empire again rang out in the land and British Canada snapped to attention. From 1908 to 1913 the Parliament of a country that had never launched a gunboat spent more hours debating naval policy than any other subject. Great Britain let it be known that help from the dominions in maintaining global naval supremacy would be appreciated. How would Canada best contribute to the defence of the British Empire and its own shores?

The Laurier government's policy was to launch a Canadian navy, which would help the Royal Navy in wartime. Borden, whose solid common sense was often an antidote to imperialist flag-waving, at first seemed to favour this moderately nationalist approach. Then the red-blooded imperialists in the Conservative Party, including several provincial premiers who fancied themselves world statesmen, raised a hue and cry for an immediate contribution to imperial defence. Borden reconsidered; in 1910 the Tories opposed Laurier's naval bill, calling instead for a huge cash contribution to the British Treasury to finance two battleships. The naval debate was fervid and acrimonious, with more Tory reliance on the imperial anthem, "God Save the King," as a substitute for reasoned argument.

Borden's decision to respond to *l'appel de la race* seemed to complete the destruction of the Conservative Party in French Canada. It had been precarious there since at least the dithering over Manitoba schools, perhaps as far back as the execution of Riel or even the death of Cartier. Borden had inherited a mess: Quebec Conservatism was a drifting, dispirited, divided shadow of the big Bleu machine which had been so useful to Macdonald. Every issue involving imperial or cultural relations—South Africa, the autonomy bills, the Lord's Day Act, now the wretched navy—further isolated French-Canadian Conservatives from their Anglo-Saxon colleagues. Laurier had happily welcomed the lost camels of Quebec conservatism into his pan-Canadian Liberal tent, and spread its canvas to envelop his home province.

Borden knew the party needed to be strong in Quebec, and he played the game as best he could, working on his own French, attending to the Quebec organization, trying to find a Quebec lieutenant who could be a second Cartier. At times the effort was almost comically futile, for the French Quebecers got along neither with each other nor with the English Conservatives, who in turn had neither patience nor significant reserves of good will. "Frenchmen are so variable and unstable," Borden confided to his diary when he was prime minister.

The 1896 election had left the Conservatives with 16 of the 65 seats in Quebec. After 1900 they had seven seats. All of Borden's efforts succeeded in raising the total to eleven Quebec members in 1904 and eleven again in 1908, many of them from English-dominated ridings. French Canada had contributed so little for so long to national Conservatism that few of Borden's supporters were inclined even to notice, let alone bend to accommodate, its particular sentiments on issues like naval policy. When Borden's sometime Quebec lieutenant, Frederick Monk, broke with the party on the issue in 1910, it was an unfortunate but hardly a crippling development. From Ontario and Western Canada support was pouring in from Anglo-Canadians disgusted with Laurier's design for a "tin-pot" navy.

Then it happened, more or less fortuitously, that Borden and his party were carried to power in 1911, standing on their old National Policy platform of high tariffs and mowing down the Liberals on reciprocity. The Borden Tories had always talked protectionism and boosted economic nationalism, even in the Halifax platform, but so long as the Laurier Liberals used the same hymn book the voters could not tell the singers apart. In 1911, reciprocity delightfully split the Liberal Party, bringing a phalanx of rich and powerful and fairly progressive business interests, mostly central Canadian, back to the Conservative camp. The big electoral swing was in Ontario.

In Quebec, Borden's party did slightly worse than usual—no matter, because it had a parliamentary majority without Quebec—though it gained almost twenty more French-Canadian adherents. The latter group were Nationaliste followers of Henri Bourassa who had run mostly against anything to do with navies. Liberals claimed that Borden had concluded a tacit "unholy alliance" with the Bourassa group in the interests of defeating Laurier. After careful examination of the evidence, Borden's scholarly biographer concludes that the truth of the matter may never be known. We do know that the leader of the Conservative Party was content not to campaign in Quebec in 1911, and we know that the idea of Conservatives allying themselves with Quebec nationalists would attract several of Borden's successors.

When Borden became prime minister in 1911, it was not because of the progressive ideas of the Halifax platform, his sympathies for reform, or his leadership of the Opposition since 1901. His party defeated a tired Liberal government that was out of touch with English Canadians' love affair with the Empire and had abandoned the National Policy. Help from the renegade Liberal businessmen was very important, particularly in Ontario. Much of the electoral machinery for the victory was supplied by Conservative provincial governments in Ontario, Manitoba, British Columbia, and New Brunswick. Over the years the Tories had taken in some key Liberal "fixers," Israel Tarte and in 1911 the notorious Clifford Sifton. The provincial administrations now contributed some of their legendary organizers, notably "Silent" Frank Cochrane from Ontario and Robert Rogers, "minister of elections" in the Manitoba government, both of whom wound up in Borden's Cabinet. Some of Borden's more progressive supporters could not understand how the new prime minister could give high office to a man as politically immoral and offensive as the "Hon. Bob" Rogers. Had the lust for power overwhelmed Borden's commitment to the politics of high principle?

*   *   *

Borden did try to be a reformer. Drawing from his Halifax platform, he began to implement civil-service reform, appointed better men to regulatory bodies, extended rural free postal delivery, and got the federal government into the construction of terminal grain elevators. Some provincial governments had wanted easy funding for new programs. Responding to that, the Borden government proposed to offer grants to provinces on condition that the money be used to build highways. This was the first use of the federal spending power to encourage provinces to initiate programs in their sphere of jurisdiction. The initiative had come from the provinces. The Liberals opposed the grants as encroaching on provincial autonomy. Anxious to build rural support, the government proposed other conditional grants to support agricultural education.

What the Borden government would not do was get government off farmers' and other taxpayers' backs by lowering the tariff. Nor were any of the state's other activities being cut back. Borden was like most of his colleagues, like the Laurier Liberals he had replaced, and like the legendary Sir John A. himself, in having no qualms about the vigorous use of power by the state. In fact his enthusiasm for government ownership meant the state would do more, not less in the modern economy. The few Canadians who wanted to shrink the state and/or transfer power to more vigorous democratic institutions, such as co-operatives, could not find a home in either the Liberal or the Liberal-Conservative parties. Some of them, notably westerners furious at having lost the fight for free trade, were beginning to talk about the need for their own political party.

As it hit its stride the Borden government appeared to combine moderate progressivism with free-spending development nationalism, in the mode of Macdonald and Laurier. Times were very good. "The phenomenal development and progress of the country seems likely to continue in even greater measure for many years to come," Borden wrote privately in 1912. His ministers began papering the country with promises of more public works—better harbours, better roads, more railways, more public buildings, and a lot of steel shipbuilding, whether or not the vessels were naval warships.

They were too late. Small "l" liberal Canada, like liberal England in the last years before the onset of the Great War, was about to fall apart. The assumptions that had governed the political game for decades, in some cases since Confederation, began crumbling.

More than a decade of easy growth finally petered out in 1913. Canada suddenly seemed overbuilt, overborrowed, overextended. By 1914 the country was in a depression, suffering from high unemployment, a sharp decline in foreign investment, and much higher borrowing costs. The two unfinished transcontinental railways found themselves on the verge of bankruptcy, and their executives were on politicians' doorsteps seeking handouts, and then more handouts, and then just a bit more.... Turn them away and the collapse of their ventures would possibly drag down at least one major chartered bank, perhaps throw several provinces into insolvency, and certainly tarnish the reputation of Canada in the eyes of foreign investors. The Conservatives cursed the Laurier government's railway recklessness six ways to Sunday as they tried to nurse the desperately sick systems through to completion and the return of good times.

Politics turned bitter and rancorous. The Conservatives were appalled when the Senate, completely dominated by Laurier's appointees, became less co-operative than it had ever been in the past. A whole series of government bills were amended or rejected. This posed for the first time since Confederation the fundamental question of the legitimacy of the undemocratic upper house. The naval question resurfaced as the government proposed to spend $35 million on three battleships that would be turned over to the Royal Navy; the debate on naval policy degenerated into one of the most ill-tempered confrontations in Canadian parliamentary history.

The Liberals decided to stop passage of the Naval Aid Bill, arguing (as the Tories had with the reciprocity legislation in 1911) that such a fundamental issue ought to be put to the people for approval in an election. They kept the debate going twenty-four hours a day in the House of Commons for a full two weeks, an unprecedented filibuster. Tempers flared, manners deteriorated. Normally polite MPs nearly came to blows. Borden's iron determination, fully harnessed to a heavy load of partisanship and imperial patriotism, led to a decision to introduce limits on debate, for the first time in the history of the Canadian House of Commons.

The only way to stop a filibuster on the new closure rules was to apply a form of closure immediately upon their introduction. The first person effectively to be gagged was the country's greatest parliamentarian, Laurier himself. Ever since the winning of responsible government, there had been a basic comity about the rules of the game. Now it was shattered. Partisan bitterness—even Laurier lost his temper and cried, "Shame," at Conservative tactics—had never been so intense. "Both sides wanted a physical conflict. Primeval passions," the Prime Minister noted coolly in his diary after one of the more difficult days.

What would the Senate do after the House passed the Naval Aid Bill? Borden hoped there were enough imperialists among Liberal Senators to force an acceptable compromise. He was wrong. The Senate threw back the legislation.

Borden tried to plaster the gaping division between his English and French supporters with promises of generous shipbuilding contracts, spurious claims that Canada would have a real voice in the making of imperial foreign policy, and indications that in certain circumstances he might support the use of plebiscites on defence matters. But the Conservatives lost most of their French-Canadian friends in the early stages of the naval debate, and, in truth, few of them cared. Prominent Tories calmly contemplated a future for the party without French-Canadian support. "Surely it is in the West that the Conservative party must chiefly build for the future," J.S. Willison wrote to Borden in 1911. In early 1914 the Prime Minister twice chewed out his Postmaster-General, Louis-Philippe Pelletier, for having alarmed Anglo-Protestants by authorizing the post office's sale of bilingual postcards outside Quebec.

The political system was in deadlock, near breakdown. One party controlled the House, the other the Senate, and the division between them was fundamental. The Tories were the party of flag-waving Anglo-Canada; the Liberals spoke for French Canada, many recent immigrants from outside the United Kingdom, and pockets of isolationists and agrarian dissidents. In the early months of 1914 Borden prepared to try the politician's last resort, an appeal to the people. Either at the polls or through a special plebiscite, he would call for Senate reform—an elected Senate. At the last moment, in July, the Conservatives hesitated, unsure that they could actually carry the country. That they would bitterly divide the country along its cultural fault-lines, destroying prospects of Anglo-French co-operation for years, did not seem to be a major concern.

Somewhat reluctantly, for he was afraid that it would hurt him politically, Borden acquiesced in King George V's wish that he accept a knighthood. He was enjoying a pleasant holiday in Muskoka, hoping he would soon get over a prolonged bout of carbuncles, when news of an impending European war caused him to rush back to Ottawa.

* * *

Canada had no say in the matter. When Britain went to war against the German Empire on August 4, 1914, her Dominions, not yet autonomous in matters of foreign policy, were also at war. Such legalities were irrelevant in one sense, for popular and political sentiment in the country was overwhelmingly in favour of war. No one was more eloquent about the unity of Canadians and their commitment to the fight for freedom than the leader of the Opposition, Laurier. Canada's answer to the call, he told the House of Commons, could only be couched in the classic British phrase "Ready, aye, ready!" On the willingness to go to war, there was in Canada "but one mind and one heart." Splendid rhetorical sentiments, almost certainly not felt by a majority of French Canadians.

The government moved quickly to put the country on a war footing. War immediately centralized power in the hands of the federal government, in the hands of the Prime Minister and his Cabinet. Borden described his activities in the last two days of peace:

> On Sunday and Monday we spent practically the whole day in Council. We established censorship, declared bank notes legal tender, authorized excess issue of dominion notes, empowered the proper officers to detain enemy ships, prohibited the export of articles necessary or useful for war purposes and generally took upon ourselves responsibilities far exceeding our legal powers. All these measures, which were wholly without legal validity until they were

afterwards ratified by Parliament, were accepted throughout the country as if Council had possessed the necessary authority.

Parliament not only ratified the steps the Cabinet had taken, but passed an Emergency War Measures Act authorizing Cabinet to do virtually anything that was necessary for the "security, defence, peace, order and welfare of Canada." In peacetime you could take your time, and take counsel, and take holidays. During a storm at sea the men on the bridge took charge.

In the autumn of 1914 Canada sent an expeditionary force of more than 30,000 soldiers to Britain, the largest single army that had ever crossed the Atlantic. Despite this remarkable contribution and despite his near-dictatorial powers at home, Prime Minister Borden found himself unable to steer or even influence the British Empire's conduct of the war. There had been much blather over the years about giving the Dominions a voice in the making of imperial foreign policy, but nothing of any significance was in place when Canada began sending men to fight and die in Europe. "In the most critical area of war policy the Canadian leader was a frustrated follower...," Robert Craig Brown writes.

> The Canadian government's role was confined to the recruitment and initial training of Canada's soldiers. In the field they were under British command. Borden was not consulted about the battles.... He was not consulted about the strategy or the tactics adopted by the British High Command. He was not consulted about any significant aspect of the imperial government's war policy. With very few exceptions Borden and his critics got their information from the same censored source: the public press.

If the war had been neat and short Canada's voicelessness might not have mattered. When the fighting bogged down into mutual slaughter by massive immobile armies, no self-respecting leader could tolerate the old ways—especially after realizing that the old ways were confused, amateurish, and bloodily expensive. After seventeen months of war, many thousands of Canadian casualties, and innumerable evasions and procrastinations from the British, Borden let his impatience boil over in a letter to the Canadian High Commissioner in Britain, Sir George Perley:

During the past four months since my return from Great Britain, the Canadian Government ... have had just what information could be gleaned from the daily Press and no more.... Plans of campaign have been made and unmade, measures adopted and apparently abandoned and generally speaking steps of the most important and even vital character have been taken, postponed or rejected without the slightest consultation with the authorities of this Dominion.

It can hardly be expected that we shall put 400,000 or 500,000 men in the field and willingly accept the position of having no more voice and receiving no more consideration than if we were toy automata. Any person cherishing such an expectation harbours an unfortunate and even dangerous delusion. Is this war being waged by the United Kingdom alone, or is it a war waged by the whole Empire? ... if we are expected to continue in the role of automata the whole situation must be reconsidered.

Procrastination, indecision, inertia, doubt, hesitation and many other undesirable qualities have made themselves entirely too conspicuous in this War. During my recent visit to England a ... very able Cabinet Minister spoke of the shortage of guns, rifles, munitions, etc., but declared that the chief shortage was of brains.

The letter was not made public, but the Canadians' determination to have a voice in the affairs that concerned them was quietly insistent and effective. The Canadian army was fighting as a distinct corps in the British forces, and eventually would have a Canadian commander and become one of the most effective and respected forces in the Allied armies. The British government conceded the justice of Borden's complaints by convening a new institution, the Imperial War Cabinet, which might function as the long-dreamed-of Imperial Council. When Borden went to England in 1917 it was as prime minister of the senior Dominion, a self-governing nation, conferring with the other prime ministers on an equal footing. Canada and the Dominions had an entirely new status. Borden and the South African leader, General J.C. Smuts, helped formalize that status by sponsoring Resolution IX of the later Imperial War Conference, which committed the Empire to full recognition of the autonomy of the Dominions and the need for continuous consultation on all common imperial matters. "You and I have transformed the structure of the British Empire," Smuts later said to Borden.

To the end of the war and beyond, Borden pressed for complete formal and *de facto* recognition of Canada's autonomy. The greatest work of his career, he thought, took place out of the country as he participated in imperial councils in Britain and then at the Paris Peace Conference. Because of Borden, Canada's Parliament ratified the Treaty of Versailles. Because of Borden, Canada was a full member of the League of Nations. More than Laurier, who preceded him, or King, who came after and took all the credit he could get away with, Borden has a compelling claim to be the father of Canada's effective independence. The valour and sacrifice of Canadian soldiers on the battlefields of Flanders were the real cause of the final breaking of the colonial tie, he maintained.

*   *   *

Borden's achievements in fighting Canada's way into the councils of the Empire were not well advertised or appreciated at home. Never a charismatic politician at the best of times, Borden could not rise to eminence as a war leader like David Lloyd George in Great Britain or even Woodrow Wilson in the United States. He was always on duty, was hardworking and fair-minded and almost universally respected, but neither loved nor hated. He did not rant or rage, usually keeping in check a temper which, he wrote in his memoirs, "has always been rather violent but which, throughout my life, I have kept in almost perfect discipline." When he had had enough of his lieutenants, he simply dismissed them. After a trying Cabinet meeting in 1917, "The discussion was lengthy and eventually became so wearisome that I interposed, informing my colleagues that they had made me sufficiently acquainted with their views, that the duty of decision rested with me, and that I would subsequently make them acquainted with my conclusion."

The foolishness Borden had to suffer was sometimes avenged with dry, devastating comments in his daily diary. His ostensibly tedious memoirs are often bitingly acerbic. Consider as a single, sufficient example this passage about his Minister of Militia, Sam Hughes:

> When I formed my Government in 1911 I was extremely doubtful as to including Hughes; while he was a man of marked ability and sound judgement in many respects, his temperament was so peculiar, and his actions and language so unusual on many important occasions that

one was inclined to doubt his usefulness as a Minister.... I discussed with Hughes when I appointed him his extraordinary eccentricities.... He was under constant illusions that enemies were working against him. I told him on one occasion that I thoroughly agreed that he was beset by two unceasing enemies. Expecting a revelation he was intensely disappointed when I told him that they were his tongue and his pen.... during about half of the time he was an able, reasonable, and useful colleague, working with excellent judgement and indefatigable energy; for a certain other portion of the time he was extremely excitable, impatient of control and almost impossible to work with; and during the remainder his conduct and speech were so eccentric as to justify the conclusion that his mind was unbalanced.

Some of the politicians and businessmen who were close to Borden complained about his caution and indecision—just as their counterparts had about Macdonald and Laurier. During the war Borden was more beset than his predecessors by businessmen impatient for action, idealists who wanted him to lead them into battle, and a volume of business that constantly threatened to overwhelm him. His diaries and memoirs portray a prime minister stretching his large capacity for work to the breaking-point, operating often on the edge of collapse. Borden not only had a war to manage, but for the whole period of it had a national economic crisis to deal with because of the legacy of Laurier's railways. His "minor" problem, to be wrestled with in the time the PM could spare from the war, was the fact that close to two-thirds of Canada's transportation system was insolvent and needed constant infusions of capital; the banking system and the credit-worthiness of several provincial governments were also at risk.

Borden's worst mistake, a decision he ought to have reversed long before any shot was fired, was to maintain Sam Hughes as Minister of Militia (the equivalent of today's minister of defence). At best, Hughes was possibly qualified to be Minister of Militia in Stephen Leacock's "Mariposa." As minister responsible for the Canadian divisions in a world war Hughes was pathetically and obviously out of his depth. Borden knew it and yet bore with Hughes for more than two years, before finally firing him in November 1916. The most defensive passages in the *Memoirs* are attempts to explain Borden's forbearance with Hughes. Robert Craig Brown concludes that Borden stayed with Hughes for so long because under his bluff exterior the Prime Minister was actually sentimental and tender-hearted. Borden claimed that he worried about Hughes' political power—it seemed better to have a mad cannon more or less under control in his Cabinet than careering around the country firing publicly at the government. Ironically, Borden's soft-hearted, perhaps soft-headed tolerance of Sir Sam (*le roi s'amuse*, Henri Bourassa punned brilliantly on hearing that Hughes had been knighted) probably cost more of the Canadian lives the Prime Minister cared about so deeply.

The need to worry about his political base further drained Borden's strength and patience. He had been near to calling an election before war broke out. Should he have a wartime election? His government's mandate would expire in 1916. Even if the two parties agreed not to disagree on the war effort, could they fight an election campaign without damaging national unity? Much more to the point, how was the situation changed by the fact that Laurier and Borden came to disagree on a central strategic issue, Canada's manpower policy?

Borden was determined to provide all the reinforcements Canada's frontline soldiers needed. As the pool of willing volunteers was used up, recruiting became very difficult. By the summer of 1917 Borden concluded that the government would have to compel Canadian men to fight abroad, in other words, to conscript them for overseas service. He knew that conscription would be controversial and divisive to implement. He hoped to persuade Laurier to support the policy and join with him in a coalition government, along the lines of Britain's wartime administration. With overwhelming political strength, such a coalition would easily win the 1917 election (there had been an agreement to extend the life of Parliament into 1917) and would implement conscription with the least amount of disunity.

Laurier did not agree. Complex negotiations between the two leaders foundered on Laurier's refusal to campaign for conscription. Laurier did not believe he could carry Quebec on the issue; he seems personally not to have believed that Canada ought to take such a drastic step.

Determined to broaden political support for conscription, Borden continued talks with prominent English-speaking Liberals, many times offering to step aside in a coalition for the sake of the greater cause. Laurier loyalists were appalled at the prospect of their party being broken again, as it had been when the protectionist Liberals defected in 1911. Many partisan Tories were also shocked by the idea of getting into bed with their political enemies. Some backbenchers, and at least one minister, Bob Rogers, were outraged that Borden was literally conspiring to destroy the traditional party system.

> My supporters were convinced that the Liberals with whom I had been negotiating were not acting in good faith; that I was altogether too guileless and was being deluded by conversations and promises which were wholly insincere; and the reproach was cast upon me that my foolish trust in certain elements of the Liberal party could be of no advantage to the country and must certainly end in the destruction of the Liberal-Conservative Party.... it was almost impossible to withstand the pressure of opinion that I was betraying a party which had given unlimited confidence and support to my leadership. A more difficult and even tragic situation for a party leader could hardly be imagined.

If negotiations failed and it had to fight a united Liberal Party on conscription, the government resolved not to be beaten by the votes of people identifiably unwilling or ineligible to fight. It brought in new electoral legislation that disfranchised conscientious objectors and citizens born in enemy countries who had come to Canada since 1902. The right to vote was given, on the other hand, to the female relatives of overseas soldiers. In his memoirs Borden justified enfranchising these women

> upon the considerations that a large number of soldiers overseas would probably be unable to vote, that many of them fighting in allied armies had not the legal right to vote, that thousands had fallen in battle whose voices were stilled, that some thousands were prisoners of war, and finally that the men fighting overseas were stripped of the influence which under normal circumstances they could exert among their fellows in an election contest.

More pithily, he told his diary of his ministers' fears that in a straight party fight "we would be beaten by French, foreigners and slackers."

In October Borden finally broke the crust of the party system and put together a coalition. The Union government consisted of Borden as prime minister and a Cabinet composed of twelve former Conservatives, eight former Liberals, and one labour representative. The conscription legislation had already been passed by Parliament, but not proclaimed. The Union government went to the country seeking a mandate for conscription, the vigorous prosecution of the war effort generally, and a program of other reforms. The 1917 election was the most bitter in Canadian history, viciously fought on both sides. Virtually everyone's loyalty and morality were called into question—although neither Borden nor Laurier sacrificed his dignity. The Unionists carried the country easily, taking 153 seats to the Liberals' 82. Sixty-two of the Liberal seats were in Quebec; the government elected only three MPs from that province.

Borden has been given a rough ride by critics who argue that he brought on the conscription crisis by combining reckless commitment to a huge Canadian army with inefficient Anglo-centric recruiting policies. Was his personal decision at the end of 1915 to double the authorized size of the Canadian forces to 500,000 men irresponsible? Did his too-cautious tolerance of Hughes mean the continuance of recruiting methods that systematically discouraged French-Canadian enlistment? If he had been a more cautious warrior on the one hand, a better administrator on the other, could he have kept out of the quicksands of conscription and coalition?

Probably not. The 500,000 authorization was a dramatic gesture, but was nothing more than a filling-in of the "blank cheque" Canada had given when it pledged all-out support for the war effort in 1914. C.P. Stacey argues that the Canadian forces would have grown to this total and beyond (they eventually reached 620,000, a much smaller contribution in proportion to population than Great Britain's) in response to the needs of the war. Most serious students of the manpower problem doubt that any amount of improvement in the recruiting campaigns would have brought forth the needed volunteers.

Most important, as Brown underlines in his biography of Borden, the Prime Minister would never have agreed to limit the support that the Dominion gave to its soldiers. He would never have broken faith with the men or the cause.

The conscription decision was a moment of truth for Borden and his generation of politicians, and for the country itself. Canadians who sent their sons to die, and the sons who faced death, had little patience with the regime of compromises and half-measures so often deemed essential for national unity. Borden had no illusions about the unpopularity of conscription in Quebec. He knew that it had the potential to spark unrest amounting to civil war. In words anticipating one of Mackenzie King's most famous comments in the next war, Borden told Charles Hibbert Tupper in January 1917, "It may be necessary to resort to compulsion. I hope not; but if the necessity arises I shall not hesitate to act accordingly."

Conscription isolated Quebec. Intense resistance to the draft boiled over in riots in Quebec City in the spring of 1918, and the government did "act accordingly," using English-speaking troops armed with machine guns to keep order. Four civilians were killed in clashes with the soldiers. Politically, Conservatism had committed suicide among French Canadians, and might not be resurrected for decades, if at all.

Perhaps the alternative would have been worse. Borden shared a widely held belief about the consequences if Canada let its fighting men down. He spelled it out in the debate on the conscription bill:

> If we do not pass this measure, if we do not provide reinforcements, if we do not keep our plighted faith, with what countenance shall we meet them on their return? ... They went forth splendid in their youth and confidence. They will come back silent, grim, determined men who, not once or twice, but fifty times, have gone over the parapet to seek their rendezvous with death. If what are left of 400,000 such men come back to Canada with fierce resentment and even rage in their hearts, conscious that they have been deserted or betrayed, how shall we meet them when they ask the reason? I am not so much concerned for the day when this Bill becomes law, as for the day when these men return if it is rejected.

In 1917 Borden believed that if Laurier returned to power he would face "an impossible situation which might precipitate rebellion." Had Borden and his friends lost touch with reality in their judgement of the situation? Possibly. Possibly not. We do know that 1917 was one of the most desperate, bloody years in the history of Western civilization. Men and nations were staking everything—their honour, their sense of duty, their love of country, their sense of comradeship and religious obligation—on seeing the war through no matter what the cost. Robert Borden was not a publicly passionate man. But on this matter he was an unwavering war leader.

*   *   *

Borden liked to hope that there was a silver lining in the coalition situation. It seemed to him that Canada's most patriotic politicians had agreed to submerge their differences for the good of the country. They had abandoned narrow partisanship, abandoned "party," stopped playing politics.

Union government seemed to be the ideal that generations of political reformers had dreamed about, a government by moderate, right-thinking men of good will and public spirit and overwhelming strength in Parliament. Other idealistic Unionists, such as the Ontario Liberal N.W. Rowell, shared Borden's hopes, and invested their reputations in what they hoped would be the best government Canada had ever seen, non-partisan, non-political. Union government would be not only a win-the-war government; it would would also be a manage-the-country, nationalize-the-railways, reform-the-social-order government, a new kind of government for a new postwar Canada. Unionism would be a way of political life; there would be no return to the old days of bitter partisanship and patronage. As prime minister of the Union government Borden established a national franchise in which all adults over age twenty-one could vote, abolished traditional patronage, brought in the most drastic civil-service reform yet, and proposed to have all future government purchasing done without regard to party. The Union government effectively completed the nationalization of the bankrupt railways, developed path-breaking programs of veterans' benefits, and toyed with schemes of extensive economic regulation to try to control war-born inflation.

Borden did not give his full attention to creating the new political order in Canada because in 1918 and 1919 he spent most of his time abroad, working on the larger question of winning the war and designing a new world order. He took immense pride in his participation in the Imperial War Cabinet and in Canada's status as a full member of the British delegation at the Paris Peace Conference, and was certain that his contributions to these deliberations were the most important work of his career.

There was no doubt in his mind that Canada was now, practically speaking, independent—though formal constitutional ratification by Great Britain of the Dominion's independence had yet to follow. But Canada was still a British country. Borden believed he was seeing the British *Empire* evolve into a British *Commonwealth* of independent nations that would freely agree, because of the strength of their common ties, to implement common foreign and defence policies. He saw himself as the Canadian spokesman at the Commonwealth councils developing such policies.

The dream of Commonwealth harmony was fraught with difficulties, constitutional and otherwise, that only gradually became apparent. What if a member nation of the Commonwealth did not agree with the majority's view? The logic, with which Borden agreed, was that dissenters would swallow their doubts and support decisions freely taken. Thus he found himself agreeing that Canada, because it had a voice in the planning, should be a major contributor to an Allied expedition to Russia to find ways of getting that country back into the war (Russia made peace with Germany after the Communist revolution of 1917). The generals and statesmen who conceived the Russian venture had only the foggiest idea of what they were doing; the Canadian people had none. The first Canadian conscript soldiers arrived in Vladivostok two weeks before the war ended. The British government pressed hard to keep forces in Siberia to help thwart the forces of Bolshevism. The Canadian Cabinet made clear to Borden that public opinion would not support a continued intervention; he eventually insisted that the Canadian contingent be brought home. The British were not happy. It was not an auspicious beginning to the idea of a common Commonwealth policy.

Borden should have seen the writing on the wall anyway. He had been angered by the British so often during the war that he should have asked himself about the foundations of Commonwealth solidarity. Did being "British" mean that Canada had enough common interests with Great Britain to support common policies? Despite his reluctance to face up to the issue, he clearly had his doubts. At the Imperial War Cabinet in 1918, for example, he spoke strongly against the thought of any future British Empire policies that might jeopardize Canada's relations with the United States. He was outraged at the proposal, popular in Britain, that the Kaiser should be put on trial for war crimes. He was well aware of the British government's tendency to make decisions first and then talk about them with the Dominions later. "I am beginning to feel more and more," he wrote in his diary in 1918, "that in the end, and perhaps sooner than later, Canada must assume full sovereignty. She can give better service to G.B. and U.S. and to the world in that way."

Borden became the first prime minister to see Canada as having vitally important ties with both the United States and Great Britain. Canada must never have to choose one over the other—ideally it might be a mediator or linch-pin between the two, the hypotenuse in what Canadian statesmen came to call the "North Atlantic triangle." This shifting focus of Canada's vision reflected broad cultural and economic realignments (there was significant integration of the North American war effort after the United States joined the conflict in 1917). On a more personal level, Borden became the first prime minister to take regular holidays in the United States. He was not uncomfortable in that country, and he became increasingly impatient with what he found in the motherland. During an Imperial War Cabinet meeting Lord Curzon asked him, "What is Canadian opinion with respect to the social order prevailing in this country?" "If you wish me to speak frankly," the North American prime minister replied, "we regard your social order as little more than a glorified feudal system." Conversation stopped. In the spring of 1918 the Borden government abolished the granting of hereditary titles to Canadians as being "entirely incompatible with the ideas of democracy as they have developed in this country." In his retirement Borden concluded that titles for Canadians should be abolished entirely, and would have cheerfully surrendered his own knighthood.

The façade of postwar unity was as fragile at home as it was abroad. The Union government was the child of war and its peacetime future was dubious at best, almost certainly nonexistent without Borden's leadership. The more Borden stayed abroad, the more his ministers urged him to come home. "We are launched on a troubled sea without chart, compass or captain," the aged minister Sir George Foster wrote at the beginning of 1920, as the government staggered on while Borden tried to regain strength on a holiday.

Torn between exhaustion and determination to do his duty—everyone kept saying that he was indispensable—Borden hoped that the Unionists could create a political organization and a platform that would sustain them electorally. The vision of an alliance of moderate, non-partisan politicians working for the public good energized him as late as June 1919, when he suggested to caucus the formal creation of a Unionist Party, and outlined an eleven-point platform. The government's greatest problem was lack of Quebec support—Borden and some of the ministers approached the Quebec premier, Sir Lomer Gouin, and several other French-Canadian Liberals known to have conservative sympathies, about coming on board.

The Quebecers refused to join forces with the ministers who had imposed conscription. Most of the other bases for Unionist rejuvenation were fragile. Borden's proposed platform, for example, was full of generalities and clichés.

("The adoption of such policies and measures as will tend to compose differences, to harmonize divergence and to unite all our scattered communities in the common ideal and purpose of true national endeavour.") An ageing progressive whose best statement of his ideas had been in the Halifax platform more than a decade earlier, Borden now had no new ideas in domestic policy, no ideological or practical response to a wave of social, democratic, and populist ferment that was sweeping the country.

Even so, the government had made sweeping changes, including bringing in serious civil-service reform and conceding women's right to vote. Borden tried to bring in one last progressive measure, a bill to abolish patronage in government purchasing by creating an independent purchasing commission. Politicians on both sides of the House rejected the idea, and he realized the government might lose its majority if it forced the matter. He surrendered to the forces of the old politics of Macdonald and Laurier, but not without lecturing the House of Commons in a moral tone no other prime minister would have used:

> It really does seem remarkable that when a Government is making a most earnest attempt ... to rid itself and future governments of the evils of patronage ... the attempt should be met with such resistance on both sides of the House.... The elimination of political patronage, whether in the appointment of public servants or in the purchase of public supplies, is eminently in the public interest.... I do not know ... of any other means by which the evil can be eliminated.... If anyone, in or out of the House, can suggest a better method, I am ready to consider and accept it. For the purpose, not the method, I am in earnest, in deadly earnest.

*   *   *

Borden finally decided to leave the job of reshaping Canadian politics to a younger man. On July 10, 1920, he attended his last Cabinet meeting as prime minister and went to the swearing-in of his successor, Arthur Meighen. "So ended ... my public life of twenty-four years," he wrote in his *Memoirs*, "during which, doubtless, I had made many mistakes but in which I had always striven to do my duty as God gave me to see it." Borden retired to private life, accepted a few directorships, emerged on several occasions to undertake assignments as a respected elder statesman, and in the privacy of his study proved a wry observer of the passing scene—writing a series of "letters to Limbo" (an imaginary newspaper) for his own amusement. He died in 1937.

If Macdonald had been a British politician in Canada, and Laurier a Canadian politician, Borden had been a British-Canadian politician. Though he came to dislike the Old Country's social structure, he never doubted the underlying excellence of Canada's British parliamentary system of government, and he never doubted the permanence of the British connection through Canadian adherence to the monarchy and the Empire or Commonwealth. As a progressive, twentieth-century citizen, Borden hoped to reform the abuses of the political system. He followed Macdonald and Laurier, especially the former, in believing in big, active government. He would go further. In a new age he was ready to extend government into bold new realms of ownership and regulation—and also to extend democracy itself by granting the universal suffrage that both Macdonald and Laurier had disliked.

As part of the world's tragedy of 1914–1918 Borden found himself extending the arm of government into Canadian institutions and lives in the worst possible ways. "It is not an agreeable duty to summon the splendid youth and manhood of our country by the hundred thousand to take up arms, to undergo untold hardship and suffering, to make perchance the supreme sacrifice," he said in 1917. He never wanted to be a war leader, but Canada was fortunate to be led by him during the Great War. He made his share of mistakes, some of them serious, but his integrity, his earnestness, his capacity for hard work, his determination to rise above party and above politics, all struck the right notes. Borden never became a beloved Canadian institution; he did win most Canadians' respect.

The best Conservative prime minister of the twentieth century ("best of a bad lot, surely," one of my Liberal friends scribbles in the margin of this manuscript), both as war leader and as reformer, Borden was also one of the more successfully authoritarian leaders. He fended off several challenges to his leadership while in opposition, and once in government became the man at the top who made decisions and expected his supporters to fall into line. "Political partisanship is closely allied with absolute stupidity," he wrote in his retirement. Unlike Macdonald and Laurier, he was not a devoted party man, and made little effort to jolly along the rank and file—who often chafed under his leadership. There is at least one documented case of the Prime Minister mistaking one of his backbenchers for a page boy.

At the same time, Borden did more than any other prime minister before Brian Mulroney to disrupt the Canadian political system. He engineered a coalition government, and fought the 1917 election out of his sense of duty to the fighting men and because he did not believe very much in political parties anyway. At the end of the war his Union government led a victorious nation marching to full independence. But Quebec was estranged and there were deep new wounds between members of the country's major ethnic groups. Other powerful interests, notably farmers and labour, had war-heightened expectations while nursing old grievances. They, too, began to revolt against the traditional political system. Partisanship would not end; it would simply put on new clothes.

But these were problems others could handle. Under Robert Laird Borden's leadership Canada had survived. As a people at war, their hopes and fears and fondest Christian ideals carried into battle by the flower of their youth, Canadians had achieved great things. Like the soldiers, the Prime Minister had done his duty in a time of trial, and had kept faith with the men buried in Flanders fields.

Dale/Winnipeg/Free Press/19 January 1931

"My Government"

R.B. Bennett's one-man band

4

MEIGHEN AND BENNETT
The Crisis of the Self-Made Leader

There were ordinary everyday fools, and there were damned fools. Between the wars there were ordinary everyday Conservatives, and there were the two men who led the party: Arthur Meighen and Richard Bedford Bennett. Quite a few of the ordinary Conservatives suspected that Meighen and Bennett were damned fools. Quite a few ordinary Canadians thought all Conservatives were fools anyway, backward and out of touch with the common man in a democratic century.

Perhaps the majority was right. The half-century from the 1920s to the 1970s was a hard time, in Canada and many other countries, for conservative people. Many of them yearned to return to an old order that seemed to have ended so abruptly that beautiful summer of 1914. Conservatives seemed to have few answers to urgent problems of economic security, liberty, and authority in a world shaken by economic disorder and awash with ideological passion. Nothing is more futile in politics or life than trying to turn the clock back. Conservatives seemed to be clock-turners.

Canadian Conservatives were bound to have a hard time coping with the country's confusions after the Great War, not least because they had been in power during it and could be blamed for many of the disruptions it had created, including the near-collapse of the traditional party system. It would be a Liberal politician, Mackenzie King, who rebuilt and adapted the system and became the "master spirit" of Canadian politics in the democratic age. The poor Tories took decades to recover. Perhaps they were not in touch again with the spirit of the times until the 1980s—and then only briefly.

Could the debacle have been avoided? Did things have to be quite so bad? Surely it would have helped a lot if the interwar leadership of the party had not seemed to be acting on a Freudian death wish. Arthur Meighen and R.B. Bennett were disasters as leaders of men; their author-itarian stewardship nearly ruined their party. Theirs was the kind of lead-ership that helped give "conservatism," both the small-c and the big-C variety, a bad name.

One reason why they failed was that they had been so successful in their personal lives. Meighen and Bennett were both self-made men of immense raw energy and awesome self-discipline. Both developed an outlook on life that was narrow, self-centred, righteous, and profoundly anti-political. Borden had had much the same background and some of the same charac-ter traits, but had managed to overcome his weaknesses in a period of enlightened leadership—which had, however, left in its wake a nearly ruined political party. Possessed of all Borden's flaws and few of his strengths, Meighen and Bennett made the situation worse. The Conservative Party would have been hard-pressed to survive war and depression and the advent of mass democracy under the most creative leadership. Under Meighen and Bennett, both of whom believed in the mission of men of great ability to govern the usually foolish masses, there was almost no hope.

*   *   *

Let us start by mentioning the Conservative prime minister who might have been. When Borden canvassed the Union government's parliamen-tary caucus in July of 1920 to gather opinion on a successor, the over-whelming choice of his Cabinet ministers was Sir Thomas White, the Minister of Finance. White had held the job since 1911. He was fifty-four, a lawyer and businessman, formerly a Liberal, one of the "Toronto Eighteen" who had come over to the Conservatives on the reciprocity issue. White was able and sensible, was reasonably popular with his col-leagues and respected across Canada, and was a non-partisan politician much like Borden. Borden personally favoured White.

Tom White became the only Canadian to turn down a request from the Governor-General that he form a government. His years in public life had exhausted him (Borden and White were among the few politicians anywhere to have held such high positions in their country from the first to the last days of the Great War), and imperilled his financial security. A stint as acting prime minister while Borden was abroad quenched any lingering ambition for the top job; the worry and strain convinced him that he was temperamentally unfit. He refused an offer of a trust fund from his friends, saying he was going to leave politics.

Borden thought it important at least to go through the formality of having the Governor-General ask White to form a ministry. Many of his colleagues would not serve with anyone else until White had refused; there was always a chance that he was playing coy, and would surrender to rekindled ambition or sense of duty.

He did not. White turned down the Duke of Devonshire's request and returned to private life. He lived for another thirty-four years. Some of his friends thought that if he had had a stronger sense of moral obligation to serve his country, he might have become a great leader. In fact, it is doubtful that anyone could have led the Conservatives to victory in 1921. White would probably have fought the best fight in a lost cause. The course he chose itself became an important tradition in Canadian life—of the high-achieving, talented individual who turns his back on politics. White's uniqueness was to have served so long near the top and then to refuse a direct offer of the prime-ministership. Today many of the Tom Whites never serve at all, and the country is the poorer.*

*   *   *

Arthur Meighen believed that any sensible Canadian boy would aspire to become prime minister. He shared the old-fashioned view of politics as a noble calling. He was like Macdonald and Laurier in moving quickly into politics, virtually as a career choice.

Meighen was born on a farm in south-western Ontario in 1874. His parents were hard-working and God-fearing and respectful of education

---

* There was some evidence of that tendency beginning to be reversed in the 1993 general election. The Liberals, in particular, attracted a number of highly talented candidates who appeared to be risking considerable pecuniary and professional sacrifice out of a sense of public service.

and ambition. They instilled in Arthur an intense commitment to hard work, Protestant moral precepts, and the desire to get ahead. He single-mindedly applied himself to his studies at the University of Toronto, forgoing extra-curricular activities, to earn a first-class honours degree in mathematics in 1896. He found a job teaching high school, but quit after a year of feuding with trustees about his insistence on disciplining their children—a kind of microcosm of his future.

Meighen went west, read law in Winnipeg, and settled down to practise it in Portage la Prairie. He did well in the booming Manitoba town, made a happy marriage, joined the Conservative Party, was elected to Parliament in 1908, and quickly made an impressive mark in the House of Commons. "Borden has found a man," Laurier said after Meighen's maiden speech.

Meighen's strengths were debating and hard work. From his high school days he had enjoyed debating as a kind of intellectual swordsman-ship. Not sword*play*, in the tradition of stretching minds and wits in friendly rivalry, but sword*fighting* as deadly combat between those in the right and those in the wrong. Meighen had the sharp and narrow mind of the trained mathematician, honed by school-teaching and legal advocacy. Propositions were either true or false. If false they were nonsensical, absurd, ridiculous, contemptible. He believed that the views he held were intellectually and morally right, and his opponents' views were similarly wrong. In the political arena that righteousness translated into intense partisanship, readily appreciated in party circles. "Meighen made a magnificent speech which greatly enthused all our men," Borden told his diary one night in 1913. "Have decided to make him Solicitor General."

Ironically, Meighen was promoted for a speech explaining why the government was limiting debate, at the time of the Liberal filibustering on the naval question. As one of the architects of closure, Meighen broke sharply with the traditions of the Canadian Parliament—angering in passing the most revered of Commons debaters, Laurier himself.

Meighen's reputation as a parliamentarian became absurdly inflated in the reminiscences of his handful of admirers. As a debater in the House of Commons, he was no more the equal of Macdonald or Laurier than liquor-store alcohol resembles good scotch. His speeches lacked any semblance of wit, breadth of learning, or rhetorical eloquence. They were fact-filled, earnest, logical, intense, and arrogant, much like their author. Meighen saw debate as an instrument of intellectual power in the cause of political dominance. When it came time to put an end to tiresome speechifying by the Opposition, he saw no reason not to apply closure. At best, he was a throwback to the Grit moralists of the nineteenth century, Edward Blake and Richard Cartwright. At worst, he stood out as an arrogant, verbose orator who furthered the decline of parliamentary debate in the twentieth century.

As Solicitor-General, Meighen became Borden's workhorse, drafting and defending complex and often controversial pieces of legislation. He designed both the conscription act and the special electoral laws of 1917, and thus would become a politician without Francophone friends in Quebec. His work on nationalizing the bankrupt private railways and melding them into the Canadian National Railways made him the father of the CNR, and thus cost him many Tory CPR friends in Montreal. The draconian measures he introduced to punish leaders of the Winnipeg General Strike in 1919 won him the enduring hostility of the labour movement. In all of these debates Meighen, a gaunt, ramrod, often poorly dressed man (one journalist compared him to a "moulting bobolink"), scored points only on the floor of the House and with the government's backbenchers.

It was the backbenchers who in 1920 told Borden they wanted Meighen to be their leader. Meighen was not an old-fashioned machine politician. Neither was he in any way a reformer. He toed, expounded, and clarified the party line, acting like a good Conservative in a government that was still nominally a coalition. Thoughtful Unionists, such as Saskatchewan's James A. Calder, could not see him as their leader: "Meighen is absolutely out of the question in so far as Quebec is concerned," he wrote Borden. "... I do not think Meighen possesses the necessary qualities to ensure his success as a leader at any time in the future." Borden himself wondered privately: "Meighen is a man of brilliant ability, high courage, inflexible determination and great persistence. He has a fair fund of patience, but I am not sure whether it will stand very numerous draughts thereon in the years immediately in front of him." Even Meighen's father apparently let Borden know he thought Arthur was too young and too ambitious to become prime minister. And the new Liberal leader, Mackenzie King, told his diary that "for the country's sake" White should replace Borden, while Meighen's leadership would be best for the Liberal Party.

The best judgement on Meighen's capacity to be prime minister was passed by one of the Conservative Party's elder statesmen, Sir Joseph Flavelle, a few years later:

Meighen is clever, destructive in debate, crushing in criticism, but there it ends. No one possessed of such qualities can command heart loyalty…. He is by qualification intended for first lieutenant, in place of commander-in-chief. He should be the fighting mate of a big, simple, human man, who would win the affection and command the respect of his party. He is the terrier who worries the other fellow, the auditor who discovers mistakes in the man of constructive imagination.

Even Thomas White did not exactly fill Flavelle's specification of a "big, simple, human man," and there was no one else but Meighen. So the caucus went with him, and on July 10, 1920, Arthur Meighen, a hard-working small-town lawyer, became prime minister. The Union coalition disappeared in all but name (it was formally dissolved just before the 1921 election). The Conservatives had chosen a leader from the second team. "It is too good to be true," Mackenzie King exclaimed to himself, relishing the thought of fighting against "a Tory through and through."

*   *   *

Lacking imagination, judgement, and reform instincts, Meighen did not know what to do with power. His liabilities included the groups who disliked him—French Canadians, Montreal business interests, organized labour. Beyond his own intellectual abilities, he had one obvious advantage: the sundered Liberal Party was only gradually reuniting under its inexperienced, insecure leader, King.

There was a second possible asset in the alienation of farmers across Canada. They were fed up with the old parties' neglect of agriculture. They were worried about the future of farming and farm prices in a city-dominated, consumer-oriented country. Now that the war and the Union government had shattered the old allegiances, farmers were leaving the Liberals and Conservatives in droves to form their own political movements—United Farmers of Alberta, of Ontario, of Saskatchewan, of Manitoba; for national politics they called themselves Progressives. The sprawling farmlands of Western Canada were their spawning-ground and spiritual home. When the farmers of the prairie lands began marching in their might, Canada would surely wake up and take notice.

The farmers' movements generated windy rhetoric about change, and prescient ideas about the desirability of bringing political parties under closer democratic control. But on most matters of social policy farmers were deeply conservative. Like most of Arthur Meighen's followers, they were not interested in the radicalism being pushed by the left and pondered by King's Liberals. Were there prospects, then, of the Conservatives cultivating their natural ties with farmers? Could they unite on a platform of reforms to the political system—loosening discipline and partisanship, strengthening ties back to constituents—to make the parties more responsive to agrarian interests, as a young Borden might have favoured? Could the Conservatives support greater economic freedom, such as the open markets and tariff reductions that many farmers wanted? Arthur Meighen was the first Canadian prime minister to call Western Canada his home. Could he become the west's authentic voice in Ottawa?

Not a chance. Meighen's spiritual home was somewhere back in the nineteenth century. In the United States Warren Harding and the Republicans were urging a return to "normalcy" after the disruptions of war. So, in Canada, was Arthur Meighen. Here is the voice of Canadian Conservatism at the beginning of the 1920s:

> The great task before the people of Canada is to get back ... to old time sanity of thought and action, to get back to our old high standards of living and character—standards handed down to us by our forebears. We have been living for the last six years in a highly abnormal and artificial age, and the sooner we get to normal conditions the better it will be for all of us.... in our hearts we know that much of that which is new is superficial and transitory, some of it unreal and based upon insecure foundations. The public mind is confused with a veritable Babel of uninformed tongues. A great many people seem to have lost all sense of values, of proportion and of numbers; extravagance in thought is as great as the undoubted extravagance in living. It is an age of indulgence, in Isms and theories. Thousands of people are mentally chasing rainbows, striving for the unattainable, anxious to better their lot and seemingly unwilling to do it in the old fashioned way by hard honest intelligent effort. Dangerous doctrines taught by dangerous men, enemies of the State, poison and pollute the air....

Meighen boiled the yearning for "old time sanity" down into one major idea—support for protective tariffs! Macdonald's old National Policy had carried the Tory party through thick and thin in the past, and he, Meighen, was going to take his stand on it for the future.

So much for the farm movement. The new PM's uncompromising protectionism, accompanied by his thinly veiled contempt for the Progressives as "a dilapidated annex to the Liberal party," meant that he had turned his back on the one constituency that might have spelled the difference between manageable defeat and the disaster approaching for his government.

He would not even fudge his protectionism, or any of his other positions, deliberately dulling his debating sword for the sake of popularity. That, he thought, would be dishonest and immoral. "I know that another stand would be more popular in the West," he told a follower afterwards, "but a great party cannot shuffle and a leader worthy of the name never shuffles." Meighen would not shuffle, in the west or in Quebec: "I favoured conscription ... I introduced the Military Service Act.... I spoke for it time and time again ... I did it because I thought it right," he told Quebecers, asking for their votes in the 1921 election. He did not get many.

Not unlike Kim Campbell's ill-fated administration seventy years later, Meighen's was a government of burnt-out and out-of-touch Tories. Meighen looked for a Quebec "Cartier" and could not find one. When he rebuilt his Cabinet before the election, he appointed four French-Canadian ministers, none of whom had as yet been elected. Only one of them had ever sat in Parliament, and that had been from 1896 to 1900. "Canada Needs Meighen" was the government's slogan on the hustings. Canadians disagreed: the government was crushed, clinging to only 50 seats, compared with 117 for the Liberals and 65 for the Progressives. Meighen, who had been prime minister for eighteen months, carried no seats in Quebec, no seats on the prairies.

*   *   *

Desperation leads otherwise sane politicians into wild contradictions and risk-taking. Later in life it was important to Arthur Meighen that he be known as a man of the highest integrity and consistency. He was fortunate in finding a history professor, Roger Graham, willing to argue that position with great conviction through three volumes of biography. In reality, and Graham was too honest to fully hide it in his own pages,

Meighen careered from scheme to scheme, stratagem to stratagem, in his search to regain power in the 1920s. He baffled and sometimes angered other Conservatives. He maintained consistency only in his own eyes.

Thanks to Borden, Meighen was the first prime minister of an independent Canada. A few constitutional wrinkles remained to be ironed out, but few doubted that Canada could now act on the world stage as its government decided. Meighen was like Borden and their Conservative predecessors, however, in believing that Canada was a British nation, bound by ties of history, blood, culture, institutions, and sentiment to a family of British nations. The Commonwealth ought to act as one unit, he believed, in its relations with other countries. Could this doctrine of Empire or Commonwealth solidarity be meshed with real Canadian independence?

Perhaps it could, so long as no vital interests were at stake. Arthur Meighen's one significant contribution to Commonwealth affairs came at the 1921 Imperial Conference in London, which some went so far as to call a meeting of the "Imperial Cabinet." Meighen argued with some force and effect that Great Britain ought to reconsider the future of its alliance with Japan in view of the need for the best possible relations with the United States. The British agreed, despite the objections of Australia and New Zealand, and the Anglo-Japanese alliance ended.

At this conference and at the Washington naval conference later in the year, Canada's special role was to be particularly sensitive to the Empire's relationship with the United States. Perhaps Canada might have a distinct voice in the Commonwealth as the member most in touch with American aspirations. On the other hand, what would have happened if the prime ministers had been unable to agree on the future of the Anglo-Japanese alliance? There was little evidence in 1921 of any Commonwealth will to establish formal mechanisms to ensure solidarity on future matters. In principle, everyone hoped there would continue to be a common imperial foreign policy, but no one, including Canada, was willing to be bound to one.

Arthur Meighen felt bound to Britain by all the traditional ties that had influenced Canadian Conservatives since 1763. His first trip to England, in 1917, was marred by intense seasickness. But his feelings on landing, as Roger Graham beautifully describes them, shrank the ordeal to little more than crossing a millpond:

It was worth all his discomfort to see England at last. It was in a way like a homecoming to his second, spiritual home, with which he felt instinctively and deeply a kinship that nothing would ever destroy. For him England, whose history and literature he had read and loved, was always a shining citadel of all that was worthwhile in life. It was Mother England, from whose long experience had come those blessings of parliamentary government and ordered liberty and those examples of courage, good sense and wisdom which were at once the hope and envy of the world. As he walked the streets of London, meeting scenes familiar to him through word and picture, the old farms near St. Marys, the drab surroundings and small affairs of Portage la Prairie—even the more glamorous, exciting life of Parliament Hill—seemed remote, part of another world. But, at the same time, his trip to England brought home to him more forcibly the truth of what he had always felt: that Canada was a vital part of a great communion that bridged the oceans and brought the continents together, a fellowship to which she must remain true if she were to be true to herself. Mere geography could never destroy the ties of sentiment, tradition and self-interest which bound the old land and the new together.

Given these feelings, Meighen's response as leader of the Opposition to 1922's imperial crisis was probably predictable. Britain and Turkey were near a confrontation over the stronghold of Chanak. Framing a scenario of war with Turkey over Chanak, and not bothering to consult anyone, the British government asked the dominions how they would help. Prime Minister Mackenzie King, who learned of the request from journalists, was furious, and stated coldly that Canada's Parliament would decide what, if any, help might be forthcoming. Meighen saw only a troubled motherland asking for help, and declared that Canada ought to have answered Britain with the same phrase Laurier had used in 1914: "Ready, aye, ready!"

This was lunacy. The price of loyalty in 1914 had been 60,000 Canadian graves in Flanders. Who in his right mind would volunteer to fight for the British Empire in Turkey?

A few years later Meighen went to the opposite extreme. In calmer moments he knew that French Canadians would not vote Conservative so long as they thought the party might impose conscription again. In a major speech in Hamilton, *after* the election campaign of 1925, Meighen announced a new policy about sending Canadian troops abroad: none should ever be dispatched until the government had received Parliament's consent *and* had gone to the people in a general election.

If the response to Chanak had confirmed French-Canadian doubts about Meighen, the Hamilton proposal caused thousands of Anglophone Conservatives to wonder if their leader had any judgement at all. The idea seemed madly impractical. Worse, Meighen had said nothing in this vein during the election campaign, and now offered his Hamilton stance just before a crucial by-election in Quebec. Was this the politics of principle and consistency? Or was it a desperate reversal to catch French-Canadian votes? And what was to be said of the Conservative leader's overall conduct of the 1925 election, in which he had made a deal to allow a Quebec "lieutenant," E.L. Patenaude, to run an independent campaign while he, Meighen, stayed out of the province! Courage and consistency? Crass office-seeking? Perhaps a speeding bobsled, lurching from one side of the run to the other, uncontrolled by judgement or balance?

Whatever their motivation, all of Meighen's Quebec stratagems failed dismally. While he was leader the party failed to win a single non-English constituency in Quebec. Patenaude went nowhere. The provincial Conservative Party usually ignored the federal party. Promoting Quebec Conservatism at the national level was little more than an expensive hobby for cantankerous Montreal millionaires. For a time in the 1920s, the party's Quebec headquarters was a suite at the Mount Royal Hotel.

Meighen held firm to some other principles he might have profitably abandoned. He fudged a little, but never really backed away from high-tariff protectionism. Grudgingly admitting that some regions of the country might not benefit from high tariffs, the Tories proposed more, rather than less, state paternalism, in the form of subsidized railway freight rates. Some Conservatives in the 1920s, like some of the farmers, were beginning to suggest that enterprise should be liberated from excessive entanglement with the state (Howard Ferguson's Ontario government best caught the new spirit) but Meighen was firmly in the Macdonald–Laurier–Borden tradition of big government. In and out of power he continued to defend the decision to create the sprawling, debt-laden, publicly owned CNR. He would not entertain proposals that it be privatized, possibly under the management of the CPR, because that might mean an effective railway monopoly. Montreal's CPR interests remained alienated from the Conservative Party, but at least Meighen had been consistent. In the late 1930s he would change his mind and conclude that government ownership of a major railway system had been bound to fail.

The clumsy attempts to court the French-Canadian vote were not matched by initiatives, slick or otherwise, to find farmer support in Western Canada. Meighen's rigid views on the tariff were a barrier, and so was his unwillingness to consider any reform of Canada's parliamentary system. Its rigidity was one of the Progressives' main grievances. They wanted to break open the top-down, Cabinet–caucus control of parties to allow MPs more independence. At the least the Progressives wanted to see more free votes in the House; many of them wanted Canada to experiment with such direct democratic devices as referenda, voter initiation of legislative proposals, and schemes to recall MPs who disregarded constituents' wishes.

Anticipating the Tory mentality that finally killed the party in the 1990s, Meighen could not understand the need for reform. His idea of governing was to govern, and let the people judge, later, how well you had done. None of the Progressives' populist proposals for extending democracy were of the slightest interest to the Conservative Party during his leadership. Mackenzie King, on the other hand, who held power in a minority situation after 1921, knew the precariousness of his situation and often revised his policies after hearing opinion in the House of Commons. Meighen condemned King for running a "guess-work government" that trimmed its policies to court support from elected MPs.

There was a particularly revealing exchange of views one day in the 1922 session, when the King government seemed to be waffling, trying to discern MPs' views on the future of oleomargarine (many farmers were fiercely opposed to legalizing the butter substitute). The leader of the Opposition lost patience:

> Mr. MEIGHEN: ... The function of the Government is to come to Parliament with definite proposals on public questions, submit them to Parliament, and ask for its judgement upon them. That has been the practice in the world, and in this country, until we had the present phantom of a government in office....
>
> Mr. CRERAR: ... if the view of my hon. friend is held to the letter, it simply means that a dozen gentlemen composing the Government of this country will decide in Cabinet Council what is good for

the country, and then come to Parliament and say; you must take this or turn us out.

Mr. CASGRAIN: Toryism.

Mr. MEIGHEN: That is right.... The Government is virtually standing up and asserting "... We ask that we be mere clerks of the House of Commons; we ask that we do not have the responsibilities of government at all; we ask that we be allowed to sit here and ask Parliament, by a vote, to decide what we ought to do as a government." ... You cannot carry on government that way....

Mr. KING: ... The whole evolution of constitutional government has been that it is gradually subjecting the executive to the will of Parliament and there is an effort to make Parliament more and more an expression of the will of the people. I contend that is exactly what we are attempting to do to-day and if it means further evolution in giving expression to the constitutional rights of the people we will do all that we can to develop that evolution.

When the chips were down and Meighen's future hinged on his understanding of the will of the House of Commons, he failed. The Liberals had fewer seats than the Conservatives after the 1925 election, but kept on governing with wobbly Progressive support. A customs scandal in 1926 set the stage for certain defeat of the Liberals in the Commons. The wily King asked Governor-General Lord Byng for a dissolution instead, which would mean another election. Byng refused, arguing that Meighen ought to have a chance to form a government. King resigned. Meighen thought he would be able to get enough support in the House of Commons to survive for a decent interval and went ahead and formed a government. It lasted three days before being defeated.

In the election that followed, King alleged that Lord Byng's behaviour had been constitutionally wrong. It was probably not. The real mistake had been Meighen's miscalculation in thinking he could carry on government for more than a few hours. The leader with an honours degree in mathematics was unable to make a reliable count of the sympathies of members of Parliament. His opponent, King, understood Meighen's situation far better than Meighen did. In his diary King had earlier recorded these thoughts, after a discussion with the Governor-General about the possibility of Meighen some day being asked to form a government in the narrowly balanced Parliament:

He added he did not know whether Mr. Meighen would accept. I did not say anything but I thought at once if he did—that would be his doom for ever—office for the sake of office—he will find it hard if not impossible to resist & if he accepts and our men stand firm they can defeat him in the H. of C. on the first div'n.... Of course what he will seek will be to get control of the election machinery—let him have that if I have the people.

Meighen was humiliated by his party's defeat in 1926 and King's return to power with a working majority. He did not believe that he had failed; instead it was the voters who had let him down. "The people of Canada are on trial," he had written in *Maclean's* on the eve of the election. "On the integrity of their thinking, as reflected in the verdict of tomorrow, will depend in no small measure the standard of our public life for years to come."

He resigned his leadership, but in years to come he never admitted a mistake in 1926. It was Canadian public life, in his view, that proved deficient. Another consideration about the 1926 verdict, that it was not really a judgement on the King–Byng controversy at all, never occurred to Meighen. But the fact was that the Tories were defeated in that election because farmer voters, some of the most conservative people in Canada, chose to support the friendly Mackenzie King government rather than the aloof party led by a man who called the west his home.

He had been introverted and authoritarian, neglectful of organization, and out of touch with ordinary Canadians as well as his caucus. His contemptuous manner in debate created sympathy for his opponents. Roger Graham, Eugene Forsey, and a few other admirers later gave him a wholly undeserved reputation as a great Conservative. A then unknown Conservative in Saskatchewan, John Diefenbaker, was much more sensitive to some of the needs of struggling Canadians in the 1920s. In 1926 the Liberals had promised to bring in modest old-age pensions for the needy. Meighen was not impressed. Diefenbaker recalled:

I was a candidate twice under Mr. Meighen when I had to try publicly to explain matters that were unexplainable. During the 1926 campaign, Meighen had a tremendous meeting in the Third Avenue Methodist Church in Saskatoon. During the question period, an elderly gentleman by the name of Eby, something of a local institution and much beloved ... rose and asked, "Why are you opposed to old age pensions?" For ten minutes Meighen took apart the man as only he could. Support in the audience went down the drain.... And they tell me today that the Meighen name is magic in Canadian politics.

In 1927 the Conservative Party held a convention to choose a new leader and consider new policies. It was the first broadly based convention the Conservatives had ever held. As retiring leader, Meighen was of course invited to speak. He ought to have made a gracious swansong. Instead he chose to defend his Hamilton speech, which, until this speech in its defence, had been the most foolish of his career. As any sensible man would have anticipated, Meighen outraged many of the party's most stalwart followers. Howard Ferguson, the popular Premier of Ontario, insisted on taking the podium after Meighen finished, and publicly scolded him. There had been some feeling that Meighen's speech was an attempt to rouse the convention to re-acclaim him leader. "If the Convention chooses to endorse Mr. Meighen, I would dissociate myself entirely from the activities of this Convention," Ferguson proclaimed, putting an end to any hope Meighen might have had of succeeding himself. Thoughtful Conservatives judged that Arthur Meighen's last act of leadership had been almost unbelievably self-centred and stupid, a damn fool way to behave in politics.

At age fifty-two Arthur Meighen left the public arena, his faith in democracy severely shaken. He had aimed too high, for a position requiring judgemental and brokerage skills he did not have. Arthur Meighen should have served loyally as chairman of the math department and coach of the debating team. Like Joe Clark and Brian Mulroney in the 1980s, he was born to be a lieutenant, not a general.

*   *   *

"It has been said that I am a man of great wealth. It is true. I got it by my own untiring efforts.... "

It was easy to parody the new Tory leader, R.B. Bennett, as a plutocrat of plutocrats. He was a rotund, pin-striped millionaire who as a youth had deliberately overeaten to give himself the dignity of flesh. He had a rich, deep speaking voice, and he liked the sound of it, especially in the first person singular. He was a workaholic with no interest in recreations, a bachelor with no home of his own, a Calgarian who was the spitting image of a Montreal tycoon, a largely friendless man loved by Conservatives because they thought he might be a winner and because he had a wide-open chequebook. The party got its money, like its ideas, in those years, from a few insiders. Bennett claimed to have spent half a million dollars of his own money on the party between 1927 and the 1930 election call:

> I look upon it [wealth] as a solemn trust to enable me to serve my country without fear or regard for the future ... henceforth I must dedicate my talent and my time and such qualities as I may have, the fortune that God has been good enough to give me, to the interests of my country....

The difference between Bennett and some well-to-do politicians was that he really did mean it. He was an ambitious man, but he did not go into politics to feather his nest or even to defend the interests of his species. Like Borden, he entered politics from a sense that it was natural for the rich and successful to use their talents to give something back to the country. Bennett was more inconsistent than his predecessors about the political calling, sometimes dropping out to nurse his large and fragile ego, but in 1927 decided he was ready to give his all to save the Conservative Party, and through it to improve Canada.

By the 1930 election, the job seemed to be to save a country with a serious unemployment problem from the *laissez-faire* attitudes of the Liberals. Within months it became evident that a major depression was imperilling the standard of living of millions of Canadians. Fighting the Great Depression became the central theme of Bennett's prime-ministership. During the worst economic crisis of the twentieth century, Canada was governed by a millionaire with either a messiah complex or horrible judgement, perhaps both. Certainly no ordinary politician would make the personal commitment R.B. Bennett did in 1930—to end unemployment or perish in the attempt.

*   *   *

Well, Dick Bennett was a Methodist, and Methodists were taught that all things could come to those who believed and worked. And Bennett was another of the relatively poor Canadian boys of the late nineteenth century who made spectacularly good, not unlike the heroes of Horatio Alger's popular novels.

He was born in 1870 in eastern New Brunswick, not fifty miles from Borden's Nova Scotia village. Like Borden and Meighen, Bennett took family, church, and school seriously, and worked hard. The Atlantic provinces were a seedbed of bright young men on the make. Two of Bennett's friends from his New Brunswick years, Max Aitken and James Dunn, also became enormously successful businessmen. All three eventually became titled. Sir James Dunn made millions as a stockbroker in Britain and came home to Canada to be the caesar of the Algoma Steel Company. Aitken became Lord Beaverbrook, politician and press magnate and bon vivant extraordinaire, and played out his life on the grand stage at the centre of the Empire. Bennett, we will see, finished his life as Beaverbrook's neighbour in the next mansion over, but took a roundabout, more Canadian, and more earnest way of getting there.

Beaverbrook was probably the best friend that Bennett ever had, and later wrote an affectionate memoir of their relationship entitled *Friends*. Save us from our friends, as Beaverbrook draws attention to young Bennett's austerity, egotism, quick temper, and flair for self-dramatization. "First there came Bennett, conceited and young/Who never knew quite when to hold his quick tongue," his classmates at teachers' college wrote of him. "He was a young man of too many negatives—no smoking, no drinking, no dancing, no games of chance," wrote Beaverbrook (for whom there were no negatives). After school-teaching, Bennett read law at Dalhousie, where he was an outstanding and unpopular student. He excelled in Mock Parliament and Moot Court, but developed a verbose speaking style characteristic of old-fashioned platform politicians and revivalist preachers. Even friendly listeners noticed the "windyness" of his rapidly delivered and very long speeches.

Like Meighen, Bennett went west to find his fortune, moving to Calgary in 1896. The fortune was his for the finding: he prospered in real-estate speculations, company promotions, and law practice as a partner of the city's most prominent Conservative, James A. (later Senator Sir James) Lougheed. Naturally Bennett drifted into electoral politics, serving in the territorial legislature (Alberta became a province in 1905) and running for Parliament in 1911. Bob Edwards, editor of the *Calgary Eye Opener*, commented that Bennett "would be a very clever fellow if he did not know it," and many agreed. The *Albertan* referred to him as the "wind instrument."

Somebody nicknamed him "Bonfire Bennett" because of his speaking style. He burned most hotly on imperial questions. He was the most British of Canada's British Conservatives, an imperialist to the core, who believed passionately in imperial free trade as the alternative to freer trade with the United States. The *Globe* described Bennett in the 1913 debate on the Naval Aid Bill as "lashing himself into paroxysms of fortissimo oratory, pounding his desk, shaking his fists and declaiming the great peril, the great menace that threatened to wipe out the whole British Empire."

Backbencher Bennett was a little too emotional and erratic for Prime Minister Borden's taste (he did not help himself by damning the government's railway policy and calling Arthur Meighen a "gramophone" for the Canadian Northern), and was not promoted to the Cabinet in the manner he expected. When he was not given the Senate seat he believed Borden had promised him, he threw epistolary temper tantrums so severe that Borden (and others) wondered about his mental balance. Ernest Watkins, a biographer almost as friendly to Bennett as Beaverbrook, labels him moody, unstable, solitary, insecure, and neurotic.

Bennett left politics in 1917, made more money, inherited a controlling interest in the E.B. Eddy pulp and paper company in Hull, Quebec, from a widowed friend of his youth, and was lured back to Ottawa by Meighen to be Minister of Justice in his 1921 government. In the election that year he was beaten by sixteen votes on a judicial recount that hinged on whether ballots could be marked with fountain pens and coloured pencils. Bennett appealed the negative ruling to the Supreme Court of Canada and lost.

He was so bombastic and pompous, a near comic figure, that he never would have returned as a senior Tory if the party had not been in such a mess. Meighen, who admired Bennett's memory and financial acumen—Bennett admired Meighen's intelligence—promised him a major portfolio if he would run in 1925. He was Minister of Finance in Meighen's aborted 1926 government, the only Conservative elected from the prairies that year, and about all the Tories had left to succeed Meighen in 1927.

Surprisingly, he seemed to have matured after mid-life, at least for a few years, as a more rounded and contained person. Borden was no special fan of Bennett's, but he was impressed as the new leader displayed "excellent judgement and ... ability in parliamentary debate." The Bennett-led Conservatives began a major revival.

Bennett was more innovative than Meighen. With a handful of brilliant organizers who borrowed from recent U.S. presidential politics, Bennett put together the best central party headquarters Canada had yet seen. By election time in 1930 the Conservatives had developed sophisticated, mechanized mailing systems, were publishing a regular party newspaper and press service, had discovered the mass-mailing uses of free postage for MPs (the King government belatedly put a stop to the Tories' most liberal abuses), and were making creative use of the new medium of radio.

In policy Bennett was at first less belligerent and divisive than Meighen, then far more activist. Canadians didn't care about the national debt, his chief organizer advised him; they would be happy to support expansive spending programs. As the happy days of the late twenties drifted into nostalgic memory, the Conservative leader became a strident advocate of government action to build a national highway, create a great St. Lawrence seaway, and promote jobs, jobs, jobs. Mackenzie King, a cautious federalist, had turned down the provinces' requests that Ottawa spend money to help them with the burden of unemployment relief; Bennett pledged that his government would intervene. King had introduced old-age pensions for the needy on a shared-cost basis; Meighen had opposed the scheme; Bennett now promised that Ottawa would assume a larger share of the costs. Most important, and in perfect harmony with his Tory forefathers, including Meighen, Bennett promised to use the tariff to protect Canadians from foreign competition in their marketplace.

The timing of his agenda could not have been more fortunate. Years of prosperity and debt and tax reduction had made it seem possible for Ottawa to loosen the purse-strings in good causes, while the recent economic downturn was making the problem of unemployment more serious than the King government (and probably Bennett too) realized. In effect, the Bennett Conservatives ran another National Policy election in 1930. The campaign echoed that of 1878, Macdonald's great comeback, as dynamic, caring Conservatives swept aside low-tariff *laissez-faire* Liberals who seemed to lack compassion:

... I say to you business men and clerks, women, housewives, and office girls, after July 28, at the first session of the new government we will pass a tariff law that will give Canadians a fair chance with their neighbours, that, or we perish in the attempt. There is no evasion, that is our promise.... Do you believe Canadian industry should have the opportunity to supply the wants of Canadian consumers? If you do, vote for us. But if you believe our boys and girls should grow up to manhood and womanhood estate and then have to go to the United States to find jobs, vote for the Liberals. If you want to give work to Japan, Czechoslovakia or some other country in place of Canada, vote for the Liberals.... What does the government do to-day to help you? ... Oh what an opportunity there is at the present time for bold, constructive leadership! This opportunity the Conservative party will seize.

Listen you agriculturalists from the west and all the other parts of Canada, you have been taught to mock at tariffs and applaud free trade. Tell me, when did free trade fight for you? You say tariffs are only for the manufacturers. I will make them fight for you as well. I will use them to blast a way into the markets that have been closed to you.

The confidence, extravagance, and conceit of Bennett's campaign were striking to observers. Sometimes he sounded like an Old Testament prophet, preaching damnation to free-traders and foreigners, offering himself and his ideas as salvation. Plus another $250,000 from his personal fortune to help with the campaign funds! The combination, and a lacklustre, disorganized Liberal campaign, made him unbeatable. The Conservatives won their first clear majority since 1911. The tide even brought in a surprising twenty-four seats in Quebec.

*　　*　　*

Five years later Bennett was overwhelmingly rejected by Canadians, and his party was shatteringly defeated. Historians' verdict on his government has been more quizzically negative. He failed to save Canada from the Great Depression, and he duly perished. But does he get credit for honest effort? Did he know what he was doing? Was he incompetent? Insensitive? Both? Was he a genuine social reformer who hit a long patch of bad luck?

Bennett's unattractive personality clouds attempts at judgement, and helps explain why at the time of writing he still awaits a thorough biography. Soon after becoming prime minister he reverted to his old form— erratic, emotional, insensitive, conceited, self-obsessed. He was a one-man band, without capacity to share success and responsibilities with his ministers. The story went round that when Bennett was seen mumbling to himself he was holding a Cabinet meeting. "He was not above asking the opinions of others," the Tory journalist Grattan O'Leary remembered wryly. "He was only above accepting them."

His popularity went down like a stone as the country sank into the worst depression in its history. The Prime Minister became a symbol of, perhaps a scapegoat for, all the sins of capitalism and capitalists throughout the land. Public-opinion polls had not yet come to Canada; Bennett's standing may have been worse than even Brian Mulroney's low of twelve per cent sixty years later. Bennett was rich, fat, self-satisfied, and, in some of his policies, apparently uncaring. Left-wingers made much of his plea to Canadians "to put the iron heel of ruthlessness" against agitators seeking to overthrow the established order. Newspaper reporters, with whom he had no patience, and to whom he threatened censorship, saw him as a menace to freedom of the press. Liberal journalist J.W. Dafoe characterized him as "Alger boy hero plus Mussolini." Liberal MP Chubby Power told the House of Commons in 1932 that the Prime Minister "in his public relations ... often exhibits the manners of a Chicago policeman, and the temperament of a Hollywood actor." The most damning slurs were the ones uttered behind his back by Conservatives. "Too bad he's such a damn fool," said one MP. "The sun never sets on the day on which the Prime Minister hasn't insulted some good and loyal Conservative," said the good Conservative C.H. Cahan, Bennett's Secretary of State.

The confounding fact was that Bennett, with more support from his ministers than he ever acknowledged, was a whirlwind of activity. No one could say that his government drifted or dithered, as King's had before 1930. In *Reaction and Reform: The Politics of the Conservative Party under R.B. Bennett*, Larry Glassford offers a convincing argument that the Bennett government went through three stages: (a) implementation of virtually all of its campaign promises; (b) "a desperate defence of the basic social order" when the Depression worsened; (c) a major attempt at social reform.

The main promise, to use tariff increases to protect jobs and then negotiate reciprocal tariff reductions to secure foreign markets, was inherently contradictory. Bennett tried to implement it anyway. He sharply raised the tariff, and then hinged his external commercial strategy on building closer trade links in the British Empire. Over in England, Beaverbrook campaigned frantically and quixotically for what he called Empire Free Trade, and assumed Bennett agreed with him. In fact, for all their voluble loyalties, Canadian protectionists never wanted the Mother Country's products to come into Canada freely. Their idea of imperial tariff preferences was to levy even higher duties against non-imperial countries. At the Ottawa Imperial Economic Conference of 1932, chaired by Bennett, the British, in particular, were outraged to learn of the depth and selfishness of Canadian protectionism. The Ottawa agreements somewhat strengthened the imperial preferential trading system, and a few Canadian exporters benefitted spectacularly. But no one felt that genuine imperial economic unity had been achieved. The British delegation burned with resentment at Canada's ungenerous bargaining stance and its prime minister's unlovely personality. Chubby Power's view of Bennett was much quoted.

No one said it frankly, but the Ottawa Conference was yet another turning-point in the evolution of the Empire/Commonwealth. It was one final, serious attempt to create a significant economic partnership. Bennett, Beaverbrook, and company were the last drinkers at the jingo bar, still fantasizing about substitutes for the failed dream of political union through imperial federation. After 1932 their ideas gurgled down the drain of history. Bennett's government turned reluctantly to ponder the tariff walls guarding the forty-ninth parallel, and opened talks on trade liberalization—the hated reciprocity—with the United States. Sensibly, the Americans thought they might get a better deal if they kept talking until he was out of office.

Bennett's "defence of the social order" has yet to be fully explored. Historians tend to concentrate on the government's relief policies and its emphasis on law and order, ignoring the seriousness of the autumn 1931 world economic crisis. The government did all it could to mask the latter problem, and some key documents recording Bennett's actions have yet to come to light, if they still exist. Briefly, when the British pound collapsed in 1931 the Canadian dollar went down with it, and the world-wide flight to convert investments into cash left the country's financial system technically insolvent and the government's foreign borrowing capacity in jeopardy. "At this critical and anxious time," Beaverbrook wrote, "Bennett carried a frightful burden of responsibility and exerted his authority to the limit." Beaverbrook refers to a "round robin charter" which approved "drastic, astonishing and even incredible measures for maintaining stability."

The "charter" has never been found. We know that Bennett's government pushed its legislative authority under the Unemployment and Farm Relief Act to fantastic lengths to permit a temporary suspension by banks and life insurance companies of market valuations of the securities they held. The "round robin" was probably a signed agreement to respect the artificial convention. Then the Government of Canada, to protect its own credit standing, raised a $200 million special "National Service Loan" from the Canadian people, using patriotic appeals as though it were a time of war. In Bennett's mind, at least, a financial catastrophe of staggering proportions was narrowly avoided, and a great service done to the country. Perhaps he was right.

Debate about Bennett as a "Reformer" usually centres on the intentions and sincerity underlying the sweeping changes he suddenly advocated in a series of radio addresses in January 1935. Pronouncing that the age of *laissez-faire* capitalism had failed and was at an end, the Prime Minister proposed to bring in unemployment insurance, legislation regulating hours of work and minimum wages, consumer and investment protection laws, fair trade requirements, and other changes. The package was instantly labelled a "New Deal" like Franklin D. Roosevelt's reform package in the United States. But the Bennett version was dismissed by many as an insincere, deathbed conversion. History has been a bit more kind, and several scholars see the package as an expression of the Prime Minister's activist, reform bent.

Bennett was an old "progressive," somewhat in the Borden mould, never a small-government or free-enterprise Conservative. As a Methodist with a social conscience, he had proclivities that today get labelled "Red Tory." The 1935 program, as Glassford shows, was in some ways the culmination of proposals that had been fermenting in the government for several years. Earlier the Bennett government had become the father of the Bank of Canada, and of public broadcasting in Canada, by creating the Canadian Radio Broadcasting Commission. Both were new and potentially powerful central institutions. When his government's actions raised constitutional questions, Bennett threw his weight on the side of strengthening Ottawa's powers to intervene in Canadian life. National problems, he believed, required vigorous national solutions.

Bennett's 1935 attack on capitalism was both fierce and, coming from his mouth, bizarre. It almost seemed as though the Prime Minister had been converted to the socialism being advocated by J.S. Woodsworth, leader of the fledgling Co-operative Commonwealth Federation. In fact, Bennett was adopting a bundle of collectivist nostrums that had been floating around on both the left and the right of politics in the 1930s and had achieved temporary North American legitimacy in Roosevelt's attempt to "codify" the U.S. economy under the National Reconstruction Administration. The advocates' hope was to stop the downward economic spiral by setting floors on prices and wages, or in the case of agriculture by creating marketing boards to control both supplies and prices. If you could freeze enterprise, perhaps you could impede its decline. Much of Bennett's legislative program echoed price- and wage-fixing ideas that small businessmen and farmers had been pushing for some time, and that were newly prominent thanks to a sensational witch-hunt being carried on against big business by Bennett's Minister of Trade and Commerce, H.H. Stevens.

Glassford's study of Bennett shows how waffling and uncertain he actually was in 1935—now a man of the left, then again somewhat to the right, perhaps really in the centre. Erratic as ever, he had no capacity to build a coalition of support for his ideas. "A leader skilled in the arts of conciliation and compromise would have squared these circles somehow," Glassford comments, "but the task was beyond Bennett, who alienated nearly everyone." Neither his Cabinet nor his caucus had had any warning of the 1935 reform proposals. Bennett's ministers did not even know how many radio talks he planned to give.

Glassford and others nonetheless see Bennett as a genuine progressive-conservative, trying, as his party did, to reconcile instincts to change and instincts to preserve. This view may credit Bennett with more depth and stability and coherence than the evidence warrants. The one common theme of his leadership was that government had to do something, had to help solve people's problems. It was a squishy, vaguely collectivist, anti-liberal notion that somehow the visible hand of the state had to be used to stop the invisible forces of the market economy from doing so much damage. It would have an enduring appeal to many of Bennett's successors, from Diefenbaker through Campbell.

When Bennett's deepest instincts surfaced, they appeared to be tinged with nostalgia for the nineteenth-century world of striving, self-sufficient individuals he remembered from his youth.

> The difficulty about all these matters [he wrote in 1931] is that too much reliance is being placed upon the Government. The people are not bearing their share of the load. Half a century ago people would work their way out of their difficulties rather than look to a government to take care of them. The fibre of some of our people has grown softer and they are not willing to turn in and save themselves. They now complain because they have no money. When they were earning money many of them spent it in speculation and in luxury. "Luxury" means anything a man has not an immediate need for, having regard to his financial position.
>
> I do not know what the result of the present movement may be, but unless it induces men and women to think in terms of honest toil rather than in terms of bewilderment because of conditions which they helped to create, the end of organized society is not far distant.

Another way of reading those thoughts is to note that a politician is complaining about the inadequacies of the people. Government was doing its job; the people were not doing theirs. No doubt government would have to try some more expedients, because Tory paternalists had always suspected that the peasantry would have trouble fending for itself. Bennett spent millions on relief and helped set the stage for vast future programs of social welfare for Canadians, but he was probably at his most characteristic in sending out two-dollar bills to poor Canadians, and then dozens of boxes of chocolates to his friends at Christmas.

Bennett's authoritarianism was a combination of two hierarchical traditions. Drawing on the world of business, he saw himself as a kind of managing director of Canada Inc., running the show, at times appearing to own a controlling interest in the country. His position shaded into making himself lord of the manor, working hard to help lesser breeds because religion dictated that the *noblesse* should *oblige* (while at the same time keeping the sheriff well armed in case the unstable peasantry rioted against law and order). "Bennett is more of an aristocrat than a democrat," his former secretary wrote in an adulatory biography in

1934. "He believes in government by the ablest and best—not government by the will of the people—who are often wrong ... only Mackenzie King makes any attempt to carry out government *by* the people." In that depression year, Bennett decided that the time had come to reintroduce the practice of honouring the ablest and best Canadians by having the monarch grant them titles. His political judgement had completely deserted him.

Since the 1930 election the leader had almost completely deserted his party. The Tories' superb organization was shut down literally the day after it delivered the goods, and Bennett showed no interest in reviving it until the last possible moment. He made no efforts to cultivate long-term support anywhere in the country, and was particularly neglectful of Quebec. He spoke no French and had no inclination to work closely with any of his Quebec ministers. He was the kind of British Canadian who was outraged at the thought that the Bank of Canada might issue bilingual banknotes. The Tories' minor breakthrough in Quebec, their most encouraging result since 1891, was squandered.

And there were worse problems. By 1935 the party was badly split. H.H. Stevens, a crude demagogue beside whom Bennett was a model of intellect and modesty, had been fired from the Cabinet for his wild attacks on responsible businesses, and had decided to found his own party, the Reconstruction Party. Many of the Tory millionaires, including Bennett, were quite a bit poorer in 1935 than they had been in 1930. Some of them, such as Sir Joseph Flavelle, were so fed up with Bennett's inconsistencies and his attacks on capitalism that they decided to support the Liberals. The party's elder statesman, Sir Robert Borden, had the best vantage point on the Tories' agony. In 1934 he observed,

> Some of Bennett's colleagues impute to him lack of sense of proportion, vacillation, a tendency to waste time and to postpone decisions, failure to consult them on matters of utmost importance, extreme discourtesy on occasion, lack of self-control, temperamental outbursts tending to sap their loyalty.
>
> On the other hand, they agree on his high courage, his remarkable ability, his amazing energy, his tireless industry. They acknowledge that on occasions of supreme moment he has shown himself skillful and masterful, dominating the situation to the undoubted and lasting advantage of our country's welfare. And they concede his

kindliness of heart and his generous instincts. However, they believe
that his neglect to direct or to authorize effective or indeed any
organization is guiding the party to ultimate overwhelming defeat.

Bennett manfully threw himself into the 1935 campaign, and may have
saved a few seats that would otherwise have been lost. But the defeat was
the worst the party had ever suffered. The Conservative Party elected
only forty members of Parliament. In Quebec they were back to five
seats in English-dominated ridings. Seeing the defeat coming, many
Tory MPs had retired to the Senate or other patronage positions. "I
went down with the ship and did not seek to evade punishment," Bennett wrote Borden. A view that Stevens' defection and the Reconstruction vote are all that prevented the Tories from being re-elected is
fanciful nonsense from historians who can't count.

*   *   *

Both Bennett and Meighen were tempted to blame the people. In the
fourth decade of the twentieth century, both of these Conservatives
expressed doubts about democracy, particularly about universal suffrage.
They belonged to what might be called the "rotten moral fibre" school
of conservatism, as they bemoaned the failure of the people to rise to
their responsibilities and defer to the good sense of their rulers.

Neither man gave up lightly or made his peace with the verdict of
his countrymen. Bennett clung to the Tory leadership until 1938, and at
the convention called to choose his successor he made a last-minute plea
for resurrection. Meighen, who had worked loyally for him as government leader in the Senate, had the good sense to urge him to desist.
Three years later, after R.J. Manion had led the party to another crushing defeat, Meighen had the bad sense to agree to resume the leadership.
He was beaten by a CCF candidate in his attempt to return to the House
of Commons and stepped down again, humiliated. Bennett retired to
Great Britain, where Beaverbrook sold him a manor house and arranged
to have him made a peer.

Dick Bennett of Hopewell Cape, New Brunswick, finished his days
as Viscount Bennett of Mickleham. His last windy speeches were delivered in the House of Lords. He died in his bathtub in 1947, almost forgotten by Canadians. In his swansong to the 1938 Tory leadership

convention he had said, "My friends, I have nothing to regret and nothing to retract—not a thing."

Arthur Meighen lived on through the 1950s. After leaving full-time politics he did very well in business. In the late 1930s and throughout World War II he increasingly bemoaned the country's drift towards socialism, complaining bitterly of high taxes and the disrespect for property rights. Meighen became the classic angry rich man, a kind of mirror image of Marx's alienated proletarian but without the excuse of ignorance and poverty, seething with resentment at a world he could not control. Conservatives in the Meighen mould were such unhappy people. The shrewd Liberal politician Ernest Lapointe had caught their mood back in 1919 when he told his party's convention, "A Liberal is a Liberal because he likes something or somebody; a Tory is a Tory because he hates somebody or something."

There seems to have been a softer, more reflective and regretful side of Arthur Meighen, hinted at in brief passages in some of his speeches,* in the stability and happiness of his family life, in his resolve that his descendants become bilingual. But it remained mostly hidden. His public visage was the hard, embittered face of the right-wing man of rectitude wronged by Mackenzie King and the Canadian people. The self-made man, especially the insecure one, hated to admit ever having made mistakes. When Meighen published a collection of his speeches in 1949, he used as their title a phrase from his final speech to a Conservative leadership convention: "Whether now judged right or wrong, whatever I have said, whatever I have done, is going to remain unrevised and unrepented." One of his granddaughters picked up the volume, sounded out the title, *Unrevised and Unrepented*, and offered a last word on the book: "Uninteresting."

---

* In a 1941 speech commemorating Sir John A. Macdonald, Meighen said, "We read in many places of his tact and his urbanity, of the amiability and gentleness of his nature, of the kindness, humour and forbearance which seemed the only weapons he would turn to attacks from those who should have been his friends. From every source we learn of his patience, his unbounded and unending patience. These are virtues possessed by a few—a very favoured few—but possessed in equal degree by Sir John's great rival and successor [Laurier]. They are virtues in public life of almost unbelievable importance, virtues valued most by those to whom they are denied."

Like many moderately conservative Canadians, Sir Robert Borden was not unduly upset at the result of the 1935 election. He knew that Mackenzie King was a sensible, mainstream politician, anything but a wild-eyed radical. Borden rather appreciated King's political adroitness, as well as his attention to detail, including the niceties of manners. He noted in his diary that King "never fails in courtesy or in the observance of social convention. Unfortunately Bennett usually fails in both these respects. Like Meighen he lacks that indefinable but very distinctive quality called breeding." Borden, whose background and temperament were not unlike Meighen's and Bennett's, had managed to develop that quality. Which is an oddity, because surely Meighen and Bennett were closer to the norm. It is inherently contradictory to be both self-made and well-bred.

Chambers/Halifax/Herald/1944

"And that's that!"

5

KING
Dividing Us Least

My late colleague Colonel C.P. Stacey did a shabby thing to Mackenzie King, the greatest and most interesting of Canada's prime ministers.

Charles Stacey was Canada's most distinguished military historian, author of most of the official history of the Canadian army in World War II, and of several other good books. He was a historian's historian—imbued with respect for documents, passionate about accuracy, properly cautious about generalizations, deeply in love with his subject (his memoirs are titled *A Date with History*). After retiring from the Department of National Defence he joined the University of Toronto's history department, where he became a loved and respected grand old man of our discipline. He was unusually gracious and friendly towards young historians. Lunch with Charles was a treasured time of genial historical gossip.

In the early 1970s Stacey's table-talk began to centre obsessively on the diaries of Mackenzie King, which he was reading with growing astonishment and excitement. Everyone knew that King had kept an exhaustive personal diary from his years as a college student in the 1890s until just before his death in 1950. As an intimate record of the daily life of the longest-serving prime minister in Canadian history, revealing not only his own thoughts but those of his friends, Cabinet colleagues, and foreign visitors, the tens of thousands of pages of King diaries had been instantly recognized as one of the more remarkable political documents in the Western world. His literary executors had surely made a responsible decision in ignoring, after much soul-searching, the provision in King's will that his diaries should be destroyed except for the marked passages. Their excuse was that King in his retirement had not had the time or energy to mark any passages.

The diaries were used to good effect by King's official biographers, R. McGregor Dawson and Blair Neatby, who in three volumes told the story of his life to 1939. Four thick volumes of edited excerpts from the diaries were published to cover the years 1939 to 1948. Stacey himself used the diaries for his major works on Canadian war policies and the history of Canadian external relations.

Everyone who has ever read an old newspaper knows how easy it is to become sidetracked by the colourful trivia of history. While ranging through the King diaries, Stacey found himself reading seemingly endless passages about the Prime Minister's relations with women, his interpretations of his dreams as "visions" in which the spirits of the dead appeared to him, and his serious interest in other forms of spiritualism. When Stacey turned to King's college years, he was surprised to find detailed descriptions of nocturnal excursions through the streets of Toronto in search of prostitutes. "As the picture expanded," Stacey wrote in his memoirs, "I was more and more astonished: it was clear that King, the solid, stolid, stodgy figure, the dullest personality in modern Canadian history, had unsuspected depths." Stacey decided that King's biographers had not properly explored these depths, that a book about King's private life was there for the writing, that franker times now made possible discussions of prime-ministerial sexuality, that he, Stacey, was more qualified than some to write the book, and—"one might as well be frank—here was a subject which might have sufficient public appeal that a little money might be made out of it, a rare event in the life of a Canadian historian."

In 1976 Stacey published the book we had heard so much about at lunch, *A Very Double Life: The Private World of Mackenzie King.* Its "revelations" about the prostitutes, the married women in King's life while he was prime minister, and his explorations in spiritualism were given extensive coverage in the media. Charles did not say how much money he made from the book, but it certainly outsold his more solid works, and it was widely discussed among historians, history buffs, and politicos. It is still the first book about King that curious Canadians are apt to pick up. It has had immense impact in further vulgarizing the image of the man who was Prime Minister of Canada from 1921 to 1930 and from 1935 to 1948.

History was already being unkind to King. Soon after his death, journalists had revealed the broad outline of his spiritualist interests. Both the popular and the official biographies mentioned these and other idiosyncrasies: his extremely close relationship with his mother, his construction of ruins at his country estate, his fascination with the positioning of the hands of the clock when he was making important decisions. King was obviously an odd duck.

Serious critics from both the left and the right had continued the assaults on him that King had faced throughout his career. They portrayed him as a pudgy waffler whose only principles were love of power for himself and, if a scornful critic like Donald Creighton was being charitable, the Liberal Party. The most devastating and most quoted lines in Canadian satirical poetry were written about King in 1954 by the McGill constitutional lawyer, socialist activist, and poet Frank Scott:

W.L.M.K.

How shall we speak of Canada,
Mackenzie King dead?
The Mother's boy in the lonely room
With his dog, his medium and his ruins?

He blunted us.

We had no shape
Because he never took sides,
And no sides
Because he never allowed them to take shape.

He skillfully avoided what was wrong
Without saying what was right,
And never let his on the one hand
Know what his on the other hand was doing.

The height of his ambition
Was to pile a Parliamentary Committee on a Royal Commission,

To have "conscription if necessary
But not necessarily conscription",
To let Parliament decide—
Later.

Postpone, postpone, abstain.

Only one thread was certain:
After World War I
Business as usual,
After World War II
Orderly decontrol.
Always he led us back to where we were before.

He seemed to be in the centre
Because we had no centre,
No vision
To pierce the smoke-screen of his politics.

Truly he will be remembered
Wherever men honour ingenuity,
Ambiguity, inactivity, and political longevity.

Let us raise up a temple
To the cult of mediocrity,
Do nothing by halves
Which can be done by quarters.

For many readers, Stacey's book became the clinching nail in the coffin of Mackenzie King's reputation as a human being. For those who only read the critical books (the official biographies were thick and scholarly and not very sexy) this dull, odd, egotistical political mediocrity was now revealed as a sex-crazed, hypocritical, and truly weird egotistical political mediocrity. A semi-comic figure, now to be ridiculed in historical fiction and even in Dennis Lee's children's poetry.

William Lyon Mackenzie King,
Sat in the middle and played with string,

> And he loved his mother like *any*thing—
> William Lyon Mackenzie King.

The few current politicians with a sense of history were happy to place themselves in the Macdonald, Laurier, Borden, Pearson, Diefenbaker traditions. Hardly anyone, even in the Liberal Party, mentioned Mackenzie King. Who wanted to be seen to be in the tradition of the sex-crazed spiritualist in our political attic, loving his mother and playing with string?

* * *

Some historians and some of the surviving politicians and civil servants from King's era had known better all along. The official biographies were judicious and scholarly and largely favourable to King. Charles Stacey himself had always had a grudging regard for King's talents as a politician. He conceded that King was a remarkably successful political leader whose abilities were high by comparison with other Canadian politicians, but thought that King had a second-rate mind, and that his experiments with ouija boards, table-rapping, and mediums proved it. The historian and founding father of the Co-operative Commonwealth Federation, Frank Underhill, wrote a series of appraisals of King that became increasingly favourable. "Mr. King for twenty-five years was the leader who divided us least," Underhill finally concluded. It was not lavish praise, except that he added, presciently, "Perhaps this is as much as we shall ever be able to say, for a long time to come, about Canadian unity."

The distinguished political scientist H.S. Ferns had worked for a time in King's office, and in the 1950s had co-authored a harshly critical book on King's early ambition (he, too, was trying to make money with his book, Ferns admitted). In his 1983 memoirs Ferns made a point of correcting the impression Stacey had gleaned from the diaries, "that Canada was governed by a superstitious lunatic":

> This is not at all the impression that members of his secretarial staff, observers in the Parliamentary Press Gallery, or members of Parliament had of the Prime Minister at that time. He appeared to us as ... a sensitive, clear-headed, political technician with an unrivalled sense of the nuances of Canadian politics. One did not need to agree with Mackenzie King about everything he said or did to acknowledge that

he was an extremely able politician. Even his worst enemies paid him the compliment of saying "Willy is always too clever by half," and many of them considered it grossly unfair that the Prime Minister had been endowed with better brains, quicker responses, and more guile than themselves. In terms of understanding the political problems of Canada and in knowing what the Canadian people as a whole were willing to accept from a government, Mackenzie King was miles ahead of any of the active participants in politics.

... It will take a long time to rescue the reputation of Mackenzie King from the psychologists and the pornographers, and to leave it to the judgement of those interested in what is truly relevant in the man: his activity as a Canadian politician in a period of extreme political disturbance....

Some of King's defenders, including Ferns, thought history should concern itself only with the public side of what King himself had called his "very double life." So what if he had been lecherous, silly, or immature in private? No one, including Stacey, had shown that these activities had the slightest effect on King's conduct of government. Yes, he had occasionally asked a medium to predict the political future, but he disregarded intuitions that disagreed with his own. So what if he sowed wild oats in his youth (if he actually did), had lady friends in old age, and became superstitious, self-absorbed, and maudlin about his dogs? Does not our tolerant age understand the normality of a little harmless deviance? Surely we understand the ache of sexual need, the tortures of loneliness.

Surely with a little remembrance and reading we understand the force of the belief in the immortality of the spirit, and how it led millions of lonely people into intense efforts to communicate with the souls of loved ones who had gone before. Yes, there was always a silly, fraudulent side to organized spiritualism, from its origins on the American frontier in the 1850s, but there was also a serious interest in life after death, psychic powers, the possibility of spiritual communication. Intellectual spiritualists were not an oxymoron. No one ever said, for example, that Arthur Conan Doyle, creator of Sherlock Holmes, was a stupid man. Nor was he alone in his beliefs: artists, intellectuals, political and literary figures, even some scientists, embraced aspects of spiritualist doctrine in the English-speaking world in the late nineteenth and early twentieth centuries. And the carnage of the Great War tremendously intensified the yearning of good folk for communion with those who would not grow old, their dead sons and lovers.

Why was Charles Stacey not more tolerant or understanding of King in *A Very Double Life?* The answer seems to lie in the contempt that so many Canadian soldiers developed for the King government during World War II, particularly its handling of the conscription crisis. Stacey was a soldier and the historian of Canada's soldiers. He controlled his feelings in his official histories, but he allowed them to colour and direct *A Very Double Life*. After Colonel Stacey had concluded from the diaries that Mackenzie King was out walking the streets of Ottawa looking for sex on Easter Monday, April 9, 1917—the day that thousands of Canadian soldiers died storming Vimy Ridge—there was little hope he would work hard to balance his judgements.

Much of what Stacey wrote about King, and much of what "the psychologists and pornographers" have found in the private King, is at best half true. The King diaries are not the record of a public success and a private failure. King's life is not a Jekyll-and-Hyde epic. Carefully read, his public and private records portray an extraordinarily gifted and sensitive man, the product of a certain moment in cultural history, who dedicated his life to public service and succeeded beyond even his own ambitious dreams. Willie King did a good job both as a politician and as a human being.

*   *   *

William Lyon Mackenzie King was Canada's most highly-educated prime minister. In his early years he fashioned a career of extraordinary achievement, unrivalled by any other prime minister except possibly Lester Pearson. King was better educated and smarter than Pearson, and had better judgement.

He was born in Berlin (now Kitchener), Ontario, in 1874. His mother, Isabel Grace Mackenzie, was the youngest daughter of William Lyon Mackenzie, the hot-headed leader of the Upper Canadian rebellion of 1837. Isabel had been born while Mackenzie was in exile in New York, and had inherited some of her father's wilfulness and instability. She married John King, a lawyer, also of Scottish descent, who was somewhat more stable and with a scholarly bent, but uninterested either in the rough-and-tumble of legal practice or in maximizing his income.

The Kings were gentlefolk but not rich. They were a close and loving and deeply Presbyterian family. The parents, particularly Isabel, were ambitious for their four children—especially Willie, who seemed unusually gifted.

King took a Bachelor of Arts degree at the University of Toronto, graduating with first-class honours in 1895. He studied political science, history, economics, and law, stood at or near the top of his class, and found time for a wide variety of extra-curricular activities, including leadership in a student strike against nepotism and incompetent administration. He took a Bachelor of Laws degree at Toronto in 1896, an MA there in 1897, studied at the University of Chicago on a fellowship, then went to Harvard, where he took another MA and commenced doctoral studies. His Harvard fellowship also allowed for study abroad, which he did at the London School of Economics. King's professors included many of the leading economists and political scientists in three countries. As an enquiring, sociable, and ambitious young man, King made the acquaintance during his student years of dozens of the leading lights of the Anglo-American intellectual and political world.

In 1900 he ended his formal studies to take a position as a civil servant in the Canadian government. He was to edit the newly founded *Labour Gazette* and get the new Department of Labour, supervised by the Postmaster-General, off the ground. Within a few months he was named Deputy Minister of Labour. In the next eight years King had a spectacular career as a conciliator in major industrial disputes. He roamed the country as the government's peacemaker in bitter, often violent confrontations between desperate trade unions and determined, angry employers. He was the architect of the 1907 Industrial Disputes Investigation Act, the most significant Canadian legislation in the field of industrial relations. He also became a kind of roving diplomat, undertaking missions to China, Washington, and London, even helping out U.S. president Theodore Roosevelt in certain Anglo-American matters. King was one of the first and most glittering and creative of Canada's great twentieth-century civil servants. In 1909 Harvard accepted a government report he had written on Oriental immigration to Canada as a doctoral thesis (choosing it from a ream of other reports he submitted) and awarded him its degree of Doctor of Philosophy. No other Canadian prime minister has had a Ph.D.

During these years King was twice offered professorships at Harvard. Laurier advised him "not to think of it, that a man with the blood I had in my veins, my talents, etc. had a great future in this country, that I would be lost as a professor, even if I did write books." In 1908 Laurier encouraged King to leave the civil service and stand for Parliament. He was elected and, as had been half-promised, entered the Cabinet in 1909 as Canada's first Minister of Labour. He aspired to the prime-ministership. Many of his friends—the Governor-General was at the top of the list—were certain he was a prime minister in the making. It was only a matter of time.

What about the whores he writes about in his diaries? The place to find sexual excess in a young galahad, a political saviour in intellectual training among the North American elite, is in recent biographies of John F. Kennedy. Mackenzie King's sexual awakening was entirely different, possibly more Canadian, certainly more Victorian, and a lot less sensational.

When Mackenzie King went down on his knees, as he did almost every day of his life, it was to pray for guidance and strength to be a better man. He was intensely religious and idealistic. His mind was shaped by nineteenth-century Presbyterianism impregnated with philosophical idealism, and he was nurtured by his parents' love and ambition for him. His student diaries portray a sensitive, hard-working, and naively self-conscious young man struggling to set a course for his future. He knew he had ability, he knew he had a moral obligation to dedicate his life to higher things, and he thought he discerned, in the old Calvinist sense, that God had destined him for something special. He had been taught to believe that the "highest" or "truest" realities were things of the spirit; ideas and ideals were more important than matter and material concerns. Serving God and serving mankind were the two highest callings available. During his student years he seemed more inclined to become a minister or an academic than a politician.

The best service to humanity seemed to be work for the downtrodden and neglected. Young King, the rebel's grandson, was drawn to the gospel of Christian service as expressed in early social-work experiments. He was involved in some of the pioneering "settlement" houses, notably Hull House in Chicago, which saw young idealists attempting to work in urban ghettos. He visited prisons and hospitals, took an interest in various charities, and tried to work personally with the neglected denizens of the streets. Newsboys were one group of street people King tried to befriend; prostitutes were another. As Britain's greatest Liberal politician, W.E. Gladstone, had done before him, and innumerable humanitarians have tried to do over the years, King experimented a few times with efforts to rescue "fallen" women.

While helping others cope with the base, sordid side of life, King had to deal with his own appetites. His diaries contain a sometimes moving record of a Christian's struggles with sin and temptation, a pilgrim's efforts to progress. King wrote the now famous line "There is no doubt that I lead a very double life" in 1898. He added by way of explanation: "I strive to do right and continually do wrong." All his life he from time to time berated himself for his failings, endlessly seeking perfection, endlessly falling short. What Stacey dismissed as "orgies of self-contempt" had a lot to do with ideas of sin and salvation and the impulse to Christian perfectionism.

(The same ideas later meant that the Prime Minister of Canada regularly criticized himself for not being a better speaker, for not being better read, for having wasted too much time. At the end of a day he would get down on his knees and ask for the strength to do a better job—a form of self-abasement probably foreign to most Ottawa bedrooms in our time.)

Without knowing it, nineteenth-century physicians and counsellors perpetrated a painful hoax on young men in the ideas they spread about male sexuality. They taught that sexual energy was vital energy, life-force. Semen was the essence of life itself. When semen was emitted in the sex act, it was draining and enervating (thus the old rule that athletes must abstain from sex during training), though necessary and wonderful as part of procreation. When semen was repeatedly drained away in acts of onanism, masturbation, or "self-abuse," or even in nocturnal emissions, it was exhausting, debilitating, and worse. All the late-nineteenth-century "sex manuals" taught that habitual masturbation would probably lead to insanity. You mustn't do it. Conquer, control the animal instincts. Avoid the lascivious thoughts that give rise to evil practices.

Mackenzie King was a normal male animal. His career suggests that he was an enormously energetic male, not unlike a Kennedy or a Clinton. He never married; he may never have had sexual intercourse, or he may have slept with a woman once or twice in his life. Most of the sexual torments recorded in his diaries seem obviously a record of agonized attempts to avoid seminal emissions that he thought would destroy his body and his mind. The hours he spent talking and praying on several occasions with poor Toronto prostitutes were apparently followed by nocturnal seminal emissions, then by intense remorse and worry. On other occasions King may have surrendered to lustful thoughts, perhaps by buying some of the "French" postcards of the era. Possibly he gave in and masturbated. He had been taught to abhor waste of all kinds. The time spent wrestling with lascivious physical thoughts was "wasted." When he succumbed, the time was "worse than wasted."

When Stacey wrote *A Very Double Life* he made no allowance for the hyperbole that sensitive spirits, including idealistic nineteenth-century Christians, use to describe their feelings. He seemed to know nothing about sexual attitudes of the period, or the historical literature on the idea of masturbatory insanity. He concluded that King's remorse came from having had intercourse with the prostitutes, which made him a ridiculous, albeit regretful, hypocrite. It is far more likely that King's problems in his youth, and for much of the rest of his life, came from trying so hard to maintain unnatural sexual continence.

Many saintly priests could have kept diaries much like Mackenzie King's. As part of an exhaustive medical examination during a period of intense stress and fatigue in 1916 he was told by his doctors "that what was health, I was mistaking for an evil passion." Their main advice to him was not to worry about it. In 1933 he told his diary that his tensions stemmed from "the unnaturalness of a celibate life with strong animal passions to contend with, and a highly sensitive nature." He could have added, as his doctors had sometimes noted, that for his physical well-being alone it was too bad he had never married.

King was not repugnant to or repelled by women. He was good-looking (arguably one of the more handsome of a pack of fairly unattractive prime ministers), well dressed, and charming, though perhaps too earnest for certain tastes, perhaps too vain for others. He loved to dance and party, and was invariably considerate and thoughtful. He fell madly in love at least once during his student days (his family strongly opposed the idea of marriage to a Chicago nurse), and never lacked female company in the Ottawa social whirl. Sir Wilfrid and Lady Laurier were among the many matchmakers who tried to find a suitable wife for this most eligible bachelor. Nobody would have been surprised if King had married well and married long. He thought a lot about marriage, hoped he would find the ideal wife, and deeply regretted that he never did. In the meantime he got on with his career of public service.

*   *   *

The Liberal defeat in the 1911 election appeared to derail King's political career. He had been an active Minister of Labour, organizing pioneering investigations into technical education and sponsoring Canada's first effective anti-combines act. But as MP for the fairly industrialized central Ontario riding of North Waterloo he became one of the victims of the reciprocity agreement, beaten by a protectionist Conservative and out of a job.

He kept his hand in Liberal politics, bided his time, thought about getting married, and in 1914 began a remarkable new career when the John D. Rockefeller family asked him to advise on industrial relations in their violence-torn Colorado mines. His success in helping bring peace to the bloody Colorado camps led to a considerable reputation and many more assignments in the United States, as well as lifelong friendship and support from John D. Rockefeller, Jr.

At any time during the next five years King could have moved to the United States. He turned down several attractive offers, including the directorship of Alexander Carnegie's vast philanthropies. If King had moved in the right way at the right time and become an American, he might well have later built a successful political career. He is the only Canadian prime minister who, had he been born an American, had a mix of talents rich enough to take him all the way to the presidency. Some of the others might have become senators or state governors.

King did not want to become an American, was not attracted by the lure of money and an easy life, and told his diary he did not really care for the association with families of great wealth. He made a conscious decision to carry on a career of political service in Canada. The fact that he spent much of the Great War substantially aiding industrial productivity in the United States—he was too old to serve in the army—ought to have been a feather in his cap rather than another question mark in the eyes of his critics. In 1917 he was a party insider in the intense Liberal debate on coalition and conscription. After much soul-searching—he believed in the essential fairness of conscription—King decided to stay with Laurier. It was an act of some courage, for the party's official opposition to conscription meant political suicide in Ontario. King ran in the 1917 election and was beaten again.

In 1918 he published a thick book, ostensibly his final report to the Rockefeller Foundation, entitled *Industry and Humanity*. Most readers, then and since, found it dull, platitudinous, and dense, evidence to some that King had missed his calling by not becoming a professor. The book is 540 pages long, King wrote it all himself, and it sold about 10,000 copies in four Canadian printings in its first year, no mean feat of authorship by either a professor or a politician. King knew while writing the book that he was not cut out for more efforts in that line: "The truth is I am not suited to theoretical work, but to practical, and need the active touch with men and affairs to give vitality to what I write."

His desire for practical work was more than satisfied a few months after *Industry and Humanity*'s publication, when he was chosen to succeed the deceased Laurier as leader of the Liberal Party. He won the mantle in a close convention contest with the septuagenarian former finance minister, W.S. Fielding. The support he got from Quebec for having been loyal to Laurier and against conscription in 1917 made the difference. After becoming Liberal leader, King mostly suspended his search for a wife. He was wedded to politics and public service.

*   *   *

For all of his achievements, King was still largely an unknown quantity when he became prime minister in 1921 at age forty-seven. The Canadian political system had become an unknown quantity too, with the comfortable old Liberal-Conservative duopoly in ruins. Sixty-five members of Parliament, most from the west, called themselves "Progressives." In many ways the spiritual forebears of today's Reformers, they were the second-largest group in the House of Commons after the Liberals, but refused to form the official Opposition or even call themselves a party. The Progressives wanted to do more for rural Canada, passionately disliked protective tariffs, and offered a reasoned critique of the old parties, the old politics, and the old politicians. They held the balance of power in the House of Commons, and could at any time unite with the Conservatives to defeat the government—though there was never any guarantee that a group that despised party discipline would act as a unit. This was the first minority government situation since Confederation, and one of the trickiest Canada has ever seen. There was much speculation that one or more of the old parties would crumble, and that almost anything could happen.

King was a relatively young, inexperienced, and suspect player. "His political amateurishness in view of the position he holds is almost unbelievable," wrote J.W. Dafoe, the normally astute editor of the *Winnipeg Free Press*, in 1922. In that year Dafoe was a leading mouthpiece of Manitoba Progressivism. The next year, the crusading editor spent several weeks in London as part of the Canadian delegation to an Imperial Conference, at the invitation of Mackenzie King—a demonstration of prime-ministerial "amateurishness" that must have caused both Macdonald and Laurier to smile in their graves. Dafoe was soon writing that King was surprisingly able.

Canadians might have known more about Mackenzie King if *Industry and Humanity* had not been so difficult to read, or if they had been aware of his sophisticated work in industrial relations. He had been a serious student of advanced currents of European and American social thought. His Liberalism, despite being filtered through a sometimes befogged intellect, was better expressed than the ideas of any of his predecessors or successors, possibly excepting Pierre Trudeau.

King abhorred conflict. He was the first Canadian politician to work and think in terms of classes and their struggles. His profession as a conciliator was to bring the classes together, reconciling labour and capital, not just intellectually but in the midst of real and often violent struggles. The resort to coercion in industrial disputes—strikes, strike-breaking, intimidation, calling out the militia—was usually a sign of failure. King's job was to convince leaders to return to the bargaining table. He resolved conflict by restoring personal contact and facilitating consensus. In practice and in his book, he preached a gospel of reducing class conflict through rational investigation, the accumulation of knowledge, and improved personal relations.

Though King was a conciliator, he was not neutral at heart or in his Liberalism. In the broad conflict of the masses versus the big interests, the people against the plutocracy, Mackenzie King was usually on the people's side, often self-consciously so, in the tradition of his grandfather. He believed in the advancement of the interests of the working classes as circumstances reasonably permitted. While rejecting the extreme of state socialism, he argued that industry had to serve the needs of humanity, including and especially its workers. From influential reports on sweatshops for the Government of Canada in his student days, to highly paid consultancies in which he urged American corporations to work with trade unions, King proposed approaches to industrial problems that almost always meant gains for workers.

Later the left criticized him as an advocate of company unions, a stop-gap, halfway measure. King's sensible view was that a company union was better than no union. In situations with more options, he recommended that firms recognize unions and learn to work with them. Industrial harmony through collective bargaining was the wave of the future.

While believing that the state's role in industrial disputes should ideally be limited to bringing people together, King was the first Canadian prime minister to advocate that the state also assume major social-welfare responsibilities. Bismarck in Germany in the 1880s and the Asquith/Lloyd George Liberals in England after 1906 had pioneered in the introduction of social-insurance schemes. But before the war no one thought that bustling, growing, prosperous Canada needed such Old World solutions. Then, after four years of fighting and sacrifice, many Canadians had come to believe that building a better world would have to involve much more in the way of social justice. King was one of several Canadian intellectuals calling for a national commitment to insurance against the ravages of old age, sickness, and unemployment (Stephen Leacock, a Conservative, was another early advocate, in his 1919 book, *The Unsolved Riddle of Social Justice*; the CCF, Canada's socialist party, did not yet exist, and it is a myth to credit it with first putting the welfare state on the political agenda). King was influential in having these proposals written into the Liberal Party's platform at the 1919 convention. Bringing the welfare state to Canada was to become a main part of the thrust of Liberalism in the next several decades.

A style that stressed conciliation, healing, soothing, and restoring bonds of unity and harmony fit neatly into the tradition set by Macdonald and Laurier. Already a master at dealing with industrial conflict, King saw democratic government as charged with the job of handling all forms of interest-group rivalry. Canadians had a multitude of interests— class, ethnic, religious—and very marked regional differences. An issue like the tariff triggered complicated considerations of region, occupation, and class. Religion was beginning to wane as a force that divided Canadians politically, but ethnicity, or race, as most people called it, seemed more divisive than ever. Conscription and war had split Canada down its fundamental fault-line. Quebec was alienated and sullen, not sure that there was a basis for real co-operation in national politics. The war had stimulated every other kind of conflict—the west, farmers, workers, veterans, the middle classes—everyone it seemed. The times cried out for healing and conciliation.

King's political model was Laurier, the great conciliator and compromiser. The domestic history of King's governments in the 1920s is a study in the skilful balancing of interests. Meighen wanted to divide Canadians on fundamental principles; King wanted to bring them together. Meighen's were the politics of confrontation and conflict and contempt, King's of co-operation, consensus, and conciliation. Meighen scored in verbal battles in the House of Commons; King ducked and evaded, retreated and sallied, and won the political wars. "The extreme man is always more or less dangerous, but nowhere more so than in politics," he once told his diary about R.B. Bennett. "In a country like ours it is particularly true that the art of government is largely one of seeking to reconcile rather than to exaggerate differences—to come as near as may be possible to the happy mean."

His strategy for healing the political system was practically flawless. He wooed the Progressives without becoming trapped by them. He was always friendly to the western agrarians, whom he characterized as Liberals in a hurry; Meighen was usually contemptuous. The farmers felt most strongly about the tariff, which Meighen would have raised. King's governments tinkered and adjusted, usually in the direction of lower tariffs, but without driving away the high-tariff men in the Liberal caucus. Many of these were from Quebec, where the party's stand on conscription paid golden, almost effortless dividends. French Canadians simply would not leave the Liberal Party to support the man and the party that had imposed the tax of blood in 1917.

An inexperienced prime minister in a broken party system that most believed would further fragment or realign, King navigated through four years of minority government, the longest uninterrupted minority in Canadian history. He survived the 1925 election, outmanoeuvred Meighen in the trickiest minority situation ever, and won his first majority in 1926. By then the Progressives had almost disappeared. Both the west and Quebec were solidly Liberal. Two-party dominance had been restored. Britain's wartime coalition under the charismatic David Lloyd George had irredeemably split that country's Liberal Party, and in the aftermath of war it continued to disintegrate and decline. In Canada the Liberal Party that had been split and reduced to a Quebec rump in 1917 now drew support from every region of the country.

The delicacy of conciliatory politics, of working to bring people together, inevitably put a premium on personal relations. Laurier and

Macdonald had understood the politics of charm. Borden, Meighen, and Bennett charmed no one. To understand Mackenzie King we must put aside the false image of a self-centred, second-rate, neurotic wimp, and realize that he was as pure a practitioner of the politics of charm and good will as Canada has ever seen.

As leader of the Liberal Party for twenty-nine years, King almost never deliberately made an enemy (except possibly Vincent Massey, one of the most egotistic and unlovable of all Liberals; King despised Massey's British arse-kissing and airs and let him know it, but did make him a Cabinet minister, minister to Washington, and High Commissioner in London). King's manners were impeccable, his thoughtfulness, especially on the great occasions of joy and sorrow—weddings, funerals, births—was legendary. His secretaries joked and cursed about his immense Christmas card list, and the attention he gave to keeping it up to date. He signed all the cards himself, and as a sentimental Christian he bestowed tidings of joy and salvation upon friends and enemies alike. We have trouble understanding this because in recent times politicians' Christmas card lists have become mammoth and out of date. Machines do all the signing. The senders have replaced portraits of the Holy Family with pictures of themselves and their families. And they wonder why we laugh at them.

King's notorious lack of consideration of his personal staff, particularly in his later years, seems to belie the image of a thoughtful, considerate man. He expected his aides to be on call all hours of the day and night; he could drive university graduates to distraction with his fussing about the dishes to be served at a state dinner. It was not hard to hate working for Mackenzie King. Why, then, did so many smart men serve him so long and so devotedly? Because they knew a prime minister has the right to be well served, they understood that some of his fussiness was related to age, they were impressed that he drove himself as hard as he drove them, and, especially in the later years, they knew they were working for a winner.

More than all that, King had a way of charming his staff. Flattery was a favourite weapon—"He covered me with whipped cream and bullshit," Leonard Brockington remembered. When a secretary, F.A. McGregor, couldn't stand it any more one day in 1924, he threw a bundle of papers into the air and ran out of the Prime Minister's office. King gave him a leave of absence, a junket to Atlantic City, a junket to England, and eventually a twenty-five-year sinecure in the civil service. McGregor wrote a very good and affectionate book about his former master. Chubby Power, a Liberal insider and Cabinet minister, remarked in his memoirs, "I doubt that anyone would have taken off his coat to fight for Meighen had his name been mentioned with disrespect, but such a thing could easily have happened for Laurier or even for King."

King mastered the necessities as well as the niceties of working with people in politics. He had no hesitation about surrounding himself with powerful Cabinet ministers, the strongest and ablest men he could find (there was never a woman in a King cabinet; there were still hardly any in Parliament). He was better than either Macdonald or Laurier at working with powerful personalities, knowing how to delegate authority in Cabinet, knowing when to massage bruised egos, when to defer to better judgement, when to overrule, and, as we will see, when to fire. Ageing leaders usually lose touch with the young and like to surround themselves with sycophants. Macdonald, Laurier, and possibly Trudeau had that tendency. Incredibly, King's Cabinets got stronger as he got older. Some of the ministers occasionally resisted him on points of high principle; he fought back and always won. When he left office he engineered a smooth transition of power to one of the most competent Cabinets in Canadian history. By comparison with this consummate professional, Meighen and most of King's other opponents were rank amateurs.

King's greatest weakness was his inability to write or deliver a good speech in public. He had no oratorical or personal charisma, and was intensely self-conscious and nervous whenever he had to give a formal speech or lead off debate in the House. He compensated by using his caucus masterfully. Paul Martin senior first attended caucus as a rookie MP in the 1930s:

> Mr. King was seemingly secure as leader of the party, but the caucus had no sooner opened than there began all kinds of speeches which suggested that we were anything but a united party. Westerners complained about agricultural policy and members from the Maritimes criticized all kinds of policies.... I soon realized ... that, in reality, Mr. King's use of the caucus was a manifestation of his great skills as a leader.... At a time when national differences and grievances were so great, Mackenzie King allowed members to air their dissatisfactions in the party caucus. In that way he preserved the very thing I

believed was being disturbed during that first caucus, party unity. Every caucus was a political meeting which Mr. King would always end with a rousing speech which invariably provoked resounding cheers from the members. Reinvigorated, they would return to the backbenches and urge on Mr. King and the cabinet....

Other former ministers have written that King's best speeches were delivered behind closed doors to caucus. While he did not rise to similar heights in public, he came to understand the House of Commons and parliamentary tactics as thoroughly as any of his predecessors. When H.S. Ferns had the job of briefing King before question period, he found it was like carrying coals to Newcastle. "The Prime Minister had a preternatural sense of what was up in the House of Commons and could anticipate a question before the opposition had even thought of it." King became legendary, inside and outside of Canada, for his political smarts. "He was incredible, uncannily shrewd," the British High Commissioner to Canada during World War II remembered. "His political instincts were virtually always sound. It was as if he were endowed with antennae which somehow informed him as he sat alone and undisturbed exactly what all the millions of his fellow-countrymen throughout the colossal dominion were thinking." J.L. Granatstein, the historian who has written most widely about the King era, is not given to lavish praise, but he concludes that "Mackenzie King perhaps brought prime-ministership to its tactical perfection."

These were not the skills of a man with a warped or inadequate personality. Mackenzie King did not have an ego problem that interfered with his work. Compared with Meighen and Bennett he was a paragon of humility, publicly and privately. The endless self-examination, the apparent self-obsession of many of his diary entries, may seem like conceit mixed with crippling insecurity. But it was actually King's way of working out his thoughts and feelings, of relaxing through self-expression. Other politicians would stay up late with buddies, soaking their egos in rye and scotch. King wrote and thought, went to bed, and dreamed that Laurier or his mother wanted him to do a better job.

He needed approval, as do most of us. He recorded compliments and honours in his diary and became more conscious of recognition as he neared the end of his career. Sadly, he came to know that Canadians would never love or revere him, just as he knew that he would never have loving intimacy with a wife. All of this is a long way from the insatiable psychic-hunger of some of his contemporaries and many of his successors, men and women who needed constant stroking and gratification from crowds, cameras, and cronies. He was publicity-conscious, to be sure, but King could live with himself.

He thrived on solitude, preferring to work at Laurier House, his Ottawa home, or his Gatineau retreat, "Kingsmere." He had political and personal friends who were as close to him as he chose to allow. His Quebec lieutenant, Ernest Lapointe, was his most important party comrade; Joan Patteson, an Ottawa banker's wife, was a platonic soul-mate. Stacey found King's friendships with married women shocking. The surprise surely is that King did not have sexual affairs with other people's wives,* did not boink female secretaries on their desks or in closets, did not, for that matter, show the slightest hint of sexual interest in his male secretaries.

"I've always found that you can control people better if you don't see too much of them," King told an early biographer. Several political and personal acquaintances noticed that he preferred to keep people at a distance. His loneliness was as much a source of strength as a problem. King, remember, was a bachelor by choice, not necessity. "He draws his strength from loneliness and God, this remote and quiet place, not public meetings," wrote the Reverend William Heeney, who often visited King at Kingsmere, where they would pray together under the stars. "He needed to be alone to build up reserves of physical, nervous, and spiritual strength," F.A. McGregor, recalled, adding, "one could never imagine him sitting back in the lounge of his club, sipping a cocktail, smoking a cigarette, swapping stories with the boys, or drawing himself up to the table for a foursome at bridge." Jack Pickersgill, who also thought King was reclusive by choice, noted that he was a superb host and fine company when he wanted to be, but usually regretted having wasted time on the vanities of the world.

King used his solitude to study devotional literature, pray, talk to himself through his diaries, and meditate on how to do a better job. Sometimes when politics was not absorbing too much of his time—

---

* The possible exception is his relationship with Joan Patteson, which may, briefly, have become physical. That presumption rests on purely negative evidence, however—pages later torn from the diary and destroyed.

especially during the years of Bennett's government—he experimented with psychic phenomena. He attended séances, and with his close friend Joan Patteson he used a ouija board and engaged in table-rapping. He was a metaphysical idealist who believed that spirit was real and eternal. Like hosts of intelligent and progressive people of the late nineteenth and early twentieth centuries, many of them reacting against old Christian beliefs in a literal heaven and hell, he hoped that the spirit world did intersect from time to time with the material one. He was certain that ultimately spirit controlled matter, a conviction underlying his sense of events being foreordained. Coincidence, such as the movement of the hands of the clock, became important to him as a sign of an order out there greater than random chance. Perhaps it was possible to make contact with the spirits of the dead, through mediums or even through the interpretation of dreams.

His diaries do not suggest that King was completely gullible. He hoped more than he believed. He yearned for mystical, transcendent experiences, and he knew that the experiments with automatic writing and at séances did no one any harm. When the duties of his office called, he put aside most of those foolish things.

*　　*　　*

In most of his cultural tastes King was a Victorian British Canadian. But he was too well educated, too travelled, too familiar with the United States, to share the uncritical Anglophilia of many Canadians. His grandfather had led a rebellion against the British government; King doubted that William Lyon Mackenzie had ever been really disloyal, and he saw no disloyalty in his own critical attitude towards some aspects of British life.

He knew too much about classes, for example, to believe that all Englishmen thought alike or that the attitudes of a few Britons ought to command instant colonial deference. The motherland's governing class, he concluded early in his life, was trained to rule, and to rule the dominions, and "I can see wherein it will be many years before it will ever come to fully appreciate what self-government means." King intended to follow in the footsteps of his grandfather and Sir Wilfrid, and help the British appreciate real Dominion self-government.

In charitable moments he may have admitted that Borden and the Great War had done a fair bit to educate Britain and the world. Borden certainly thought they had, and considered Resolution IX of the Imperial

War Conference to be *de facto* recognition of Canada's independence. The remaining problem, in Borden's view, was to develop mechanisms through which a commonwealth of independent nations could express a common foreign policy. How would such mechanisms evolve?

King thought they could not and should not be defined. Real self-government for Canada and the other dominions meant that each would be free to make its own decisions in all the affairs of the world. The sovereign body for Canadians was the Canadian Parliament. It ought not to limit its sovereignty by giving open-ended commitments, or blank cheques, to be bound by foreign policy developed by anyone, including the other members of the Commonwealth.

King sometimes had doubts about taking an independent course. He had a vague, lingering faith in the unity of the British Commonwealth, and did not use the word "independence" to describe Canada's status. But most of his hesitations were lost early in his prime-ministership when, practically out of nowhere, in the autumn of 1922, he was asked by reporters how Canada would respond to Britain's invitation to send troops to the Near East to help in the impending showdown with Turkey over the city of Chanak. It seemed a classic case of British bungling and arrogance: with no consultation and not even a sense of diplomatic propriety, the London government was calling on the dominions for support in a crisis mostly of its own making.

Chanak was the test case of Canadians' willingness to rally still to the old flag of Empire. Meighen was "Ready, aye, ready!" King was furious. He refused several British requests for a firm statement of support, and, with the backing of Cabinet, took the position that Parliament would decide the extent, if any, of a Canadian contribution. While the romantic imperialists wrung their hands at the negativism of a position that appeared to shatter the unity of the world's greatest empire, it was quickly obvious that King was perfectly in tune with the wishes of most Canadians, who had no desire to be involved in warfare in a far-off place to defend obscure British interests.

After Chanak the last steps in British recognition of the complete autonomy of the dominions, culminating in the Statute of Westminster in 1931, were just a matter of timing. At the several Imperial Conferences he attended in the 1920s, Mackenzie King was sometimes a leader in resisting the imperialists' rearguard attempts to salvage a façade of common commitment, at other times a conciliator when the Irish and

South Africans wanted to move further and faster. By the end of the 1920s no one doubted that Canada was an independent nation on the stage of the world. Credit for parentage in the matter—to Borden or to King?—was left for historical dispute.*

King would always be sensitive to the Tory charge that he was a smasher and breaker of the British Empire—showing the disloyalty you could expect from a rebel's grandson. He believed that the British had caused imperial disunity by continuing to treat the dominions as adolescent nations. As in other relations among autonomous individuals, the precondition of effective co-operation was mutual respect. King was determined to make Britain respect Canada.

*   *   *

Having secured Canada's right to go its own way in world affairs, King was extremely cautious about charting a course. Canadians were deeply divided when they thought about the big issues of war and peace in the 1920s and 1930s. The price of having gone to war at Britain's side in 1914 was 60,000 dead men, years of economic sacrifice, and the most bitter crisis in the country's political history. The United States, neutral until 1917, had avoided most of the war and much of the sacrifice. As war loomed again in Europe—a false alarm over Turkey, increasingly real concerns about Germany and Italy in the 1930s—millions of Canadians, particularly French Canadians, wanted to have nothing to do with commitments of any kind. Millions of other Canadians were still moved by cultural and racial ties to Britain. Their instinct would always be to take a stand at her side when danger threatened.

King's conduct of foreign policy after returning to office in 1935 was a textbook example of putting national unity first. "Canada's first duty to the League [of Nations] and to the British Empire, with respect to all the great issues that come up," he told the House in 1936, "is, if possible, to keep this country united." The storm clouds gathering over Europe alarmed him, and the search for a silver lining helped prompt him to make some truly absurd misjudgements about the personality of Adolf

---

* Meighen had the best line, in quipping that after Borden all King had done was to "burst heroically through open doors."

Hitler after he met the German dictator in 1937. King wrote them down in his diary, and of course they have been exhumed to make him look ridiculous. (King on Hitler: "I am convinced he is a spiritualist—that he has a vision to which he is being true ... his devotion to his mother ... the world will yet come to see a very great man—mystic in Hitler ... much I cannot abide in Nazism—the regimentation—cruelty—oppression of Jews ... but Hitler ... will rank some day with Joan of Arc among the deliverers of his people....") In fact King understood the menace of Germany to the peace of Europe in the late 1930s, and prayed that Hitler would stop or be stopped.

It was up to the rest of the world, particularly Britain and France, to find a way of containing Hitler. King had to think beyond peace-making to the prospect of war, and of Canadian reaction to being asked again to fight and die on foreign soil. Suppose Britain got deeply involved in a European conflict, he told a private session of the Commonwealth prime ministers in 1937:

> There would be the strong pull of kinship, the pride in common tra-
> ditions, the desire to save democratic institutions.... The influence of
> trade interests, of campaigns by a part of the press, the legal anom-
> alies of abstention, the appeal of war to adventurous spirits, would
> make in the same direction.
>
> On the other hand, opposition to participation in war, any war, is
> growing. It is not believed that Canada itself is in any danger. It is
> felt that the burdens left by our participation in the last war are
> largely responsible for present financial difficulties. There is outspo-
> ken rejection of the theory that whenever and wherever conflict
> arises in Europe, Canada can be expected to send armed forces over-
> seas to help solve the quarrels of continental countries about which
> Canadians know little and which, they feel, know and care less about
> Canada's difficulties—and particularly if a powerful country like the
> United States assumes no similar obligations.

King dared not commit Canada in advance to a course of action that would involve automatic participation in a European war. The best Canada could do was support the hope that Hitler could be appeased by appropriate concessions in Europe. If it did come to force, King always believed that Canada would have to stand with Britain. He believed

Canada *should* stand with Britain—and, to his great credit, told Hitler during their 1937 meeting that Canada would fight (Hitler was not noticeably deterred). The justification of King's timid, almost nonexistent foreign policy in the 1930s was that when Britain did go to war in 1939, formally to protect the sovereignty of far-off, undemocratic Poland, Canada rallied to its side.

King had no regrets about the course the country had taken, evolving through caution and attempts at appeasement to a state of war against the evil of Nazism.* In September 1939 Canada was the only country in the Americas that took sides in the conflict with Hitler. The United States remained neutral for more than two years, finally going to war when it was attacked by Japan. As they had in World War I, Canadians contributed proportionately much more of their wealth and blood to the defeat of European totalitarianism than did the people of the United States.

* * *

Two days after the United States entered World War II, Conservative House leader R.B. Hanson had lunch with King to discuss the future. Hanson urged King to form a National Government, bringing Meighen and other prominent opponents into the Cabinet on a policy of waging total war. A total war effort would include conscription.

King had promised that conscription for overseas service would not be used in this war. The government felt it had to make this commitment to obtain even grudging support of the war effort in Quebec, where memories of the last conflict ran deep and enthusiasm for fighting Hitler ran shallow. In September 1939 Quebec's nationalist premier,

---

* He did have some mild regrets that Canada had not been more willing to accept Jewish refugees from Nazism. Although by no means free from racist preconceptions ("It is fortunate that the use of the bomb should have been upon the Japanese rather than upon the white races of Europe," he wrote in his diary after hearing the news of Hiroshima), King was more liberal than many of his advisers on the issue of Jewish immigration. But he allowed himself to be persuaded that the voices advising a restrictive policy, especially those emanating from Quebec, were too strong to be resisted. He swallowed similar doubts about the wisdom of evacuating the Japanese Canadians in 1942, but achieved a small victory later by persuading Cabinet not to continue to restrict their right to vote.

Maurice Duplessis, had called a provincial election, which everyone saw as a referendum on Quebec's support of the federal government's war policy. Repudiation of the war effort by the country's second-largest province would have been a crushing blow to Ottawa. King's Quebec ministers intervened openly in the Quebec election to help oust Duplessis. Without the no-conscription promise they could not have done it.

On his other flank King was harassed by those who believed Canada was not doing enough. Pressure grew insistently as Germany conquered Europe and laid siege to Britain. In early 1940 King seized upon a resolution of the Ontario legislature condemning Ottawa's war policies as reason to call an election to renew his mandate. Campaigning largely on the need for national unity, he won the greatest victory of any prime minister to that time, 184 out of 245 seats.

In their luncheon on December 9, 1941, Hanson used arguments to King that became familiar to Canadians during the Mulroney years of the late 1980s. King had a mandate, Hanson said. He controlled the House of Commons, he could reverse his policies if he so desired, as, in fact, Hanson and most of the Conservatives had reversed theirs since the 1940 election. "Hanson said, at one stage, that with my large following I could do anything I wished." King answered Hanson with an impromptu sermon on Canadian leadership, distinguishing himself from the dominant Tory tradition:

> I replied to him that my views of the source of power were very different to those of some other men. I cited Bennett in particular. I said that such successes I had had, I believed, came from the fact that I believed my power came from the people; that it was not something that arose from some "superman" power which I myself possessed; that I felt I had held that power by being true to the people and to the promises I had given to them. That they trusted me because they knew I would not break faith with respect to their own views and wishes.
>
> Hanson then said: "Then you feel that you should not lead?" To which I replied: That is not the case. That I believed the people had a true instinct in most matters of government when left alone. That they were not swayed, as specially favoured individuals were, by personal interest, but rather by a sense of what best served the common good. That they recognized the truth when it was put before them,

and that a leader can guide so long as he kept to the right lines. I did not think it was a mark of leadership to try to make the people do what one wanted them to do....

Hanson then asked me if I had completely closed my mind to any other course. I replied that I had an open mind in regard to everything. That I would meet situations as I found it necessary and desirable to meet them, but that I would try to view everything in the light of all circumstances, past, present and future.

King soon realized that circumstances were making it necessary to reconsider his no-conscription pledge. Consistent with his sense of a bond between government and the people, he asked Canadians in a national plebiscite on April 27, 1942, if they favoured releasing the government from its promise. Nationally they agreed, by a very big majority. Quebec dissented, equally firmly.

Some of King's ministers, notably J.L. Ralston, the strong-minded Minister of National Defence, interpreted the plebiscite as a mandate to begin conscripting men at any time. King was convinced that the degree of disunity shown in the plebiscite and known to exist in the country, pointed in the direction of more caution. The sixty-eight-year-old prime minister presided over weeks of intense debate among tough, passionate men in his Cabinet, by the end of which he had support for an ongoing policy he described as "not necessarily conscription, but conscription if necessary." The phrase has become notorious in Canadian history as the ultimate in evasiveness, the purest waffle. In fact the words were precise, the policy was clear, and the approach sensible. Conscription would divide Canada. King would do it if he found it necessary, but he would not do it unless it was absolutely necessary, as it was not in 1942. "If we can only keep off putting conscription into force," he wrote in his diary in July 1942, "we will have little trouble when the time comes for that to be necessary."

Two years later, with Canadian infantry fully engaged in Europe and taking heavy casualties, Ralston and the military became convinced that they owed it to the soldiers to insist that conscription be implemented to keep units at proper fighting strength. There were more weeks of intense, exhausting discussions in Cabinet. On November 1, 1944, the Prime Minister told Cabinet that he was accepting the resignation of his Minister of National Defence and had asked General A.G.L. McNaughton to assume the portfolio and make a final plea for volunteers to meet man-power requirements. It soon became clear that McNaughton's campaign had failed. Facing the prospect that further delay might induce resignations in the military and in his Cabinet, King finally decided that a limited measure of conscription was necessary. The required order-in-council was issued, and the decision was confirmed in Parliament. Most French-Canadian members of Parliament voted against it, but the leading Quebec minister, Louis St. Laurent, stayed in the Cabinet. The government retained the confidence of the House and, in the 1945 general election, the confidence of the country, including massive support from Quebec.

Had King tried to "lead" Canada into conscription earlier, Quebec would have resisted. In 1942 and 1944 the Cabinet discussed the possibility of civil war as the worst outcome, and the likelihood of a repetition of the Easter 1918 use of martial law and machine guns to enforce the policy in Quebec. No doubt the will of the majority could have been enforced. In the eyes of many of Canada's soldiers and their loved ones, who despised wavering politicians, it should have been enforced much earlier—and would have been if King had not been such a political weaseller. Perhaps a few Canadian lives were lost because of the delay in bringing units back up to strength.

Perhaps the country was saved. For all of King's struggles to maintain unity, Hitler's war still left a legacy of deep bitterness in Quebec. Justifiably or not, the promise to avoid conscription had been abandoned, the will of a great majority of the French people of Canada had been overridden. On this issue there was no common ground between Canada's two main cultural groups. Memories of conscription crises, Louis Riel, and other perceived acts of "injustice" burned deeply into the consciousness of people whose provincial motto was not to forget. Within twenty years of the end of the war Quebec had an active separatist movement, whose principal argument was that English and French had too little in common to maintain the political bonds. A more vigorous approach to conscription during the war would surely have fanned the flames of separatism in the 1940s and again when they reappeared in the 1960s. The Conservative approach to fighting the war, the Conservative idea of leadership, would have left postwar Canadian unity in a shambles.

*   *   *

King did more than divide Canadians least. His career was so long and complex that he alone in the prime-ministerial group requires more consideration. This chapter has challenged the Stacey image of King the warped second-rater. Much more has to be said about Frank Scott's untrue line, "Always he led us back to where we were before."

A final kick at those who misread the diaries. Was King a lonely, unhappy, unfulfilled human being? Yes, often. He was too human and too normal and too devoted to the memory of his own loving and close-knit family not to have intense regrets about staying a bachelor. His commitment to his diary—like his maudlin love for his dogs in his last years, like his attempts to commune with the spirit world—was a catharsis for his loneliness.

King would have liked to have squeezed love out of the Canadian people, but he knew his limitations. He had too much self-respect and intelligence, and concern for the welfare of the Liberal Party and the country, to cling to office after his time was gone. When he decided to retire in 1948 there was no goodbye tour of world capitals, no lavish gala celebration. Instead there were standing ovations after his farewell speech to the Liberal convention, and, on the first day, a garden party on the grounds of the Dominion Experimental Farm. At the end of the affair he drove off into one of the most glorious sunsets he had ever seen—and wrote poignantly in his diary:

> I quite enjoyed the drive home but kept regretting that I was so completely alone in sharing the great events of a day like today. I could have wished that some members of the family might have been down with me but still more that I might have had a family of my own. I felt that particularly today. However I cannot say that I feel really lonely. I feel a sense of the fulness of life, tremendous satisfaction and pride in the fact that all has gone so well.

VOTE LIBERAL

THE WELDER

6

KING
Welfare Liberalism

"You are going to be as bad as the rest of them, give public buildings before elections, etc.," his friend the Governor-General told Mackenzie King in 1908. Lord Grey was both right and wrong. He was wrong in that Mackenzie King's lofty view of the political calling left little room for the squalid job of distributing favours. In many parts of Canada it was becoming less important anyway, by the 1920s, to distribute traditional patronage in the old-fashioned blatant way, at least at the national level (new provincially based industries such as highway improvement and liquor control became a patronage bonanza). King's governments maintained some of the old patron–client relationships, but the Prime Minister stayed as aloof as possible.

Grey was right, though, in sensing that the Liberals would continue to work hard to win voters' gratitude by doing favours for them. King's governments developed new methods of manipulation and organization and they built support with new forms of state intervention. Instead of funnelling government money to a few thousand friends of the party, they initiated national programs of unemployment insurance and family allowances that turned practically every Canadian into a client of government.

Giving Canada a welfare state seemed to be enlightened and humanitarian. It seemed consistent with notions of a broadening economic democracy and citizen entitlement for the state to stand behind everyone's

153

welfare. But it was democratization with this twist: in doing good for the average person, the politicians were profoundly entrenching themselves as the distributors and redistributors of Canadians' money. As the country became wealthier and citizens developed a greater capacity to look after themselves, the state was not withering away—it was becoming even more important. In fact the politicians of King's era went further: as disciples of the new economists who had been taught by the great British economist John Maynard Keynes, they were even claiming that they knew how to manage the whole economy. Government could end unemployment and guarantee perpetual prosperity for its clients. Wow—some patronage!

Mackenzie King presided over the coming of the welfare state and was immensely proud of it. He helped protect Canadians from poverty and insecurity, fulfilling in large measure the promises of the Liberal platform of 1919. He was even prouder of his party's string of electoral successes, and had a canny sense of how the good things given to the voters rebounded to the Liberals' benefit at the polls.

But sometimes he was not sure that developments were entirely for the best. In his late years, we will see, he occasionally fretted about his ministers' and his civil servants' commitment to big, active government. There was often tension in his governments, as Cabinet and the bureaucracy, egged on by a generation of intellectuals who believed in expanding the state's activities, tried to do and spend more and more, while a cautious leader tried to hold back the tide. Mackenzie King had to be dragged kicking and screaming into the modern world, the younger Liberals felt. They discounted the wisdom of an old fox who was not sure that the young pups knew what they were doing, or that their activities were always good for Canadians.

*   *   *

The Prime Minister did not like some of the names on the list for Senate appointments in 1940. "One might say: why, then, appoint these men?" he asked himself in his diary. "The answer is: it wd. be impossible to keep one's colleagues together unless their collective will to some extent in matters of this kind was recognized." He went ahead and appointed more political hacks to the Senate.

In his ideal world Mackenzie King would have rallied Canadians to the spiritual values underlying Liberal principles. He would have appealed to his countrymen's idealism, their sense of service, the duties of citizenship, compassion for the less fortunate—the sense of a higher calling that undoubtedly motivated him. But he knew too much about the real world and the base motivations of too many of his fellow men, even some Liberals. So he made his peace with the conventions of Canadian politics, going along, more realistically perhaps than Borden had, with many of the traditional uses of patronage.

Like Borden, King wanted to keep his own hands clean. He left the details of party organization, fund-raising, and mundane patronage to his ministers, and increasingly to paid specialists, while he as Prime Minister tried to float above politics.* His disdain for the men who handled the grubby details of organizing and fund-raising was ill-concealed, his gratitude uncharacteristically ill-expressed.

King did occasionally put his own hands gently into the muck. He believed it important that government bodies, such as the boards of Crown corporations, be "representative" of Canada. So the first directors of the CNR, for example, were a nice cross-section of regional representatives (who happened to be all Liberals), rather than the high-powered group of disinterested businessmen dreamed of by the friends of efficient public ownership. In 1935 King advised his novice Minister of Transport, Clarence Decatur Howe, to take account of groups like women and youth and labour in making appointments, and also to "keep the party forces in mind ... keep the political point of view in mind, to cultivate it in addition to the business method...."

C.D. Howe probably didn't need the advice. In his previous career constructing grain elevators, Howe had mastered the highly political game of getting government contracts. His instincts were to reward his

* Unlike Macdonald and Laurier, King did not have any regional or provincial power base, any fiefdom of his own. He sat for various ridings, from Prince Edward Island to Saskatchewan, wherever he was easily electable. Meighen and Bennett were similarly rootless, and some of King's young men, notably Jack Pickersgill and Lester Pearson, were later parachuted into ridings they had never heard of. The King Liberals did maintain a crucial power base in Quebec, and a lesser one in Saskatchewan, but made much of their appeal to all regions of the country. An emerging nation seemed to be generating truly national parties and national political figures, advocating broad national policies.

friends and punish his enemies. For twenty-two years Howe was a central figure in King's and St. Laurent's cabinets; he developed a larger-than-life reputation as the personification of business values in government. In fact he was not and never had been a pure free-enterpriser. Howe was one of the most political of the senior Liberal ministers. He encouraged partisanship and cronyism in appointments at the highest level, and in the 1940s and afterwards acted as the party's senior bagman.

Men and firms that got major government contracts from C.D. Howe's departments would be systematically approached by the minister himself when the party needed money. The Liberals did not "tollgate" on contracts in the sense of requiring a contribution as a precondition of success; instead, they expected money as a condition of gratitude—switching, as Jeffrey Simpson puts it, from "money-before-contracts to money-after-contracts." The growth of government activities, particularly during World War II, meant an ever-expanding pool of grateful contractors.*

"Gratefulness was always regarded as an important factor in dealing with democratic governments." This was the testimony of R.O. Sweezey, the worldly promoter of power developments at Beauharnois on the St. Lawrence River, as he explained why his firm had contributed $600,000 to $700,000 (about $6 million to $7 million in today's values) to the Liberal Party in the 1930 election campaign—thinking, wrongly, that it would retain power. The Beauharnois Scandal of 1931 was a major embarrassment to the Liberals, the worst of the King years. It became a major embarrassment to King himself when it was revealed that one of his rich friends, Senator W.L. McDougald, who had happily paid the Prime Minister's hotel bill on a recent trip to Bermuda, had passed the receipt on to the Beauharnois corporation for reimbursement. "It was mighty generous of McDougald," King had naively diarized. "All he seems to seek in return is recognition and friendship which he craves."

King apologized abjectly to the House of Commons for his party's and his own sloppiness in the Beauharnois affair. He told the House that he and the party were in the "valley of humiliation," a reference to John Bunyan's *Pilgrim's Progress*. They would not let it happen again.

---

* Political scientist Reg Whitaker notes that the Liberals got much of their money from contractors, while the Tories traditionally drew on manufacturers interested in maintaining the tariff.

Nor did they. While the fund-raising methods of Howe and other ministers and organizers are unacceptable by today's standards, they were a cut above the crudities of earlier times. King became fanatical about his personal expenses, either paying his way himself or having another politician or civil servant look after his bills. The Prime Minister of Canada seemed a model penny-pincher; his expense account after one state trip was lower than his valet's.

Canadian political parties never descended into selling senatorships the way that twentieth-century British politicians began selling memberships in the House of Lords. But one practice that King was surprisingly willing to continue was accepting gifts from wealthy friends. Like Macdonald and Laurier and many other national and provincial politicians, he accepted money in trust. Peter C. Larkin, the Salada Tea millionaire whom King appointed High Commissioner to Great Britain, organized the presentation to King in the 1920s of a fund of $225,000. It was kept in a trust company in Boston. Even after Beauharnois, King thought trust funds an exception. He advised St. Laurent to have no qualms about the purse that was being raised for him, arguing that nearly every Canadian political leader got similar compensation for the loss of income involved in public service. In our time, of course, the sinecure of the directorship has become a kind of after-the-fact compensation. No Canadian prime ministers have died in poverty.

(Mackenzie King was particularly careful with money. His mother had grown up in poverty and his father's improvidence had kept the whole family on the edge of hardship. He lived within his salary, reinvested his interest and dividends, and was worth over $700,000 when he died. Most of his wealth was left to the nation, which has not been typical. Even the eccentric ruins adorning his country estate, Kingsmere, were partly an economy measure during the Great Depression. "No one is likely to be critical of a ruin as an extravagance," King told his diary.)

Some of King's ministers thought they were fighting a losing battle to maintain political control of patronage in the old-fashioned and, in their view, the proper way. Jimmy Gardiner, a former premier of Saskatchewan and in his biographer's phrase a "relentless Liberal," was, as Minister of Agriculture from 1935 to 1957, the rural equivalent to C.D. Howe. Gardiner was one of many Liberals who complained about King's wartime order to suspend patronage and appoint only the best people to agencies doing war work. Some of the new appendages of government were also non-political. Gardiner was upset, for example, to learn that the new air-fields being built all over flat Saskatchewan were being created without anyone asking politicians to contribute to location, tendering, or hiring. Non-Liberals in high positions were giving jobs to relatives, and the Liberal minister responsible for Saskatchewan didn't even know about it! In 1955 Gardiner was still complaining about public-works officials' reluctance to hire locally because of their "weakness for wishing to get someone who has engineering or some other technical knowledge." King had long since written off Gardiner as a machine politician, given to "betraying the very principles of Liberalism which all of us are trying to uphold in public life."

*   *   *

What were the principles of King's Liberalism, other than smoothing over conflict? There was an Ontario Grit/Victorian liberal side of King that made him a believer in honest, efficient government and free trade. He disliked big interests, special interests, and Tories, all reeking of special privilege. Most of the time he was also a classic federalist, content to respect the dividing lines between levels of government.

In the 1920s and into the Great Depression, King tried to govern within these parameters. World War I had led to what then seemed to be unsustainably high levels of public debt and taxation. Prudent public finance afterwards seemed to King to involve cutting spending, reducing taxes, and paying down the national debt. During the 1920s Canada gradually reduced the burden of its war debts. In the boom years after 1926 the King administration handed back money to Canadians in the form of substantial annual tax reductions while still running budgetary surpluses. Finance minister J.A. Robb based his budgets on maxims like "Work and thrift are the only sure roads to success." By 1928 he was ready to eliminate the national sales and income taxes totally. King preferred to reduce the tariff.

The tariff was the trickiest of all political issues. King's governments, like Laurier's, dared not tackle the forces of protectionism head on. After his personal experience in 1911, King would never rush into free trade, even when he had the chance. But trade liberalization was close to his heart and the goal of his tariff policy. Most of the tariff changes during the 1920s were in a gradual downward direction. In the 1930s he fiercely opposed Bennett's high-tariff strategy, and when the Liberals came back to power in 1935 one of their first acts was to sign an important trade treaty with the United States; it mandated the first significant reciprocal tariff reductions since 1854. King governments stood for lower tariffs within and without the Empire. After World War II the Liberals fully supported the international thrust for free trade that resulted in the General Agreement on Tariffs and Trade.

Standing for the leadership in 1919, King had presented himself as a progressive reformer, committed to his party's idealistic platform of comprehensive social insurance. In the flush of war-born idealism—why not make war on poverty, on social injustice, on inequalities at home?— the ambitious notion of creating a welfare state seemed, briefly, to have become practical politics. A year or two later, much of that idealism had dissipated across the country. In a climate of longing for "normalcy" and prosperity, the idea of remaking society through government action became postponable. Mackenzie King had few qualms about tempering his commitment to change with a cautious concern for the state of public opinion. He would initiate reform when the public was ready to support reform, not before.

Social-policy initiatives at the national level would be largely unconstitutional anyway, King also realized. The British North America Act had been interpreted by the courts as giving the provincial governments responsibility for most areas of social welfare, including old-age pensions and unemployment relief. The Ottawa government could not bring in national social programs without changing the constitution or persuading the provinces to co-operate. Quebec's government was particularly opposed to interference with its prerogatives, and had no interest in secular social-welfare programs.

The old-age pension question was wending a slow way through the Ottawa machinery until the 1925 election left the balance of power in the House of Commons in the hands of the "Ginger Group" of independent and labour MPs. Needing their support, King promised to bring in a bill to share with the provinces the costs of giving needy Canadians over age seventy $20-a-month pensions. The old-age pension bill was defeated in the Senate, reintroduced after the 1926 election, and passed without opposition—except from the provincial governments, most of which felt they were being levered into new spending commitments or were having to say no to the elderly. The provinces grudgingly fell into line, with Quebec's Liberal premier, L.A. Taschereau, being particularly aggrieved. It was a major diplomatic achievement for King to prevent an open breach with Quebec.

The government briefly canvassed provincial opinion about national unemployment insurance, found no interest, and dropped the matter. King was soon eager to remind the provinces that care of the unemployed was solely their responsibility. As depression conditions began to take hold after 1929, he scorned new requests from provincial governments—mostly Tory and habitually spendthrift—for money for the unemployed. He sailed into the 1930 election proud of his record of financial stewardship, believing the country needed little more than another term of good, prudent government.

Ottawa did take an important initiative after 1926 in its support for Atlantic Canada. The Maritime region was in serious decline by the 1920s and was clamouring for help. Agitation for "Maritime Rights" expressed itself politically in declining support for the Liberals. King responded with a royal commission on Maritime claims; it recommended that the Atlantic provinces be given special subsidies and that the government reduce freight rates on the old Intercolonial Railway as a measure of regional aid.

King worried that the commission had gone too far. "The whole problem seems a futile effort to combat geographical and other economic conditions," he told his diary. He agreed to go along with the proposals solely to gain political support in that region. When Maritime politicians asked for more, he refused, arguing that a policy of more concessions to one region would hurt the party in other parts of the country. But he had already whetted regional appetites, and without considering the long-term consequences of the policy—which haunt and rob taxpayers to this day—the Government of Canada had apparently bought the idea of a right to special regional welfare policies.

King's complacency in 1930 was the worst misreading of Canada's situation in his career. He and his ministers simply failed to grasp the extent of the economic downturn (a partly understandable error; the Wall Street stock market crash seemed a one-time adjustment, probably without serious consequences for Canada. In Ottawa the Dominion Bureau of Statistics was only four years old and there were still no national unemployment figures). Bennett and the Conservatives were the activists in that election, promising more federal money for old-age pensions, emergency grants to the provinces for unemployment relief, and, above all, tariff intervention that would end unemployment. King thought the Tories were being irresponsible, proposing to bribe the voters with federal funds.

The voters wanted the pay-off. Cautious Liberalism had become the conservative choice. It was swept aside as voters chose a government that promised to do great things.

*   *   *

There is no truth in the story that King foresaw how bad the Depression would be and deliberately lost the 1930 election. But he did write to himself after that defeat: "I shall be glad to throw on to Bennett's shoulders the formation of a govt. & finding a solution for unemployment & other problems. My guess is he will go to pieces under the strain. He has promised impossible things.... It looks as tho' it might mean Bennett for a while then a Liberal party with a long lease of power later on."

While waiting to take up its lease, King's party began to debate the meaning of Liberalism. The Depression posed fundamental questions about the future of capitalism, the role of the state, and, in Canada, the future of Dominion–provincial relations. A younger generation of Canadian intellectuals, many of them bound for senior positions in the civil service and/or the Liberal Party, called for government leadership in managing the economy and providing for the disadvantaged. From the left came a clamour for public ownership and economic planning. On the right there was growing interest in artificially inflating the currency, perhaps by providing "social credit" to stimulate the economy. From the universities came disciples of John Maynard Keynes, preaching that governments could implement effective fiscal and monetary policies to counter fluctuations in the business cycle.

Meanwhile the country seemed mired in stagnation, and worse. Unemployment hovered around twenty per cent of the work force, and comparatively few women even bothered looking for salaried work. The prairies were destitute and literally dirty as soil eroded and blew. Several provinces were almost bankrupt. Several provinces had elected demagogic, unstable premiers (Mitch Hepburn in Ontario, Duff Pattullo in British Columbia, soon to be joined by William Aberhart in Alberta and Maurice Duplessis in Quebec), who were apt to lash out in any direction, apt to try wild legislative experiments. The whole world was in a gloomy mess, with many predicting the permanent eclipse of capitalism and liberal society. In Canada many of Bennett's proposed reforms were unconstitutional. If the Liberals came to power again, as they probably would, what the hell would they do?

In the policy discussions of the 1930s King drifted to the right wing of the Liberal Party. He did not like most collectivist approaches to economic recovery, for he disapproved of their coercive features. Agricultural marketing boards, for example, with their strict limits on production and prices and their rigid licensing systems, seemed to him a menace, little more than "self-appointed soviets" tramping on individual freedom. King had been trained in economics, but he was sixty years old in 1934 and had no interest in immersing himself in the new interventionist doctrines. He believed that sound public finance was as relevant to Canada in the 1930s as it had been in the 1920s. The other great needs of a trading country were improved commodity prices and open access to global markets.

As prime minister again after 1935, King became alarmed at his ministers' persistence in submitting increased estimates for their departments at budget time. Why weren't they concentrating on restraint? "The truth is," he reflected in 1937, "the Ministers have lost all sense of responsibility to the tax-payer, and are thinking only of making a showing in their particular fields, with public monies. All have got into the habit of yielding to pressure, and particularly with unemployment, doing the thing that is likely to help some Province." The next year was worse, as heated debates about the good things to be achieved by spending gradually eroded the resistance of King and his finance minister, Charles Dunning. The 1938 budget featured the first planned deficit in Canadian history— a projected $23 million shortfall. The government defended the unorthodox policy because of the stimulating effect the extra spending would have on the economy.

Having largely lost his struggle against the spenders, the Prime Minister was philosophic and pragmatic:

> In politics one has to continually deal with situations as they are in the light of conditions as they develop from time to time. The world situation has headed the countries more and more in the direction of the extension of State authority and enterprise, and I am afraid Canada will not be able to resist the pressure of the tide. The most

> we can do is to hope to go only sufficiently far with it as to prevent
> the power of Government passing to those who would go much far-
> ther, and holding the situation where it can be remedied most
> quickly in the future, should conditions improve.

"Those who would go much farther" included, in King's mind, some of
the provincial politicians the Depression had brought to the fore. Debt
and spending had pushed Alberta and Saskatchewan to the brink of bankruptcy. British Columbia under Liberal premier Duff Pattullo seemed not
far behind. "Would spend millions—no sort of person to govern," King
noted about Pattullo. The Prime Minister fought his ministers to a stand-
still on their desire to support some of Pattullo's public-works projects,
and the B.C. situation was the occasion of more homilies on the spending
problem: "I really do not know what is going to happen to the country in
the course of time with the kind of men who are gaining control of public
affairs, and who use the public treasury as if it was something to be given
away rather than guarded." This dimension of Mackenzie King's pre-
science did not begin to be appreciated by Canadians until in the 1990s
they began to count the cost of decades of giveaways.

The financial woes of several provinces and the growing belief that
social welfare was a national responsibility caused the King government to
begin to lay the groundwork for constitutional reform. A royal commission was created to undertake the most comprehensive review since 1867
of the division of powers and responsibilities in the Canadian federation.
The 1940 report of the Rowell–Sirois Commission recommended a complex rewiring of the system to recognize that human well-being was a
national problem, and to give the national government the financial
resources to cope with that problem. To preserve the balance, the actual
delivery of most social services would be through the provinces.

Rowell–Sirois was more than a document in the history of Canadian
federalism. The report's recommendation that the Government of
Canada ensure for all citizens uniform national standards of welfare services was a major turning-point in the history of the welfare state in
Canada. In tandem with the 1943 *Report on Social Security for Canada* it
marked acceptance of the idea that Canadians had a right to a state-pro-
vided safety net. Support could be extended in various ways—to only the
needy or to everyone, in time of need or continuously, through national
benefits or with regional adjustments, and so on—but philosophically the

breakthrough had come. There is little distance between 1940s concepts of a "National Minimum" and debates in our time about the concept of a guaranteed annual income.

In this central area of social policy King was not a conservative. The Conservative Party and many conservative individuals would wrestle for years with worries about the danger to the moral fibre of individuals whose welfare was looked after by the state. King often reminded himself and his ministers that he had set out a welfare state agenda in *Industry and Humanity*. He was more conscious than some of the enthusiasts of the problems of timing and provincial co-operation. But it was only a matter of patience and negotiation, not principle. In the best sense it was a matter of opportunism.

*   *   *

The activists, the spenders, the interventionists, and the centralizers had their opportunity thrown to them by the requirements of another world war. From 1939 to 1945 the Canadian government ran a command economy, intervening in the nation's life whenever and wherever it decided it was necessary to get things done. After a slow start in 1939–40, when there was little fighting anywhere, the government found itself having to divert more resources to war-making than anyone had thought possible. "War socialism" in Canada meant heavy taxes, huge increases in government spending and borrowing, wage and price controls throughout the economy, rationing of foodstuffs and gasoline, regulation of pant cuffs and hemlines, no new cars or tires, and barrages of propaganda aimed at reminding Canadians of their patriotic duty to obey the regulations, suffer and sacrifice, and support the nation's magnificent war effort.

Dissent from wartime orthodoxy was severely controlled. Censorship inhibited the flow of bad news. Internment severely restricted the activities of suspect men and women, that is, those who might advance the enemy's cause; the spectrum of potential enemies ranged from the mayor of Montreal to all the Japanese Canadians living in British Columbia. The line between harmful and legitimate dissent became exceedingly fine: both Conservative conscriptionists and French-Canadian anti-conscriptionists were denied access to CBC Radio so that the war effort, and the government's program, would not be disrupted.

World War II, then, saw the advent of big, authoritarian government in Canada. Historians have not yet written a balanced history of the war years, one which acknowledges that the controls were unpopular, the munitions supply programs less than spectacularly effective, the organization and command of the fighting forces not up to the standards of our Allies. Someday a case will be made that big government did not work very well in Canada during the war.

Such revisionism would be an attack on the way the Liberals and their friends tried to write the history of those times. During the war and for decades afterwards, conventional wisdom held that Mackenzie King's governments had done an excellent job of organizing the war economy. After all, we put a million fighting men in the field, we put all the unemployed back to work (wasn't it the war that really saved Canada from the Depression?), we turned a depressed agricultural country into a mighty industrial giant, we avoided scandals, avoided inflation, got through a crisis on conscription, and even brought in the welfare state.

C.D. Howe, the Minister of Munitions and Supply, was the truest believer in Canada's and his own wartime achievements. For Howe and other entrepreneurial spirits interested in the creative uses of government power, the war was a kind of ultimate megaproject, a great development job. Money didn't matter, production did. Achievement was measured by counting the output of Canadian industry—thousands of planes and tanks, millions of tons of steel and aluminum ingots, hundreds of millions of shells, uranium for the Manhattan Project, which built the atom bomb. Long-term calculations of cost-benefit (some of the costs included low standards of civilian living, barely above Depression levels; suppressed inflation; depletion of natural resources; lives lost from defective equipment and leadership) hardly seemed possible or relevant. We won the war, didn't we, and wasn't that the only thing? Big government had not let us down; it had carried us through. The interesting question was how best to apply methods of state intervention to winning the peace. How, for example, could we create more megaprojects to stock the economy? Howe's answers included pouring hundreds of millions into the peaceful uses of atomic energy and laying the foundation for what he hoped would be a great Canadian aviation industry.

The Liberal politicians thought they were doing a fairly good job, but hearing Winston Churchill's speeches always reminded Mackenzie King of his inadequacies as a war leader. He knew he was no Churchill or

Franklin D. Roosevelt, and worried that Canadians would see him as no leader at all. (The nightmare apparently came true in 1947, when the Niagara Parks Commission installed carillon bells inscribed "in memory of our nation's leaders, Winston Spencer Churchill and Franklin Delano Roosevelt." King's distress at the inscription was hardly less than his anger at the failure of Liberals everywhere to rise in protest against what could only be another manoeuvre by the Conservative government of Ontario.) He knew that the soldiers did not like him, partly because of conscription, partly because he was so thoroughly unmilitary. On one occasion while inspecting Canadian troops in England in 1941 the Prime Minister was met with scattered boos. His anxieties increased. As he explained, honourably, in his diary,

> I really felt too moved at the thought of all this young life being possibly destroyed to be able to give proper expression to my thoughts. I cannot talk their jargon of war. There is no use attempting it. My words inevitably get into those of thought, and prayer, and Providence, which is not the conventional thing, but the only thing which I feel at heart. I have held to those words, rather than to others. I cannot tell them what we are expecting of them in the way of service. Offering their lives is infinitely greater than anything I myself am called upon to do.

King's respect for ministerial autonomy and the collective will of Cabinet—a team approach to leadership—reached its height of effectiveness during the war. He had strong ministers bolstered by strong civil servants, and for the most part he gave them their head. His government did not try to dictate grand strategy to the senior allies, or even ask for more than a *pro forma*, photo-opportunity share in the making of overall war policy. The young diplomatic corps was quietly insistent on Canada having a say in matters of real concern to the Dominion; men such as Lester Pearson, Hume Wrong, and Norman Robertson garnered significant respect in chancelleries and state departments as professional spokesmen for the interests of a country that had mobilized a fair amount of military muscle. The Roosevelt–King relationship became particularly warm and reasonably personal—probably the closest relationship there has been between a president and a prime minister—as Americans and Canadians worked on joint problems of continental defence and defence production.

The war years were hog heaven for the new class of Keynesian economists, ambitious interventionist politicians, and expansion-minded bureaucrats who had been filtering into Ottawa during the Depression. Many of them owed their jobs, directly or indirectly, to the Prime Minister's instinct for recruiting well-trained young men.

King respected the intelligence and the energy of the new men around him, but had seen too much of government and politics to share all their enthusiasms. As the Department of Finance developed plans for managing the economy after the war, as ministers pushed for consideration of ambitious social programs, as diplomats proposed a more aggressive role for Canada in the postwar world, the Prime Minister wrote note after cautionary note in his diary about the power-hunger of those around him. He feared that ministers might become the tools of civil servants, that both groups liked power too much, and that nobody paid enough attention to the political element as expressed through Parliament.

> I can see in [Norman] Robertson always a tendency to get things into the hands of the permanent officials rather than to leave them to the judgment of the government....
>
> Howe too is interested mainly in power that the position gives him, not in public service for its sake....
>
> Dr. [W.C.] Clark is really the one who is responsible for members of Government not doing what I think the judgment of most of them inclines them to do....
>
> ... There is a danger of a government growing up which is not a government. A bureaucracy which will try to control things from Embassies rather than having Embassies the agents of government....
>
> ... In some way or another, it seems impossible to get Ministers to give up this little authority which they have exercised during times of war and leave it to the body to which it belongs, namely Parliament. I do not object to the Opposition forcing our people to fall properly into line on the supremacy of Parliament.

King focused his limited stock of enthusiasm on plans for social reform. By 1940, through a considerable feat of personal diplomacy, he had managed to obtain provincial agreement to a constitutional amendment giving the federal government responsibility for unemployment insurance. The necessary federal legislation was put through immediately, and King was very proud:

> This is really a great achievement for the Liberal Party. We inaugurated social legislation, the old age pensions measure. Set out to get a federal measure of unemployment insurance. Got the B.N.A. Act amended to give power to the federal government to legislate; got consent of all provinces of Canada to this end, and have now got the bill through both Houses.... For all time to come, that will remain to the credit of the Liberal Party under my leadership.

Wartime paved the way for more reform because Canadians, like most combatants, had their dreams of a better world rekindled by the bloodshed and sacrifice. Canadians were in close touch with British schemes for "cradle-to-grave" social security, and the Cabinet commissioned home-grown studies of appropriate programs. Everyone worried about a return to depression conditions after the war, and the economists in the Department of Finance were eager to develop ways to stimulate peacetime purchasing power.

By 1943 King was more eager than many of his ministers to go ahead with further reforms. "I get very fatigued when I encounter a strong opposition to what seems to me the obvious and right thing for a liberal party to pursue," he wrote of social-security legislation. "Little by little the effect of the war on some members of the government is to make them so reactionary as to cause the party generally to lose ground right along to the C.C.F." When several by-election defeats and a September 1943 opinion poll showed that the electorate was moving leftwards very quickly, King and the Cabinet decided to recapture liberal ground and become vigorous reformers.

There would no return to *laissez-faire* after the war. New departments were created to look after veterans, housing, health and welfare. The right of collective bargaining was fully accepted for the first time in federal jurisdiction as an order-in-council created a framework for the certification of unions and the conduct of industrial relations. Reconstruction planners prepared a White Paper on employment and income explaining how the government would conquer unemployment in peacetime by the appropriate use of fiscal and monetary policy, including the deliberate use of budget deficits in difficult times.

Other civil servants were drafting schemes of comprehensive health insurance.

The linchpin of the new Canadian welfare state was to be the family allowance program, or the "baby bonus." In 1944 the government introduced legislation to provide monthly payments ranging from $5 to $8 per child, depending on age, to all Canadian families. The worst hardships endured by large families having to survive on low wages (the core poverty group, next to the aged) would instantly be overcome. At once the masses would have a monthly jolt of purchasing power. And without anyone quite realizing it, the decision to pay the allowances to the mother, rather than to the traditional "head" of the household, created another kind of social revolution, giving hundreds of thousands of women the first money they had ever controlled.

Nobody dared vote against family allowance legislation in the House of Commons, though a fair number of Conservatives tarred their party by carping about moral fibre and bribes to the province where people had the largest families (i.e., Quebec). Even King had had some doubts about the whole exercise, grumbling at times when his MPs seemed to be calling for "more and more of expenditures ... less and less of taxation." Sometimes he had to be prodded by his parliamentary secretary, Brooke Claxton, or the young idea man in his office, Jack Pickersgill. Most of the time he was solidly behind reform. To have written "the doctrine of national minimum standard of life," as set out in *Industry and Humanity*, into government policy seemed to make life worthwhile, he told his diary. The rich and even the middle classes might be upset, but "at least the great numbers of people ... will see that I have been true to them from the beginning of my public life."

The politicians, naturally, realized that great numbers of people would have pleasant feelings towards the government that gave them their baby bonuses. King wrote pages and pages in his diary about his satisfaction at doing good for Canadians. To his Cabinet, discussing the timing of the first baby-bonus cheques in relation to the next election, he reasoned,

> I did not like the idea of spending public money immediately before an election. Also ... people were likely to be more grateful for what they were about to receive than anything they might have been given in advance. I believe that politically they will be more likely to support

our administration by having the Act on the Statutes with the understanding we were committed to carry it out than they would be had the provisions gone into effect with possible delays and comments upon the amounts and their varying effects on various families.

An opinion survey disclosed that twenty-nine per cent of Canadians thought family allowances were "a political bribe," thirty-four per cent considered them "a necessary law," and sixteen per cent thought they were both necessary and a bribe. In later elections Liberals hinted that Tories would do away with family allowances, and probably other benefits as well.

The family allowances were thought to be a full enough plate for 1944–45. Health insurance would require more planning and more provincial co-operation (quite a lot more of both, it turned out). Cabinet also decided, King recorded, "that we had gone as far as we should on public expenditures and on social security matters, and that to announce further large new expenditures in view of outlay for family allowances, would only alarm one side of the electorate in the matter of taxation, and no further thanks from the other."

The voters were asked to give thanks to the government in the June 11, 1945, general election. After six years of war, suffering, regulation, and a conscription crisis that had angered everyone, it was not at all clear that they would be grateful. Many observers thought the government would be beaten. The British were soon to dismiss their war leader, Churchill, from further conduct of their affairs.

The Liberals were helped immeasurably by the plight of the Conservatives, now led by the former Liberal-Progressive premier of Manitoba, John Bracken, and calling themselves the Progressive Conservatives. Bracken's personality made King seem a paragon of charisma. Most of the election campaign was fought after Germany's defeat and, incredibly, the PCs made conscription for the war with Japan the central issue. They effectively gave up on Quebec, fielding only thirty-one candidates in that province and garnering less than nine per cent of the vote. The Liberals took many more seats in Quebec than anyone had expected, largely because various splinter groups fizzled. Liberal national campaigning centred on the baby bonus as the key to "Building a New Social Order for Canada." Voters were reminded of all the money that a benevolent government would be putting into their pockets. Like the Liberals in

1930, the Conservatives were known to have grave doubts about the morality of giving money to voters.

The Liberals won another majority, to many of them an amazing victory. For Mackenzie King, this sixth electoral triumph was particularly satisfying. He had led his country through war and had a mandate to lead it into peace. Roosevelt was dead, Churchill would soon be defeated. King alone carried on—though he had to find a new riding when his personal victory in Prince Albert was overturned by the military vote.

*   *   *

The 1945 election campaign saw the first full-scale use of advertising agencies by Canadian political parties. In Mackenzie King's final attack on the Progressive Conservatives, he charged them with this sin:

> It is now perfectly clear that there has been a highly financed campaign of modern publicity, with special write-ups in the press, endless photography in the magazines; with radio, films, posters and what not, to sell John Bracken, the new leader of the Progressive-Conservative party, by the same methods that are used in selling a new breakfast food, or a new brand of soap.

This section of King's speech was apparently written by his own party's advertising agency.

The Conservatives employed McKim Advertising to plan their campaign. The Liberals had developed their connection with Cockfield, Brown, Canada's largest advertising agency, in the late 1930s. Agencies had earlier been used to place party advertisements during election campaigns; now wartime propaganda and publicity efforts tremendously multiplied government's use of their services. By 1945 the Government of Canada was the country's largest advertiser. It awarded advertising contracts without tender. Public-opinion polling had also come to Canada during the war. The emergence of these new specialists laid the foundation for a new age of political marketing.

Whether their records were clean or dirty, politicians could indeed be sold like soap. The Walsh Advertising Agency of New Brunswick made this pitch for Liberal business in 1948:

> Walsh has always approached its political assignments with the same techniques that it employs successfully to sell automobiles, fountain pens, hosiery, etc. for other clients. Perhaps that is the secret of the agency's success in the political field. After all, voters are human beings. And all human beings are motivated, in all their actions, by a comparatively few well-known and measurable impulses. These may be broadly defined as Fear, Hunger, Sex, and Rage. To reach and incite these impulses, there are five portals of entry—sight, sound, touch, taste, and smell....
>
> Given a free hand, Walsh proceed[s] to formulate a plan that would sell a Government to a people, just as we would sell any other product or service....

Walsh stayed mainly provincial, because the national Liberal account was sewed up by Cockfield Brown. H.E. Kidd of that agency had worked closely for years with Brooke Claxton, a rising force in the party whom King promoted as his parliamentary secretary and then into the Cabinet. Cockfield Brown ran general elections and by-elections for the Liberals, organized dinners and conferences, monitored the press, did research, wrote speeches, and, from 1948, supplied the services of Kidd, who stayed on payroll, as secretary of the National Liberal Federation. The firm billed the party directly for some of its services and donated many others. It became the advertising agency of choice not only for the government but for many of its Crown corporations and client firms. Liberals took some pains, Reginald Whitaker notes in his fine study, *The Government Party*, to cover up details of the relationship between the government and its advertising agency.

The admen were not yet political gurus (Dalton Camp was still learning the game in New Brunswick), but some of the old politicians realized that a new era was dawning. Political intelligence used to be picked up by MPs gladhanding on Main Street; now it was being gathered and analysed by professionals. Old-fashioned machine politicians like Jimmy Gardiner and Chubby Power were becoming anachronisms in their own lifetimes.

*   *   *

So was the Prime Minister. In 1945 King turned seventy-one, and he was worn out. It would take time to plan a smooth transition of power. In the meantime the government had no respite from the problems of reconstruction at home and the attempt to create a new world order abroad.

King continued to be very well served by his Cabinet. Veterans like C.D. Howe wanted no more than to be left alone to plan big postwar industrial developments. Young men like Claxton and Paul Martin were eager to carry the ball on social policy. Louis St. Laurent, whom King had brought into the government as his new Quebec lieutenant and Minister of Justice in 1941, was a particularly good find, and soon emerged as King's likely successor. In 1946 King made St. Laurent Secretary of State for External Affairs, the first non–prime minister to hold that portfolio.

Domestically, King's government soldiered on with the attempt to build a social welfare state managed according to Keynesian principles of deficits in hard times, surpluses in good ones. The war had elevated the dominion government to clear primacy over the provinces, for obvious reasons. In peace, however, "the sleeping dogs of provincial power" awoke and began to snarl at the Ottawa Grits. The premiers of Ontario and Quebec led intense objections to Ottawa's desire to monopolize income and corporate taxation to fund comprehensive social security. King privately sympathized with provincial resentment at the centralizers in the Department of Finance. He did not think it was possible or desirable for Ottawa to reduce the provinces to subsidy-dependence, or even to introduce social programs that involved transferring large sums to the provinces. He fought for classic "separate sphere" federalism, in which each government would raise for itself the money necessary to carry out its responsibilities:

> a great mistake has been made by taking vast sums from the federal treasury and giving them to provinces by way of subsidies. Much better for everyone [to have] the body spending the money, the body required to raise the necessary taxation.... I said I felt all my Liberal training ... caused me to feel the wisdom of not allowing an issue to be raised on the endeavour on the part of the Federal Government to centralize everything in Ottawa but to keep to certain measures of provincial autonomy. That the Liberal background was all in that direction and that we were going far too rapidly with some of our social legislation.... all these grants to the Provinces for different health measures, etc., were simply handing from the Federal Treasury

so much money to Provinces to spend in ways which were helping them to fight us politically and were not economical.

King's doubts about his colleagues' judgement came close to paranoia as he contemplated the mess the world was in after the war. Peace had hardly broken out when great-power politics resumed, East–West conflict sharpened (with a major spy scandal, the Gouzenko affair, in, of all places, Canada!), and the possibility of World War III began to loom. In the 1930s King and many of his senior advisers had leaned towards North American isolationism. By 1945 the diplomatic corps and most of the Cabinet, including many former isolationists, were firmly committed to internationalism. Canada would do all it could to play an active role in world affairs, especially at the United Nations and in other international bodies. King dissented, sometimes obsessively and irrationally. He wanted to go back to the policies of the thirties, but with even less international involvement.

His isolationism sparked an open clash with his ministers in 1947, when St. Laurent approved a proposal for Canada to serve on a United Nations temporary commission to supervise free elections in Korea. Day after day King battered his ministers, and his stenographers, with rants against the rashness and danger of all these involvements in far-away places:

> I thought I ought to say I felt a great mistake was being made by Canada being brought into situations in Asia and Europe of which she knew nothing whatever.... I asked why should we attempt to go in and settle a situation as had arisen in Korea. Have our country drawn into or possible consequences [*sic*] that would come from war....
>
> St. Laurent said ... that we could, of course, withdraw from the United Nations if we wished, but that, being a member of it, we were now going to take a seat on the Security Council and we had to assume other obligations, etc. I replied that I thought the United Nations counted for nothing so far as any help in the world was concerned....
>
> I said ... that I did not see how I could place on my soul the burden of being responsible in any way for bringing Canada into a situation that might make this country responsible for war.... It all arose from being unwilling to say we did not know anything about these matters and therefore would not assume responsibility in connection

with them. Canada's role was not that of Sir Galahad to save the whole world unless we were in a position to do it....

The truth is our country has no business trying to play a world role in the affairs of nations, the very location of some of which our people know little or nothing about. So far as External Affairs is concerned, they have been allowed to be run far too much on [Lester] Pearson's sole say so, and Pearson himself moved far too much by the kind of influences that are brought to bear upon him. He is young, idealistic, etc., but has not responsibility. I am thankful I held responsibility for External Affairs as long as I did. At least, I did not get the country into trouble by keeping it out of things it had no business to interfere with....

King only gave in and sanctioned the Korean commission, with many caveats, when St. Laurent and other ministers threatened to resign.

As King aged and reflected on his career, he was increasingly given to telling young Liberals and his diary that the secret of governing well was in preventing things from happening rather than in taking positive steps. "It is what we prevent often more than what we accomplish that tells for most in the end." He could cite examples large and small—how he had prevented the collapse of the political system in the 1920s, how he had blocked a lieutenant-governor from dismissing Alberta's Social Credit government in the 1930s, how he had stopped the country from flying apart by being so cautious on conscription in the 1940s, how often he had persuaded ministers to reconsider ill-conceived, reckless schemes, how he had saved the British Commonwealth from all the centralizing plans of the old imperialists.

When King's reputation was collapsing in the 1960s and 1970s, he was blamed by some of the new nationalists for not having prevented the American domination of Canada. During and after the war, they argued, King's government had snuggled up too close to the Yanks, and the country had never recovered. The PM was too busy snipping the last colonial ties to England to realize that his friends the Rockefellers and Roosevelts were reducing Canada to a new kind of colonial status. From colony to nation to colony again, in a few short years.

In fact Mackenzie King was one of Canada's charter postwar anti-Americans. He was not particularly comfortable with U.S. activities in the Canadian north during the war (the building of the Alaska Highway by the United States had caused a fair amount of friction), and as he thought about Canada's future he worried about the prospect of sharing the continent with a powerful, expansive neighbour. As he prepared for a Commonwealth Conference in 1946 he told his Cabinet that

> I believed the long range policy of the Americans was to absorb Canada. They would seek to get this hemisphere as completely one as possible. They are already in one way or another building up military strength in the North of Canada. It was inevitable that for their own protection, they would have to do that. We should not shut our eyes to the fact that this was going on consciously as part of the American policy....

King distrusted American domination of the United Nations, and he was not sure that Canada ought to follow the American lead in all matters involving East–West relations. Lester Pearson and some of his other diplomats, he thought, were too dazzled and dominated by their counterparts in the U.S. State Department.

On the other hand, there was no question of the primacy of Canada's relations with the United States, especially now that continental defence against the Soviet menace was more important than ever. In King's ideal world Canada would preserve and develop a role as both British and American, becoming a linchpin in the Anglo-American relationship.

Early in 1948 the old man was informed that U.S.–Canadian trade discussions, looking towards free trade across the border, were going very well. There was a distinct possibility of a major agreement. King mulled the matter over and decided that, even though Canada had initiated the talks, he was going to stop them. He told his senior advisers again and again that he believed the Americans wanted to take over Canada, that he was not going to be accused, as Laurier had been, of being an annexationist, and that, whether prime minister or not, he wanted never to cease being a "British citizen." (In fact he had finally become a "Canadian citizen" a year earlier, receiving the first certificate of citizenship under his government's Canadian Citizenship Act. One clause in the act, later removed, did state that Canadian citizens remained "British subjects.") The reciprocity discussions were shelved for another thirty-five years. It was King's last act of prevention.

Sir John A. Macdonald:
Setting the genetic code for being
a Prime Minister of Canada.

Macdonald, 1891:
In old age a Victorian, "ethnic" politician.

Sir Wilfrid Laurier,
with admirers:
A charmer who
learned to deliver
the rough stuff.

Sir Robert Laird Borden:
The best Conservative Prime Minister
of the twentieth century.

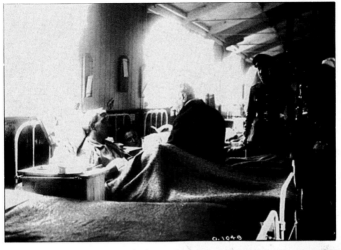

Borden visiting wounded
Canadian soldiers: His duty was
to keep faith with the men in
Flanders fields.

Arthur Meighen:
Narrow and self-righteous
and baffled by his failures.

Richard Bedford Bennett:
Self-made, would-be saviour of the
Conservatives and Canada.

William Lyon Mackenzie King (with dog, Pat):
Canada's most successful and most misunderstood Prime Minister.

John Diefenbaker, 1958:
He said there was nowhere to go but down, and he was right.

John Diefenbaker at the Conservative convention, 1966,
glaring at Dalton Camp. About to be deposed by
men who sometimes questioned his sanity.

Lester Bowles Pearson and Maryon Pearson (second from left), 1948.
Everyone liked "Mike" until he became Prime Minister.

Pearson, Pierre Trudeau, and Quebec Premier Daniel Johnson (senior)
before the 1968 constitutional conference. Trudeau supplied the toughness.

Pierre Elliott Trudeau.
"A weird bugger but a smart one."

Trudeau in retirement:
An elite of one.

Brian and Mila Mulroney with Ronald and Nancy Reagan
at the Shamrock summit. He would have been an excellent
mayor of Boston in the 1940s.

King was so obviously out of sympathy with the trends of the times, especially the activism of his ministers, that he began to question his own judgement and realized it was time to retire. He indulged in the harmless vanity of staying in office until he had beaten Walpole's record as the longest-serving prime minister in the history of British government. At a national Liberal convention in August 1948, St. Laurent was chosen to succeed him. There were no surprises at the convention, partly because of King's advance manoeuvring. No one doubted his private support for St. Laurent. The convention also went smoothly because logistical arrangements were in the capable hands of the men from Cockfield Brown.

*   *   *

King left the scene just as Canada was embarking on an unprecedented, unpredicted era of wonderful affluence. The grey years of hard times and sacrifice gave way to happy days of full employment, shopping centres, television, teen dances, and high incomes. Rock-and-roll was almost at hand. The baby boom began literally rejuvenating the country. European immigrants, many of them "DPs" (displaced persons) from Hitler's war, began changing its face.

It wasn't much of a Liberal rejuvenation to replace a leader aged seventy-three with one aged sixty-six. But those who worked closely with the prime ministers saw the advent of Louis Stephen St. Laurent as a breath of fresh air (except at Cabinet meetings, after St. Laurent reversed King's ban on smoking). Gone was the fussiness, the dithering, the moralizing, the obfuscation, the timidity, the living in the past. St. Laurent was smart and self-effacing, dignified, friendly, totally bilingual; he did his homework, liked to run a tight ship in Cabinet, but was also happy to give his ministers their head.

The St. Laurent years to 1957 became a rich, golden autumn of Mackenzie King Liberalism. All of the Liberal commitments—to national unity, the welfare state, modern economic management, prosperity, prosperity, prosperity—seemed to come up trumps, beating everything the hapless Tories and socialist CCFers offered in the 1949 and 1953 elections. The Liberal Party of Canada was arguably the most successful political party in any democracy. Canada was one of the most successful countries in the world, and, as Liberals saw it, one of the best governed. The popular slogan in the 1949 campaign, "You never had it so good," applied to Canadians and Liberals alike, and explains why most Canadians were Liberals.

Mackenzie King did not live to see the full apotheosis of Canadian Liberalism. Exhausted when he retired, he died at Kingsmere on July 22, 1950. He had an impressive state funeral, but the country did not plunge itself into mourning. Most Canadians had respected King; few had loved him. Almost immediately, Canadian politicians began losing touch with his spirit.

The St. Laurent government's activist course in external relations must have had King tossing in his grave. War had broken out in Korea just as he lay dying. His last words could have been, "I warned you." On the train back to Ottawa from King's burial, St. Laurent and his Secretary of State for External Relations, Lester Pearson, began planning Canada's contribution to the effort to save South Korea. Soon Canadian troops were fighting and dying in yet another far-off land.

The government had no realistic option other than to support the American–U.N. initiative in Korea. But Pearsonian diplomacy was aimed in that direction anyway. The Canadian government now wanted to and did play an engaged role on the world stage, and it became respected for that role. The new diplomacy of international activism culminated in the Suez Crisis of 1956, when Canada and Pearson were instrumental in establishing a U.N. peacekeeping force in the Near East, for which Pearson received the Nobel Peace Prize. Suez has been enshrined in national memory as Canada's finest peacetime hour in world affairs.

At the time it was much more controversial. The Anglo-French assault on Egypt provoked the last crisis of Commonwealth foreign policy. Many English Canadians thought Canada still owed "ready, aye, ready" loyalty to the motherland, especially in an easy battle against a pushy third-world country. Goaded by Tory critics who still lived in the nineteenth century, St. Laurent commented acidly in the House of Commons that "the era when the supermen of Europe could govern the whole world is coming pretty close to an end." King would have approved the sentiment, but not its indiscreet expression. The veneer of Canadian unity on such matters was still thin. The government's stand on Suez cost it support outside of Quebec.

On the domestic front, the continuities with King Liberalism were almost total. During the King years a modern, professional civil service had evolved that served his administrations very well. To the Liberals the civil service was a source of talent as well as ideas, a training ground for running the country. King himself had begun the tradition of moving from the civil service to electoral politics. J.W. Pickersgill and Lester Pearson were the most prominent of several former public servants para-chuted into Liberal politics and the Cabinet during the St. Laurent years, and the practice became habit-forming.

Inside the bureaucracy the Department of Finance believed that it was managing or "fine-tuning" the economy consistently with the prin-ciples of Keynesian economics. It was probably not able to do this, but the country's tremendous postwar prosperity, based on global hunger for its natural resources, made all jobs easy and all theories apparently work-able. By the early 1950s the finance minister had the pleasant annual embarrassment of having to defend each year's budgetary surplus. Omi-nously, the Opposition scored political points by arguing that surpluses were too high, that governments should find ways of giving the money back to citizens instead. Surely a good and popular idea—but if you did not bank the surpluses from the good years to cover the deficits you planned to run in the bad years, what would eventually happen?

The welfare state continued to be built. In 1951 seventy-year-old Canadians began receiving $40 a month in old-age pension, as a matter of right; by 1957 the federal government was beginning to fund hospital insurance. St. Laurent worried a bit about the pension scheme being effectively non-contributory, funded out of general revenue. He rightly predicted that elections might become an auction for the votes of old-age pensioners. Similarly, the unemployment insurance fund contained a huge surplus because there had been so little unemployment. Members of Parliament saw no reason why the scheme ought not to give more generous benefits to voters, and in 1950 the government began offering unemployment insurance to certain seasonal workers, thus subverting the insurance principle. Jack Pickersgill, who had become the MP for Bonavista-Twillingate in the new province of Newfoundland, used the precedent to begin pressing for UI for fishermen.

Pickersgill's career was a classic study in the new politics of welfare Liberalism. A former mandarin, a charter member of the Liberal elite, he would normally not have gone near Newfoundland except for holidays. But once Newfoundlanders had become his constituents, he could be counted on to scatter favours in return for their support. In 1956 the government began allowing fishermen to go on "pogey." "I regarded my part in securing the extension of unemployment insurance to fishermen as my most substantial contribution to the welfare of my constituents, and of Newfoundland in general, and evidently the electors had similar feelings," Pickersgill wrote years later.

The welfare of Canadian cultural producers was also taken in hand by benevolent Liberals. In 1951 the Royal Commission on National Development in the Arts, Letters, and Sciences recommended grants to stimulate Canadian cultural expressions which might otherwise be swamped by lowbrow Americanism. The Canada Council was established in 1957. The government also began granting money to the provinces to support the universities. In both of these areas St. Laurent allowed himself to be persuaded by his ministers. He had doubts about getting into the business of "subsidizing ballet dancing" (King would certainly have shared those doubts), and federal involvement in education provoked intense resentment in Quebec. Many Liberals believed, however, that a flourishing national culture, aiming at excellence in the arts and education, was one of the next steps in building an independent Canada. There would have been a distinctive Canadian flag, the Red Ensign, in the 1940s had not King pulled back at the last moment.

Some of the Liberals who came to maturity during the St. Laurent years have argued that "Uncle Louis," as he came to be known, was a great prime minister in his own right. With characteristic cleverness, Pickersgill claimed in *My Years with Louis St. Laurent* that St. Laurent ran Canada so efficiently, solving problems before they developed, that he created the myth of a country so easy to govern that it hardly needed a prime minister (and could even risk a Tory regime after 1957). But it's surely special pleading to suggest, for example, that handling a national railway strike was as great a triumph as wrestling with conscription. Governments always have hard decisions to make. The fact is that booming, united postwar Canada really was easy to govern. For much of the time it did not have a prime minister—at least, not a PM who was more than the chairman of Cabinet.

Louis St. Laurent's political ideas were traditionally Liberal, a little bit of Laurier, a dollop of King, diplomacy by Pearson. His leadership style was relaxed at the beginning of his tenure, virtually nonexistent by the end. He took no interest in political organization, leaving everything to his ministers and the ubiquitous men from Cockfield Brown. The advertising agency, which Pickersgill neglects to mention, seems to have played the dominant role in organizing the Liberals' 1953 and 1957 campaigns, and in creating the fanciful image of St. Laurent as an amiable French-Canadian "uncle" to the country (Josef Stalin had earlier been avuncularized when the Russians became North America's allies against Hitler). The real St. Laurent was aristocratic, aloof, and, whenever removed from Ottawa, out of touch. On forays to meet ordinary Canadians, he was usually accompanied, advised, and packaged by a Cockfield Brown representative.

Many of the Ottawa men were out of touch by the mid-1950s. Twenty years of governance, always with a majority, had taught Liberal Cabinet ministers that parliamentary approval of their measures was virtually automatic. Debate was little more than ritual. The key decisions were made in Cabinet, rubber-stamped in caucus, rubber-stamped again in the House. Power rested in the hands of ministers working with likeminded bureaucrats. C.D. Howe was notorious for having elevated the idea of personal power for himself into a principle of government: he insisted on legislative confirmation of war-born emergency powers long after all emergencies had ended. "Howe's essence was power," his biographers write. He was terribly frustrated when anyone, be it the president of the CBC or the Conservatives in Parliament, stood in the way of his use of power. Once when the Tories were complaining in the House that the Liberals would end preferential tariffs if the people would let them, Howe snapped, "Who would stop us? ... Don't take yourself too seriously. If we wanted to get away with it who would stop us?"

Who indeed? The Conservative opposition often seemed pathetically ill-informed, badly led, factious, and silly. The CCF were righteous fringe politicians still fighting the battles of the Depression. The Ottawa press corps was subsidized and usually supine. The best and most prominent Ottawa journalists, Grant Dexter, Blair Fraser, Bruce Hutchison, were thinly camouflaged Liberal insiders. Canadian business leaders, many of whom did not like C.D. Howe's public entrepreneurship, knew that they could not deal with the Government of Canada without sucking up to "C.D." and his "boys." Provincial governments, more and more of which were not Liberal, seemed inferior and usually incompetent, obstacles to the good governance of Canada rather than partners in the federation.

St. Laurent failed in his duty to his party, and perhaps to his country, by clinging to power much too long. He talked often about retiring, but did nothing. Several of his ministers urged him to stay on because they saw him as the party's greatest asset. This was a foolish, palpably untrue counsel of despair, for the party was bursting with younger talent. The advice may have reflected senior ministers' love of the power St. Laurent was happy to let them exercise.

St. Laurent ought to have retired before the 1953 election, and certainly should have left soon after that victory. By 1954 and probably earlier (we will not know until a thorough, objective biography appears) he was prone to serious bouts of depression. We do not know how often the septuagenarian prime minister was clear-headed and in command of the government between 1953 and 1957. Like the British Cabinet during Churchill's final years as a senile figurehead in the early 1950s, St. Laurent's ministers had every interest in minimizing his debilities.*

When C.D. Howe decided that it would be necessary to invoke closure at every stage of parliamentary debate on a bill to subsidize construction of a natural-gas pipeline, St. Laurent offered no objection. The other ministers went along; a few, including Pickersgill, went along enthusiastically. The pipeline debate of 1956 sparked a dramatic opposition stand on the importance of free parliamentary debate. Their arrogance did the Grits enormous damage, contributing heavily to the government's problems in the 1957 general election. Under the glare of television cameras in that campaign, St. Laurent, Howe, and company now appeared to be a lot of wooden, tired old men who had lost touch with Canada. The voters decided to stop them.

*   *   *

Mackenzie King would never have allowed the government to self-destruct the way it did. He believed too deeply in the sovereignty of the people through Parliament to have ever sanctioned the tactics used in the pipeline debate. He would never have allowed himself to lose touch with the mood of the country as St. Laurent had. King may have been

---

* Mackenzie King's last two years in power may have been characterized by similar ministerial covering for a leader whose powers were failing markedly. Nobody, to my knowledge, has considered the impact of age and failing health on Canadian political leadership, yet questions can also be raised about Macdonald, Laurier, Diefenbaker, and Pearson.

more of a mystical than a modern populist, but, like his grandfather, he would have been appalled at politicians who seemed to think they governed by divine right. He knew when it was time to give up his power.

Many of the Liberals whose careers were made by Mackenzie King became contemptuous, condescending, or smirkingly nervous in their references to him in later years. Eventually he became almost a non-person in the litany of Canadian Liberal heroes. Under close historical scrutiny, though, King appears to have been smarter and more successful, doing more for both party and country than Laurier, St. Laurent, or, we will see, Lester Pearson. We will also see that Trudeau, who marched to a different drummer, was the other Liberal prime minister whose abilities and achievement vied with King's.

King not only divided Canada least, but he led governments that accepted a responsibility for ensuring Canadians a national minimum standard of living. The King Liberals gave Canada the welfare state. They expected the thanks of a grateful population at election time and got it. From Macdonald's day the essence of Canadian electoral politics—perhaps the essence of electoral politics in most countries—had been the trading of favours for voter support. King took the system to new levels of sophistication and complexity and—it has to be said—idealistic service to the less fortunate.

Earl Grey had predicted that King would be "as bad as the rest of them, give public buildings before elections, etc." Perhaps in giving baby-bonus cheques to mothers, before, during, and after elections, Mackenzie King was not as bad as the rest of them. The welfare state cemented the people to their government. For citizens in time of trouble it gave new content to the meaning of being Canadian. In later years the relationship between a paternal government and dependent citizens would be expanded and abused, and would finally become unsustainable. King had vaguely sensed some of those perils ahead. The other Liberals had scoffed at the old man's fretting and caution about too much spending and activism. He proved to have had the better foresight. The qualities that he brought to governing Canada—high intelligence, immense knowledge of government and politics, canniness, wariness, and utter dedication to his calling—helped him keep the ship of state on course and prevent disasters in stormy, shark-infested waters. Beginning with St. Laurent, his successors lacked Mackenzie King's unique package of political skills.

"WHAT HAPPENED TO MY STRAWBERRIES?"

The reference is to the mentally unbalanced Captain Queeg in
Herman Wouk's bestselling *The Caine Mutiny*

7

DIEFENBAKER
Trying Tory Populism

They butchered his name, talking of Diefenbucks and Diefenbubbles, calling him Diefenbacon, Diefenboulanger, Diefenbacker, Diefenbawker (that by President Kennedy), Studebaker, and Diefenburger. It was not hard to imagine a "Diefenballet," an amazing concatenation of styles and steps. Snatches of hymns and square dances, triumphant classical symphonies, dissonances, cacophony. A Nijinsky figure in the title role, a demagogue of dance, spinning and pointing and shaking.

Attacked by dark men from a mad world bearing nuclear swords and footballs. Minor female leads named Edna and Olive, the first treated for craziness. A chorus of average Canadians, simple and uncomprehending at first, divides into urban sophisticates and country loyalists and then falls into disharmony. Camp followers finally drag the old man from his leadership. As the curtain falls he is dancing a *pas de deux* with the ghost of Sir John A.

There was a palpable touch of madness to the Diefenbaker years. They were the height of the Cold War. East and West bristled with atomic and hydrogen bombs and missiles capable of destroying life on earth. Strategists talked of first-strike capacity, massive retaliation, megadeaths. Governments encouraged us to build bomb shelters—the Ottawa one for Cabinet was nicknamed the "Diefenbunker"—and scientists talked about what the strontium-90 released in nuclear testing was doing to our bones and our genes. During the Cuban Missile Crisis of October 1962, senior ministers, including perhaps the Prime Minister, expected the bombs to go off and the world to come to an end.

Some of the senior ministers thought the Prime Minister himself was mad in 1962–63. His mood swings and temper tantrums were beyond belief, his physical appearance increasingly demented, almost satanic. He became paralysed by indecision, and in the Cuban affair, the most tense military crisis in the history of the world, would not order Canada's armed forces to prepare to fight. They went on the alert anyway, in spite of a government that had given them missile batteries without warheads.

After Cuba, the government of the United States considered Canada an unreliable ally in the defence of North America. In John Diefenbaker's version of history the Americans then conspired with the Canadian Liberal Party and with the media and with the big interests to get rid of him. Everyone said the unstable old man was paranoiac, and many felt righteous and sane enough to cast the stones that drove him from office. "Sometimes I really do believe he's crazy," Leslie Frost, the Premier of Ontario, said to Eddie Goodman, a leading party organizer, in 1961. "Why only sometimes?" Goodman responded.

From the distance of our time, Diefenbaker's role as a prairie populist who tried to revolutionize the Conservative Party begins to loom larger than his personal idiosyncrasies. The difficulties he faced in the form of significant historical dilemmas seem less easy to resolve than Liberals and hostile journalists opined at the time. If Diefenbaker defies rehabilitation, he can at least be appreciated. He stood for a fascinating and still relevant combination of individualistic and egalitarian values. He anticipated leaders as diverse as Pierre Trudeau and Preston Manning.

But his contemporaries were also right in seeing some kind of disorder near the centre of his personality and his prime-ministership. The problems of leadership, authority, power, ego, and a mad time in history overwhelmed the prairie politician with the odd name.

*   *   *

His name helped shape his life. A man called Diefenbaker, no matter how pedigreed a Canadian (Ontario-born in 1895, Pennsylvania Dutch immigrants on his father's side, Scots Bannermans on his mother's), was an outsider the moment his name was uttered. Not necessarily in the

Saskatchewan country, where the Diefenbakers went pioneering in 1903 amidst Ukrainians, Hungarians, Doukhobors, Mennonites, Métis, and hosts of other nationalities. But certainly in Ottawa in the 1940s—it was not an asset to have a German name during the war—and 1950s and on national radio and television, where names and accents were English or French, and the rest were "foreign." In the land of Kings and Howes and Pearsons and Heeneys and St. Laurents and Drews, a Diefenbaker would surely speak with a thick accent. Quaint that Mr. Diefensomething had aspired to the leadership of the Progressive Conservative Party in 1942 and again in 1948. Not the least surprising that he had been beaten badly both times. "My name will prevent me from becoming prime minister," he complained to his wife.

When he stood for a third time in 1956, a coterie of Conservative establishmentarians rallied round the president of the University of Toronto, Sidney Smith, as a stopper. But Smith would not run, and Canadians learned how to pronounce the long, strange name, and learned that John Diefenbaker spoke their language perfectly, spoke it to a fault and with a vengeance.

His speech was his greatest strength. Diefenbaker had aspired to the prime-ministership from age six. When he told his strong-minded mother that he intended to be prime minister, she did not laugh. The Diefenbakers were much like the Kings—a bookish, impractical father, a tough and ambitious and domineering mother, who appears to have lacked Isabel King's soft edges and love of culture—and a boy carrying a burden of high hopes and boundless ambition. Naturally he became a good public speaker and debater, naturally he studied law at the University of Saskatchewan, naturally he ran for Parliament.

But unlike the fair-haired King, John Diefenbaker seemed destined to fail. He was defeated as a Conservative candidate for the House of Commons in the 1925 election. He was defeated again—by Mackenzie King himself—in the 1926 election. In 1929 he was defeated as a candidate in the provincial election. In 1933 he could not even get elected mayor of Prince Albert. In 1938, as provincial leader of the hapless Saskatchewan Conservatives, he failed again to win a seat. When he finally made it to the House of Commons in the 1940 general election he was forty-five years old, the age at which King first became prime minister.

By the mid-1950s the sixty-year-old opposition MP seemed to have missed the boat for good. He had always been a bit of a lone wolf in

Parliament, an outsider with an exaggerated, histrionic speaking style, never close to the Conservative Party's well-bred, well-to-do, Ontario-based establishment. After 1948 the party had never seemed more well-bred, well-to-do, and Ontario-based than under the leadership of former Ontario premier George Drew—"Gorgeous George" as the Liberals nicknamed him, after a professional wrestler.

Drew had no more luck against the Liberals than his several predecessors, partly because he seemed to be cut from exactly the same cloth as men like Bennett and Meighen—blue serge and shirt-stuffing. Drew was proudly British, proudly private school and upper class, humbly questioning about whether the welfare state and all those Liberal social programs didn't sap the morale of the honest working man. His followers said George Drew was a shy and great-souled patrician, but the Canadian people never saw beyond his aura of pomposity and arrogance. Drew might have put up a good fight against the equally arrogant Grits in the 1957 election—he and his lieutenants had done well in the pipeline debate (without much help from Diefenbaker, who had never been much of a team player in the House), and they had Canadians' resentments about Suez going for them. But Drew suddenly became mysteriously ill and was pressured by family and friends into resigning.*

Nobody in the Conservative Party expected actually to beat the Liberals in the coming election. Some thought Diefenbaker would be a risky choice as leader, and asked coded, serious questions about his "stability," especially his fitness to deal with world affairs. But nobody with better credentials stood against him. There was a sense that John's turn had finally come. It would probably be a caretaker leadership for a few years while the party bred a younger successor. And a real westerner with an "ethnic" name might even help broaden the appeal of a party not known for inclusiveness after the days of Macdonald. The old Tory power-brokers resigned themselves. "People want John Diefenbaker," said one of the Ontario kingmakers, "and there is no use kicking against the pricks."

*   *   *

* Drew's illness and much else about his personality remain elusive, partly because his family has not released his papers.

The Diefenbaker revival came in two stages. In the 1957 election Diefenbaker lost the popular vote to the Liberals (who piled up wasted majorities in Quebec), but squeaked through to a minority government. The country shifted slightly to the Tories out of a sense that it was time for a change. Ten months later, John George Diefenbaker won the most stupendous landslide yet seen in Canadian politics (only Brian Mulroney in 1984 would better it), 208 of 265 seats, on the strength of his own and his party's appeal. What a political revolution! For Conservatives— for huge numbers of Canadians—John Diefenbaker seemed to be a political messiah ushering in a new age.

He and most of the country interpreted the 1958 victory as a personal, not a party, triumph. No wonder. The Conservative Party had not asked Canadians to vote Conservative; it had asked them to "Follow John." Dief the Chief was everywhere, crisscrossing the country, coming right into Canadians' living rooms on their black-and-white TV screens. He was an intensely magnetic, preacher-like orator at a time when millions admired the crusading of the American revivalist Billy Graham, and he had a vision of a new Canada that was immensely appealing to a people raised on Liberal pablum.

What would candidate Jack Horner talk about to the electors of Acadia riding in Alberta?

"Do you know Diefenbaker?" his riding head asked him.

"I know Diefenbaker well."

"Then just get up there and say his name as many times as you can."

It had a dominant note and an overpowering soloist, but the Conservative Party in 1957–58 was not a one-man band. Its campaigns were heavily influenced by professional advertising men, including Allister Grosart from McKim's and a smart New Brunswicker, Dalton Camp, who was compiling a good record of winning campaigns down east. Other firms also lobbied for a piece of the action. Camp quipped that Diefenbaker had more advertising men working for him than General Motors. They wrote memos in which they solemnly concluded that "in actual fact there is every evidence that what we describe as the average voter appears to have an intuitive confidence and liking for this party's leader," and they decided they liked the candidate's name. No one could make disparaging rhymes on it. And, Camp wrote, the word "Diefenbaker ... suggested ethnic origins, a social order other than Toronto, and politics other than Conservative."

The admen were becoming active Tory backroom strategists by the 1950s. Grosart was responsible for pushing the view in 1957 that it was foolish to waste resources on futile battles in Quebec when victory could be achieved outside that province. Camp, a former Liberal without strong ideological convictions, was trying to teach Tories to be more positive, to understand the creative uses of government, to promise to outdo the Liberals in founding programs and organizing spending that would improve people's lives. The leader had his own bias in these directions. He deeply believed in the duty of government to help the little man, and he had no record of catering to special claims made by Quebecers.

A young economist from Saskatchewan named Merril Menzies supplied the most creative ideas for the 1957–58 campaigns, suggesting what he originally called a "new frontier policy" of northern development. Menzies, like Camp, was a strong believer in positive government. He hoped to revive Conservatism's activist past by linking new national development policies to the days of Sir John A. and the building of the CPR. The Conservatives would again don the mantle of visionary, frontier politics—building "roads to resources," exploring for oil and gas in the north, encouraging mineral development and the maximum processing of raw materials inside the country. The north was the last new frontier, a land of opportunity and hope as surely as the west had been in Macdonald's and Laurier's and young John Diefenbaker's time. Alvin Hamilton, Diefenbaker's first Minister of Northern Development, was the most visionary of the Tories, seeing a nation of two hundred million people in the future, and the Arctic as "the Mediterranean of the modern world." When Liberal leader Lester Pearson mocked the Tories for proposing to build roads "from igloo to igloo," he sounded like Edward Blake dumping on the CPR all over again—Liberals as do-nothing, *laissez-faire* men of little faith.

The nationalism of the appeal was palpable, and when John Diefenbaker proclaimed his "Vision" on the platform in 1958 the impact was often electrifying. The young country that had suffered and achieved so much in the war was on the march again, to God-given greatness, its northern destiny. There were new opportunities for the next generation. There was a leader, a chief, a man who stood for and seemed to define the aspirations of a people. No one—not Macdonald, not Laurier, not Borden, certainly not Mackenzie King—had ever personified

Canada the way Diefenbaker did in 1958. "I saw people kneel and kiss his coat," former Tory minister Pierre Sévigny wrote of the launching of the campaign in Winnipeg. "Not one, but many. People were in tears. People were delirious. And this happened many a time after."*

*   *   *

"There is no place left to go but down," Diefenbaker sensibly told his caucus after 1958. The tragedy of the Conservative Party in the next few years was that they could not control or limit the downward slide. The government was trapped at home and abroad in devilishly difficult, maddeningly unstable times. And Conservatives had tied their fortunes to a leader whose personal judgement and stability proved inadequate to meet those challenges.

Diefenbaker appears to have had few doubts about his capacities— or, if he had, unlike King he did not write them down. He took his job seriously, was hard-working and considerate of his aides, had a good memory and an excellent sense of humour, and was a quick study when he chose to be. He was one of the first Canadian politicians to use the telephone for constant networking, and the only prime minister whose office door was often literally open to ordinary people. In the early days he and the Cabinet were vigorous and decisive. They began dozens of new programs, and they shot down one enormous white elephant left

---

* "I have never seen such adulation before or since in political gatherings in this country," Tory organizer Eddie Goodman wrote in his memoirs. "While Pierre Trudeau drew huge enthusiastic turnouts in the 1968 election he did not establish the same type of rapport with the public. Ordinary people never felt that Trudeau was one of them, but Diefenbaker's admirers certainly did. It was small wonder that their affection touched him. When we would arrive back on the railway car or in the hotel room, he would turn and say, 'Did you see them? Did you see them? They believe in me. They have confidence that I will carry out my promises.' He would shake his long finger and swear solemnly, 'I will not let them down. I will not let them down.'" Heath MacQuarrie, who had eked out a narrow victory in his P.E.I. riding in 1957, and now waltzed home, remembered that in this campaign "the Diefenbaker coat-tails were like a flying carpet."

over from the Liberals, the "Arrow" supersonic jet fighter being built for the RCAF by the A.V. Roe Company of Toronto. On his own, without consulting Cabinet, Diefenbaker approved an agreement with the United States developed by the Liberals, to enter into a joint defence arrangement, the North American Air Defense (NORAD) Agreement. He looked forward to dealing with other external affairs issues, an area in which he had always taken a special interest.

In its domestic policies the Diefenbaker government reversed the Conservative Party's twenty-year habit of bitching about the welfare state. No more Meighenesque worries about moral fibre or bribes to have babies. Diefenbaker had been an early supporter of old-age pensions and family allowances, and had been criticized in caucus for this position. Suddenly in the 1957 election the Conservatives criticized the Liberals for having been too stingy with old-age pensions. Once in power they immediately bumped the pension entitlement higher. Other social-assistance grants were raised by a government happy to cut the melon after years of Liberal surpluses, and Ottawa for a time still had money to return to Canadians in the form of tax cuts.

Diefenbaker continued a course the Liberals had set after the war in viewing government grants, handouts, and job creation programs not as social welfare but as social justice. It became fashionable to state that Canadians had a claim to benefits from their government as a right, not as a favour from the condescending well-to-do. The Diefenbaker government also argued that the "rights" of the poorer areas of the country— Atlantic Canada and rural regions—should now be recognized through special programs to raise incomes and living standards. The serious attempt to equalize income across Canada, overcoming the barriers of geography, was begun in the Diefenbaker years.

The farmers of Canada, whose single-minded lobbying had been rewarded with a myriad of programs since the 1930s, were blessed to overflowing by the prime minister from Saskatchewan. The Conservatives not only launched new programs to subsidize farmers in hard times, but negotiated huge wheat sales to Communist China that caused very good times for grain growers. With the building of the South Saskatchewan Dam the river literally overflowed, creating Lake Diefenbaker as the largest new body of water in the west. "It'll be a dam sight sooner if John is elected," the Tories had promised.

As a friend of the little man, Diefenbaker sometimes saw himself as a

Tory paternalist in a nineteenth-century British tradition, or even a John A. Macdonald tradition.* During the Diefenbaker years some intellectuals discerned what has been called a "Red Tory" tradition in Canadian politics. As a strong free-enterpriser and avowed enemy of socialism, not to mention Communism, Diefenbaker was not much of a "Red." The badge he most happily and aptly wore was that of a populist. He liked to say that he knew what was on the mind of the average Canadian because he was one. Just a Canadian, not a German- or an English- or a French- or any kind of hyphenated Canadian. All his life he had talked about one Canada, one common Canadianism. As party leader and then prime minister he was intensely proud that his party and government were open to Canadians of all nationalities, including native peoples. He was often photographed in the robes and headdress of an honorary chief. The Conservative Party began finally to overcome its image of WASP exclusivity. With luck it would no longer be an ethnically based party.

The new openness was not a prescription for a lasting Tory regime in Quebec. To have won 50 of the province's 75 seats in 1958, a wonderful gain from 9 in 1957, was both a triumph and an opportunity. But this part of the victory was not primarily Diefenbaker's. Many of the new MPs owed their seats to the energies of Maurice Duplessis's Union Nationale machine, unleashed by the conservative Quebec premier to join a rising tide now that St. Laurent had retired. By 1959 Duplessis was dead. By 1960 the Union Nationale was out of office and everything "conservative" was in bad odour in Quebec as Jean Lesage's Liberals began a rapid modernization of the province that was soon labelled the "Quiet Revolution."

* Diefenbaker cheerfully presented himself as the high priest of a Macdonald cult, surrounding himself with letters, furnishings, and other memorabilia of the man the Tories wanted to see idolized as the father of the country. Satirists said that his suits had also belonged to Sir John A.

The appearance of D.G. Creighton's nationalistic two-volume biography of Macdonald in the early 1950s had helped pave the way for the Macdonald revival. Creighton, however, who had a good claim to being Canada's leading Conservative intellectual, felt shabbily ignored by Diefenbaker, as he told me at great length one day in 1967 when I came across him standing on the sidelines at one of the Centennial celebrations.

It was said that Diefenbaker never understood how thoroughly Quebec was changing in those years. His defenders reasonably point out that no one else understood events in Quebec either. The Diefenbaker government installed simultaneous translation in the House of Commons, making parliamentary debate truly bilingual for the first time. It commenced using bilingual cheques, an innovation the King–St. Laurent Liberals had apparently considered too expensive. Quebec had its usual share of federal patronage. Diefenbaker appointed the first French-Canadian Governor-General, Georges Vanier.

That was about as far as the Prime Minister thought he should go. He did not believe Quebec had "special" requirements because he did not believe in treating French Canadians as a distinct group of hyphenated Canadians. He did not see Confederation as an Anglo-French compact. His notion of equality was the equality of individuals, not of collectivities. His populist Conservatism had strong overtones of nineteenth-century liberalism. No group should get special treatment, special privileges, except the poor and the oppressed.

French Canadians would not have special privileges in the Conservative Party, either. At the 1956 leadership convention Diefenbaker chose to have an easterner and a westerner nominate him, breaking the tradition of a French-Canadian seconder. French-Canadian Conservatives were deeply offended. Diefenbaker did not get along well with his most prominent Quebec minister, Léon Balcer, and while fancying himself as a reborn John A. Macdonald, had no interest in finding another Cartier. During the Diefenbaker years nothing was done by way of intense organizational efforts or the cultivation of young talent to reroot the Conservative Party in the exceptionally difficult soil of Quebec. Quebec nationalists scorned the government's bilingualism gestures as "table scraps."

During his career as a trial lawyer Diefenbaker had fought often against the power and privileges of the Crown. Here was the most authentic source of his populism—struggling in court for the rights of the accused. He championed individual liberties, becoming a skeptical observer of the tendencies of governments to use special powers, take legal shortcuts, and otherwise flex royal prerogatives to get their way. In the House of Commons Diefenbaker had opposed the extraordinary powers King and St. Laurent had used in rooting out Soviet spies after the war, had spoken against C.D. Howe's penchant for making his "emergency" powers permanent, and had complained about the use of

Duplessis's notorious "Padlock Law" to gag Jehovah's Witnesses and alleged Communists.* One of his apparent quixoticisms in the 1940s had been to call for a "Bill of Rights" for Canadians. Most Conservatives, and Liberals, thought the idea was irrelevant or positively wrongheaded. Parliament was supposed to be the revered guardian of freedoms in Canada's British-style system of government. Parliamentarians could be counted on to protect the liberties of the subject.

Not, as Diefenbaker had observed it, under arrogant men who liked power. In a 1948 radio talk he spelled out the need to limit Parliament:

> The time has come to assure that this government shall be shorn of its arrogant disregard of the rights of the people. It does not rule by Divine right as did the Stuart Kings.... A Bill of Rights for Canada is the only way in which to stop the march on the part of the government towards arbitrary power, and to curb the arrogance of men "clad in a little brief authority"....
>
> ... Some say that it is unnecessary and our unwritten constitutional rights protect us. They have not in the past. They can not unless you and I have a right to the protection of law in the courts of the land. There are others who claim that the Parliament of Canada cannot pass laws to preserve the constitutional freedom of Canadians. If that be true, then Canadian citizenship is a provincial variable. There will be nine kinds of Canadians in Canada whose freedoms will be based on the home address of each of us. If that contention be true, Canadian unity is a meaningless term.

In 1960 the Diefenbaker government passed the Canadian Bill of Rights through Parliament. It guaranteed Canadians human rights and fundamental freedoms, with special emphasis on the rights of accused persons. The document was severely limited: as a statute of the Government of Canada it had no constitutional impact on the powers of the provinces, which included huge spheres of civil liberties. In strict terms Diefenbaker's Bill of Rights had not done anything about his 1948 concern about rights as a provincial variable. Hostile critics dismissed it as a public

* He later also claimed to have spoken out for the rights of Japanese Canadians during the war, but had not.

relations exercise (a handsome copy of the document, signed by the Prime Minister, found its way into the hands of every schoolchild). "The Diefenbaker Bill of Rights provides protection to all Canadians, just so long as they don't live in any of the provinces," a lawyer quipped.

In fact the Bill of Rights was an important symbolic declaration. It had a limited but useful effect at the federal level, and was a harbinger of growing concern for human rights throughout the federation. Diefenbaker was ahead of his time in expounding a doctrine of rights that was to have profoundly populist, profoundly individualistic and anti-hierarchical, even anti-parliamentary implications. He fired the first Canadian shot in the human-rights revolution of our times, which is a crucial ingredient in the broadening of our concept of the meaning of democracy, and he should be seen as the direct predecessor of the more focused and effective revolutionary, Pierre Trudeau.

*   *   *

Another form of state power that Diefenbaker opposed was Communist dictatorship. As he fulminated against Soviet tyranny and called for the "liberation" of the "enslaved colonial peoples of the Soviet Union," he seemed to be another right-wing, mid-western anti-Communist, of which there were large numbers in the United States. It happened that he was also influenced by the large Ukrainian population of Saskatchewan. While his anti-Communism occasionally verged on red-baiting—in the 1962 election campaign he accused Lester Pearson of being "soft on Communism"—his concern for civil liberties usually countered the temptation to become a Canadian Joe McCarthy.*

There was little doubt that Diefenbaker would be a staunch supporter of the John Foster Dulles/Dwight D. Eisenhower hard line in the

---

* He skirted the line thus: "I did come close to getting into serious trouble during the 1949 election when I stated over the radio that all the Communists in Lake Centre were going to vote for my CCF opponent. I was challenged by the Premier of Saskatchewan, T.C. Douglas, to name them. I could have, for I had in my possession the Communist Party list of members and contributors.... My response to Tommy Douglas, however, was to point out that it would cost too much money to read out all the names on the radio ... but that if he wanted to give me a list of the Communists who were not going to vote CCF, I would read that."

Cold War. From an American point of view the 1957 change of government in Canada seemed likely to have little significance. The personal relationship between Diefenbaker and Eisenhower, for example, developed easily and well.

But Diefenbaker was also the last believer in the British Empire. His Canada was now quite different from Great Britain in cultural and ethnic ways; but politically, historically, and through a fairly significant web of trade preferences, it was in Diefenbaker's and many other Canadians' minds an integral part of a living, meaningful British Commonwealth. Commonwealth conferences were still important, more important to Diefenbaker than the activities of the United Nations or discussions among the NATO allies. The notion of Canada as a bridge between the Commonwealth and the United States was as important to Diefenbaker as it had been to predecessors stretching back to Borden, and still was to many Liberals, including Lester Pearson. The popular doctrine of the "North Atlantic triangle," with Canada forming a sort of hypotenuse helping the British and Americans understand each other, was as clear a concept of a distinctive Canadian role in international affairs as the country has ever achieved.

And it never had a chance. Great powers talked to one another; they did not need interpreters. Lesser powers were expected to be loyal and helpful allies. In certain fluid international situations there *might* be scope for creative diplomatic efforts by the Canadians. Pearson had won the Nobel Prize for his mediatory efforts during the Suez crisis, but British politicians had intensely resented Canada's defection. The affair was a turning-point in the evolution of the Commonwealth, the last time the British dared to hope that the dominions would rally in an emergency. The most creative exercise of diplomacy in Canadian history had annoyed the old motherland and lost votes at home. There was no reason to believe that a similar act against American interests in a crisis would be any more successful.

John Diefenbaker would have liked to rebuild the Commonwealth in all of its glory. He viewed with alarm Canada's increasing economic integration with the United States, and hoped to strengthen the old transatlantic trading connection. In a rash moment after coming home from the 1957 Commonwealth Conference he promised to divert fifteen per cent of Canada's trade from the United States to the United Kingdom. It was a thoroughly impractical idea that went nowhere. A British suggestion of complete free trade with Canada was kayoed by the old protectionist fist in the velvet glove of Tory imperialism. The Empire, yes, but Canada first, had always been the motto of those who relied on the tariff to keep out competitors.

After Suez, Britain itself began to come to terms with the new global realities. By the end of the 1950s it was preparing to apply for admission to the European Economic Community, a kind of opting-out from the Commonwealth community. In one of the last acts in the drama of the dissolution of the old British Empire, the Conservative government of Canada was more loyal to the old dream than Britannia herself. Diefenbaker publicly and privately objected to Britain abandoning the imperial preferential trading system. Canada opposed her application to join the Common Market, like a daughter telling her mother she can't have a second marriage.

Important economic interests were at stake in Canada's defence of imperial preferences, as well as the ongoing concern about too much dependency on the United States, but most Canadians thought the Diefenbaker government was foolishly pursuing a lost cause. The British were not impressed either.

Canada's close alliance with the United States had not been seriously disturbed since the war. Canadian diplomats had worked hard to preserve breathing-room from the Americans on issues ranging from NATO to Korea and intervention in Vietnam. This was often achieved by supporting British concerns about U.S. foreign policy. Neither ally seriously questioned U.S. leadership in the world struggle against Communist power. Given Diefenbaker's anti-Communism, given the fact that Britain was not inclined to rock many boats after Suez, given some good luck, the disparities of power and expectation in the North Atlantic triangle might not come into play.

The luck ran out. Two changes in the climate of Canadian opinion ended the golden age of Canadian–American relations and snared the Diefenbaker government. The first change was global in scope, a wave of reaction against the terrors of nuclear weapons. The second was indigenous, a resurgence of anti-Americanism by a people and a Prime Minister who didn't like being pushed around by their big, rich, and powerful neighbour.

In its honeymoon years, roughly between 1957 and 1959, the Diefenbaker government agreed to rearm Canada's forces, including the NATO and NORAD units, with weapons systems that could not be fully effective without nuclear warheads. Who would object to

Canada, like the United States and several other NATO countries, defending itself with the most advanced weapons? Canada had chosen not to develop its own atomic bombs and bomblets (it had the scientific capacity to be in on the ground floor of the nuclear club, and by the 1950s was the world's largest producer of uranium, the essential raw material), but the United States was happy to supply nuclear warheads under joint control.

The peace movement seemed to surge out of nowhere in the late 1950s. A phenomenon mostly of youth and the left, it also struck responsive chords in the minds and hearts of sensitive people of all ages and parties—indeed it was the beginning of what became wave after wave of popular protest against social injustices in the 1960s. No rational person could calmly contemplate the destruction of millions of human beings, perhaps of all life on earth, in a war between the superpowers. How could a world teetering on the brink of nuclear catastrophe be restored to sanity and safety? How could we overcome the fear of bringing children into a doomed world?

The answer, the peace marchers said, simplistically, was to ban the bomb. A more practical first step might be to limit ownership of the bombs. Canada would not exactly be joining the nuclear club by taking U.S.-made warheads, for the Americans could still veto their use. To many that seemed a distinction without a difference. If Canada took atomic weapons, they felt, one more country would have surrendered its nuclear virginity and it would be that much harder to stop other nations from doing the same.

Diefenbaker's first Minister of External Affairs, Sidney Smith, was an incompetent disappointment and he died suddenly in office in 1959. Smith's successor, Howard Green, was a recent convert to the peace movement. Green lobbied single-mindedly within the Cabinet for a less committed stance on nuclear weapons. It was possible to write him off as a rogue minister, a parochial idealist out of his depth in External Affairs, except that many of Green's tactics were being suggested by Norman A. Robertson, Canada's former High Commissioner in London, former clerk of the Privy Council, former ambassador to Washington, adviser to four previous prime ministers, most brilliant of his generation of civil servants, then serving as Under-Secretary of State for External Affairs, and also a convert to the anti-nuclear movement. Robertson had become convinced that the world was on a course to "global suicide" and that Canada had to change its policies to help change that course.

While Robertson and Green schemed within the government to stop the march towards a nuclear destiny, opposition politicians raised public objections. Nobody was surprised that the New Democratic Party, new-born child of the CCF, was full of "peaceniks." But when the Liberals themselves, the architects of Canada's Cold War alliances and military commitments, began flirting with anti-nuclear ideas, it was obvious that the Canadian people were beginning to divide on fundamental principles of defence and foreign policy.

Diefenbaker found himself caught in a divisive situation, rather as King had been with foreign policy in the late 1930s. He knew he had to be careful. Some of his advisers fretted at the attention he seemed to pay to public opinion, arguing that he was tailoring foreign policy to fit domestic political cloth. He certainly was, just as King had, just as any government ultimately must. In language almost exactly like King's, Diefenbaker regularly reassured the Americans that Canada was a good ally and would live up to its word on nuclear weapons, but had to achieve greater consensus first. This was a stalling tactic.

The patience of the American leadership began to wear thin as fighter planes and missiles were delivered to Canada without an agreement on firepower. Bomarc surface-to-air missiles, intended to intercept Soviet bombers, would have to be installed in Canadian bases with sand in their warheads. In January 1961 the United States inaugurated a new adminis-tration led by the young, vigorous Democrat John F. Kennedy, who promised that his people would "pay any price, bear any burden" in the cause of freedom. When the Kennedy men looked north, they saw former friends who seemed increasingly unwilling to bear their share of the burden.

Anti-Americanism had not been an influential force in Canadian politics since the 1911 election. For forty-five years the political and economic and military ties between the North American neighbours had been strengthening. Americans could usually take Canadian co-operation and good will for granted. Canadians, for the most part, liked American democracy, liked American investment, wallowed in American popular culture, and supported the American determination to contain Communist expansion.

Canadians had not liked the visibility of American troops who built the Alaska Highway and DEW-line radar bases in the Canadian north.

They did not like loud and brassy Americans anywhere, as tourists, businessmen, soldiers, or diplomats. They worried that the United States had a tendency to be too blunt and pushy in world affairs. Many Canadians, both on the left and among the intellectual elites, abhorred the anti-Communist witch-hunts of Senator Joe McCarthy, thought it unrealistic of the United States to refuse to recognize the Communist government of the world's most populous country (China), and worried that the U.S. was going overboard again when it broke off relations with Castro's Cuba and even sponsored an abortive invasion. Canada did not ban its Communist Party, it made hundreds of millions selling wheat to Red China, and it maintained normal trading and diplomatic relations with Cuba. Canadians were particularly anxious to make their own decisions on trade matters because high levels of American ownership of certain Canadian industries was causing some critics to wonder how much real decision-making power remained in Canada.

When Americans tried to press Canada on some of these issues (the Prime Minister might reasonably have been expected, for example, to have some concern for the enslaved Cuban people), they found that John Diefenbaker did not like being pushed around. He was a suspicious, irascible old codger, whom the Kennedy people soon came to dislike intensely. There were no rude marginal notes on the famous briefing memorandum that Kennedy's party accidentally left behind during the President's May 1961 Ottawa visit. But in it the President was advised to "push" the Canadians on several issues. Diefenbaker underlined the word in the memo. Instead of having it returned to the Americans, he filed it away in his special "vault." During the 1962 election campaign he appalled everyone around him by threatening to reveal the contents of the document, in a crude, wildly improper attempt to blackmail the United States government. What the hell had gone wrong up in Canada, the Americans asked themselves. So did some of Diefenbaker's closest advisers. Was the old man completely losing his balance?

*   *   *

It is not clear whether Diefenbaker's personal debilities were always with him or developed as a result of the stresses of his life. He had always been an introverted loner, seldom at ease in social situations. He became a good platform showman and raconteur,* but had few close male friendships, and depended heavily on support from his mother and his doting wives, first Edna,** then Olive. The long series of humiliating political defeats he suffered, the slurs on his name, the slights by the eastern establishment, could only have been borne by a man with either a streak of masochism or an unquenchable sense of personal destiny. Diefenbaker had a little of both. By the time he became prime minister he had spent almost a lifetime standing alone against the world.

The victories were a vindication that went to his head, some colleagues believed. To his friends he stopped being good old "John" and asked to be called "Mr. Prime Minister." "John, you could sit on your hands until they become attached to your ass before I call you Mr. Prime Minister," one of them replied. Bruce Hutchison neatly capsuled the two most striking sides of the prairie PM's image: "In his humor, as a story teller, he had few equals. In his ego ... he had none." Some thought he developed a case of megalomania, perhaps a messiah complex. Journalists found that a back-slapping story-teller was turning into a prima donna prone to hysteria. In the Tory caucus Prime Minister Diefenbaker acted more like a saviour than a consensus-builder (he

---

* Most of his anecdotes were political and folksy. According to Sean O'Sullivan, whenever he told off-colour stories he would attribute them to George Hees. Later the story-telling edged into malicious character assassination of many of his former associates. In the early years one of his best stories was of meeting a western Liberal MP who was parading up and down Main Street in his riding shouting, "No! No! No!" "It was one of C.D. Howe's yes-men on holiday," Dief would chortle.

** Diefenbaker married his Saskatchewan sweetheart, Edna May Brower, in 1929. She was a personable wife, ambitious for her husband's political success. But in the 1940s her personality began to disintegrate, and for a time she was hospitalized in a private asylum. She died of leukemia in 1951. Three years later Diefenbaker married an old friend, Olive Palmer. She was his devoted helpmate for the rest of his career, utterly loyal and a fierce and active enemy of all of his enemies. Diefenbaker's neglect of Edna in all of his authorized biographies and in his memoirs, along with her own evident unhappiness in the later years, has led journalists to argue that he treated her shamefully. A balanced verdict, based on all the evidence, is not yet in. Diefenbaker almost certainly felt he owed it to Olive not to say much of Edna. There were no children from either marriage.

liked to arrive halfway through caucus, to be greeted by a standing ovation), seldom sharing Cabinet's or his own deliberations about policy directions. Like Bennett and Meighen and Borden before him, he simply delivered the word from on high. "He took full credit for the party victories in 1957 and 1958," his former finance minister, Donald Fleming, wrote of Diefenbaker in his memoirs. "He had all the instincts of the prima donna. He was instinctively selfish and self-centred, the most egocentric person I have ever met."

Sean O'Sullivan, the most loyal of all the Diefenbaker loyalists, summed up the problem of trying to like Diefenbaker: "Those of us who worked for him wanted to be his friends, and he would have said we were. In truth, however, we were not his friends. We were his fans. That was as close as he would let anyone come. Somewhere amid the demands of the daily performance for his fans and for himself he misplaced the ability to make or maintain anything like a genuine, warm and intimate friendship with anyone. For all his populism and honest love of people, he simply couldn't make lasting friends."

Diefenbaker was intensely partisan. It was not paranoiac of him to believe that the Grits were conspiring to bring down his government. They were. That was their job. Problems arose because Diefenbaker and a fair number of his supporters believed that the professional civil service was collaborating with the Liberals. King, St. Laurent, and company seemed to have politicized the civil service by using it as a farm team for Cabinet material. Where had Jack Pickersgill and Lester Pearson come from? Where did their social contacts, their personal friendships, still lie? Was the government being undermined, sabotaged, by the machinations of other "Pearsonalities" in the civil service? Diefenbaker often thought so, and he found it difficult to work cordially with public servants in whom he placed little trust.

The leading members of his party had slighted him so often in the past that he was suspicious of them too. The common idea that Diefenbaker never forgave any slights seems exaggerated; he gave major Cabinet positions to his 1956 opponents, for example. According to Ellen Fairclough (the first woman appointed to Cabinet), he did complain about the difficulty of selecting his first ministry: "Looks to me as if I have to compose a cabinet of my enemies." He had a disturbing habit of encouraging petty and malicious gossip about his ministers. "I didn't answer," Fairclough said of the "enemies" comment. "I wouldn't feed that fire of his." After he became prime minister, Diefenbaker lost the charm and outgoing nature he had sometimes shown in opposition. His idea of courtesy was to ask Miss Fairclough to leave the room when the Cabinet was discussing a death sentence for a case of rape and murder.

They spent hours in Cabinet reviewing death sentences, ministers remembered, an area of his responsibilities that the Prime Minister took very seriously. In fact he took all his responsibilities seriously, and ministers eventually complained that they met too often and talked too much. After the first year or two they realized that the problem with their lone wolf of a leader was that he had trouble making hard decisions. Diefenbaker became a prime minister who could not decide where he wanted to go.

Here he was trapped by cruel domestic ironies. The postwar boom began faltering just about the time that Diefenbaker led the Tories into power. Unemployment rose, growth fell off, a period of relative stagnation began. As in foreign policy, experts were divided on how to handle the problem. The sense that Canada had been living beyond its means and ought to retrench to maintain investor confidence in hard times was very strong. It was reflected in Donald Fleming's intense desire as Minister of Finance to balance the budget, and James Coyne's equal determination as Governor of the Bank of Canada to maintain a moderately tight money policy to hold down inflation. Many members of the Tory caucus, however, were more comfortable when they could continue spending and spurring development in the name of jobs and social justice. They had powerful intellectual backing from Canada's Keynesian economists, who saw the recession as a classic instance of the need to goose an economy with easier fiscal and monetary policies.

The 1959 decision to cancel the Avro Arrow fighter program cost the government tremendous political capital in the proud heartland of the country. Everyone in authority knew the Arrow had to go—costs had soared, there were no foreign orders, A.V. Roe Canada was a ramshackle, disorganized company whose president, Crawford Gordon, was an alcoholic. The military budget could not absorb the favouritism to the air force that continuing the Arrow would have meant. C.D. Howe, who knew that the Arrow had been one of his worst follies, intended to can it after winning re-election. Avro had all sorts of advance notice to diversify its business, but had no competence in the private sector. Instead it lobbied fiercely for the right to continue wasting public money. When the Diefenbaker government shut down what had become a technological megaproject, the company brutally dismissed all 14,000 of its employees (quickly and quietly rehiring 5,000 of them to wind down the contract).

Only a few romantic engineers and aerospace buffs wept for an aircraft that had never been properly flight-tested. But all that unemployment, "caused" by a government that was supposed to have a vision of jobs for all Canadians, made it hard to be a Diefenbaker Conservative in once-Tory Toronto.

The trendy Toronto and Montreal and professorial elites wanted Diefenbaker to take one more person out of the labour force, the Governor of the Bank of Canada. Just as the Arrow was a mess created largely by the Liberals, similarly James Coyne was a Liberal appointee in a relationship with the government that the Liberals had never bothered to define. The government vaguely knew that it would be next to impossible to dismiss the country's senior banker without causing a crisis of confidence. No government would try it today except in an emergency no government would bend to the dubious tactics that academic economists used in signing a round-robin letter expressing lack of confidence in Coyne because of his advocacy of a tight-money policy during a recession—an academic conspiracy to get rid of him. The government issued contradictory statements about its responsibility for monetary policy and its powers over the governor. Then it botched the attempt to fire Coyne, stating the wrong reasons for trying to fire him, giving him a martyr's day in court before the Senate, losing face by the minute, and ending up with a new governor but no satisfaction.

By the dawning of the 1960s, Diefenbaker was showing the wear and tear of age and the stresses of office. He was in his sixty-first year when he became prime minister, and had never managed any organization more complex than a small law office. His personal health was good, but he was hard of hearing and habitually disorganized. He had had a sharp but actual broad or a deep mind, and he had few relaxations and limited in pan and and cultural interests. He did little socializing. His attention capacity for decision-making tended to shorten as a working day wore on. The bureaucracy served his government professionally but the Prime Minister's advisers consisted of a Saskatchewan mafi one or two old cronies, and his wife Olive. The Conservative Party seemed as anti-intellectual as it had been under Drew and Bennett. The Prime Minister's disposition was erratic, mercurial. Some party insiders had wondered about his emotional instability before he became leader. Their doubts grew; so did those of civil servants such as Basil Robinson, seconded from External Affairs to work with the PM on foreign policy.

The deterioration seemed visible to many Canadians. The Prime Minister's head would tremble as he talked, as though he were suffering from Parkinson's disease.* Ageing and shaky, his jowls sagging and his eyes bugging, he began to resemble the brilliantly savage caricatures drawn by Duncan Macpherson of the Toronto *Star*. The man of the hour in 1958, Diefenbaker in two or three years had become yesterday's man, a strange old duck, out of touch, it seemed, with the Canada of the 1960s and the world of John F. Kennedy and the new frontiers of youth.

The contrast with the glamorous Kennedys was painful to the many Canadians who were attracted by the American leader's sophistication, precise expression, love of physical and mental culture, and apparent appetite for vigorous decision-making. The Kennedy presidency instantly gave the United States an image of being on the move again. Diefenbaker's prime-ministership reeked of depression Saskatchewan, stagnation, down-home folksiness, and indecision. Unlike that other folksy mid-westerner of his generation, Harry Truman, Diefenbaker did not seem to have risen to his office. Instead he was being worn down by it. As the government moved into an election in 1962 it was clear that the Conservatives had lost their appeal in much of urban and young Canada.

Diefenbaker's prime-ministerial models were Macdonald and King, both of whom had developed reputations for procrastinating, and eventually for weaselling out of tight situations. "When a matter was difficult and complex, when there was deep uncertainty, I took my time before deciding. Time is often the politician's best friend. Sir John Macdonald was called 'Old Tomorrow'," Diefenbaker wrote in his memoirs. Instead of lending creative or even acceptably temporizing solutions to his problems, though, Diefenbaker's character led him towards demagoguery, lashing out. Feeling besieged by 1962, he often thought back to the first

---

* It was apparently a nervous habit. In *History on the Run* Knowlton Nash tells the story of one of the Saskatchewan campaign managers who in the 1965 election denied there was anything wrong with Diefenbaker's health: "Why, I've known and worked with John for forty years and he has been shaking like that ever since I first met him."

election he remembered well, 1911, when the Conservatives had wrapped themselves in the flag and played on Canadians' loyalties to the Empire, and their deep anti-Americanism.

The 1962 campaign was no sooner under way than loss of confidence in the Bank of Canada's ability to keep the Canadian dollar fixed at parity with the American dollar forced a 7½ cent devaluation. At the least it was a humiliating loss of face for the government. The image of incompetence grew. "Diefenbucks" were only worth 92½ cents. The Prime Minister snapped irritably at the powerful forces doing these things to him, but stayed more or less under control during the campaign—in fact, raising principled small-c conservative objections to Liberal enthusiasm for state planning. The Conservatives dropped 92 seats from their 1958 total and clung to power by their fingernails in a minority situation. A second foreign-exchange crisis immediately after the election forced the imposition of emergency controls on imports and spending abroad. The United States increased its pressure on Canada to make up its mind on nuclear weapons.

*   *   *

Dalton Camp attended a meeting of the Conservative Party's national executive committee shortly after the 1962 election, and later described it to an interviewer:

> Diefenbaker launched into a long self-pitying tirade in which he told us that Mrs. Diefenbaker had sent back her credit card to Eaton's. In that election, Eaton's, for the first time in its history apparently, did not contribute to the national party. He also said that she had cancelled her subscription to *Maclean's* and he said to us we should all do the same—cut off our credit at Eaton's and cancel our subscriptions to *Maclean's*. And he was shaking, and he was terrible.
>
> We were terribly uncomfortable. When it was over and we came out, Finlay MacDonald said, "He's certified mad. We've got a prime minister who's a lunatic."

After the election Diefenbaker stepped into a gopher hole at Harrington Lake and was immobilized for weeks with a broken ankle and a broken spirit. His depression was acute, and it was not only enemies-to-be like

Camp who wondered if the Prime Minister of Canada had lost his sanity. "He was completely off his rocker for three or four months!" Alvin Hamilton commented. "You had to admit it, he was unstable...." Richard Bell, another minister, denied that they had speculated about mental illness, "but certainly all of us ... knew that he was subject to fits of depression and to a much greater emotional instability than had been the case previously."

The government drifted, and some thought it was disintegrating. Some ministers and backbenchers wondered about replacing Diefenbaker; they were not sure he was fit to govern. In seclusion and despair Diefenbaker gained comfort by reading Donald Creighton's biography of Macdonald, especially appreciating Sir John A.'s triumph over the "malignant host" of his enemies.

There is no evidence that Diefenbaker behaved irrationally during the Cuban Missile Crisis.* On October 22, 1962, the Government of Canada had two hours' formal notice that the United States was mounting a blockade of Cuba to prevent the introduction of more Russian nuclear missiles. In his first statement to the House of Commons that evening Diefenbaker implied that Canada's policy was to encourage a U.N. investigation to ascertain the truth of the American charge against Cuba and the U.S.S.R. Later that evening, when the Prime Minister was asked by his Minister of Defence, Douglas Harkness, about ordering Canada's air defence forces to the same level of readiness as the U.S. forces, he decided to wait and consult Cabinet. On October 23 and 24 Cabinet decided to continue to delay action on the level of readiness. The final resolution of the military situation has been described authoritatively by Basil Robinson:

> Only after Harkness had been informed in the late morning of the 24th that US Strategic Air Command forces had been placed on the second highest level of alert (imminent enemy attack expected) was the nettle grasped. After the cabinet meeting on that morning, Harkness confronted Diefenbaker personally and Diefenbaker grudgingly gave the minister the authority he had been seeking. By

---

* Professor David Bercuson, one of my critic-readers, comments, "There is no evidence that he behaved rationally either."

that time Harkness and the chiefs of staff had long since taken infor-mal measures to bring the forces to a state of maximum prepared-ness short of declaring the formal alert. Whether Diefenbaker knew that this was happening is a point of some interest. Harkness recalls that he did not tell the prime minister. Bryce [R.B. Bryce, Secretary to the Cabinet at the time] thinks that Diefenbaker had a pretty good idea of what was going on and preferred to let it happen in a less than formal way.*

Canada's doubts and delays were widely publicized. The Americans were furious at appearing to have been let down in a crisis by Canada, the only one of their allies that seemed publicly to question Kennedy's judge-ment. Diefenbaker and his defenders later argued that the Kennedy administration had broken all of its commitments to meaningful consul-tation. "We were to be accused by our critics of defaulting on our NORAD commitments," Diefenbaker wrote in his memoirs. "Nothing of the kind! It was the Kennedy government that rendered our joint arrangements ineffective. We were not a satellite state at the beck and call of an imperial master."

In his view the Americans had acted unilaterally and, like imperialists of old, had expected their allies to snap to attention and salute. It was Chanak again; it was Suez again. The government's determination to make up its own mind was fully in the traditions of King and St. Laurent and those previous crises. In fact, Diefenbaker's controversial statement to the House of Commons had been loosely based on an External Affairs memorandum naively suggesting that Canada and the U.N. might play a role in defusing this crisis, roughly analogous to the Suez diplomacy.

The politicians and the diplomats still lived in the age of gunboats, diplomatic notes, and worthwhile initiatives at the U.N. The Canadian

---

*In his later and very well researched study of these events, *Kennedy and Diefenbaker*, Knowlton Nash concluded that "Diefenbaker may have been aware of the situation, but he was not in control of it. Harkness had gone farther than Diefenbaker wanted or knew, the chiefs of staff had gone farther than Harkness himself realized; the deputies to the chiefs of staff had gone even farther; and the RCAF and RCN opera-tional officers in charge of various commands had gone farther than anybody in Ottawa knew.... everybody in the military chain of command winked and nudged and went on a war footing, and said to hell with Diefenbaker's indecisiveness."

military had realized that there was no historic parallel to a crisis like this, no time to discuss, delay, manoeuvre. Without orders it had prepared to fight. If serious warfare had begun, Canadian forces might have been involved without authorization from the civilian power. In a confrontation on the eve of Armageddon, there really was nothing for Canada to do but stand to arms. Knowlton Nash's conclusion about the lesson of the Cuban Missile Crisis is surely sound: "In truth, when John Diefenbaker signed the NORAD Agreement, Canada lost most of its ability to act independently of the United States in a military crisis."

Canadian decision-making in the Cuban Missile Crisis was a mess. The apparent breakdown in command between the civilian and military authorities was unprecedented in the country's history. So was the damage to Canadian–American relations. If Mackenzie King had been in power during those critical days, he would have instantly realized that Canada had no choice but to support the Americans. A few years earlier, however, King would not have made a snap decision to sign an agreement as fraught with perils as NORAD. He would have lectured his aides on the need to avoid rash open-ended commitments, and maintained the country's freedom of action as far as possible.

Neither King nor any other prime minister would have allowed personal relations to collapse as completely as they had between Diefenbaker and John F. Kennedy. Sources differ on the numbers and vulgarity of the epithets Kennedy used to describe Diefenbaker. The best summary appears to be Robert Kennedy's comment to Knowlton Nash that "the President felt Diefenbaker was a grandstanding, insincere, sanctimonious bore. In time he came to believe he was also a liar, a blackmailer, and a betrayer." The important point is that the Americans could get along with a Canadian who was only being sanctimonious and boring. They would not tolerate a man who hit below the belt.

The minority government collapsed early in 1963 when Diefenbaker would not bow to pressures to make up his mind on nuclear weapons. In this crisis his instability may have been a factor. Perhaps everyone was unstable. Ministers were principled rebels one hour, Diefenbaker loyalists the next. The leader of the Opposition, Lester Pearson, abruptly reversed his party's stand on nuclear weapons (thus proving himself, in Patrick Nicholson's phrase, "decisively inconsistent" while Diefenbaker was "consistently indecisive"). U.S. officials allowed their contempt for the Canadian government to lead them into diplomatic improprieties almost as gross as any of Diefenbaker's. Canadian public opinion seemed loony, too, appearing to be anti-nuclear and anti-American one minute, violently pro-American and pro-Kennedy the next. It was a mad time, as a disintegrating government faced defeat in the House of Commons and almost certain annihilation at the polls. At the press gallery's annual dinner, the Prime Minister of Canada sat and watched while his infirmities were satirized as "Harkness's disease." A reporter who escorted him out of the dinner said he was literally frothing at the mouth in rage.

The final Cabinet meeting before the government fell, at 24 Sussex Drive on February 3, 1963, was probably the most tumultuous in Canadian history. Ministers shouted and swore at one another, called each other liars, sons of bitches, shits. Harkness resigned. King Lear at bay, Diefenbaker raged and pounded the table, said he was resigning, and stormed out. So did several of his followers. One of the cooler heads noted that they soon would not have a Cabinet left to fight an election. At least two ministers described the Prime Minister as seeming like a "raging lunatic." The next day the Diefenbaker government was defeated in the House of Commons, and the Prime Minister asked for a dissolution.

There were more Cabinet resignations and a bizarre proposal by the dissidents that Diefenbaker should resign to become Chief Justice of the Supreme Court (a position for which they apparently did not think mental instability a handicap). Diefenbaker clung to his leadership, blaming his problems on a vast conspiracy of his enemies. As Bruce Hutchison put it, the enemies mostly wielded rubber knives. The prospect of being able to strike back at them on the hustings revived Dief's spirits. He was a one-man dervish in 1963, raging against the Americans, the media, big business, the Liberals, elevating paranoia into a political platform, wallowing in a crude anti-Americanism that would have seemed demagogic even in the days of Macdonald and Borden. Everyone was against him but the people, Diefenbaker said over and over again.

Enough of the people believed him—especially the ageing and rural folk, and some of the poor and some recent immigrants—to prevent the complete collapse of the Conservative Party. The Liberals won in 1963, but had to form a minority government. Later Diefenbaker was happy to spread the myth that he had lost his prime-ministership because of the Kennedy administration's interference in Canadian affairs. The truth was that he had lost the confidence of the new Canada of urban dwellers, the young, and the well educated. Since 1958 he had had a run of bad luck and tricky problems that he could not master. He had been tested in the kinds of situations that Macdonald had slipped out of, Borden had ploughed through, and King had manipulated brilliantly. Diefenbaker had failed the tests. He had proved to be an incompetent prime minister, whose failures in international crises had become shameful in the eyes of many Canadians. He was not mad, he did not have Parkinson's disease. He had been too narrow and too temperamental, perhaps too old, to get the job done. "I consider his disappearance a deliverance," the Canadian ambassador to Washington, Charles Ritchie, told his diary. "There should be prayers of thanksgiving in the churches. And these sentiments do not come from a Liberal."

*   *   *

Diefenbaker left office at a time when the Canadian economy was prospering again and jobs were being created by the tens of thousands. Neither the devaluation nor the emergency austerity measures of 1962 had hurt the economy. Possibly they had helped. The rest of the 1960s would be very good years, to the political profit of the Liberals.

Some of the Diefenbaker government's programs had been obvious successes—the northern road-building, the South Saskatchewan Dam, "winter works" to reduce seasonal unemployment, the wheat sales and other props to the agricultural economy. Cancelling the "Arrow" had been a sensible decision, the more remarkable in view of later governments' inability to make hard choices. There were no major scandals during the Diefenbaker years—no horses on the government payroll, he liked to remind audiences, referring to a minor defence department scandal under St. Laurent. There was no more contempt for Parliament, either, no more pipeline debates, no more "Who's to stop us?"

Diefenbaker believed he had done more for the Progressive Conservative Party than any leader since at least Borden. He had led it to two election victories and the largest majority in Canadian history. He had wiped out its image as the party of eastern privilege and Anglo exclusivity, and had caused at least a temporary revolution in Canadians' voting habits. Even in defeat he had fought the Grits almost to a stalemate, doing far better in 1963 than anyone had thought possible. The Tory caucus was the key to his ongoing power. Many of the members knew they owed their seats to Diefenbaker, many of them believed in loyalty to the leader as a profound principle of both politics and life. Diefenbaker believed his leadership had opened the party to Canadians from all regions, all walks of life, all nationalities.

Some aspects of his vision of Canada seemed more important than ever to the old man. As Quebec nationalism became more intense during the early 1960s, his emphasis on "One Canada," an ethnically blind country with human rights for all and collective privileges for none, was a sharp contrast to many Liberals' interest in recognizing a special status for the government of French Canada. For the 1961 census Diefenbaker had tried to make it possible for Canadians to register themselves simply as Canadians. Protests from French Canada forced the government to back away. Liberals and even some Conservatives were talking about Canada as being "two nations," a "Siamese twins" view of the country radically different from Diefenbaker nationalism.

In opposition again, Diefenbaker was a devastating critic, a holy terror to the Liberals in the House of Commons and in the stalemated election of 1965. The old warrior comforted himself with thoughts of having fought the good fight for principles and party against a host of malignant enemies.

To those outside the Diefenbaker circle, there was little difference between this extreme individualist's view of reality and what Richard Hofstadter called "the paranoid style" in politics. Away from Parliament Hill, increasing numbers of Conservatives doubted that the party had any long-term future as a haven for only the rural and ageing, as a vehicle only for opposition from Diefenbaker and a rump of "cowboy" MPs. "In some quarters we are branded an anti-intellectual 'Peasants' Party'," wrote young Alberta Conservative Joe Clark in 1963. Diefenbaker saw himself as a great democrat and a humble servant of the party; others saw erratic autocracy by an unstable leader whose ego would not allow him to let go. Tory organizers in 1965 joked that their campaign slogan should be "Give the old bugger another chance." Dalton Camp organized the opposition that seized control of the party apparatus and forced a leadership convention in 1967.

One of the last straws had been Diefenbaker's emotional, last-ditch stand against the government's introduction of a distinctive Canadian flag in 1964. The Tories screamed that the disappearance of the Union Jack from Canadian flags was an unacceptable assault on the country's heritage, probably inspired by the need to appease Quebec. Canadians would never accept the new maple-leaf rag, they argued. As in resisting Britain's decision to enter the Common Market, Diefenbaker had completely misread the course of Canadian history, and fought with increasing irrelevance and rhetorical violence in a lost cause. At times he was Clarence Darrow for the defence; at times he was William Jennings Bryan on the witness stand. Reverting to the old ethnic fundamentalism, the Tories sang "God Save the Queen" in the House of Commons, surely for the last time. Prime Minister Harold Macmillan, the realistic old duffer who was for British Conservatism everything Diefenbaker was not for Canada, saw him as a "mountebank" and a "caricature," intoxicated by ego and verbosity. "Poor old Diefenbaker," Macmillan said.

He stood again for leader in 1967. He did it, he said, to oppose the party's adoption of a "*deux nations*" view of Canada. Others said he suffered from egomania. Both views were probably true. One of the greatest of all Diefenbaker loyalists, Sean O'Sullivan (he later developed a higher loyalty to Jesus Christ and became a priest), quoted approvingly in his memoirs a friend who said of the old chieftain at that convention, "John Diefenbaker is a madman who thinks he's John Diefenbaker."

He was humiliatingly rejected by the party, which eventually chose former Nova Scotia premier Robert Stanfield to lead it to rejuvenation. In the 1968 general election the "*deux nations*" policy was a disaster for the Conservatives, Stanfield proved no match for Trudeau, and the party did worse than it had in any of John Diefenbaker's campaigns. As a Diefenbaker loyalist put it, the notion that the party was more popular than the leader was wrong. There was, as they said, a fate worse than Dief.

John Diefenbaker never left the House of Commons he had worked so hard to enter. He became a legend in his own lifetime, still capable from time to time of rousing himself to undercut his leader. The last page of his memoirs is a list of Tory MPs who were disloyal to him. He died in 1979, during the brief Conservative government of Joe Clark, a few years before Pierre Elliott Trudeau succeeded in having the Charter of Rights and Freedoms written into the constitution.

He had left detailed directions for "Operation Hope Not," an elaborate, pretentious state funeral. Winston Churchill's funeral plans had had the same code name. Although Diefenbaker was a Baptist, he directed that the Ottawa service be held in the Anglican cathedral, because of the anticipated crowds. He wanted his coffin to be draped with his flag, the Red Ensign, but in a state funeral the Canadian flag had to be used. So both flags covered his body. The body of Olive, who had predeceased him, was disinterred and taken to Saskatchewan for reburial with him. On the funeral train that carried the former prime minister across Canada to his final resting-place, his friends and executors drank heavily and argued loudly about control of his personal papers and the trust fund supporters had created for him. Some claimed that his last will should be declared void because he had not been mentally competent when he drew it up.

At the Ottawa service the climactic singing came with these lines from the recessional hymn: "He hath loosed the fateful lightning of His terrible swift sword/His truth is marching on." This anthem, of course, was "The Battle Hymn of the Republic."

8

PEARSON
Middle Innings

Lester Bowles Pearson had trouble with his first name. The Royal Flying Corps wanted jaunty, tough pilots. At first roll-call a Canadian minister's son named "Lester" did not appear to be ideal raw material. So his commander at flying school in 1917 started calling him "Mike." The nickname stuck.

Thirty-five years later, as he was preparing for political wars in his native land, Pearson's advisers decided to toughen his image further by persuading him to stop wearing bow ties. He also had a slight speech impediment, a hint of a lisp. So they tinkered with word selection in his speeches, banning phrases like "seven successive deficits."

They did not minimize Pearson's public appearances as leader of the Liberal Party in the 1962 and 1963 elections, but they knew he was no match in one-on-one combat with the old raging baron, Diefenbaker. So the Liberals emphasized the team of strong men at Mike's shoulder, some of them veterans of the King–St. Laurent years, others experienced civil servants who had signed on with the Liberals, and a number of talented new recruits from private life. The Pearson team would give Canada another era of political peace and good government, a return to "normalcy" after the Diefenbaker chaos.

"I like Mike" was a favourite slogan in all the Pearson election campaigns (not always fully understood, he remembered, at least not by the little boy in one town who kept chanting, "I like milk"), and it was true. Almost everyone did like Mike Pearson, the most amiable, charming, and self-deprecating prime minister since Macdonald. Many of his followers loved him deeply.

But there was always a murmur, louder than a whisper, about Lester B. Pearson's toughness and the quality of his judgement. He gets a rough ride in the memoirs of some of his closest associates—Tom Kent, Walter Gordon, Judy LaMarsh—who felt he was a weak and vacillating prime minister. Did he commit the unpardonable sin of letting down his comrades? Perhaps he did not have the right stuff after all, his old friends imply—usually in sorrow, sometimes in anger.

In England in 1917 an accident and possibly a collapse of spirit—at bottom he may not have been at all jaunty*—had kept young Pearson from seeing aerial combat with the Royal Flying Corps. Some of his friends came to wonder if they and the Liberal Party would not have been better off without him in the tumultuous 1960s. He had lived a full life as Canada's greatest diplomat, and perhaps ought to have retired in the late 1950s, a job well done. Instead, his critics felt, he tried to soar too high.

*   *   *

For most of his life the only kinds of toughness Pearson needed were physical stamina and the capacity to suffer fools gladly. He qualified, and he also had a good mind and a usually sunny disposition. His childhood in Ontario Methodist manses had been as idyllic and innocent as the age that ended in 1914. "God was in his heaven and Queen Victoria on her throne. All was well," he began his memoirs, referring to 1897, the year of his birth. His youth was unremarkable, or perhaps it was remarkable in its normality. Lester was an obedient and loving son, did very well in

---

* There are hints and stories, mostly told off the record, to the effect that Pearson was sometimes depressive—whether more than is normal with sensitive, high-achieving males is hard to tell. In a recent study of his father's diplomacy, *Seize the Day*, Geoffrey Pearson doubts "that any mystery lurked behind the façade of reticence. He witnessed at an early age the brutality and squalor of World War I and, like others, may have suffered some darkness of the soul, to be repressed or overcome by a quick wit and a sense of paradox."

school, and excelled on high school and university playing fields. The Reverend Edwin A. Pearson was a bit other-worldly, as might be expected in a minister. Lester's mother, Annie, was perhaps the more determined of the parents, a moderate repetition of the weak father/strong mother pattern that had shaped several previous prime ministers. Lester Pearson was a well-brought-up middle-class kid who naturally hoped to have a good life and do some good for his country.

After the wars he finished his education at Victoria College of the University of Toronto, sampled and spat out the business life, won a fellowship for a couple of years' study at Oxford, and settled back into a teaching job in the U. of T.'s history department. Not a disciplined scholar, he was most successful as the coach of several of the university's athletic teams. In 1927 Pearson excelled on competitive examinations for positions in the Department of External Affairs, and gave up on the academic life. The only hesitant note in acquaintances' appraisal of his qualifications was struck by Vincent Massey, who found "something curiously loose-jointed and sloppy about his mental make-up which, as a matter of fact, is reflected in some measure in his physical bearing."

For the next twenty years hardly anyone was that critical of Pearson as he climbed the ladder at External, rung by rung, posting by posting— Ottawa, London, Ottawa, Washington, Ottawa—learning his craft, retaining a healthy sense of proportion. Of the early diplomatic life in London, he remembered

> I could soon balance a tea-cup, a cocktail shaker, or a champagne glass as though I had never been brought up in a Methodist parsonage.... I became accustomed to the costume of my trade: black homburg, short black coat, striped trousers, and furled umbrella. Anyone watching me enter my club, The Travellers, might have thought I was the patterned product of Eton, Oxford, and the Foreign Office, unless he heard me speak.... I still talked Canadian. I had enough sense not to follow the unseemly example of some adult Canadians whom I watched as they tried to switch to English.

Pearson was almost always impressive, not least to Mackenzie King, the shrewdest of all Liberal talent scouts, who saw the makings of a future prime minister. King may have had his own youthful vigour and assurance in mind when he noted the "light which shone through his countenance" when Pearson came into his office. Other friends thought that Mike "glowed" with good spirits. Everyone liked him. They were not so sure they liked his more outspoken, sometimes abrasive wife, Maryon. No shrinking violet, she was nonetheless devoted to her husband's career, was more interesting to talk to than the trophy and paper-doll wives of the diplomatic circuit, and became a good hater of Mike's enemies.

In the superficially genteel world of the diplomats it was inappropriate to appear to be pushing for advancement. Do a good job and the rewards would follow naturally. Current biographers have swung over to emphasizing the ambitious Pearson, who aimed high, reaching for the brass ring, Maryon helping him extend a bit farther. Fair enough, but Pearson does not appear to have been a driven man, in the mode of a Diefenbaker or even a King. He seemed reasonably happy with whatever job he was doing, but saw no reason not to aim for promotion.

In 1948 he had few qualms about trying the leap into active politics. He jumped from Under-Secretary of External Affairs to the House of Commons—he was parachuted into the safe Liberal riding of Algoma East in Ontario (at first he was not exactly sure where it was)—and back to External as minister. "How long, Mr. Pearson, have you been a member of the Liberal Party?" he was asked at his first press conference. "Since I was sworn in as a minister a couple of hours ago," he answered. His friend Walter Gordon remembered Pearson wondering if he would be tough enough to handle the cut-and-thrust of politics.

*   *   *

The Secretary of State for External Affairs stayed largely above the political fray for almost ten years. Until the Suez Crisis the Opposition seldom criticized the handling of Canadian foreign policy. The old isolationist, Mackenzie King, was probably the sharpest opponent of Canada's postwar commitment to collective security and a more active role on the world stage. After his departure, there was a broad consensus in Ottawa to the effect that Canada ought to work hard to advance peace, that it was a staunch ally of the two great Western powers, the United Kingdom and the United States, and that with luck it could play a useful mediating role between them. With bow tie and happy face, Mike Pearson was a universally respected Canadian—the best known of all Canadians. His visage even appeared on a bubble-gum card in a series portraying great men of world history.

The Canadian diplomatic corps as a whole had an enviable reputation at the U.N. and in world chancelleries for intelligent professionalism. In a crisis it was worthwhile to know what the Canadians thought and proposed. In 1948 and again in 1953 Pearson almost became Secretary-General of the United Nations. His mediation during the Suez Crisis in 1956 was exactly what the international affairs community had come to expect from Canada. The announcement that he had won the Nobel Peace Prize for those efforts seemed entirely appropriate. Too bad, some of the U.N. types said, that Mike was giving up the great game to become party leader back in Canada. In their eyes it was a kind of retirement, like giving up a law career to become a house-husband today.

Few doubted that the Liberal leadership was Pearson's for the taking. To most Canadians it seemed entirely natural that the man who had led the country on the world stage should lead his party at home. The other Liberal notables, men like Paul Martin or Jack Pickersgill, were "nothing but old pols," one party member put it. "Pearson was a prince." He was also, to a remarkable degree, an outsider with few political skills or inclinations—a house-husband who had never ironed a shirt or cleaned a toilet.

Pearson got his first real taste of domestic politics when the Conservatives went on the attack over Suez, accusing the government of being the Americans' "chore boy" in knifing Britain and France in the back. "Any feeling of exaltation and conceit or euphoria at our success in avoiding a general war in the Middle East (if in fact we had avoided it in our actions) was dissipated for me by the vigour of the assaults on my conduct, my wisdom, my rectitude, my integrity, and my everything else," he remembered. Worse was in store, notably the scathing tongue-lashing John Diefenbaker gave Pearson after the new leader of the Opposition moved that the minority Conservatives resign and let the Liberals govern again without an election. "Mike, it is sad to see you come to this," an old friend on the Tory side of the House said. "Mr. Pearson, you are a very nice man, but go home," a friendly voter told him during a stop in the 1958 election campaign, "you're wasting your time." And when news of the unprecedented Diefenbaker landslide came in, Maryon had the last word: "We've lost everything. We've even won our own constituency!"

Had he been unseated in 1958, Pearson would probably have exited back to service in the broader world. His son has written that he had not been sure he wanted the leadership in the first place. "His heart belonged to global, not national politics." Now he was condemned to at least another term in the Ottawa kitchen.

*   *   *

Somebody rebuilt the Liberal Party during the next four years, and the credit must properly be given to Pearson. He was the official leader, and he did have a knack of inspiring people to work with him. He was not tough, or decisive, or very well organized, or very good in the House of Commons, or at all interested in the minutiae of political organization—so he could appear to be little more than a famous figurehead, a kind of chairman of the board. The day-to-day job of party rebuilding was handled by veterans like Jack Pickersgill and Paul Martin in the House of Commons, and newcomers like idea-man Tom Kent and businessman Walter Gordon.

Gordon was a rich Toronto chartered accountant who had been dabbling in public service for years. One of his contributions was to raise a fund in 1948 to supplement Mike Pearson's salary as a politician. The effort was cutely named the Algoma Fishing and Conservation Society. Gordon became increasingly active in the party in the late 1950s, raising funds, encouraging promising young men to become involved, and finally agreeing to run in return for a promise that he would become Minister of Finance. Gordon did not have a modest opinion of his abilities. He expected to be the real managing director of a Pearson government, just as he thought he was the driving force of the Liberal revival in opposition.

What would Liberals stand for, now that the King epoch was over and, shocking to contemplate, a Diefenbaker era seemed to be at hand? The Tories had caught the prospering country's yearning for a new northern nationalism and charismatic leadership. Pearson, by contrast, had not expressed any views on domestic questions before taking his party's helm. In foreign affairs he believed in tolerance, open societies, respect for human rights, and the need to temper *realpolitik* with a certain amount of idealism. He was never much of an ideologue of any kind, partly because he had an intellectual's and a diplomat's ability to see both sides of an issue. During the St. Laurent years, according to Pickersgill, Pearson took little interest in economic policy or in the government's refinements of welfare policies. "He was interested in international affairs and in the ideas of his 'civilized' friends, who ranged all over the ideological map." No one ever felt he could comfortably nail down Mike Pearson's essential beliefs. It was "like stabbing a sponge," one former colleague said, or as Pearson himself once observed of the diplomatic art, he could say no in such a way that it sounded like yes. Others noted more coldly that his agreeableness led to his reflecting the ideas of the last person who had spoken to him.

In opposition and the early months of his post-1962 government, that tendency often meant sounding like Walter Gordon or Tom Kent. Kent, a smart Englishman who left the editorship of the *Winnipeg Free Press* to work with Pearson, believed that the mission of modern Liberalism was to use the state to create greater social equality. Like the hugely influential expatriate Canadian John Kenneth Galbraith, who coined a term to describe a new age with his 1958 bestseller, *The Affluent Society*, Kent believed in expanding the public sector's role to compensate for inequalities created by private-enterprise capitalism. The state should intervene more, control more, spend more—using its powers to make war against poverty and injustice just as it had made all-out war against fascism. Government's material aid to ordinary citizens would expand the realm of freedom by liberating them from poverty, ignorance, and other disadvantages. Its planning and regulatory efforts would lead to the final triumph of economic expertise—the visible hands of modern management—over the harsh, impersonal forces of the business cycle.

These moderately social-democratic ideas were hardly startling to welfare-state Liberals of the King/St. Laurent generation. The new Liberalism seemed to translate into programs for better pensions, health insurance (the party had first promised this in 1919), and vigorous activity by politicians and government generally. A few Liberal old-timers, notably some journalists from King's generation, did wonder about the costs of bigger government and the party's tendency to promise more than it could deliver. They were brushed aside. Pearson mused that Canada was now in "the age of grants."* His shadow finance minister,

---

* When Diefenbaker announced emergency grants to western grain farmers in 1958, Pearson's response was to ask whether the $40 million payout was large enough. Perhaps there ought to be a national policy of such payments that would include other primary producers, such as fishermen, he suggested. Newfoundland MPs immediately began lobbying for such grants, with Pickersgill talking of the need to compensate the fishermen for "crop failure" in their industry. A few cynics began talking of politicians manoeuvring to bribe voters with their own money.

Gordon, was one of the trendiest of Galbraithians, with few qualms about major new spending programs. If government was run by politicians of high purpose and pure spirit—politicians much like themselves—the Liberals believed it could work wonders in modern society.

The recession of the late 1950s had caused the first postwar flurry of alarm about job prospects for Canadians. In the 1962 election campaign Kent persuaded Pearson to promise to cure unemployment, which stood in the seven to eight per cent range, or resign. Few noticed the echo of another activist Methodist's pledges in 1930. R.B. Bennett would also have approved of the Liberals' 1963 commitment to take immediate action to solve Canada's problems in "Sixty Days of Decision."

Walter Gordon was known to have an ideological hobby-horse in being a little bit anti-American. No: they were pro-Canadian, Gordon and his friends would always say. They worried about the extent of American economic and cultural influence on Canada, and thought the Canadian state should take a few modest steps to safeguard Canadians' control of their national destiny. Pearson seemed to see no problems with Gordon's stance. Who could quarrel with nationalism in a country that had so little of it? Who could dispute the need to keep an eye on American penetration of Canada? As a diplomat Pearson had been a wary friend of the United States; as early as 1951 he had said publicly that the days of easy and automatic dealings with the United States were over. By the late 1950s his party's position on accepting U.S.-controlled nuclear arms was at least as confused as the Conservatives'. Many Liberals, Maryon Pearson among them, were deeply involved in the international peace movement.

Nobody in the Liberal Party seriously believed that a dose of pro-Canadianism would mean closing the forty-ninth parallel. More than most Canadians, in fact, Liberals were fascinated by the American political revolution that brought John F. Kennedy and the Democratic Party to victory in 1960. Gordon and his friends avidly read Theodore White's instant classic, *The Making of the President, 1960,* and part of their modernization of the Liberal Party included adopting the most up-to-date U.S. image-making techniques. They even hired Kennedy's favourite polling firm, the Lou Harris organization, to show them how to make a prime minister. Harris and others advised the recasting of the leader's image, and emphasis on a Liberal *team* preparing to restore competence and dynamism to Canadian government in an even shorter period than Franklin D. Roosevelt's famous "Hundred Days" back in the 1930s.

Pearson's about-face on nuclear arms in January 1963—suddenly committing his party to carrying out Canada's existing obligations—was the boldest single step he took in five years as opposition leader. On his own he reversed party policy, turned up the heat on the faltering Conservatives, assured his party the good will of the Kennedy Democrats, and came into accord with the mainstream of Canadian opinion. Many of his followers, including the Kent–Gordon crowd and some French Canadians who had been almost ready to enter active politics, saw Pearson's tough-mindedness as an unnecessary betrayal of cherished ideals. The government was collapsing anyway, they felt, and the U-turn played too neatly into Diefenbaker's politics of paranoia.

No one was more scathing in his condemnation of Pearson than the Quebec lawyer and political writer Pierre Elliott Trudeau, for whom this was a matter of high principle. "Power offered itself to Mr. Pearson," Trudeau wrote of the affair in *Cité Libre*. "He had nothing to lose except his honor. He lost it." Trudeau, who would reverse his course on several later occasions, had nothing to do with the Liberal team in 1963. He worked and voted for the New Democratic Party.

*　*　*

The Pearson government began unravelling on the fifty-third day of decision, June 13, 1963, when Walter Gordon introduced his first budget. Gordon bungled budget-making more thoroughly than any finance minister in the country's history. He bypassed his senior officials to bring in outside consultants, proposed harsh measures to limit foreign ownership of Canadian industries (most notably a thirty per cent takeover tax on sales of Canadian companies to outsiders), disregarded clear warnings that his schemes were unworkable, learned from an enraged business community that they really were unworkable, and then bungled their withdrawal. In a few days this deeply foolish finance minister destroyed his own reputation and crippled the government's. The Liberals' heady promises about a quick return to dynamic, effective government had become a joke.

Gordon was a gentle and generous man who attracted a number of spiritual disciples and intellectual hangers-on, as well as the powerful editorial support of the Toronto *Star*. He and his supporters believed that Pearson and most of the other ministers were delinquent in not having leapt to his defence in the House. Pearson's real mistake was in not having accepted Gordon's resignation. Gordon's further mistake was in not having insisted on resigning. He and several of Pearson's other troubled ministers developed a curious doctrine of collective responsibility, trying to hold the whole Cabinet responsible for the mistakes of any individual. Perhaps it was a consequence of having billed the government as a team operation. The Prime Minister's job, they seemed to think, was to act as cheerleader for the squad.

Many members of the Pearson team went about their business earnestly and competently and got results. The Minister of National Defence, Paul Hellyer, for example, unified the army, navy, and air force into a single organization, the Canadian Forces, in the teeth of tremendous entrenched resistance and hostile lobbying—one of the few examples in modern Canadian government which prove that a determined minister actually can beat down special interests. There have been so few examples because there have been so few determined ministers. Hellyer described how he kept the Prime Minister on his side:

> Pearson himself said he was influenced by the last book he had read or the last person he had talked to.... I went through it on unification ... when it became politically difficult he almost backed off. I put a stop to that by threatening to resign.... I took a very tough stand and he responded to that by backing me up....

Other ministers were bloody-minded but bumbling. As Minister of Health and Welfare, the mercurial Judy LaMarsh fumbled repeatedly in trying to rush an ill-conceived Canada Pension Plan (CPP) into law. She bumped into her own blocking bureaucrats, then was tackled and downed by provincial resistance, led by Quebec. Pearson had to intervene and carry the ball himself, negotiating a compromise that saved the day. LaMarsh slammed back in her memoirs:

> When I heard that we were to make an accommodation with Quebec ... I blew up ... I was so angry I picked up the autographed photo of Pearson that stood on my desk and slammed it face down. The long shards of smashed glass skittered across the desk....
> ... I felt that I had been shamefully treated by my Leader. Pearson did not then, nor has he ever, even acknowledged what a dirty trick

he played.... But if he let Walter Gordon down in the time of his trouble, why should I expect more? I know leaders have enough on their plates without spending time to "baby" temperamental ministers, but I have always thought that one of the signs of natural leaders of men (and women) was their readiness to take the necessary pains to keep their followers with them. Pearson just let his ministers lie where the axes had felled them, and he harmed not only himself but his administration by doing so. He lost their affection but, more importantly, their respect and loyalty.

Some party potentates, on the other hand, felt that Pearson was much too patient with the likes of LaMarsh. Eugene Whelan in his memoirs recalled a time when caucus was so angry with the Honourable Judy than even the senators were aroused. "Mike, you're not enough of a son of a bitch to be Prime Minister," their respected spokesman, David Croll, told him.

Since Laurier's day, the Liberals had been particularly sensitive to their Quebec base. Pearson paid far more attention to Quebec than Diefenbaker did. His first Cabinet contained ten French Canadians, the highest number since Confederation (in the largest Cabinet since Confederation). We see in a moment how hard Pearson worked to accommodate the highly visible aspirations of the "new" Liberal-dominated Quebec. Ironically, several of the Quebec ministers disgraced themselves and embarrassed the Pearson government through involvement in a series of minor scandals involving conflict of interest, special pleading, and influence-peddling.

The worst mess was created when the over-burdened justice minister, Guy Favreau, mishandled investigations into the attempts of a convicted dope pedlar, Lucien Rivard, to bribe his way out of jail. There had not been major scandals in federal politics since Beauharnois in the 1930s, and the Liberals did not know how to react to waves of righteous Tory witch-hunting in the House of Commons. No one seriously questioned the Prime Minister's basic personal integrity, but in his confusion and forgetfulness he did mislead the House of Commons about his knowledge of the Rivard affair, and he knew it. Having allowed a judicial inquiry into his justice minister's judgement to be established, Pearson was excruciatingly slow in acknowledging his own error. Favreau took the heat, was broken by it, and died in 1967. "Never has Pearson so dishonoured himself, nor earned greater condemnation from his colleagues, and the scorn of history," Judy LaMarsh wrote, "as he did in shrinking from his duty and leaving to sacrifice a great soul in his place."

The vaunted Pearson team deteriorated into a herd of quarrelling, petulant individualists, more disorganized than the Diefenbaker Cabinet had been. The competent ministers got on with their business and resented the antics of the prima donnas. Journalists began analysing the factions in the Cabinet—old guard, new guard, left wing, right wing, nationalists, continentalists—aided by rivers of leaks from half a dozen ministers. Pearson could not rise above the factions and establish control. Instead he accepted the Gordon group's argument that the government's problems were mostly the Opposition's fault. If the Liberals could only get a majority and rid themselves of the terrors Diefenbaker had wrought, Gordon and his friends argued, political calm would be restored and the ship of state would return to an even keel. Pearson agreed to go to the people in the autumn of 1965, appealing above all for a majority government.

It was a disastrous campaign. Neither Pearson's head nor his heart was in it, and his performances were visibly dispirited. Reporters joked about "poor old pooper Pearson." Diefenbaker joked about Lucien Rivard (who, after his political friends failed to get him out of jail, simply climbed over the wall and escaped), saying the government's only possible campaign slogan had to be "Throw the rascals in." Students at Trent University greeted Pearson with cries of "Crime Minister." When he spoke English in Montreal the crowd shouted *"En français"*; when he switched to French they still shouted *"En français."* The parties frantically bid for support of the aged with promises of better pensions ("In all my years of politics I never found a more effective promise," Heath MacQuarrie remembered of the Tories' commitment to a huge cash increase; the Liberal angle was to reduce the age of eligibility and begin to index pensions to the cost of living). The electorate was angry and dismayed at the unnecessary election and the Diefenbaker–Pearson political circus. The government picked up only two seats, still short of a majority, while slightly declining in the popular vote. "I had never been so depressed in my political life.... We had gone through it all for nothing!" Demoralized and feeling the full weight of his sixty-eight years, Pearson wanted to resign.

His dejection at his inability to master the office of prime minister appears to have been profound. He camouflaged it with his endearing sense of humour ("How have I messed things up today?" ... "We'll jump off that bridge when we come to it") and, at least in retrospect, developed a fairly good understanding of his problem:

> My difficulty was that most Canadians ... wanted me to continue to wear the mantle of international statesmanship. At the same time, they wanted me to show guts and strength in domestic leadership. They wanted a fighter in the political struggle, inside and outside Parliament, but not to the point of becoming "just another politician" interested only in votes and office. This created for me a dilemma I was never able to resolve.

Walter Gordon, the architect of the 1965 election strategy, finally accepted responsibility for his incompetence and left the Cabinet in the aftermath. The Pearson–Gordon friendship had soured. Gordon was very unpopular within the Liberal Party and outside of central Canadian nationalist circles. To his devoted followers he was the prophet of a new Canadianism. To his critics he was just another Toronto protectionist, scheming to strengthen Ontario's grip on the nation's business. In reality he was a little of both.

Pearson went too far with Gordon, politically, intellectually, and personally. Having accepted the trust-fund monies, he ought never to have encouraged Gordon to become an active politician. The moral complexities of that relationship were too thick and prickly. Pearson ought to have fired Gordon from the Cabinet in 1963. Perhaps he should have known enough about the impracticality of Gordon's economic nationalism never to have encouraged him to believe he could be Minister of Finance. There are shades here of the Borden/Sam Hughes relationship.

Pearson's lack of interest in economic questions, large and small, helps to explain his excessive trust in Gordon. They were both good nationalists. But, as Jack Pickersgill recalled, Pearson was not a doctrinaire economic nationalist. Like King, he was a "status" nationalist, interested in the signs and symbols of nationhood. His own personal crusade in the first government was to fulfil a promise to create a distinctive Canadian flag. In 1964 he insisted on putting Parliament through months of bruising debate over a piece of cloth with a maple leaf on it. Some of the Gordonite ministers saw the flag debate as an irrelevant sidetrack, more evidence of Pearson's unwillingness to face the hard questions of power and programs. Within two years Canadians were flying the maple-leaf flag everywhere and wearing it on lapel pins and backpacks, and the world had accepted it as a symbol of the young country. Long after all of Walter Gordon's ideas had fallen into the dustbin of history, Pearson's flag was a revered symbol of his country.

*   *   *

That he was happier being a diplomat in office than trying to be a tough guy was most evident in federal–provincial relations. Pearson inaugurated the era of what came to be called "co-operative federalism," an open-ended phrase that usually meant constant, respectful consultation between the two levels of government. In the past they had been thought of as the junior and senior levels of government, and Ottawa had treated the juniors accordingly. But in the Pearson years, students of Canadian federalism began writing of "federal–provincial diplomacy," deliberately using a model drawn from the affairs of independent nations. Journalist Peter C. Newman wrote of Pearson acting as a kind of Secretary-General for Canada. There were more dominion–provincial consultations in the first eighteen months of the Pearson government than in the preceding six years of Conservative rule.

The need to accommodate the "Quiet Revolution" in Quebec seemed the most visible cause of the new federalism. Under Liberal premier Jean Lesage, who had defeated the old Union Nationale machine in 1960, Quebec was experiencing a wave of secularization, state-led modernization, and, increasingly, French-Canadian nationalism. To pay for its expensive new programs the Lesage government was demanding greater financial capacities than existing tax "rental" arrangements with Ottawa provided. To help make French Canadians *maîtres chez nous*, Lesage and his ministers wanted control of most of the powers and resources of the modern state. Many ministers, especially René Lévesque, saw the Quebec government as the "national" government of French Canadians. Ottawa was almost a foreign power, the representative of the rest of Canada.

Most of the other provinces were experiencing socio-demographic changes similar to Quebec's as the baby-boom generation came of age, though few of them made quite so much noise about it. From British Columbia to Newfoundland hordes of children were moving through a school system that required modernization from kindergarten to graduate school. Canadians old and young wanted better health care—more hospital beds, more physicians, more diagnostic services. They wanted to drive on better highways, and they were happy to vote for provincial politicians who promised them more and better jobs. Education and health, both provincial responsibilities, were the fastest-growing areas of social spending. All provincial politicians and civil servants thought "province-building" was both a duty and an opportunity—mini-nation-building within the national state. Complete with mini-diplomacy: at Quebec's suggestion, in 1960 the premiers began holding annual interprovincial conferences to discuss matters of common interest. Chaste reluctance to find a common interest in criticizing Ottawa was overcome by the allure of finding new sources of revenue to continue the expansion. Ottawa became not just Quebec's enemy, but the common enemy.

Jean Lesage had been a colleague of Pearson's in the St. Laurent government. The natural inclination of the Liberal first ministers was to respect one another's concerns. Pearson also seems to have believed that the provincial role in Canadian life was going to be greater than in the past, and, much more than St. Laurent, he was willing to reconsider the centralist elements of Liberal federalism. In 1962 he told Tom Kent that if he had to advise a young man about going into public life, "I'd have to suggest that he go into provincial politics or a provincial public service. For the next decade or two, that's where there'll be most need for new programs, where the most constructive and interesting action will be." Whether or not that perspective was sound, the "action" was at least overlapping as governments intruded on each other's jurisdictions. Increased consultation and negotiation were necessary to sort out responsibilities and accountability.

Ottawa's proposed Canada Pension Plan, to be built on top of the universal old-age pension, became the acid test of "co-operative federalism." The Pearson Cabinet's idea for an unfunded "pay-as-you-go" plan was unacceptable to Quebec. *Any* plan controlled by Ottawa was unacceptable to Quebec. Pension diplomacy in the spring of 1964 took place in a deteriorating climate. Serious separatist sentiment, fronted by terrorists, was mounting in Quebec. Even moderate French-Canadian nationalists were suggesting that the logic of two founding peoples meant that Quebec ought to have a "special status," or *statut particulier*, in the Canadian federation.

The Canada Pension Plan compromise allowed any province to set up a pension plan similar to the one Ottawa would administer. Ottawa's final plan resembled the one first proposed by Quebec. Quebec was the only province to go ahead with its own plan. There would be two partially funded pension plans in the one country, Quebec's and Canada's. The Quebec government would control investment of the funds built up in its plan.

Critics rightly argued that the pension deal gave Quebec *de facto* special status.* Would similar policies of trying to appease the grievances of provinces or cultural minorities lead to a new harmony in the country, or was this the beginning of a slide towards balkanization or separation? The early results were not encouraging, as all of the provinces speedily developed an appetite for being treated like independent principalities, their premiers like little princes. Ottawa appeared to be dealing from weakness, not strength (look at the Gordon budget; look at the bungling on the CPP; look at the government's minority situation), and sharp-witted provincial politicians were happy to rake in the chips.

The erratic, alcoholic Jean Lesage, who made Charles de Gaulle seem a model of humility, became completely unpredictable. Now Quebec was suggesting it should take over family allowances. Now it wanted a voice in all diplomacy affecting provincial affairs. Now it was beginning to set up offices abroad and trying to run its own foreign affairs—just as Canada had in its gradual march towards independence from Great Britain. Terrorist bombings in Montreal supplied a violent refrain. Was co-operative federalism a one-way street? Could the cozy Canadian world of the sleepy conference chamber and the worthy compromise be maintained? Would the centre, where Cabinet ministers still took the bus to work, hold in the era of stretched provincial limousines and swollen provincial ambitions?

*   *   *

The centre did not seem to be holding in external affairs. The advent of the Pearson government was met with relief and almost visible rejoicing

---

* "I was troubled in principle, as were many of my colleagues," Mitchell Sharp, who was then Minister of Finance, writes in his memoirs, "by the fact that members of Parliament from Quebec would be eligible to debate and vote on a bill to establish or amend the Canada Pension Plan, which would operate everywhere in Canada except in their constituencies."

by the country's allies, especially the Americans. Mike was back in business, there was a firm hand again on the Canadian tiller. Jack Kennedy, who had admired Pearson as surely as he loathed Diefenbaker, was particularly pleased and had him down to bask and talk baseball in Camelot's summer sunshine.

Then Kennedy was assassinated and a crude Texan, Lyndon B. Johnson, took over the White House. And the little war in Vietnam was expanding into a major land war that many Canadians and some Americans thought was a ghastly tragedy. When Pearson visited the LBJ Ranch in 1965 he was engulfed in a vulgar display of good ol' boy swaggering and pissing by the roadside, a few weeks before the Americans began massive bombing raids against North Vietnam. Pearson had known every American president since Franklin D. Roosevelt. Johnson was the one, Pearson's biographer John English concludes, who really frightened him. The spectacle of the mightiest country in the world devastating a benighted corner of Asia seemed obscene.

Canada had tried to play its traditional role of quietly exploring ways of helping the Americans out of the Vietnam mess. But on April 2, 1965, Pearson accepted a peace award at Temple University in Philadelphia and used the occasion to suggest a pause in the bombing. His polite language could not disguise the fact that the Prime Minister of Canada was publicly criticizing American foreign policy on American soil, a stance that violated every canon of diplomatic protocol and good manners. Pearson had acted in the teeth of intense objections and threats to resign from his own Minister of External Affairs, Paul Martin. At a post-speech luncheon with Johnson, Pearson received a presidential tongue-lashing unprecedented in the history of Canadian–American relations. "You don't come here and piss on my rug," the President of the United States told the Prime Minister of Canada. In the privacy of his diary, Pearson wrote a savage comment about the President—"If there had not been a kind of 'et tu, Brute' feeling about the assault, without any personal unpleasantness of any kind, I would have felt almost like [Austrian chancellor] Schuschnigg before Hitler at Berchtesgaden!"

Johnson and his warlords had no time for private or public Canadian wimpishness about Vietnam. The Pearson government appears to have had no further influence with the United States government on the most vital issue of the day (although Canadian diplomats were still being used as quiet couriers to Hanoi). Pearson's Temple speech can be seen as a huge mistake, a stand taken in the wrong place at the wrong time. Had he stupidly upset Canada's relations with the United States as thoroughly as old Diefenbaker? Or had the minister's son decided it was time to make a public stand against evil? Many of us were glad to see the gesture at the time, and glad to have it on Canada's record of those troubled years.

There were precious few bright spots. The United Nations peace-keeping mission to the Middle East, begun by Pearson in 1956, collapsed in 1967 when Egypt insisted the force be withdrawn. Another Arab–Israeli war followed. Paul Martin was a competent external affairs minister, but had nothing memorable to do beyond getting Canada involved in another peacekeeping venture in Cyprus. Pearson was a "brilliant mediator" between Britain and the black African Commonwealth states, John English tells us, but the affairs of the British Commonwealth rate only one paragraph in his account of Pearson's prime-ministerial years. Britain was receding very quickly from Canadians' consciousness in the 1960s. The most promising international event would be Canada's invitation to the world, in 1967, to help celebrate a hundred years of survival since Confederation.

*   *   *

After the 1965 election the Pearson approach to Quebec began to change radically. His sensitivity to the new Quebec had always seemed to be one of his greatest strengths. With no one knowing exactly how to respond to the clamour for more recognition of the French presence in Canada, Pearson's first strategy was to buy time. A Royal Commission on Bilingualism and Biculturalism—the Bi-Bi Commission—spent several years helping persuade Canadians that a major rebuilding job was needed to save the country. Co-operative federalism was another, *faute-de-mieux* approach: preserve the bonds of unity by allowing them to loosen.

The Pearson government treated the Lesage government as the voice of French Canadians partly because its own French-Canadian representation was relatively weak and hamstrung by scandals. The 1965 election decisively changed that picture, as three new recruits, Jean Marchand, Gérard Pelletier, and Pierre Elliott Trudeau were easily elected in Quebec ridings. Dubbed the "Three Wise Men" of Quebec, they were soon given major responsibilities and their voices in the government became instantly important. "It was in 1966," Mitchell Sharp wrote, "during a cabinet committee discussion of shared-cost programs relating to post-secondary education, that for the first time I heard Pierre Elliott Trudeau, then parliamentary secretary to Prime Minister Pearson ... express his opposition to federal policies that resulted in special status for Quebec. That was, he contended, the slippery slope to separation. I was impressed."

In 1966 the Liberals replaced co-operative federalism with a return to classic federalism. Ottawa would not offer more concessions to Quebec or the other provinces. It would be pleased to respect the traditional division of powers. If provinces wanted more money they should set their own rates of income tax. For its part the Pearson government would recognize the new Canada by implementing real bilingualism in the public service.

The language revolution in the federal government was begun not by Trudeau but by Pearson, a man who could not conjugate the verb "*avoir*" and who deeply regretted it. The bilingualism policy was partly a response to Bi-and-Bi recommendations, partly a product of the pact with the Wise Men, partly a response to incessant nationalist agitation from Quebec, and partly a result of Lester Pearson's search for the parameters of a new Canadian identity. Of course young Canadians should learn two languages—it would be a distinctiveness that went with the maple-leaf flag on their knapsacks. Where Diefenbaker would have narrowed the definition of Canada, and destroyed the country, Pearson worked to enlarge it. He thought that he would probably be the last unilingual prime minister.

The post-1965 Cabinet was stronger and steadier, though still visibly divided on most policy questions. There was intense debate about the timing and affordability of the next big welfare program, national health insurance (or "medicare," as it was named in imitation of a Kennedy proposal in the United States). The province of Saskatchewan had led the way in experiments with universal, comprehensive health insurance, and in crushing organized resistance from the medical profession. The Liberals wanted finally to complete the structure of the welfare state they had been building since the 1920s. Some believed that health insurance was a wonderful way of liberating Canadians from the curse of the financial costs of ill health.

The Liberal right wing agonized prophetically about the costs of such a program, and the Prime Minister apparently took little interest in the issue. But even the doubters were impressed by the tremendous performance of the Canadian economy during the 1960s. Beginning about the time the Liberals came to power, the economy enjoyed the longest period of uninterrupted, month-over-month expansion since Confederation. In the early 1960s Canadian exports doubled; in the late 1960s they doubled again. Unemployment fell below four per cent in the middle of the decade, inflation creeped just above two per cent. For years Canadians had been told that theirs was one of the most richly endowed nations on the face of the earth. The prospect of northern abundance seemed unlimited, certain to generate the extra resources needed to pay for health insurance and all the other welfare entitlements. The prospective political returns from a popular program were obvious. National health insurance was approved by the House of Commons in December 1966 in a vote of 177 to 2. It came into effect on July 1, 1968.

Ottawa showed none of its recent respect for provincial sensitivities when it introduced medicare. The message to provinces was that they had to implement plans which met strict criteria of universality, comprehensiveness, and portability, or they would get no health insurance money. Take it or leave it. The provinces could not afford to take the political heat of staying out. Their resentment at being effectively blackmailed into what soon proved to be a wildly expensive leap in the dark was intense. Physicians' sensible worries about the long-term effects of socialized medicine on the delivery of health care had also been overridden, as the power to determine support for human health shifted from the private sector to the state. Politicians were now the givers of health care to their voter clients.

The state had moved into education in the mid-nineteenth century, into health in the mid-twentieth. Except for stodgy, penny-pinching finance ministers—Gordon's replacement, Mitchell Sharp, was one of these—hardly anyone doubted that the state had the capacity to offer an ever-growing menu of "free" services for its citizens. There was much talk in the 1960s of scholarships or other programs that would eliminate tuition fees for universities. At the least Ottawa could put up money to help the young do good things. The Pearsonites had high hopes that the Company of Young Canadians, called into being by federal money in 1966, would be a maple-leaf equivalent of the U.S. Peace Corps—youth in the service of the nation and humanity.

Not much was yet being said in those years about the relative positions of men and women in Canadian life. Mike had fairly traditional attitudes to women. When Pauline Jewett suggested that she might merit a place in his first Cabinet, he reminded her that there already was a female minister. But he listened to women, including his strong-minded, often cynical wife (who had joined a vaguely radical proto-feminist organization, the Voice of Women),* and he allowed Judy LaMarsh and women's groups to persuade him that the government ought to create a Royal Commission on the Status of Women. It was established early in 1967 with a sweeping mandate "to enquire, report and make recommendations to the federal government as to what steps it can take to give women equal opportunities with men in every aspect of Canadian society." The timing of this speculative exploration, an almost risk-free venture the Conservatives would never have considered, proved superb; when the new feminism burst on the North American scene in the late 1960s, there was the Canadian government apparently already on top of the matter.

Otherwise, Pearson was not much of a reformer. In 1967–68 provincial pressures forced Ottawa to resume serious discussions of constitutional reform—a promising round in the early sixties had bogged down—against the government's better judgement. Pearson left the matter in the hands of his new Minister of Justice, Trudeau. His memoirs suggest that he did hope to see the completion of Canadian independence with the patriation of the constitution and, eventually, the phasing out of the monarchy as a Canadian presence (on one visit he warned Buckingham Palace to begin thinking of that possibility; former colleagues speculate that with a parliamentary majority after 1965 he would have severed the tie).

Throughout his prime-ministership Mike Pearson liked to talk about the need for high ideals in politics, and respect for the political calling, and the need to tone down the bitter partisanship. In reality Canadian

---

* When Pearson was asked whether it bothered him when anti-Vietnam protesters blocked his car, John English notes, he said it worried him because Maryon might get out and join them. The Pearson marriage is now known to have had serious rough times—it was not a Victorian idyll—and Maryon seems to have been too unfulfilled to have been a happy woman. But in the years of her husband's prime-ministership the press still largely refrained from extensive coverage of the personal problems of politicians and their spouses.

politics began a long era of disrepute in the 1960s, partly because public-spirited citizens began expecting the ethical behaviour the politicians said they believed in. The Pearson government thought it was more important to persuade citizens to honour politicians than it was to change politicians' behaviour. Democracy is "diminished when the politician ... betrays the trust of those who elected him," Pearson wrote in his memoirs, adding, "This rarely happens in our country."

Like King, Pearson professed dislike of the sordid aspects of the political game but played it anyway. Even his ministers thought his senatorial and other patronage appointments were of low quality. Canadian citizens were constantly becoming better educated and better informed. Despite the cords of dependency being spun by the welfare state, the country's tremendous affluence made many Canadians less dependent on governments than ever before. Habits of deference to politicians, and other traditional authorities, were beginning to crumble. A ferment of interest in new forms of politics, new kinds of "participatory" democracy, was beginning to bubble towards the surface. The government's response was to offer more grants.

Pearson's attitudes towards Cabinet and caucus were fairly traditional. He jealously guarded prime-ministerial prerogatives, and in heated discussion behind closed doors was not always the nice guy. The extreme, unruly partisanship of House of Commons debates, and Canadians' obvious dislike of MPs' often silly posturing, might have stimulated a more reform-minded government to find ways of relaxing party discipline. In one notable precedent, the Pearson government did abandon tradition after it absent-mindedly found itself defeated on the third reading of a tax bill in February 1968. The government resisted opposition demands that it resign or dissolve Parliament, won a vote of confidence, and carried on. Pearson did not think speech-making in the House of Commons was very relevant or important, and Parliament's long decline as Canada's democratic forum continued.

Pierre Trudeau was one of several ministers who thought the level of disorganization in the government and Parliament was astonishingly high. "Agendas were hastily slapped together and followed only sporadically, if at all," he says in his *Memoirs*.

> The Cabinet wasted an inordinate amount of time discussing insignificant topics, and then had to whisk through questions of major

importance, often without arriving at any conclusions. And all too often we would eventually learn that Mr. Pearson, with a handful of our colleagues, had already decided everything for us anyway. In short, the decision-making process was often rendered frivolous because of a lack of organization. As for the House, it was a noisy bedlam, and the disorder that ruled there bothered me a great deal.*

The government put an end to the scandal-mongering, but in a sordid way. Pearson had the RCMP search the files on the previous government and found a sex scandal involving two ministers and a German whore, Gerda Munsinger, who was a security risk. In the tackiest encounter in Canadian prime-ministerial history, he privately warned Diefenbaker that he knew about the matter, and Diefenbaker countered by threatening to renew absurd allegations from the McCarthy era that Pearson had once been a Communist. Finally, when the Tories attacked one French-Canadian minister too many, the newly toughened Quebec contingent struck back, spilling details of the "Monsignor affair." The ensuing investigation by a Supreme Court judge of Diefenbaker's handling of the case seemed a dirty way of resolving an affair that had done no credit to anyone. But there were no more scandals. Soon, as the Conservatives moved to save their party, there was no more Diefenbaker.

Pearson was a fair-weather reformer, at best, because he personally had done so well in government. He had risen spectacularly in the public service and for forty years had moved in the most elite circles at home and abroad. He believed in careers open to talent. He believed that only small numbers of talented Canadians understood the intricacies of government. He would have been the first to say that he was not a populist in politics, if only because Diefenbaker's career seemed to have debased that term for a generation. Pearson did not even have Mackenzie King's sense of having been a tribune of the people in their struggles against the big interests.

* Jean Chrétien puts it slightly differently in *Straight from the Heart*, making the point that Pearson was less consensual than Trudeau became—"He had his own views, and most of the time he just did what he wanted to do. There would be great storms in cabinet, with ministers pounding the table and raging at each other. Then Pearson would say in the middle of the mess, 'It's time to go to lunch, so I'll take care of the matter.'"

But Pearson would have angrily denied the accusation that he had lost touch with ordinary people. In all his years as a diplomat he never lost the ability to "speak Canadian." His love of sports put him on the same plane with steelworkers and loggers in Algoma East. In election campaigns he was a happy, relaxed main-streeter, only stiffening up when required to whip a crowd into partisan frenzy. In public, and usually in private, Mike Pearson was casual, affable, instantly likeable, anything but austere, never a stuffed shirt—the world-famous diplomat who knew every left-fielder's batting average. His veins flowed with the milk of human kindness. As a human being, Lester Pearson was about the best a Canadian could hope to become. As a politician he hoped to bring out the best in his fellow Canadians. The old Methodist in him had long since mellowed. It was hard to work up a passion to rid the world of sin, if you were not sure most of your fellow men, other than Diefenbaker, really were sinners.

*   *   *

Better to celebrate goodness than to castigate evil. Centennial year was a tailor-made occasion for Mike Pearson to welcome the world to a Canada that had put on its happiest face. The economy was strong. Peace reigned throughout the land. All was well. The Montreal World's Fair, Expo 67, was a splendid success (despite having a name, "The World of Man/Terre des Hommes," that would today spark national outrage). Most Canadians' feelings about themselves and their country reached levels of well-being higher than anyone could remember—or many of them would experience again.

The President of France, Charles de Gaulle, became the serpent in the garden. On his state visit to Canada that summer he told a cheering crowd in Montreal that the reception he had received in Quebec reminded him of the liberation of France in World War II. From the balcony of Montreal's old city hall, the President of France shouted the separatist slogan *"Vive le Québec libre!"* Pearson's Temple University speech had been a model of restraint compared with this intolerable intrusion in Canadian affairs. The implied analogy between Canada and Nazi Germany was even more insulting than de Gaulle's identification with separatism. On his own, without hesitation, Pearson drafted official statements repudiating de Gaulle and making clear that he was no longer welcome in Canada.

In future the Government of Canada would show a harder face to movements to dis-integrate the country. But it was Trudeau, the Minister of Justice, who was most often the spokesman for the new policy. By the end of centennial year, Pearson was largely a lame duck, presiding over a Cabinet that had lost a sense of where it wanted to go. Ministers were in open ideological dispute (Walter Gordon had clawed his way back into the Cabinet as a spokesman for the nationalist left; everyone knew there was no consensus on economic policy), and beginning to jockey for the upcoming leadership race. Cabinet solidarity and secrecy were nonexistent. When Pearson created a Cabinet committee on secrecy, Peter C. Newman reported, the details were known to a journalist that afternoon. The Pearson government utterly lacked the quality Jeffrey Simpson later characterized as "the discipline of power." Some of the ministers admired and loved the Prime Minister, but they did not fear or respect him enough to set aside personal interests for the common good. Mackenzie King never had such a problem.

Pearson kept his distance from the contest to succeed him, although it was known he was partial to being followed by a French Canadian. In his farewell to the party at its April 1968 leadership convention, he meditated on the problems of leadership in a state where government now intervened "in practically every aspect of the citizen's life" and was expected to have an instant solution to every problem. "The Leader has merely to find these solutions," Pearson said,

> and, for this purpose, to be strong, decisive, wise, dynamic, charismatic, patient, indefatigable, kindly, and capable of inspiring unswerving loyalty, unquestioning obedience and rapturous worship.
>
> He is expected, by the image-maker, to be a combination of Abraham Lincoln and Batman, to perform instant miracles. Then, when the poor, honest, decent chap can't live up to this image, the process of demolition begins so that another superman can be erected in the ruins.

The party's last gift to the retiring prime minister was to be a white puppy. Pearson told the organizers that he and his wife didn't want one. They insisted, arguing that the presentation would look wonderful on television.

Mike Pearson's last appearance in the House of Commons was on

April 23, his seventy-first birthday and the first day of the new session. Various MPs were prepared to pay generous tribute to him. "Everyone was jovial and I was wondering what I should say when, as I expected, the Prime Minister declared this was the time to recognize the incomparable services to Canada, to the world, to the interplanetary system of his predecessor. But I was relieved of that oratorical problem. The Prime Minister quietly announced dissolution ... no one could speak, since there was no Parliament to speak to.... I noted in my last prime ministerial diary, 'Tough.'"

*   *   *

Lester Pearson was Canada's greatest diplomat in an hour in the country's evolution when its voice was most likely to be heard. If he had retired in 1957 his reputation as a great public servant and statesman would have been secure. By staying in the game and turning to domestic politics late in life, by trying to be a diplomat when he needed to be tough, and trying to be tough when he needed to be diplomatic, Pearson replaced the exclamation point after his career with that lingering question mark. If Canada had not been a relatively easy country to govern in the 1960s—many of Pearson's mistakes, such as the Canada Pension Plan and the thoughtless spending commitments, were not evident until much later—the damage to his reputation might have been worse.

He wrote good memoirs before his death in 1972, and then he was fortunate to have his life described in sensitive, almost lyrical prose by a sympathetic historian and Liberal, John English. English's argument is that, for all his faults, Pearson succeeded in making progress, particularly towards a new balance between Canada's two major cultures. "Mike Pearson barely kept his ship afloat, much less on course, as he guided it through swift rapids and perilous narrows. The journey was rough, but its direction was always forward."

Was he tough enough? It was hard, in the twentieth century, to grow up as the child of a religious faith that was losing its relevance even to many who professed it. English's biography, its volumes titled *Shadow of Heaven* and *The Worldly Years*, plays carefully on spiritual themes, building to a powerful image: "Mike reminds one of John Updike's liberal parson who can't bring himself to tell dying parishioners that there probably is no heaven." You could tell your children that they ought to grow up to have the values Mr. Pearson had, but in the same breath you might also advise them to stay out of politics. Or, if Lester Pearson really was the quintessential Canadian, the Canadian in the mind of God, then maybe Canadians really aren't tough enough. We often suspect that.

Pearson might have preferred to have been judged in the metaphor he came to love best. He was a transitional figure. Macdonald, Laurier, and King were starters who almost always went the distance, complete game men. Mike didn't have their range or stamina. Always a junk-ball pitcher, he depended on control that became harder to maintain as the game went on. He couldn't easily move batters off the plate—he never wanted to throw at anyone's head. He gave up a lot of hits and walks, but he did keep his team in the game. Good for the middle innings. What they call a set-up man. He knew his limits, and when he reached them he took himself out of the game and handed the ball to the guy who threw hard and fast.

Question Period

The first term, when everything came easy

9

TRUDEAU
The Politics of Confrontation

Pierre Elliott Trudeau did not fight for his country in World War II. That abstention from battle led critics in later years sometimes to question his brand of patriotism. No one ever questioned his toughness. Trudeau became the most formidable political warrior in Canadian history. He confronted separatists, terrorists, provincial premiers, Conservatives, anyone who disagreed with him, and he almost always won.

He did not flinch from danger when bottle-throwing separatist rioters chanting "*Trudeau au poteau*" ("Trudeau to the gallows") threatened the reviewing stand at the St. Jean Baptiste Day festivities in Montreal in 1968, the night before his government's first electoral victory. How far would he go in fighting terrorism during the October Crisis of 1970? "Just watch me.... There's a lot of bleeding hearts around who just don't like to see people with helmets and guns. All I can say is, go on and bleed...." Lester Pearson thought that "ice-water" ran in Trudeau's veins. To change Canada's constitution, the Prime Minister assaulted eight provincial premiers and prepared to take on the Mother Country itself. Twice he recovered from major political wounds to regain his majority. Twice he came out of retirement to launch devastating attacks on seemingly impregnable constitutional positions erected by all eleven first ministers.

In Lyndon Johnson and Ronald Reagan the Americans had a real cowboy and a Hollywood cowboy in the White House during the

Trudeau years. But it was the Canadian prime minister, alone and exposed on stage and television screen, jacket off, tie loosened, fingers hooked in his belt—the gunslinger on Main Street—who most resembled Clint Eastwood. Most of those who hated Trudeau, eventually a large number of Canadians, would not deny that they respected or feared him.

A fighting intellectual, a man with an extraordinarily clear vision of the structure of the Canada he wanted to mould. The father of bilingual, multicultural Canada, the father of the Charter of Fundamental Rights and Freedoms. His nation-changing, nation-building achievements were comparable only to those of Macdonald and King.

He was not, however, the father of a new social order for Canada. The "just society" the Liberals liked to talk about was not delivered during almost sixteen years of Trudeau government. What did emerge was a slow realization of the limits of government, of the inability of bureaucrats and social engineers to control the forces of the marketplace and to change people's behaviour. In the end, the Trudeau Liberals left Canada sinking in debt and facing a tidal wave of Conservative reaction. Trudeau's biography has yet to be written; his *Memoirs* are ghosted and thin; so it may be many years before we understand his feelings about the less successful side of his prime-ministership. Did he regret that the state proved unable to *give* Canadians a new equality? Or did the logic of his own free-spirited skepticism towards authority lead in directions only hinted at during his years in power—towards a withering away of the nanny state as citizens learned to empower themselves, learned the possibilities of personal freedom and self-directedness that Pierre Trudeau personally exemplified?

*   *   *

"The state has no place in the bedrooms of the nation," Trudeau quipped as Minister of Justice in 1967, and struck an intensely responsive chord. He was defending legislation to liberalize divorce (previously granted only on grounds of adultery), part of a package that also legalized homosexual acts between consenting adults and ended unenforceable prohibitions on the sale of contraceptives. Trudeau's "Omnibus Bill" was a sweeping act of deregulation, a demolition job on the state's century-long propensity to try to control private behaviour and morals.

It was perfectly in tune with the flowering of individuality in the 1960s—the new permissiveness—and Trudeau himself, though born in 1919, often seemed a child of the new age. As a rookie MP he wore sandals and ascots in the House of Commons. He drove flashy cars and liked beautiful women. He was a skier and scuba diver, a world traveller, a rich and stylish bachelor, close to the platonic ideal of the intelligent playboy. A few years after becoming prime minister he married a beautiful playmate, a flower child of twenty-two from the West Coast, Margaret Sinclair, and they settled down to live happily ever after. Their first two children were born on Christmas days. What magic there must have been in the Trudeau bedroom. Lucky Pierre!

The real Trudeau was very different, as Margaret learned to her increasing dismay. During his youth and early manhood he had created for himself an intensely self-disciplined, self-contained lifestyle. Trained by Jesuits, and driven, he sometimes admitted, by shyness and insecurities, he had developed austere, almost ascetic personal habits. He was a rich man's son—Charles Trudeau had become a millionaire as the founding owner of an automobile service club—who learned to do without. He paddled to Hudson Bay; he roamed Canada, and the world, on a few hundred dollars. He conditioned his body through individualistic sports—canoeing, boxing, judo—and his mind by reading classical moral and political philosophy.

"I wanted to know everything and experience everything, in every realm." Some of Trudeau's mentors suspected he was a closet Protestant, "not only because I insisted on closely questioning the most established truths but even more because I regarded my conscience as the ultimate court of appeal." He became a Catholic individualist (adopting the philosophy of "personalism," which seemed to find a middle way between the claims of authority and the spirit of freedom), not a libertarian or hedonist. Now and then he would indulge himself in a flashy car or a flight to faraway places, but for the most part he lived simply. He despised the habit of smoking, and seldom drank alcohol. Margaret was surprised to find that Pierre would dry himself on the smallest and meanest towel he could find at 24 Sussex, which had generously stocked linen closets. "It's the training," he told her.

His father was a street-smart French Canadian who expected his kids to be tough and self-reliant; his mother, Grace Elliott, was a gracious, cultivated Scots Canadian. Trudeau seemed to have both temperaments and would move from one parental persona to the other. He could quote Greek philosophy and tell his enemies to eat shit, in either language. Private he might be, but, as the televised version of his "Memoirs" graphically demonstrated, put a camera near him and he would find a way, often by clowning, to become the centre of attention. Not a guy who would spend a lifetime avoiding the spotlight.

His lack of enthusiasm for the armed forces during the war suggests a more French-Canadian than English-Canadian cast of mind. Here was another blinkered young Québécois divorced from the great struggle against totalitarianism. "So there was a war? Tough," he says in his memoirs. "It wouldn't stop me from concentrating on my studies as long as that was possible.... if you were a French Canadian in Montreal in the early 1940s, you did not automatically believe that this was a just war ... we tended to think of this war as a settling of scores among the superpowers." Soon Trudeau got out of Quebec. He supplemented his law degree from the Université de Montréal with studies at Harvard, the London School of Economics, and the Sorbonne. He earned a Harvard MA, but never wrote his Ph.D thesis. Instead he travelled to the ends of the earth, including the forbidden kingdom of post-revolutionary China.

The outside world was fresh air compared to the stench of church and state authoritarianism in postwar Quebec. During the long premiership of Union Nationale leader Maurice Duplessis the state–church alliance seemed to dominate every parish of an intellectually stagnant province. Dissent, debate, the free flow of ideas, were discouraged. When Trudeau returned to Quebec, more aware of the dimensions of liberty, he allied himself with leftist intellectuals and trade unionists opposed to Duplessis. "I found it unacceptable that others should claim to know better than I what was good for me." He sometimes gave legal help to the union movement, he occasionally lectured and wrote about problems of federalism and civil liberties in Quebec and Canada, and he worked for a year in the Privy Council office in Ottawa on constitutional minutiae.

He worked hard at what he did, being anything but an idle rich man's son. But he had no need to forge a career—"I didn't have the temperament of a bureaucrat"—and liked to stay on the move. Nobody in the 1950s would have said that Pierre Trudeau was an ambitious man or a politician in the making. To some he was a dilettante, under-using his talents. He had wanted a university appointment, but could not get one in Quebec while Duplessis was in power. After the winds of change began to blow in 1960 he was hired to teach constitutional law at the Université de Montréal.

Five years later Trudeau went into federal politics to fight Quebec's drift towards separation. He had concluded that the emerging separatist movement in Quebec was reactionary. It seemed to him inward-looking, parochial, and, above all, based on collectivist myths of "nation" and "race" that reasserted the supremacy of the group against the individual. He was disgusted by separatists' tendencies to totalitarianism, anti-Semitism, and economic illiteracy. He found their revolutionary pretensions absurd:

> Quebec's revolution, if it had taken place, would first have consisted in freeing man from collective coercions: freeing the citizens brutalized by reactionary and arbitrary governments; freeing consciences bullied by a clericalized and obscurantist Church; freeing workers exploited by an oligarchic capitalism; freeing men crushed by authoritarian and outdated traditions. Quebec's revolution would have consisted in the triumph of the freedoms of the human being as inalienable rights, over and above capital, the nation, tradition, the Church, and even the State.

Trudeau, *philosophe*, had no use for the separatists' dream of uniting the ethnic "nation" with a political state. Governments and nation-states were, to him, political constructions whose aim should be to maximize human liberties, not to champion ethnic collectivities.

By the mid-1960s, the Quebec government was working hard to acclaim itself the champion, the spokesgovernment, for French people in Canada. Ottawa would be the government of the rest of Canada. As power and prestige slid from Ottawa to Quebec City, the demands for more power, even for some kind of special status for the Quebec government, continued to escalate. The Pearson Liberals, anxious to curb the erosion, welcomed the "star recruits" from Quebec—Trudeau, journalist Gérard Pelletier, and union leader Jean Marchand—into federal politics in 1965 to bolster the French presence in Ottawa.

Marchand, a tough, influential unionist, was the brightest star. Trudeau was a bonus in the deal, possibly a throwaway, included largely at Marchand's insistence. He was not well known or influential, and his dilettante reputation preceded him. For the 1965 election he was pitchforked into a safe, mostly English-speaking riding. When a collection of his essays, *Federalism and the French Canadians*, was issued in English early in 1968 the publishers felt that Trudeau needed to be introduced to Canada by the historian J.T. Saywell.

By the time the book was published, Trudeau had emerged from nowhere to become the leading candidate to succeed Pearson. After a brief apprenticeship as a parliamentary secretary he had been appointed Minister of Justice in 1967. The divorce bill and other moral reform bills were the first big step in his leap to prominence. The second was his remarkable televised performance at the constitutional conference Ottawa held in February 1968. Pearson chaired the meeting of first ministers. Daniel Johnson of the Union Nationale, who had replaced Jean Lesage in the 1966 Quebec election, now demanded radical constitutional reform to recognize Quebec's special status as the homeland of the French Canadians. As Pearson's constitutional adviser, Trudeau icily and publicly tore the concept apart as both unworkable and inequitable. Johnson was put firmly in his place as the premier of one of Canada's ten provinces.

Trudeau's combination of intelligence, charm, self-deprecation, good looks, and panache overwhelmed the other contenders in the race to succeed Pearson. He was also helped by the Liberal Party's preference for alternating English and French leaders. The fact that Trudeau's was a fresh face played to Canadians' sense of having been badly served by the Diefenbaker–Pearson generation of fuddy-duddy politicians. Sure he was almost an unknown, but he seemed to be a man of today and tomorrow, not yesterday. He was a terrific performer on television. Perhaps he was a harbinger of a new breed of non-political leaders, a "neo-politician." Perhaps he was a philosopher-king. Perhaps he was the man who would keep Quebec in its place. In his first election campaign he talked a lot about "one Canada," sometimes appearing even to echo old Diefenbaker, while the new Tory leader, former Nova Scotia premier Robert Stanfield, got himself all tangled up in the idea that there might be "*deux nations*" within Canada.

Many Canadians were not sure exactly what Trudeau's beliefs were, but they liked the idea that he had strong beliefs. A man of principle, not a compromising politician. "A man for this season, uncontaminated and uninhibited," Lester Pearson wrote of that perception. Peter C. Newman observed that voters could not decide whether Trudeau stood on the right or the left of the political spectrum, but thought he certainly seemed to stand for the future. Or, as a B.C. Grit put it, "We decided that he's a weird bugger but a smart one and maybe he can pull it off."

He had to overcome whispering campaigns that he was a pink pansy intellectual. This venom was more than drowned out by adoration from women, who seemed to find him a model of male attractiveness. In the 1968 campaign he became Canada's Jack Kennedy, its Yves Montand, and any of the Beatles, take your pick. "Had there ever been in Canada a national party leader quite like this?" Meighen's biographer, Roger Graham, asked. "Sir Wilfrid Laurier, let us say, sliding down a banister? Sir Robert Borden in goggles and flippers? Arthur Meighen in a Mercedes? Mackenzie King at judo? R.B. Bennett on skis?"

Young women rushed to kiss him, to touch him, to pluck hairs from his balding head. "He's cute and he's handsome and he's lovable and he's only forty-eight years old and he's going to be the greatest prime minister in history," one of the teeny-boppers gushed. Adults who did not succumb to the "Trudeaumania" of the season still felt what Trudeau biographer George Radwanski called "Trudeauphilia—a vast outpouring of visceral *liking* for this dynamic, quiet-spoken man with the tough yet hopeful words and the shy smile." They saw his toughness during that St. Jean Baptiste Day riot on June 24—members of the press gallery stood and applauded his courage—and the next day voted him the first majority government the Liberals had won since 1953. In a few years he had come from relative obscurity to win a remarkable place in the esteem of Canadians.

*   *   *

> We must separate once and for all the concepts of state and of nation, and make Canada a truly pluralistic and polyethnic society.... The English Canadians, with their own nationalism, will have to retire gracefully to their proper place, consenting to modify their own precious image of what Canada ought to be.
>
> ... I have no intention of closing my eyes to how much Canadians of British origin have to do—or rather, undo—before a pluralist state can become a reality in Canada.

Trudeau had written this in his 1962 attack on separatism. Almost all of his writing included thoughts on putting English-Canadian nationalism in its place, and of righting the wrongs done to the French in Canada. If the Quebec government must not become an ethnic government, the

Government of Canada had to stop being one. Canada could no longer be a unilingual, unicultural country with one exceptional province. Instead it had to become a country whose government respected and reflected real pluralism.

How much pluralism and why? Trudeau did not argue for linguistic or cultural rights based on history. "In terms of *realpolitik*," he wrote in 1965, "French and English are equal in Canada because each of these linguistic groups has the power to break the country. And this power cannot yet be claimed by the Iroquois, the Eskimos, or the Ukrainians." Formal equality had to be extended to the French linguistic group simply to ward off separatism. This would be the balance, the bargain, that cancelled out the separatist impulse and made Canada continuable.

Ottawa's post-1965 commitment to real bilingualism in the civil service was the first fruit of the "French power" that Trudeau, Marchand, and their friends promised to exercise. The Official Languages Act of 1969 chiselled the new vision into the statute book. In all of its activities, the Government of Canada would put the country's two official languages on an equal footing. It would do all it could to pressure the provinces into granting equal educational rights to French linguistic minorities. The office of Official Languages Commissioner was created. Keith Spicer, the first incumbent, advised Canadians that the best way to learn French was in bed. There were jokes about French having a place in the bedrooms of the nation.

Linguistic guarantees would ideally be entrenched in a new constitution, Trudeau had suggested. But he was otherwise a constitutional conservative, extremely wary of the mess that any casual attempt to rewrite the British North America Act might create. He had spelled out his caution in 1965:

> For the last hundred years ... this country and this constitution have allowed men to live in a state of freedom and prosperity which, though perhaps imperfect, has nevertheless rarely been matched in this world. And so I cannot help condemning as irresponsible those people who wish our nation to invest undetermined amounts of money, time, and energy in a constitutional adventure that they have been unable to define precisely but which would consist in more or less completely destroying Confederation to replace it with some vague form of sovereignty resulting in something like an independent

Quebec, or associate states, or "special status," or a Canadian common market, or a confederation of ten states, or some entirely different scheme that could be dreamt up on the spur of the moment, when chaos at all levels had already become inevitable.

"When Pearson told me, 'The provinces are pushing and we have to respond,' I said, 'Let them push,'" Trudeau remembered. They kept pushing, and the government finally had to respond. As Minister of Justice, Trudeau's main idea for constitutional reform was to entrench the inherent and inalienable rights of man (and woman) in a new constitution. His interest in human rights flowed from the struggles to protect them from the oppressive instincts of the Duplessis government, and from his reading of the political philosophy of the Enlightenment. The Diefenbaker Bill of Rights had been a start, he noted, but its application was obviously limited. "I am thinking of a Bill of Rights that will be so designed as to limit the exercise of all governmental power, federal and provincial," Trudeau told the Canadian Bar Association in 1967. "It will not involve any gain by one jurisdiction at the expense of the other. There would be no transfer of powers.... Instead the power of both the federal government and the provincial governments would be restrained in favour of the Canadian citizen...."

Trudeau as prime minister continued the effort at constitutional reform launched reluctantly under Pearson. It became complicated, drawn out, tedious, and unpopular. The first ministers found they could converse and dicker more comfortably in secret, so they stopped holding public meetings. Finally they hashed out a compromise package at Victoria in June 1971. The Victoria Charter contained a complex amending formula to permit patriating the constitution from Great Britain, partial entrenchment of language rights, a few sops to Trudeau's idea of a bill of rights (the provinces were not enthusiastic), and a minor rejuggling of powers between Ottawa and the provinces. Quebec's young Liberal premier, Robert Bourassa, faced a storm of nationalist protest that Victoria did not give enough to Quebec, and he exercised the option of finally rejecting it. Trudeau observed that he had always said constitution-making was a can of worms.

*   *   *

Trudeau hoped to satisfy Quebecers and all Canadians by giving them good government. This would not be inconsistent, however, with the push for "French power." French Canadians had played limited roles in the federal Cabinet and the civil service. Now there would be no doors closed to them, no treatment of the French fact or of Quebec as an afterthought. French Canadians would get their full share of government jobs and contracts, Quebec its full share of government spending.

On the other hand, the bad old days of using taxpayers' money to buy political support would be over, Trudeau hoped. He and his circle of advisers intended to put an end to the apparent excesses of the Pearson administration—endless promising, uncosted welfare programs, seat-of-the-pants decision-making. The Trudeauites intended to substitute reason and planning, while at the same time involving citizens in government to an unprecedented degree. Everyone talked about "participatory democracy" in the heady days of 1960s utopianism. The Liberals said their aim was to create a "Just Society," their campaign slogan in 1968.

Oddly, the strategy boiled down to a bigger government doing less. More staff, more experts, had to be hired to bring things under control and do the planning and tackle the problems. "We may have gone a bit overboard at times with certain new managerial methods, much in vogue at the time," Trudeau conceded in his *Memoirs*. "People took government seriously in those days," wrote Richard Gwyn, who covered Ottawa in the early Trudeau years:

> The city crackled with energy. Soon it bristled with policy analysts and program analysts; sociologists, ecologists, economists, and socio-economists; experts on communications; experts on natives; experts on native communications and native women. They manned task forces, worked as consultants, peopled the shiny new departments—Urban Affairs, Environment, Communications—the Citizenship Branch at Secretary of State, and the Policy Planning Branches that every department sprouted. They churned out earnest reports, attended endless seminars, dished out grants for community development projects, experiments in communications, experiments in political revolution. Foreign visitors were astounded: any and every policy idea seemed to be acceptable and everyone seemed to be so self-confident. By around 1970, Ottawa resembled neither Camelot nor Athens so much as a cross between

the Harvard Business School, Berkeley in the free speech era, and a
utopian commune.

At times the philosopher-king seemed to be chairing a seminar on the
first principles of government. When Charles Ritchie, Canada's High
Commissioner to Great Britain, had his first interview with Trudeau, the
Prime Minister began by asking him if the Department of External
Affairs was really necessary and, if so, why. The conduct of Canadian
diplomacy was subjected to particularly harsh scrutiny, for Trudeau was
skeptical about both the foreign-policy establishment and the policies
that had evolved in the years of Pearsonian activism—and he had a
grudge against snooty Canadian embassies from his days as a backpack-
ing student. His government's elaborate rethinking of Canada's role in
the world led to a decision to do less—to reduce Canadian forces
abroad, cut the diplomatic corps, stop trying to be a "helpful fixer" on
the world stage, and focus instead on staving off threats to Canadian
sovereignty, some of which came from within. Mackenzie King would
have been impressed by the new direction. Lester Pearson, who was not
consulted during the review, was not.

Trudeau had not made many commitments during the 1968 campaign. One of his earliest supporters, Eugene Whelan, who became his
gladhanding Minister of Agriculture, had worried that Trudeau's main
drawback was his conservatism. At times the early Trudeau seemed to be
pronouncing the end of an era, in saying that there would be no more
"free stuff" and that government could not be Santa Claus.

> We are not promising things for everybody and we are not seeing
> great visions. We are trying to make the people of the country
> understand that if they are to be governed well they will have to par-
> ticipate in the governing; that there are no magic solutions; that
> there is no charismatic leader with a magic wand....

The more his government expanded the planning exercises, the more it
listened to what Canadians wanted—it was listening now (and even giving grants to help them talk) to native groups, women's organizations,
ethnic spokespeople alarmed by bilingualism, and every regional interest
in a nation of regions—the more the Prime Minister seems to have
become alarmed at the gap between citizens' expectations and the state's

capacity to deliver. With the big Pearson programs, medicare and the Canada Pension Plan, the welfare state seemed to have reached its limits. Already it was proving far more costly than anyone had anticipated.

There was no money for such new programs as a guaranteed annual income, which most experts had thought would be the next leap forward in social policy. Well, you could free up money if you curbed well-to-do Canadians' entitlements to some of the existing programs, such as family allowances. The first Trudeau government considered allowing the baby bonus and the universal old-age pension to wither away through inflation, to be replaced eventually by a guaranteed annual income. But the 1970 White Paper *Income Security for Canadians* produced a storm of outrage, and the ideas were dropped for more than a decade. What was to be done about the dilemma of trying to build welfare programs for the less fortunate when everything was supposed to apply equally to everyone?

From 1970 Trudeau would occasionally reflect on Canadians' impossibly high expectations. He seems to have hoped that "participation," which consisted mainly of grants to interest groups to present briefs at hearings (and maybe support their benefactors at the polls), would teach citizens the limits of government. Instead it whetted their appetite for more government and more grants. At times the Prime Minister talked as though an insoluble crisis of modern statecraft was at hand. One of the ministers, Don Jamieson, recorded a remarkable prime-ministerial musing during a discussion of the CBC by the Planning and Priorities Committee of Cabinet. CBC commentators tended to be in favour of big, active government:

> [Trudeau] pointed out that the government was coming to the conclusion that the sum total of all the demands for change, improvement and reform far exceeded both the government's and the country's capacity to pay. Therefore, he maintained, one of the important steps that the government might have to take was the dampening of public enthusiasm for various new initiatives that were beyond our reach. Fostering such expectations would only lead to frustration and disappointment and would quite possibly sow the seeds of continued unrest and eventually, perhaps, revolution. He then made the case that there was something inconsistent in having the government reach such a viewpoint

only to have an agency paid for by public funds and used by a variety of advocates make further demands.

Most of his ministers and backbenchers were intellectually in awe of Trudeau.* Most of the public assumed he ran a one-man government, doing whatever he wanted. In fact, as Jamieson, Jean Chrétien, Mitchell Sharp, and other ministers noted, Trudeau spent more time than most of his predecessors listening to other people's views and searching for a consensus. The ministers, in turn, waited for him to offer a lead. It slowly dawned on some of them that he had no hidden agenda, no magic answers. Except on Quebec and on constitutional matters he had no special expertise. And Gene Whelan had been right: Trudeau's instincts were conservative.

He was not a voluble, personable prime minister either. Trudeau could be intensely charming when he wanted to be, but often he was withdrawn, businesslike, abrupt to the point of arrogance, and unforgiving. Keith Davey once urged him to drop a friendly line to one of his harshest Tory critics, Tom Cossitt, who was in the hospital after a heart attack. "Well, Keith," Trudeau replied, "I suppose that would be a nice WASP thing to do, but I have no intention of writing to that awful bastard."

His disciplined lifestyle did not include drinks with the boys after work or schmoozing with gushy Liberals at party pep rallies. On the platform, sometimes in the House, usually with the media, he could be blunt, insensitive, combative, offensive. Westerners never forgot the line, ripped out of context, "Why should I sell your wheat?" The world affairs do-gooders were deeply offended by his query "Where's Biafra?" (the Biafrans were trying to secede from Nigeria and had hired public-relations specialists who gulled many of the socially concerned into giving aid that

---

* Mitchell Sharp told historian Allan Levine, "When I sat around the cabinet table when Pearson was prime minister, I said to myself, 'The prime minister would not be here if we were not here.' You would never have said that about Trudeau." "He seemed to cast a spell over the caucus: they became like little lambs," Eugene Whelan wrote in his memoirs. Oddly, much the same comments have been made about Brian Mulroney's command of his Cabinet and caucus, but solely because of his ability to win elections and smooth over differences. The only other prime minister whose followers were often intellectually in awe of him was King after 1935.

prolonged the war and the suffering). "I'm not really governing to be re-elected," Trudeau said in 1970. "If the Canadian people don't like it, you know, they can lump it." He was trying to say that governments have to do hard, unpopular things. He was often not well understood. Sometimes he sounded like R.B. Bennett.

The hard things his government did to combat terrorism in Quebec were well understood, however, and they were applauded. In October 1970, cells of the Front de Libération du Québec (FLQ) kidnapped a British trade commissioner, James Cross, and then the Minister of Labour in the Bourassa government, Pierre Laporte, demanding various acts of ransom from the Quebec and Canadian governments. In Quebec, Ottawa, and much of the rest of the country, the sense of uncertainty and danger was unlike anything Canadians had ever experienced. No one knew how serious the terrorist menace might become. What if a car bomb went off at lunchtime at Place Ville Marie? What politician might be targeted next? Even René Lévesque is said to have asked for police protection. Many observers thought an emergency government might have to be formed in Quebec. First the Canadian Forces were called out to help the police maintain order and protect citizens, then the War Measures Act was proclaimed, giving the authorities special powers to suspend civil liberties in the face of "apprehended insurrection."

A few civil libertarians and separatists bemoaned the inconveniences suffered by those detained under the War Measures Act. The vast majority of Canadians, including Quebecers, expressed few qualms about the Prime Minister's tough stand on terrorism. Other governments that had tried to bargain with revolutionary thugs had only sunk deeper into the muck of kidnapping and intimidation.

It eventually turned out that the FLQ was not nearly as formidable as it appeared—the few ideologues who had kidnapped Cross let him go in return for free passage to Cuba—but no one knew this at the time. The cell that kidnapped Pierre Laporte murdered him in cold blood. We cannot know what would have happened had another course been followed. We do know that terrorism ended in Quebec when faced with a tough response from the Trudeau government. The country mourned Laporte, murdered in the name of Quebec independence. Margaret Trudeau recorded in her memoirs how the tears streamed down Pierre's face when he heard the news of Laporte's death. "It gave him a new bitterness; a hard sadness I had never seen before." Later he told her that he would sacrifice her and their children, if necessary, rather than give in to terrorism. "Once you do that, you're lost."

The Liberals went to the country in 1972 with the slogan "The Land Is Strong." It seemed a transparent attempt to mask the reality of a government without bold initiatives to propose, without in fact a lot of ideas on its agenda. There was no political credit to be gained in having crushed some terrorists who should have been jailed long before. Trudeau had offended a lot of Canadians since 1968 with a style that seemed more like confrontational than participatory democracy. Many others were not so sure they liked the new cost in bilingualism—all those French radio and TV stations, the expense of sending well-paid civil servants back to language school, the damage to insensitive ears caused by airport announcements in French, et cetera—of giving French Canadians equal space in Canada.

Complacent Liberal governments in Canada had proven electorally vulnerable in 1930 and 1957, and it happened again. The Trudeau Liberals survived in a tight minority situation only because Robert Stanfield's Conservatives hardly seemed a dynamic alternative. Trudeau's first term in office was a disillusioning experience for almost everyone, the Prime Minister included.

*   *   *

Trudeau said that the near defeat in 1972 shook his faith in the democratic process. It taught him that appeals to reason could be overwhelmed by emotion, and that he would have to change. He did, becoming less the man of principle, more the man who wanted to retain power. "He deliberately diminished himself into political conventionality and carefully dimmed his originality," George Radwanski noted. No more "like it or lump it" talk. Now Trudeau understood that if he wanted to be right rather than be prime minister, he should have stayed in university.

> The voters wanted a leader to guide them, and I was giving them a professor.... From then on, I resolved to demonstrate the qualities of leadership that were expected of me.... I had not yet fully accepted the role. I even found it a bit repugnant. Personally, I have never felt that I was in need of a leader, perhaps because of the authoritarianism that was so rife in Quebec during my youth, and I

must have assumed that everyone else had the same feeling as I did. But I now realized that that was an illusion; I jumped into action feet-first.

A crass, highly political, lavish, desperate side of Trudeau Liberalism emerged after 1972. It was a response not only to being a minority government depending on support from the New Democratic Party, but also to the wild economic uncertainties that came to characterize the 1970s. The quadrupling of world oil prices in the autumn of 1973 was sign and symptom of a decade of soaring inflation, intense fears of resource shortages, and persistent unemployment and lagging productivity in Canada and the other industrial countries. The relatively stable world order of the postwar quarter-century, in which Canada had done so well and all things had seemed possible politically, appeared to have collapsed. The government felt that it had to act to cushion Canadians against the global energy crisis, the impact of inflation, all the apparent failings of a market economy—and the prospect of the Tories taking over.

The second Trudeau government took the limits off public spending. Egged on by the NDP, it raised welfare payments of all kinds, indexing many of them to the cost of living. It used direct controls to limit domestic petroleum prices, levied huge taxes on petroleum exports, and spent that windfall to subsidize imports. It became more nationalistic, implementing large chunks of Walter Gordon's earlier protectionist agenda, making the Yankees out to be the villains.

Foreign-owned energy companies were a special scapegoat in the energy-obsessed 1970s. Canada's elemental fluids seemed too vital to be controlled for all time by foreigners. The public's instrument for reclaiming control of the oil patch (a bit of a redundancy, since most petroleum reserves were owned by the Crown) would be a great nationally owned petroleum company, Petro-Canada, created in 1974 and subsidized with hundreds of millions of taxpayers' dollars. The New Democrats were delighted. Trudeau had moved from the right-centre of the Liberal Party to the nationalist left, from St. Laurent conservatism to Walter Gordon/Tom Kent activism. He claimed in his *Memoirs* that NDP support had nothing to do with it.

Trudeau usually let his ministers carry the ball on economic issues. His own instincts seem to have tended towards respecting the power of markets in the real world. His governments poured billions into regional development schemes, but privately he thought it would make sense to move people out of depressed regions to where real jobs could be found (he also suggested that Liberals worried about high housing prices in Toronto could move to Regina). In the 1974 election he lambasted the hapless Stanfield for the folly of proposing an instant freeze on wages and prices in a modern economy. Within a year inflation was so serious that in spite of itself the government tried to implement wage and price controls, apparently a complete back-flip by the increasingly acrobatic PM. At the end of 1975, after having spent some time thinking about the ideas of the Canadian-born left-wing economist John Kenneth Galbraith, Trudeau mused publicly that perhaps market failure was endemic after all, and Canadians would have to become accustomed to living with "more authority in our lives," i.e., permanent controls.

He seemed less aloof and more humble in the 1974 campaign. Margaret often appeared on platforms with him, and told Canadians that Pierre had taught her a lot about loving. The Conservatives stumbled and fumbled. On retirement Robert Stanfield became a much-beloved leader, but at the time he seemed like an ageing, slow-moving butler claiming a right to sit at the head of the table. He never became credible on either economic matters or Quebec. Trudeau regained a majority in 1974, and then led his government into another prolonged planning exercise from which little emerged. The answers to most Canadian problems—the decade-long search for a credible industrial policy, for example—seemed to boil down to more grants, more studies, more civil servants.

*   *   *

In the spring of 1976 Trudeau said that separatism was dead. That November René Lévesque led the separatist Parti Québécois to power in the Quebec provincial election. Well, they had fudged the issue: Lévesque no longer called himself a separatist, speaking instead of "sovereignty association" and promising to hold a referendum before heading in that direction. Canadians were so alarmed anyway that Trudeau had to go on national television to reassure them that the country was still strong.

Many French-speaking Quebecers had not been satisfied by the advent of "French power" in Ottawa. They also wanted to strengthen

French power in Quebec, including the dominance of the French language. The English-Canadian backlash against bilingualism had been intense and often irritating to the Québécois. A bitter dispute over the use of French in the commercial airspace over Quebec swung enough votes to the PQ in 1976 to topple the weak, scandal-ridden Bourassa government. Trudeau held power in Ottawa, and now Lévesque had gained it in Quebec City: the two combatants were about to fight for the future of Canada.

Trudeau had few allies among leading politicians. For years the New Democrats, thinking with their hearts, had been willing to go to almost any lengths to appease Quebec. The Conservatives were intent on forging a politically profitable alliance with the nationalist right in Quebec, and so had flirted with special status, with the "two nations" idea, with co-operative federalism, and with any Québécois willing to call himself a Tory. Should the whole federation be further decentralized to give more powers to all of the provinces? Joe Clark, who replaced Stanfield as Conservative leader in 1976, seemed to think so, talking about the need to think of Canada as a "community of communities."

Nobody knew much about Clark, but the premiers of most of the provinces were pleased with views like his. Provincial governments had continued to expand during the early Trudeau years. Trudeau was not the Ottawa-knows-best centralist, in the mode of the old wartime civil servants, that his enemies liked to call him. He actually leaned towards a classic division-of-responsibilities federalism not seen since the days of Laurier. His government had catered to rather than interfered with the provinces' appetite to do more in their spheres. Transfer payments soared through the seventies. The provincial governments were stronger than ever, cocky, and mostly Conservative. The sense that Canadians had limited, mostly regional identities, had grown everywhere in the country, weakening citizens' sense of being Canadians first.

The new provincialism was almost as intense in Alberta as it was in Quebec. Conservative premier Peter Lougheed believed that the global energy crisis meant a long-overdue opportunity for the west finally to come into its own. As owners of their natural resources, provincial governments would dictate energy policies. Lougheed was infuriated when Ottawa, using its powers to tax and control foreign trade, intervened to create national energy policies that did not maximize Alberta's petro-wealth. Lougheed wanted Ottawa off Alberta's back only a shade less strongly than Lévesque wanted the federal presence out of Quebec. Conservative Ontario was a sleeping giant that did not want to be disturbed by anyone. Social Credit–dominated British Columbia was an occasionally self-obsessed adolescent giant. Conservative Newfoundland would soon be jabbering about control of the fishery and its other offshore resources. Even the Premier of Prince Edward Island talked about being an Islander first, a Maritimer second, and a Canadian third.

Was the crisis of Confederation finally at hand? Trudeau responded to Lévesque's victory by preparing for another attempt at constitutional change. Ottawa also poured money and patronage into Quebec, showing Lévesque and company who had the real economic and political muscles. It conspired at every turn, in one "conference war" after another, to frustrate Quebec's attempts to build an international presence. The province would not be allowed to repeat Canada's step-by-step evolution to independence. Fortunately the United States had absolutely no interest in furthering the Lévesque government's aspirations.

The constitutional discussions failed again as the provinces kept asking for more power. Trudeau complained that he had "almost given away the store." There was little enthusiasm for his pet idea of a charter of rights. Quebec did not want any deal, as the PQ government prepared to hold a referendum on sovereignty association. Some premiers thought the next federal election would see the end of Trudeau and the advent of a more accommodating regime.

In the late 1970s the Trudeau government was slouching towards failure. It had careered from one economic panacea to another—planning, controls, monetarism, industrial strategies—without taming inflation, energy problems, or unemployment. Quebec and the constitution were unresolved. Canadians' expectations were high, their grievances deep. Trudeau and his ilk were "*fédérastes*" in Quebec, "eastern bastards" in the west. Ottawa was depressed and depressing. The elected politicians had voted themselves lavish indexed pensions and whole manuals full of perks. Their idealism spent, civil servants had learned to look after themselves. The political pond was crusting over with a scum of hangers-on, ex-politicians, and former civil servants charging handsome fees to serve as consultants and lobbyists. The noble idea of the "servant state" was corroding into the politics of self-interest and manipulation. The old Ottawa elites, supposedly the best and the brightest Canada could command, now seemed self-serving and out of touch, corrupted by too many years of too much power.*

"Lucky Pierre" had lost the magic touch, perhaps even the will to get it back. In the constitutional and political wars his hard, flippant side—snarling and slapping at his enemies, the spoiled rich kid demeaning opposition MPs as "nobodies" and giving the finger to demonstrators outside his limousine—was most often to the fore. Until a definitive Trudeau biography is written, and perhaps not even then, we will not know how seriously his public life was crippled by the breakup of his marriage. After bearing three children and sampling the highs and lows of being married to the Prime Minister of Canada, Margaret Sinclair decided that she wanted more out of life than her hard-working fiftysomething husband had to offer. She left Pierre for pathetic flights with the jet set and sorry attempts at making a career. She became the first prime minister's wife to "write" memoirs, timing the publication of *Beyond Reason* to coincide with the 1979 election. In a 1982 sequel, *Consequences*, she wrote, "I shall mind all my life that I robbed Pierre of his dignity at various stages of our life together.... Pierre has more dignity than anyone I have ever met, but what I did was unpardonable. I feel ashamed...."

"What is important is the irrepressible spirit of the man—determined to be himself against all advice, all odds, all ambition," Trudeau loyalist Patrick Gossage wrote during this period. Trudeau was not surprised by the PQ's stratagems in these years; he knew the enemy as surely as Laurier had understood the ultramontane priesthood. He claims in his *Memoirs* that Lévesque's victory reinvigorated him.

---

* These tendencies, often attributed incorrectly to the Mulroney years, are nicely described by Richard Gwyn, writing in 1980 in *Northern Magus*: "Public servants watched the politicians, and learned to break the rules. More and more public servants took advantage of the indexed pensions they had engineered for themselves to retire early. Often, they signed up immediately with their old departments, on contract, or ... put their contacts and know-how to work as lobbyists, or 'consultants' as they preferred to be called. This practice, unknown in the past, became so common that in 1976, Trudeau had to issue guidelines to enjoin retired civil servants to 'ensure by their actions that the objectivity and impartiality of government service are not cast in doubt.' All down the line, middle-rank and junior civil servants took their cues from the top. Out the window went the old ideals of integrity and frugality...."

Some thought Trudeau was deeply angered by other Canadians' apparent lack of concern for the future of their country. Most thought he was just out of touch. In the 1979 general election he seemed almost as divorced from reality as Diefenbaker had been in 1963, pleading for a vision of one Canada against separatists, provincialists, and Tories. "Who shall speak for Canada?" he asked, dismissing Joe Clark as a headwaiter for the provinces. If re-elected, Trudeau promised, he would force reform of the constitution by going to the people in a referendum if the provinces still resisted.

Who cared about Trudeau's obsession with the constitution, or his apparently alarmist sense of urgency? He seemed to be like an ageing gunslinger wandering down Main Street trying to pick a fight. Joe Clark was a decent man who might have the knack of working together with other decent Canadians, including the premiers. Peacemakers all, maybe the Canadian way. Compromise rather than conflict, conciliation over confrontation.

The Conservatives took power in May 1979, though without a majority in Parliament or any particularly clear or enthusiastic mandate. At least, though, Canadians had slapped back at Pierre. He waited for a decent interval and announced his resignation. He told an interviewer that his goal in retirement would be to get to know the name of every tree in the woods. Canada's Cincinnatus would take his canoe and paddle back into the northern forest.

*   *   *

His party called him back to duty before the year was out. The Clark government was defeated in the House of Commons on the budget, and there was going to be an election.

The Trudeau resurrectionists had a hard struggle to overcome resistance in the party and from Trudeau himself. It was not clear that the tattered image could be remade. Defeat was a real possibility, especially if voters extended their sympathy to an underdog who had been given a rough ride. Trudeau came back mainly because the referendum was looming in Quebec. He had not lost his taste for fighting separatism, and if he had prime-ministerial power again he would have the high ground and a well-stocked arsenal. "Well, welcome to the eighties," he proclaimed at the Liberal victory celebration on February 18. Lucky

Pierre, indeed: in from the woods, another majority, a last chance to do it right.

Trudeau did not talk frankly about his priorities in the 1980 campaign. To regain power he did what he was told by his "handlers"—an ugly, amoral term used to describe the admen and professional pollsters and party hacks who specialized in fighting elections. The chief Liberal handler in 1980, Senator Keith Davey, later called the campaign "brilliantly cynical"—an astonishing comment by a man at the centre of the political elite in a modern democracy. Davey and Jim Coutts, the other prominent Liberal strategist, advised Trudeau not to make too much of the national unity issue in 1980, and he went along. What Jeffrey Simpson called the "palpable phoniness" of the Liberal campaign brought spectacular short-term benefits and disastrous long-term consequences, for the party, for Trudeau's reputation, for the whole Canadian political system.

*   *   *

Trudeau had decided to bring constitutional reform to a head. During the Quebec referendum campaign on sovereignty association, on May 16, 1980, he spelled out the promise:

> I can make a most solemn commitment that following a "No" vote we will immediately take action to renew the constitution and we will not stop until we have done that.
>
> And I make a solemn declaration to all Canadians in the other provinces ... that we will not agree to your interpreting a "No" vote as an indication that everything is fine and can remain as it was before.
>
> We want change and are willing to lay our seats in the House on the line to have change.

The "No" side probably would have won the referendum anyway, without Trudeau's commitment, and the government would not have been bound to act. Trudeau had probably already made a personal decision to plunge ahead. Ottawa would patriate Canada's constitution, with an amending formula and a Charter of Rights and Freedoms, whether the provinces liked it or not. From the beginning of the process there was never a question of requiring Quebec's consent, for Trudeau had resolved to go ahead without any province's consent. He did not think he was legally bound to have the provinces on side, and, if a last resort was necessary, the government could always consult the people.

The story of the twenty-three-month struggle for a new constitution has been well told in Sheppard and Valpy's *The National Deal* and the first volume of Clarkson and McCall's *Trudeau and Our Times*. No one seriously questions the argument that without Trudeau's iron determination, supported by Cabinet and caucus on this, his issue, there would have been no constitutional consensus. The provinces were still all over the map of parochial arrogance in wanting more powers from Ottawa. They had been intractable and contemptuous of the Clark government, and were now even starting to question the Prime Minister's right to chair constitutional conferences. Trudeau ridiculed their agendas as forming the basis for a "confederation of shopping centres," and forced them to focus their attention on *his* approach to constitutional reform by threatening to proceed unilaterally. With or without provincial support, the Government of Canada would formally request Great Britain to make the final amendments necessary for patriation. If the British refused, the issue could be taken directly to the Canadian people in an election or referendum, leading possibly to a unilateral declaration of independence.

"*Allons-y en Cadillac,*" one of the Quebec backbenchers had said to caucus when it was debating going for a compromise or a full charter of rights. The Premier of Manitoba warned Trudeau that his course of action would "tear the country apart." He answered:

> If the country is going to be torn apart because we bring back from Britain our own constitution after 115 years of Confederation and after more than fifty years of fruitless discussions, and because we have asked for a Canadian charter of rights, when most of you already have provincial charters, then the country deserves to be torn up.

The Trudeau express was partially derailed when the "Gang of Eight" opposing premiers (only Ontario and New Brunswick supported the Government of Canada), supported by the Conservative opposition, succeeded in having the legality of the proposed process put to the Supreme Court. It ruled that a unilateral request to Britain from Ottawa would be perfectly legal, but that it would violate a constitutional convention that had developed since Confederation. In other words, the procedure would be legal but unconstitutional.

This ruling raised the stakes considerably. If Trudeau pressed on, there was more likelihood that Britain would turn him down, quite a bit more chance of losing the only provincial support he had, and even an outside possibility that the Governor-General might precipitate a crisis by refusing to transmit an unconstitutional request. Ontario premier William Davis, as well as influential members of the Cabinet, urged the Prime Minister to compromise. The hold-out premiers had to worry about a national, nationalist referendum in which they would be painted as the enemies of human rights for Canadians. At an early stage in the negotiations the rulers of the provinces had said no to a draft of the constitution that would begin "We, the people of Canada." Trudeau's threats to actually go to the people of Canada gave them serious pause.

The final compromise was hammered out in November 1981, with Jean Chrétien playing an important role brokering the deal, and perhaps the spirit of Mackenzie King hovering over all of Canada. Trudeau agreed to water down the charter with a "notwithstanding" clause, permitting legislatures to override it in selected instances. Nine of the ten provinces then agreed to support the package. There would be no changes in the division of powers in the federation—but, as Trudeau had said back in 1967, the charter would transfer power from governments to the people (unless governments risked popularity by using the override).

Only Quebec refused to agree to what many saw as an ingenious Canadian compromise. Quebec's consent was not necessary in law or to satisfy the convention discovered by the Supreme Court. The Quebec delegation's public bitterness at having been "betrayed" by the other members of the Gang of Eight had to be tempered by the knowledge that René Lévesque, handling himself badly under pressure, had actually been the first to break ranks in the negotiations. "*Trudeau m'a fourré*," Lévesque sobbed on the way back to Quebec City, a beaten man. It was never clear that Lévesque would have signed any deal proposed by Ottawa to renew Confederation. His interest was simply to keep the pot boiling.

The resolution requesting Great Britain to patriate Canada's constitution, with an amending formula and a Charter of Fundamental Rights and Freedoms which included the entrenchment of language rights, was approved by the House of Commons on December 2, 1981, by a vote of 246 to 24. All but three of the members of Parliament from Quebec supported it, as did Joe Clark and most other Conservatives. The Quebec legislature was on record as fundamentally opposing the package. Flags were flying at half-mast on all Quebec government buildings, and the province was challenging the resolution in court (it lost). *Le Devoir* said this was a "fatal day" for Canada.

The Parliament of the United Kingdom passed the Canada Bill in March 1982, its last legislative action affecting Canada. Queen Elizabeth II signed it into law on a cloudy April 17 in Ottawa. The skies turned greyer as Trudeau spoke at the ceremony. Someone quipped, "*Après lui, le déluge.*"

It will never be known whether Trudeau could have carried a referendum—in the whole country, in the key provinces and regions, in Quebec. Many English-speaking Canadians in those years had trouble understanding his sense of urgency, his combative tactics, and the need for a charter in the first place. The confrontational style had usually been disastrous in Canadian history, as the fates of Meighen, Bennett, and Diefenbaker seemed to show. Trudeau's counter-argument was that confrontation had finally worked: "There had been a hell of a lot of nice guys since 1926 and the constitution was never patriated," he told Clarkson and McCall afterwards. "Maybe it took a nasty guy." It was an argument that the good end had justified the rough and risky means, and it would stand up so long as history validated that the end was indeed good.

* * *

History dealt cruelly and quickly with the government's other bold initiative, the National Energy Program. Announced in the autumn of 1980, the NEP was a doctrinaire attempt to take over and mould the nation's energy future. A bewilderingly complicated regime of taxes, controls, subsidies, and incentives was applied to Canadianize the oil and gas industry, keep Canadian energy prices below world levels, stimulate petroleum exploration and development on "Canada lands" in the Northwest Territories and along the continental shelf, and generate $30 billion a year or more in revenues that the federal government could use to benefit all Canadians.

The NEP had only one important economic effect. In a few months it stimulated a massive transfer of Canadian wealth to foreign investors as public and private Canadian companies were encouraged to buy up petroleum assets at what proved to be the highest prices in history. The foreigners must still be laughing at the dim-wittedness of Canadian nationalists, buying wildly at the top of the market in an orgy of Walter Gordonism.

Everything else about the NEP crashed into ruins and disrepute in 1981, as it turned out that the intellectual foundation of the government's energy strategy was completely fallacious. The NEP was based on assumptions about permanent shortages of supply and rising prices that were a total misreading of reality and the workings of the petro-market. The high prices of the seventies had dampened demand for petroleum products while vastly increasing their supply. The price of oil collapsed in 1981 and continued to decline fitfully throughout the 1980s. Hothouse Canadian oil companies like Dome Petroleum collapsed, Petro-Canada became a taxpayer-supported basket-case, the private industry blamed its considerable problems on the NEP, Alberta alienation heightened, and the federal government's reputation for intelligence and judgement was mortally wounded. The whole energy-planning elite had failed to understand elementary market economics. Their only comfort was the excuse that almost everyone else, including the sheikhs of Arabia, had also got their figures wrong.

The extreme recession of the early eighties cast a dark shadow over the remnants of other bold economic initiatives. Industrial strategies aimed at subsidizing "winners" to make Canada globally competitive had not had any noticeable effects. Industrial bailouts kept marginal companies alive at heavy costs to the taxpayer, and caused every failing firm in the country to whine for government help. Regional "equalization" had bound most of Atlantic Canada and large parts of Quebec in whining dependence on a constant flow of federal cheques. The attempt to control foreign investment had deterred it, hurting the Canadian economy. Everywhere they had been applied, the visible hands of the planning generation had been clumsy, unproductive, damaging. In 1983 Trudeau's ageing wizards unveiled a special Scientific Research Tax Credit, designed to stimulate research and development on industrial frontiers. In 1984 they suspended it in the face of $2.8 billion in losses to the federal treasury and mounting evidence of complete chaos in its administration.

The Liberals had grasped at visionary straws. They had hoped that the NEP and a wave of resource "megaprojects" would generate the revenues necessary to keep the social-service state solvent. As resource prices collapsed and the recession hit, they had no taste for retrench-ment, and just kept spending. The Government of Canada ran its last budgetary surplus in 1972–73. In 1979–80 it spent $12 billion more than it took in; in 1982–83 the deficit topped $24 billion, and the next year it was over $32 billion.

Canada's foreign trade was also beginning to seem imperilled in a bru-tally competitive world that was shaping itself into major free-trade blocs. In the 1970s the Trudeau government had dreamed of reducing Canada's reliance on the American market, but its initiatives had floundered. Now it began to consider how to make sectoral free-trade deals with the Ameri-cans to protect Canadian access to the world's richest market.

Faintly praised for its constitutional coup, the Trudeau government was roundly, widely damned for mismanaging the economy. Its popularity collapsed to the lowest levels since Canadian polling had begun. Canadi-ans remembered all the complaints they had had about the Trudeau administration in the late 1970s, and now added more anger at the thought of having been gulled by the "brilliant cynicism" of the 1980 campaign. Were all politicians intellectually and morally dishonest, or was it just Canada's discredited "government party," Mr. Trudeau's Liberals?

The Prime Minister had never been front and centre in economic policy-making. In the confusions of the early 1980s he had seemed aloof and apart, living in a world of his own, perhaps meditating on the gap between public expectations and government's ability to deliver. Perhaps he was also taking quiet satisfaction in having finally achieved constitu-tional peace in the land. None of the provinces, including Quebec, had any taste for resuming that war. It was time to get on to other problems. The Lévesque government drifted into confusion and division as decades of smoking and dissipation took their toll on the premier. Among the young and ordinary Québécois the separatist impulse seemed finally to have been quelled. The Liberals returned to power provincially in 1985.

Trudeau's most public performances after the constitution were in international affairs. He had enjoyed foreign travel and summitry, and was always a media star outside of Canada, even without Margaret, but few observers felt that his governments had played a significant role in the affairs of nations. True to the original foreign-policy review, the 1970s were a decade of retrenchment and concentration on buttressing Canadian sover-eignty. French and Parti Québécois attempts to destabilize Canada were neutralized, the American elephant was yelled at and poked and lectured.

(The Americans took the minor irritation more or less good-naturedly. Trudeau had no public quarrels with U.S. presidents. Richard Nixon privately thought he was an "asshole," but most Canadians thought worse of Nixon.) Great Britain continued to fade into an insignificance that earlier generations of Canadians would never have believed possible. On April 15, 1969, Charles Ritchie, Canada's High Commissioner in London, wrote that "there is no interest in Canada in tightening relations with the United Kingdom or in reporting home on British policies. Dispatches from Paris are read because French politics affect our future as a nation, whereas Britain has virtually no influence at all."

World leaders seemed to think that Trudeau was smart but shallow and erratic. Canada was no longer a good diplomatic soldier, carefully building "credit" through military contributions and helpful fixing with its allies. Trudeau did some of that, especially at the U.N., but often he expected his ideas to be listened to on their merits and because of his position ("I felt it was the duty of a middle power like Canada, which could not sway the world with the force of its armies, to at least try to sway the world with the force of its ideals"). Such consistency as there was in his international outlook seemed to centre on a desire to build bridges to underdeveloped countries, to help the third world, to engage in "North–South" dialogue, and to aid and abet the socialist politicians, some of whom were dreamers, some bloody dictators, who emerged from the 1950s. Nothing much resulted from these initiatives except more American irritation at Canadians cozying up to Fidel Castro.

In 1983 Trudeau decided that East–West tensions were building dangerously, and that he owed it to posterity to make one last effort to use his power to advance the cause of world peace, a commitment he had felt ever since his youth. His last fling on the world stage was a well-publicized "peace initiative," jetting from one capital to another, pleading with presidents and prime ministers to cool down world tensions. Almost no one outside of his office, and perhaps not many inside it, believed the tour had any effect. Americans were particularly scathing in semi-public comments about Canada's prime minister behaving like a leftist high on pot. Up in heaven, the spirit of Lester Pearson must have wondered at the ironies of Trudeau's "pirouette"—turning himself into a helpful fixer, but without the credibility to be heard.

J.L. Granatstein and Robert Bothwell conclude their exhaustive study of Trudeau's foreign policy with the judgement that in foreign affairs he was never a serious thinker, "only an adventurer in ideas with great articulation and little commitment." During his prime minister-ship, in their view, "Canada sank back to its normal place in the centre of the third rank." The implication of this bleak assessment is that Canada played about the same non-role in the final struggles of the Cold War as it did in response to the rise of fascism in the 1930s. When the military effort of World War II is factored in, it may be that the country's contri-bution to the defeat of Nazism contrasts sharply with its post-1962 opt-ing out of the struggle against Communist totalitarianism. Mackenzie King had done more by staying home and thinking about unity, and then having his country do its share. Canada left it up to the United States to defeat the second evil empire.

During a long walk in a snowstorm on the night of February 28, 1984, Trudeau decided to retire. The announcement came on leap-year day. He had seriously considered staying on, telling one of his ministers that politics was still fun and he couldn't think of anything else he wanted to do. Then he realized that he wanted to bring up his sons outside of public life. "Most important of all, I had done what I had come into politics to do.... I had done my best. There wasn't much more time to give.... The philosopher George Santayana defines happiness as taking 'the measure of your powers'. That night I took the measure of mine. It was time to go home."

Trudeau's self-assessment included the knowledge that he had little taste for rebuilding, as an opposition leader, if the Liberals were defeated. They would have been. After fifteen years as prime minister, Trudeau would have been formidable in opposition, if and when he had made an effort. Instead he retired, and remained formidable in private life.

*   *   *

Pierre Trudeau's era is a study in the limits of government. The Trudeau years set major limits on the role of government in Canadian life in two ways. First, the Charter of Rights and Freedoms limited the power of governments to infringe on the rights of individuals, a danger Trudeau had first come to appreciate while experiencing the abuse of government in Quebec during the Duplessis years. Second, a long and dismal record of failure by Trudeauites steeped in Galbraithian, Keynesian, socialist, and other anti-market schools of economics became an object lesson in what governments could not achieve in a competitive market economy.

Other countries—Britain in the seventies, the United States during the Carter presidency, France in the eighties—learned similar lessons. The political left everywhere entered a new period of intellectual confusion, the end of which is not yet in sight.

Trudeau's career was about enabling Canadians to take control over their lives. The state got out of their bedrooms. The state could no longer interfere with their human rights. Power was being transferred to the people. Trudeau, on the surface the most elitist of all Canadian prime ministers, turned out to be the most important populist in the country's political history—baffling to many because he was so far ahead of his time, popular in retirement, and despite himself, because he had captured the spirit of the age.

A certain amount of the populist direction of the Trudeau years emerged *faute de mieux* as Ottawa realized that it lacked the capacity to do all or even most of the things that Canadians had come to expect from their governments. More Canadians would have to take control of their destinies, in more areas of their lives, whether they wanted to or not. The future would see less dependency, less deference.

Trudeau's special characteristic was his own inner populism. He did not bother to attack such relics of the past as the monarchy, but everyone knew that he inwardly thumbed his nose at the British. Everyone knew that he was his own man entirely, not French, not English, not a wannabee American, but a citizen of the world, a student of the Western intellectual heritage, a traveller who had found his way from the kingdom of Canada to what Edith Wharton calls the "republic of the spirit." One of the reasons why Trudeau, for all his shortcomings, retained immense respect in the country was the sense that he was a pretty good role model for taking charge of one's life. In the 1950s you wanted your children to grow up to be like Mike Pearson. In the 1980s you wanted them to be as tough and self-contained and as republican as Pierre Trudeau.

The Canadian nation had been built long before Trudeau came to power. The net effect of his governments' "nation-building" economic strategies—industrial policies, regional development schemes, energy policies, and tax juggling—was to help weaken the economic sinews of a country whose golden age as a resource treasure-house was beginning to run out. In 1984 the Trudeau Liberals left public finances in a hell of a mess, with the deficit soaring close to $40 billion. It was irresponsibility and incompetence not seen since the days of Laurier's railway policies.

But the country had also been saved. With constitutional reform, the twenty-year crisis of Confederation, sparked by the Quiet Revolution of the 1960s, seemed to have been brought to a conclusion. History is not a laboratory, so we can never weigh people and events against certain knowledge of alternatives. Put negatively, there is much truth in the observation by Denise Bombardier that if Trudeau had become a separatist in the 1960s Quebec would have been independent by the eighties. Positively, it can surely be said that without his drive, without his toughness, there would have been no constitutional reform and no Charter of Rights. Without these there might have been no more Canada.

Can it be said that Trudeau saved his country? One of the premiers who sat with him in the constitutional talks remembered him to Clarkson and McCall as "A great man. And so diamond-hard he glittered." He never led his country in war, but perhaps the most apt comparison is with Abraham Lincoln.

One of the differences in the careers of the two statesmen, however, is that Andrew Johnson did not know how to begin to undo Lincoln's achievement, and perhaps did not have the will. The Conservative who followed Trudeau had both.

10

MULRONEY
Throwback

"One thing about the old Trud, he's got a lotta class." Speaking to an early biographer, Brian Mulroney offered Trudeau this kind of respect a few months before winning Trudeau's job. Years later, when Trudeau came out of retirement to help destroy Mulroney's constitutional initiatives, the Prime Minister's thoughts were darker and somewhat obsessive. Mulroney left office in 1993, nine years after Trudeau, pleading with history to blame Trudeau for what most perceived to have been one of his own central failures.

By that time Mulroney had been for years the most unpopular prime minister in Canadians' memory. They blamed him for much of what was wrong with the country. And nobody, except a small circle of old buddies and Tory party hacks, would have said that the old Mulroney had had a lotta class.

He was a man hard to place in the socio-economic sense. His was a classic North American success story, of leaving behind his roots in the working class and scrambling up economic and political ladders until he reached the very top. He was an electrician's son from Baie-Comeau, on the bleak north shore of the St. Lawrence, who by the age of forty had become president of the Iron Ore Company of Canada and bought a handsome house in Westmount. Where was his new home, a reporter asked Mulroney. "You know the mountain?" he answered. "Right on the top. Right on the fucking top."

In 1983, without descending to serve any kind of apprenticeship in any elected office, Mulroney won the leadership of the Conservative Party. In September 1984 he swept into office with the largest caucus in Canadian history, taking 211 of 282 seats. In the November 1988 election he retained a majority, making him politically the most successful Tory prime minister since Macdonald. He left office as an undefeated heavyweight champion of Canadian electoral politics, to retire back to the mountain, with holidays in resorts like Palm Beach. The Mulroneys had done it all, except win the people's respect. That, the polls showed, was still reserved for Trudeau.

Four months after Mulroney left office, voters destroyed the Progressive Conservative Party, reducing it to two seats in the House of Commons.

Mulroney's problems did not centre on questions of toughness— although Trudeau thought so, lumping Mulroney with Joe Clark as just another of the "wimps" who were afraid to stand up to separatists. Mulroney was tough enough when he felt he had to be: in his personal life when he gave up drinking and smoking; in politics when he clawed his way to the leadership, held his party together through thick and thin, took humiliating defeats on his big jaw and kept on smiling. He was clever, too, and he could be immensely charming and a true friend to people in need. A bit of a wild Irish lad in his youth, he had settled down to be a good family man, upholding the values many North Americans cherished. The Mulroneys were a model of the close-knit, loving family.

Mulroney's misfortune was to be intellectually and temperamentally out of touch with the new Canada of the 1980s. He understood the Canadian economy, better perhaps than most of his predecessors. He understood how to get to the top, how to get power. But he had no sense of how to use power in ways that Canadians would respect. Although his own mobility had been spectacular, he was not an innovator, not a breaker of moulds. Like many self-made men, he saw little wrong in the system that had made him. In the Baie-Comeau universe you deferred to the mill manager until you got that job, and then people deferred to you. In politics you got elected and then you ran the country, and if you did a good job you got respected and loved, the way people had come to love Sir John A.

But Canada had changed. Nobody deferred, to Brian Mulroney or any other politician after Trudeau. By the 1980s the democratic spirit, so thoroughly distrusted by Sir John A. and many of his successors, had spread so widely in Canada that the whole political class, the whole political system, was in danger of losing its legitimacy. Traditional ways of governing the country had broken down, as the limits of government effectiveness had long since been reached. Institutions and attitudes based on the social and political structures that had produced Mulroney and most of his ilk were now anachronisms. New groups insisted on their right to a place in the political sun.

In the new Canada, politics was no longer going to be about moving through the social classes, rising yourself, and helping others rise. In the age of the charter it would be about treating citizens as real equals. In an age of individualism, nobody had "class" any more, in the old hierarchical sense that invited patronage and deference. Everyone had rights. The coming of age of real democracy was creating conundrums for political leaders that had baffled even Trudeau. They completely flummoxed the Conservatives. Perhaps the surprising thing about Mulroney, who ought to have been born in Boston about 1900—he would have made a great Irish mayor—is that he rose so high and lasted so long in a country whose spirit had passed him by.

* * *

With one gesture, literally with a nod of his head or a wave of his hand, Joe Clark could have destroyed Mulroney's political career on June 11, 1983.

The second ballot at the Conservative leadership convention had Clark leading Mulroney, 1,085 votes to 1,021. John Crosbie, the Newfoundlander who had been Clark's finance minister in the aborted 1979 government, was a strong third at 781. David Crombie, who had come fourth with 67 votes, was eliminated and immediately went over to Crosbie. There was little doubt that on the next ballot Clark and Mulroney would hold their strength, and Crosbie would finish third and be eliminated. After that, more of his delegates would vote for Mulroney than Clark. So Mulroney was on his way to victory, unless Clark now withdrew in favour of Crosbie. If that happened there was little doubt that Clark's delegates, most of whom despised Mulroney for having undermined Clark's leadership, would have put Crosbie over the top. "Face it," Crosbie's campaign manager told the Clark camp, "you can lose to us or lose to Mulroney."

Clark refused to withdraw, and lost to Mulroney. John Crosbie served as a senior minister in Mulroney's governments. He will be remembered as the plainest-speaking federal politician of his generation, and as the last unilingual old party man to come close to being prime minister. Crosbie might have overcome the unilingualism had not the plain-spokenness led him to say during the leadership campaign that he could not understand why the Prime Minister of Canada needed to speak French any more than he needed to speak Chinese or German. As Tory leader, Crosbie would have been unacceptable to Quebec, unable to win seats there. Perhaps he would have become prime minister anyway.

But Joe Clark was too committed to reviving the Conservatives in Quebec to take that risk. He would not hazard a return to the old days when the Tories were the party of the Anglo-Saxon ethnic group. He forced Conservatives to choose between candidates, himself and Mulroney, who had a real chance of winning in Quebec. On the fourth ballot, Mulroney beat Clark, 1,584 votes to 1,325.

Joe Clark's own passable bilingualism was one of the reasons why he had come out of nowhere to snatch the Tory leadership in 1976, beating two Quebecers, Claude Wagner and Brian Mulroney, in the final balloting. It was impressive that a young politician from High River, Alberta, had taken the trouble to learn French, and was committed to making the PCs a national party again, as they had not been, for more than one term at a time, since the days of Macdonald and Cartier.

Clark was still moist behind the ears in 1976, having only been in Parliament since 1972, but everyone knew he was totally committed to building the party. His Tory roots went back to his school-days in the 1950s. At a time when other young Canadians idolized movie and rock and sports stars, he had given his heart to John Diefenbaker. From his young PC days through to his election to Parliament, Joe Clark paid so many party dues that he never found time to make an independent career in life. He was as pure a professional politician as Canadians got in the late twentieth century.

Brian Mulroney was also a party animal, having attended his first PC convention in 1956 as vice-chairman of Youth for Diefenbaker. He learned his French easily, growing up bilingual in the company pulp town of Baie-Comeau. Like Clark, Mulroney thrived on campus Tory politics and networking. Both were big men in the party before anyone outside of it knew their names. Unlike Clark, Mulroney finished his law degree and began making a name for himself practising in Montreal. Through the Stanfield years he worked doggedly in the almost hopeless cause of building the party in Quebec. When he first ran for the leadership in 1976, he could be forgiven for not having a seat in Parliament. Jesus Christ would have had trouble winning a Quebec riding as a Tory in those years, even if He had been bilingual. Why would a lesser man offer himself for crucifixion?

In both his leadership campaigns Mulroney billed himself as a man who could bring Quebec into the Conservative fold. The failures in the Stanfield years had not been for lack of trying. The leader had tried desperately to find a formula, "*deux nations,*" or a lieutenant, Marcel Faribault or Claude Wagner, who would deliver the votes of right-wing Quebecers, the constituents of the old Union Nationale and, increasingly, of the new Parti Québécois. By the early 1980s Joe Clark was still doggedly building in Quebec, collaborating in some cases with PQ sympathizers who in 1980 had voted in the Quebec referendum to break up Canada. Clark thought the prospective gains for the party were worth the risk involved in dealing with people of suspect loyalties. In compensation for *péquistes'* self-recycling into loyal Canadians, Clark would have been willing to reopen the constitution to begin to meet some of René Lévesque's terms.

Mulroney criticized Clark for cuddling up to Lévesque's people. "I'm not playing footsie with the PQ," he told delegates in 1983. "Another candidate is developing an elegant style in that regard." Lévesque made known his belief that Mulroney was a "mini-Trudeau" in taking a hard line on the constitution and that Clark would probably be the most accommodating English Canadian. Mulroney claimed he could win Quebec without having to negotiate with people like Lévesque.

To bill Mulroney as another Trudeau would have been the kiss of death in the Conservative Party. To see him as a politician *like* Trudeau, perfectly at home in either language, a Canadian and a Quebecer, above all a winner, was to make him seem a lot more attractive than poor Joe. The ultimate Tory dream, after all, was to develop and be loyal to leaders who had the royal jelly of Trudeau and the other great Liberal prime ministers.

Everyone knew that John Crosbie had a superior mind, good business sense, and, save for his habit of saying what he really felt, keen political instincts. By 1983 a fair number of knowledgeable Canadians agreed with Crosbie's leadership campaign suggestion that Canada should enter a common market–like free-trade agreement with the United States. But

Joe Clark, who had every reason to despise Mulroney, and almost certainly did, could not bring himself to throw away Quebec.

*   *   *

Conservatives were so hungry for a real winner. What a mess the party's history had been in the twentieth century, really ever since the death of Sir John A., Borden's limited success notwithstanding. John Diefenbaker, in a sense, had been the biggest disappointment of them all, because he rose so high and fell so fast and did so much harm to the party before it got rid of him. Joe Clark and Brian Mulroney had both swallowed their customary loyalty and supported the dump-Diefenbaker campaign.

It later became fashionable in Tory circles to revere Robert Stanfield as the best prime minister Canada never had. That was romantic nonsense. Stanfield, a slow-spoken and apparently slow-thinking man with an unremarkable record as Premier of Nova Scotia, had been no match at all for Trudeau in the national arena. The best that could be said of Stanfield was that he was honest and earnest, in the fashion of a John Bracken, as he bumbled around trying to find a role for his often dispirited and divided party.

Then Joe Clark had emerged as yet another nondescript Tory. "Joe Who?" the media asked. "Joe the wimp," they sniggered at a man with no chin and no achievements outside of politics and a wife who would not take her husband's name. Clark persevered. He broke through. In 1979 he brought the Tories to power for the first time in sixteen years. And then he blew it—losing the confidence of the House, losing the 1980 election, and, in the eyes of many of his followers, losing his moral right to keep on leading the party, unless you admitted that Tories always would be just a group of wimps and losers. Political scientists found a name for the phenomenon of insiders and outsiders fighting constantly about leadership in a visibly divided, perpetually out-of-power party. They called it "the Tory syndrome."

It happened that Joe Clark was beginning to grow on people by 1983. He displayed grace under pressure, a dry wit and a quick intelligence, and an apparent capacity to learn from his mistakes. He was not arrogant; he seemed to be able to relate to ordinary Canadians; he had obviously been treated badly by irresponsible media. Clark was interested in political ideas, and had worked hard to articulate a view of Canada as a "community of communities" whose central government ought to respect local identities and interests rather than ride roughshod over them. With his party far ahead of the Liberals in the polls, there was every prospect by 1983 that he would soon be prime minister again. All he had to do was keep the lid on the dissidents in the party, keep "the Tory syndrome" under control.

Clark decided to open the party to another leadership contest when he was supported by "only" 66.9 per cent of the delegates at the Winnipeg convention in January 1983. Most observers, including Brian Mulroney, thought Clark's support was solid enough for him to soldier on. They were astonished when he announced that it wasn't good enough. He was going to settle the matter of party unity once and for all.

The decision soon became more evidence that Clark was disaster-prone. Having thrown away his government, he now threw away his leadership.

The race to succeed Clark was hard and close. Many English-speaking Canadians were drawn to Crosbie's intelligence and wit, but Mulroney seemed the Tory candidate most likely to be a winner. In 1976 he had been too much the flashy, high-spending unknown, just another slick Montreal lawyer with rich friends and a lust for power. He still had all those attributes in 1983, but he had toned down the flashiness (this time running a "rusty station wagon" campaign; aides joked about the cost of putting rust on all those new Cadillacs). Although he still had not bothered to run for office, he had kept moving upward; he was now president of the Iron Ore Company. And, of course, he promised to deliver Quebec.

Take Mulroney as leader and you took a man who had shown that it was possible to win in life—to rise from the working class of a frontier town right to the top, and be bilingual and a good party man to boot, and have a beautiful wife and no apparent bad habits.

What about the dark side? Had Mulroney been disloyal to Clark, a back-stabber, sacrificing party unity to his overweening ambition? Everyone knew that many of Mulroney's friends had been active in the campaign to undermine Clark's leadership. No one ever found a smoking gun or a bloody knife in Mulroney's hands, and the truth was that Clark's most powerful opposition came from inside his own caucus, from MPs who could never forgive him for the debacle of 1980, never believe he was fit to lead them.

Yes, it was evident that Mulroney, who had grown up in the world of the Union Nationale, knew his way around the seamy side of politics. But so did Clark, whose organizers matched Mulroney's men dollar for dollar, drunk for drunk, in rounding up Quebec delegates for leadership conventions. Since the days of Macdonald and Laurier most party loyalists had understood that a little rough stuff was part of the game. Many of them appreciated skilful political swordsmanship, because they knew that winners got power and paid off. Mulroney the leadership candidate made clear, for example, that he understood how power would lead to jobs for good Conservatives. Even more than Clark, Mulroney was known as a *patroneux*, who would deliver on the judgeships and senatorships and directorships the Liberals had monopolized for twenty years. There were winks and nudges and jokes from Brian about the jobs the boys would get under his government. As he had said back in 1976, quoting Allister Grosart, "What this party needs is its two feet right in the trough."

Everyone knew that Mulroney was a people person, a networker, rather than an idea man or a policy man. His critics said he was as shallow as a bird bath and always had been,* a fair clone of Sam Malone, the Irish bartender on the popular television series "Cheers." But many who got their kicks out of being delegates at leadership conventions were also fans of sitcoms and soaps. Mulroney was obviously not dim-witted, and he had moved sensibly and fashionably with the intellectual tides—presenting himself as a moderate progressive in 1976, a more free-enterprise, market-oriented, business-friendly candidate in 1983. Want to know his views? Okay, the team recycles some speeches into a little book, *Where I Stand*. Lots of platitudes and clichés, to be sure, but nothing dangerous, nothing extreme. Brian Mulroney would not be caught playing footsie with separatists. And, he told delegates, he was not going to get Canada into another debate about free trade with the United States.

---

* A friend from Quebec days in the 1970s, Conrad Black, observed of Mulroney in his memoirs (*A Life in Progress*), "the Pollyanna flippancy of many of his positions disconcerted his friends, including me.... His knowledge of how to get ahead was geometrically greater than any notion he had of what to do when he reached his destination.... his ideas of government consisted of a few platitudes about English–French relations and labour management co-operation. It was pretty thin gruel for an aspiring prime minister."

He used Trudeau's analogy about the dangers of living with an elephant. He said the issue had been settled in the 1911 election. "It affects Canadian sovereignty, and we'll have none of it, not during leadership campaigns, nor at any other times."

*   *   *

So he won, and he was parachuted into a safe seat in Nova Scotia, and he began getting used to what he called "this House stuff." Then when the Liberals changed leaders, and momentarily surged ahead in the polls, it was not so clear that victory would be automatic. Canadians wanted to put the Trudeau years behind them, but perhaps they would conclude that John Turner's was the fresher face. Despite Mulroney's attempts to appear forward-looking, it was already apparent in 1984 that he had many old-style political traits.

He was a male-bonder, for example, whose preference for surrounding himself with old buddies from college days at St. Francis Xavier and Laval smacked of cronyism. Give him power and he would be loyal to all of his cronies in the great big Tory party. One day early in the election campaign, some of the reporters got talking to Mulroney about his promise in the leadership campaign to give some jobs to Liberals "when there isn't a living breathing Tory left without a job in this country." Mulroney told the boys, "I was talking to Tories then, and that's what they want to hear. Talking to the Canadian public during an election campaign is something else.... I'm taking the high road now."

Having thus admitted that he would take diametrically opposed views depending on his audience, Mulroney got on to the controversy over Trudeau's appointment of a tired Liberal hack, Bryce Mackasey, to an ambassadorship. Mulroney used one of his favourite phrases to excuse Mackasey: "Let's face it, there's no whore like an old whore. If I'd been in Bryce's position I'd have been right in there with my nose in the public trough like the rest of them."

One of the ubiquitous, revealing dishonesties of modern political life is politicians' habit of telling the media their real thoughts in "off-the-record" conversations—the assumption apparently being that truth is too dangerous to be reported. Mulroney thought this conversation was off the record. To his deep embarrassment, it was not. Smartly, Mulroney offered an abject apology, suggesting he had been only kidding in those informal comments.

A few days later, in formal debate on national television with John Turner, he took the high road and the high horse with a splendid rejoinder to Turner's claim of having "had no option" but to go along with Trudeau's final wave of political pay-offs:

> You had an option, sir. You could have said, "I'm not going to do it. This is wrong for Canada and I'm not going to ask Canadians to pay the price." You had an option, sir, to say "no" and you chose to say "yes" to the old attitudes and the old stories of the Liberal Party. That, sir, if I may say respectfully, that is not good enough for Canadians.

Mulroney and the Conservatives had the best strategic advice money could buy. By the 1980s advertising agencies had come to play second fiddle to professional pollsters, whose organizations monitored the public pulse and interpreted its vagaries to their masters. They still saw elections as marketing exercises. Allan Gregg, president of Decima Research, was Mulroney's master guru. He told the journalist Ron Graham that "The biggest differences between selling Brian Mulroney and selling soap are that soap doesn't talk and its competitors don't say it's a crock of shit." One of the standard jokes about modern politics holds that sincerity is everything; if you can fake that, you've got it made. The advisers worked carefully with Mulroney on the sincerity issue, and found him a quick study. The apology for the off-the-record comments worked. The television performances may have seemed overblown and oleaginous to the cynical, but the words were right there on tape for the record.

Mulroney the campaigner was happy promising people the things they wanted, and he liked to use rhetoric inflated with images of morality and sincerity. Irishman's blarney, but with a kind of pedigree: he told biographer Ian MacDonald that he had always been impressed with the ringing phrases in the speeches that Theodore Sorenson had written for John F. Kennedy back in the early 1960s. So Mulroney could talk about protecting Canada's welfare system as a "sacred trust not to be tampered with," and in a speech at Sept-Îles, Quebec, during the campaign he could promise to find a way of getting Quebec to support the Canadian constitution "with honour and enthusiasm." Whatever his promises might amount to (journalists and opponents added up the dollar value of his pledges, but Gregg's polling suggested that the voters weren't interested), the Tory leader seemed sincere, was proving himself a fresher face than tired old Turner and the Trudeau gang, and seemed to deserve a chance.

We cannot know whether Joe Clark would also have swept the country in 1984. The national mood had been so hostile to the Liberals for so long that a Conservative Party led by Mickey Mouse would probably have overcome Turner's blip in the polls and cut him down. But it was Brian Mulroney who led the landslide, and could take credit for it, and thus emerged as the Conservatives' winner extraordinaire. He led the party right to the top of the big rock-candy mountain, creating a reputation as a masterful campaigner, a real winner, that his followers never publicly doubted. All the Tories, including Joe Clark (who always played the game and always lost), were friends of Brian's now.

* * *

Conservatives blamed most of Canada's problems on the hated Trudeau and his style. Trudeau had been confrontational. He had beaten people up, divided the nation, created wounds. Conservatives would be conciliatory, healers. They would bring people together, reunite Canada. The models for the leadership style Brian Mulroney tried to effect in Ottawa included his own experience as a negotiator in industrial disputes (shades of Mackenzie King!) and the wonderful success that Ontario PCs had experienced during decades of moderately progressive leadership. Ontario's 1984 incumbent premier, William Davis, was a politician who could sit on a barbed-wire fence, puff his pipe, and say he was just rocking on his verandah. If Mulroney developed into a bilingual Bill Davis, he could go a long way as prime minister, right down the middle of the pre-Trudeau tradition of brokerage politics.

The 1980s were a decade of neoconservative ascendency in Ronald Reagan's America and Margaret Thatcher's Britain, but not, at first, in Brian Mulroney's Canada. In his first term he moved quickly to the political centre. Several of his cruder right-wing friends were cast aside, garnering senatorships or diplomatic posts as consolation prizes, as Mulroney made his peace with the moderate Tory establishment, including the strategists of the "Big Blue Machine" that had been so important to the Davis government in Ontario. Soon there was no obvious difference between Mulroney's administration and the team that a Clark government would have fielded.

"They're all geniuses when they win," Mulroney remarked disparagingly one day about his Ontario friends. "How many seats did they win in Quebec?" He poked himself in the chest: "The Big Blue is right here." Mulroney believed he understood Quebec. He had not been an active participant in the intricate constitutional debates that had raged about Quebec's place in Canada ever since his student days, but he had always thought that accommodating Quebec's aspirations was fundamental to the future of the country. When patriation put an end to the constitutional wars of the Trudeau era in 1982, most Canadians thought the issue was settled. Outside of Quebec, and even in most circles in that province, no one wanted to hear anything about the damned constitution. Mulroney had never criticized Trudeau's initiative or its results. His own vague constitutional position in the leadership race was sketched quickly one day on the back of an airline vomit bag and seemed little different from Trudeau's.

But as early as January 1984 Mulroney told friends that he wanted to be remembered in Canadian history for having achieved a final constitutional settlement. The speech at Sept-Îles on August 6, 1984, contained a clear commitment to reopen the constitution when the time seemed right, and it made clear that the would-be prime minister accepted the view that the Trudeau government had been too centralist. He, Mulroney, would base any constitutional settlement on "respect for provincial authority." The speech was largely written by a close friend from college days who had become a senior adviser to Mulroney, Lucien Bouchard. Like many Conservative candidates and workers in the 1984 election, Bouchard had well-known *péquiste* connections and he had voted for the dissolution of Canada in 1980. Mulroney had no more qualms than Clark before him about bringing separatists into the Conservative Party.

But he was not going to play footsie with the tottering PQ government. Ottawa remained uninterested in negotiating with Quebec until the 1985 victory of the provincial Liberals, led by Robert Bourassa, one of Mulroney's many friends. Trudeau had usually treated Bourassa with contempt or disdain. Mulroney and Bourassa thought it might be possible to do a deal on the constitution. Secret intergovernmental discussions began in 1986.

In the meantime, the government had moved quickly to undo some of the Liberal policies that were most unpopular with the provinces. It dismantled the remnants of the old National Energy Program, signing a formal accord with Alberta, and it made a deal with Brian Peckford's Newfoundland government on control of offshore petroleum resources. Economic nationalism was so out of vogue that the protectionist Foreign Investment Review Agency was rotated through 180 degrees to emerge as Investment Canada, with a mandate to recruit foreign capital. Canada was "open for business again," the Prime Minister told a prestigious group of New York investors in 1984.

Canadian businessmen had high hopes that the Conservatives would also put the nation's finances back on a businesslike basis. The Mulroney government inherited a projected deficit well over $35 billion, a level of borrowing far higher than that of most other industrial countries. Surely the Conservatives, safely in power with a vast majority, would prescribe the bitter medicine of deep spending cuts necessary to restore long-term health to Canadian public life. Mulroney was no doctrinaire right-winger, but he had been a company president and he appeared to know his elementary economics. In an age when everyone realized that governments could not run businesses efficiently, Mulroney would probably also go along with the selling-off of Canada's dinosaurish Crown corporations.

There were two landmarks in the Mulroney government's abandonment of the conservative agenda in economic policy. The first was the decision in April 1985 to spend taxpayers' money subsidizing expansion plans by Domtar, a profitable Quebec-based pulp and paper company. "Domtar's financial situation is better than that of the federal government," Mulroney had said, but he went ahead anyway. Soon it was evident that the Tories were just as committed as the Liberals before them to the politics of grants and subsidies—to create jobs and to buy political support. Cutbacks would be largely cosmetic. The old politics were alive and flourishing brazenly in a country whose national indebtedness was mounting at the rate of nearly $100 million a day.

Most public-finance experts knew that big savings could only be achieved by containing the generosity of the welfare state. A bureaucratic consensus against universalism in social programs had been developing for more than a decade. The advent of the Conservatives seemed the appropriate time to make the change. Finance minister Michael Wilson was anxious to reduce well-to-do Canadians' entitlements to family allowances and old-age pensions, and proposed to do so. He ran into intense criticism from some of those he would disadvantage, as well as from the political left. Opponents could take a stand on the Prime Minister's pledge to respect universality as a "sacred trust." The climax of the early debate on the future of Canada's welfare state was a June 1985 encounter between Mulroney and a sixty-three-year-old demonstrator on Parliament Hill, caught for television. "You lied to us," an angry Solange Denis told Mulroney. "You made us vote for you, then, goodbye Charlie Brown." The government backed off, forgoing the possibility of biting into social expenditures to bring down the deficit.

By mid-1985 it was clear that the Conservatives had little interest in taking the heat that would be generated by a serious attempt to return Canada to fiscal responsibility. An impressive boom had developed after the sharp recession of the early 1980s. Both Keynesian orthodoxy and conservative common sense suggested that public finances ought to be returned to a zero-deficit basis, preferably a surplus. Perhaps remembering the debacle of 1979, when the Clark government had tried to bring in "short-term pain for long-term gain," the Mulroneyites chose the short-term political benefits of continued spending over the long-term good of Canada.

As finance minister from 1984 to 1991, Michael Wilson was responsible for the accumulation of more public debt than all of his peacetime predecessors combined. His successor, Don Mazankowski, continued the borrowing spree. Budget presentations by allegedly responsible men and women became a pathetic spectacle, as the Department of Finance annually made projections of falling deficits that came nowhere near reality. Either the civil servants were thoroughly incompetent or they were deferring to the stupid optimism of incompetent politicians. Neither civil servants nor politicians had the courage or will to resign.

The ultimate responsibility for a monstrous build-up of debt during a period of relative prosperity rested with the Prime Minister. Here was a failure of intelligence and will, a betrayal of the Conservative Party's supporters and the country's children, that would burden Canada for generations to come. The government's only defence was that it was trying to exercise restraint, and doing a better job than the Liberals had. High levels of spending, the welfare and grant mentality, had been a hallmark of Canadian political culture for more than thirty years. Powerful vested interests would have screamed bloody murder if their access to regular handouts had been cut off. It would have taken a bolder, stronger, more conservative man than Brian Mulroney to turn his back on the habits of a generation and return to the sense of stewardship of, say, Mackenzie King, Louis St. Laurent, or even John Diefenbaker.

The Mulroney government's trade policy was much bolder, to the point of being almost revolutionary. Until the 1930s the historic Tory trade stance had been protectionist, the National Policy. As Mulroney had said in his leadership campaign, the issue of free trade with the United States had been settled when Borden beat Laurier in 1911. It did not go away. By 1986, despite Mulroney's earlier statements, despite trade policy not having been an issue in the election, the Government of Canada was committed to negotiating a free-trade pact with the Americans. The discussions culminated in an agreement in October 1987.

Mulroney's precise role in the coming of the Canada–U.S. Free Trade Agreement (FTA) will not be clear until the inner history of his administration is written. The public record suggests that his government was reacting to a consensus that had formed among business, academic, and civil service elites on the need to take action to safeguard Canada's access to its largest foreign market. Since the 1930s the gradual liberalization of cross-border trade had allowed natural geographic and economic relationships to create an integrated continental economy. The economic decline of Great Britain and the protectionist stance of the European Economic Community hastened these developments. By the 1980s more than three-quarters of Canadian trade was with the United States. This was at once an enormous dependence and, given that the U.S.A. was the world's richest and freest market, a golden opportunity.

The integration was so complete by the early 1980s that a serious outburst of American protectionism could have been catastrophic for the Canadian economy. During the 1981–82 recession there were signs of a protectionist surge in Congress. Canada now abandoned the fruitless effort (dating back to the Diefenbaker years) to diversify trade away from the United States. In its last years the Trudeau government talked about making sectoral free-trade deals with the Americans, along the lines of the 1965 auto pact. In the early Mulroney years one business organization after another added its voice to the pressure for a comprehensive agreement. The 1985 report of the Trudeau-established Royal Commission on the Economic Union and Development Prospects for Canada, chaired by former finance minister Donald S. Macdonald, was particularly influential in lending non-partisan support to a free-trade initiative. Governments of both western and eastern provinces, long convinced that tariffs had discriminated in favour of central Canada, looked favourably on the idea. Surprisingly, so did Quebec, whose businessmen were experiencing a honeymoon of confidence that their Hydro-based, Frenchified, and publicly subsidized economy, nicknamed "Quebec Inc.," was truly world class.

In Washington the Reagan government was also deeply committed to trade liberalization. The close personal relationship that Mulroney quickly developed with Ronald Reagan surely helped lubricate matters. Soon after his election Mulroney had told the *Wall Street Journal* that "Good relations, super relations with the United States will be the cornerstone of our foreign policy." The famous symbol of the new bond was the gala grand finale of the "Shamrock Summit" in Quebec City in March 1985, when Brian and Mila Mulroney and Ron and Nancy Reagan all linked hands on stage and joined in a chorus of "When Irish Eyes Are Smiling." To the Mulroneyites and many Conservatives the evening signalled a new era of Canadian–American amity. Other Canadians thought it a maudlin reminder of stories about how old Colonel Robert McCormick from Chicago used to pay young Brian $50 to sing to him when he visited his company town at Baie-Comeau in the 1940s. Would free trade mean permanent dependence on Yankee dollars, and perpetual toadying to the mill owner?

Confidential negotiations with and among the provinces to reopen the constitution in a "Quebec round" went ahead fairly smoothly, though many of the veteran constitutional warriors doubted the likelihood of success. By the spring of 1987 the talks seemed to have reached an impasse—Quebec was demanding more than the other provinces were willing to give—when Mulroney invited the premiers to a private meeting at the government's Meech Lake retreat. The purpose was "to take stock of the progress already made and consider next steps."

It had become fashionable to talk of the Prime Minister and the premiers as Canada's "first ministers." On April 30, 1987, the eleven elected politicians, all male, negotiated for nine and one-half hours and emerged to announce that they had wrought a miracle. They had agreed to a package of constitutional amendments that would end Quebec's isolation and bring the province back into the Canadian family. It was the first time a unanimous consensus on major constitutional issues had been reached in Canada's modern history. There was jubilation, applause, hugging, laughter, tears, and euphoria among the politicians and the members of the constitutional "community." Mulroney, the master negotiator, had done what Trudeau could not. He had brought everyone together. Mulroney declared the rebirth of a nation. He and the other first ministers would go down in history as the fathers of a new Confederation.

The terms of the Meech Lake Accord, which included recognition of Quebec as a distinct society and various limitations on Ottawa's power to control the federation, had to be translated into constitutional language that could be put before legislatures for ratification. At this stage, arguably the last chance to make changes to the deal, only the Quebec government bothered to hold public hearings. The national Liberal and New Democratic parties decided not to oppose·an agreement they assumed was wildly popular in Quebec.

A few scattered intellectuals and commentators began critically dissecting the terms of Meech Lake. On May 27 Pierre Trudeau came out of retirement to deliver a slashing attack on the accord as a "complete bungle" executed in "political stupidity" by provincialist politicians who had lost their nerve, and a "wimp" of a prime minister. "Those Canadians who fought for a single Canada, bilingual and multicultural, can say goodbye to their dream," Trudeau wrote. The Meech Lake Accord would render the Canadian state "totally impotent ... to be governed eventually by eunuchs."

In one of the most damning commentaries on the making of the Meech Lake Accord, an insider, Patrick Monahan, has argued that the deal was collapsing under its own weight (Quebec already wanted more; Manitoba and Ontario suspected they had gone too far) and would probably have fallen apart had not Trudeau challenged the competence and character of the first ministers. They all met at the Langevin Block in Ottawa on June 2 to firm up their agreement. Mulroney led an initial chorus of anti-Trudeau outcries ("He still thinks he is governing this country" from Mulroney; "I won't be called a snivelling eunuch" from the Premier of Nova Scotia), and then they settled down to prove the old man wrong.

Following classic industrial-relations tactics, Mulroney kept the premiers bargaining for nineteen hours. The Prime Minister of Canada acted as the honest broker among the premiers. Ottawa appeared to have no position of its own to advance, except the desirability of cutting a deal. At times during the night Mulroney was told by the premiers of Manitoba and Ontario, "We're fighting your battle" ... "You should speak up" ... "Surely this concerns *you*, Prime Minister. You are the Prime Minister."

Finally the last holdout, exhausted Ontario premier David Peterson, gave in out of fear of having to take the blame for the deal's collapse. Without consulting anyone other than their elite circle of advisers, the eleven first ministers announced they had finalized the Meech Lake Accord.

The Langevin meeting was a classic demonstration that even ageing and intelligent males, who should know better, sometimes play macho power games. It was more important at Langevin to prove Pierre Trudeau wrong than to take deliberate, considered decisions. To be tough boys who could stay up all night brokering the future of a great nation and exorcising the ghost of the man who scorned their ignorance and cowardice. All of them, by their own lights, speaking for Canada. All guaranteeing to use their power as first ministers to ram the accord through their legislatures. If ordinary Canadians didn't like it, tough on them. The premiers knew better. It was not so much nation-building as the politics of bruised male egos.

*   *   *

Seeking political advantage in Quebec, the opposition parties did not seriously criticize Meech Lake. They chose instead to make the free-trade agreement, which had been held up in the Senate, the central issue of the November 21, 1988, general election. John Turner and the Liberals hoped they could restage the 1911 election, with the party labels reversed, of course, and defeat free trade on a nationalist campaign.

They also hoped to take advantage of the public's growing belief that Brian Mulroney's Ottawa was a moral sewer. Throughout his first term Mulroney was dogged by a series of minor scandals leading to the resignation or dismissal of Cabinet ministers. Several of his personal friends were exposed as sleazy lobbyists, incompetents in high places, or both. Most damagingly, the Prime Minister himself lost the moral high ground, as Pearson and Trudeau never had.

As Canadians watched the public prime minister on television, they noted how sharply his rhetoric on issues like patronage and political morality seemed to clash with the appointments he had made and the behaviour of his ministers. Many of them concluded that Mulroney had been too smooth to be sincere, and that criticisms of him as another pork-barreller in the old-fashioned Union Nationale mode were essentially sound. Immense personal damage was done to the Mulroney image by Ottawa journalists who wrote about the sumptuous refurnishing of 24 Sussex Drive, including the closets full of Gucci shoes and other fine garb. Brian and Mila were no ascetics. Somebody—ostensibly the Conservative Party, but indirectly the Government of Canada—seemed to be footing some big bills to support their lavish lifestyle. How could a man who revelled in gobbling up the perks of the good life push the other pigs away from the trough?

The 1988 election campaign became largely a debate about free trade. It was splendid national discussion of a vital issue, and compared brilliantly with the moronic presidential campaign the Americans had just held. But concentration on free trade meant that other questions about the government's record faded into the background. On free trade the government was vulnerable to vulgar nationalist appeals—that Mulroney had sold out the country, that free trade would introduce U.S.-style gun dealing and health care, that Canada would eventually be gobbled up. On the other hand, it received all-out business support stemming from a view that Canada would crumble if the deal did not go through. The Conservatives benefitted from lavish financing and a final all-out advertising blitz by the interested business groups.

Mulroney led the Conservatives to a second straight majority, taking 170 of 295 seats and forty-three per cent of the popular vote. It could not be said that the victory was a personal triumph, for his own popularity trailed his party's and the business efforts had been important. But what other Tory prime minister had done so well since the days of Sir John A.?

The Canada–U.S. Free Trade Agreement was ratified by the new Parliament and came into effect on January 1, 1989. Tariff and non-tariff barriers would be reduced gradually over a ten-year period. The onset of free trade coincided almost exactly with the beginnings of a serious recession followed by years of halting, uneven growth. Canadians had not cheered at the advent of the formal age of economic continentalism—fifty-seven per cent had voted in 1988 for parties that opposed free trade—and resistance to free trade dogged the government throughout its second term. The notion that the Conservatives were agents for the complete Americanization of Canada was almost impossible to dislodge, not least because of the widespread belief that the Prime Minister was a man who, as Lawrence Martin put it, "had 'American huckster' written all over him."

In his exhaustive 1991 study of Mulroney's rise to power, John Sawatsky argued that the Prime Minister had a deep personal longing for approval, a rather desperate need to be loved. Public signs of that need seemed occasionally apparent in the first term, but dwindled as both the government and the Prime Minister rationalized their unpopularity as a sign of having made hard choices for the country. Free trade was one tough decision, and the follow-up negotiation of a North American Free Trade Agreement, to bring in Mexico, was another (which Canada would have preferred to avoid, but had to go along with for fear of being left out in the cold as a common market of the Americas evolved).

Further obviously unpopular acts, especially the 1991 introduction of a seven per cent national value-added tax on all goods and services (the GST), made the Mulroney government appear positively masochistic. In fact it had little room to manoeuvre. In 1987 it had courted popularity by matching an American reduction in income tax rates, cleverly promising to make up the revenue shortfall with a new tax to be introduced later, i.e., after the next election. By the time "later" came around, Canadians had forgotten the earlier tax cuts, partly because the provinces had raised their income taxes to capture the savings.

Many tax experts thought the GST was a sensible, long overdue replacement of the old manufacturers' sales tax. Boxed in by the unshrinking deficit, the government could not have forgone the revenues it provided. None of these thoughts consoled ordinary citizens who suddenly had to pay the national government an extra seven per cent virtually every time they spent money. Perhaps there was some comfort in the thought that history might offer long-term approval of these tariff and tax policies. Whatever the Opposition said about them, free trade and some form of a GST were irreversible. Brian Mulroney would be known as the father of both.

He expected to be especially honoured by history as the father of the Meech Lake constitutional settlement. The deal had to be ratified by Parliament and all the provinces within a three-year period, by June 1990. Opposition, however, gradually mounted. Elections in New Brunswick and Manitoba installed new governments with little enthusiasm for the accord. Many Canadians' tolerance for generous gestures to Quebec evaporated in December 1988, when the Bourassa government went ahead with a ban on English-language outdoor signs and used the "notwithstanding clause" in the constitution to neuter the Supreme Court and the charter. No other province would have considered for a moment making the use of one of the country's official languages strictly illegal. Meanwhile, Trudeau and his supporters continued sporadic media commando raids against Meech Lake.

The critics worried that Meech's recognition of Quebec as a "distinct society" would give the province a special status that would make the Canadian federation unworkable. Mulroney had persuaded the premiers to accept Quebec's other demands, such as a veto for future constitutional amendments, by conceding the same to them. Thus tiny Prince Edward Island, population 130,000, would have a veto on the constitutional future of twenty-seven million Canadians. Senators and Supreme Court justices were to be chosen from lists provided by the provinces. The federal spending power would be so constrained as to make new national social programs a utopian impracticability. The distinct-society clause would probably also give Quebec special additional ways of overriding the charter.

The defenders (outside of Quebec) argued that Quebec's gains were symbolic and unimportant. They thought a moderate loosening of the federation was merely a recognition of the regional basis of the country, for in their view Canada was indeed a "community of communities." Not much would really change in the way the country was governed— the existing division of powers, for example, was largely untouched. Above all, defenders claimed that Meech Lake was a small price to pay for getting the Quebec government back in Canada, back on board, back in the family. With Meech Lake the great "wrong," the great "injustice," the great "exclusion" of 1981–82, was to be erased. Finally, it was said there was no choice but to press ahead. The first ministers had committed their governments, the die was cast, Meech could not be changed. Turn down Quebec now, the supporters said, wielding a blunt instrument, and the resentment might be uncontrollable.

The Meech Lake debate highlighted a major defect in the working of Canadian parliamentary democracy. Without any input from the people, without any mechanism for registering popular assent or dissent, a tiny political elite—eleven men and a gaggle of advisers—had sat down behind closed doors and agreed to fundamental changes in the structure of the country. The first ministers had literally conspired not to let any feedback from Canadians change their minds. To many citizens opposed to Meech Lake the process was an outrageous abuse of power, but it was entirely legal and consistent with tradition. Power resided at the top. The people elected politicians to make big, sometimes hard, sometimes unpopular decisions. The people did not make the decisions themselves.

If they were unhappy they could bring in a new set of decision-makers at the next election.

The unabashed elitism of this argument—straight from the speeches of the eighteenth-century political philosopher Edmund Burke—was particularly galling to groups unrepresented in the elite that had made Meech Lake. Meech was a deal to enhance the powers of Quebec, of governments generally, and of politicians, civil servants, and certain constitutional experts individually. Large numbers of Canadians who felt their control of government and their own lives had been enhanced by the Charter of Rights and Freedoms worried that they would slip back if the package went through. Politicians were using their control of the strategic heights of the amending process to take power back from the people. Trudeau had given rights; Mulroney and the first ministers were trying to take them back again.

Some of the premiers who had been at Meech Lake soon realized that they had badly misjudged the temper of the time. Instead of uniting Canadians, they were seriously dividing the country, for they had ripped open the national wounds that had been slowly healing since 1982. But the conspirators remained true to their word to carry on regardless.

In the spring of 1989 a powerful new opponent appeared when Newfoundland's Brian Peckford was defeated by Liberal leader Clyde Wells. By early 1990 it was evident that a kind of showdown was nearing, as the deadline of June 23 approached and neither Manitoba nor Newfoundland appeared likely to ratify the accord. Meech's supporters began to apply pressures on the dissidents by turning their hints into threats. The fate of Canada was now said to be at stake. If Meech failed to go through, its supporters stated, the country would fall apart.

The crisis of the Meech Lake Accord became a fundamental test of prime-ministerial leadership, comparable to the conscription issue in the two world wars or the FLQ crisis of October 1970. How could Ottawa finesse its way to a happy resolution? By amending Meech? By converting its opponents? By calmly admitting and accepting failure? By rigidly staying the course?

Mulroney's exact strategy that spring is still unclear. His government seemed to waver, in appointing a special parliamentary committee that recommended some major changes in the accord. Before Ottawa could react formally to those suggestions, Lucien Bouchard, the Prime Minister's old friend and soul-mate, author of the Sept-Îles speech, former patronage appointee and now Secretary of State, resigned from the Cabinet to lobby for both Meech and separatism. Robert Bourassa was also adamant that Meech Lake must not be changed. Mulroney accepted that view. He would have to batter down the accord's opponents in a final negotiating session.

The Prime Minister treated the future of Canada as though it were another problem in industrial relations. In their friendly 1984 biography, *Brian Mulroney: The Boy from Baie-Comeau*, Rae Murphy, Robert Chodos, and Nick Auf der Maur had exactly anticipated the approach he would use in a crisis. "Mulroney's pragmatism and position as a negotiator are often expressed in gambling metaphors," they wrote. "He talks about 'not tipping your hand' or of 'keeping your high cards.'"

"I know how to bargain ... ," Mulroney told them in 1984. "The key to bargaining is that you never give anything away until you sit down at the table.... You create a climate of confidence beforehand ... and then you sit down and play poker.... "

Mulroney invited the premiers to dinner on June 3, 1990, and he kept them at the table. For seven days the eleven men argued, laughed, cried, cursed, and pushed themselves to the brink of nervous collapse behind closed doors, emerging each evening to deliver self-serving statements on the national news to supplement their aides' attempts to manipulate the media in "off-the-record" briefings. The Canadian people were passive spectators at an ultimate display of politics at the top, summitry Canadian style, "elite accommodation" in action. Many found the spectacle nauseating.

At the end of it, the final holdout, Clyde Wells, a nearly broken man, had agreed to put Meech Lake before his legislature. Believing he had succeeded brilliantly, Mulroney gave an interview to the *Globe and Mail* in which he defended his methods on the basis of what he knew about constitution-making in the nineteenth century.

> In Charlottetown the boys arrived on a ship, spent a long time in places other than the library, eh? And then they moved this travelling circus on to Quebec where, even when I was a law student, rumours abounded about how scholarly the contributions were to the great federal debates. And there's lots of evidence that the boys had been doing pretty well.

This was a pathetically one-dimensional view of Confederation. Unable to contain himself, Mulroney went on to explain his apparently successful reconfederation tactics as an exercise in constitutional brinkmanship. It had all gone according to the strategy he had disclosed to his advisers, he said:

> I told them a month ago when we were going to start meeting. It's like an election campaign, you've got to count backwards. You've got to pick your date and work backwards from it.
>   And I said, "That's the day I'm going to roll all the dice."

Within a few days of this interview Mulroney realized that he had mis-played his hand. The Manitoba legislature could not consider Meech Lake before the deadline without unanimous consent from the members to change its rules. One member, a Cree named Elijah Harper, refused his consent. The native people of Canada, like so many other Canadians, had been left out of this "Quebec round," and one of their spokesmen put an end to it. A few hours later Meech Lake died in absurd farce as Senator Lowell Murray tried to pin the blame on Clyde Wells, who was not going to wound Canada further by having Meech defeated in New-foundland. Canadians' main memory of the sordid constitutional squab-bles of June 1990 would be of a prime minister who had taken a riverboat gambler's approach to the future of Canada, rolling the dice and losing.

*   *   *

The country did not collapse after the failure of the Meech Lake Accord. But the government of Quebec started a new clock ticking by announc-ing that it would hold a referendum on the future in the autumn of 1992 unless it received an acceptable constitutional offer from Ottawa. Mulroney, whose personal credibility was in tatters, persuaded Joe Clark to come in from External Affairs and take responsibility for what came to be called the "Canada Round" of negotiations. There were multiple ironies in Clark's being given the job of putting Humpty-Dumpty together again.

Everyone agreed that this time there would be massive consultations with the public before the first ministers made their deal. Ottawa set the ball rolling by appointing a Citizens' Forum on Canada's Future. Its report indicated immense public alienation from the political elites. Apparently believing that the public had purged itself by letting off steam, the elites went on with their business.* Constitutional bargaining went forward, sometimes publicly, often privately, in an atmosphere thoroughly fouled, not least by a sense of *déjà vu*.

With Quebec's deadline fast approaching, the first ministers met behind closed doors in Charlottetown in August 1992. Without ever holding a public session, they hammered out an elaborate Charlottetown Accord, the son of Meech. The hope was to satisfy Quebec (still a "distinct society"); keep the premiers happy by not asking them to give up anything for the sake of Canadian unity (such as the elaborate non-tariff barriers the provinces had erected over the years); and buy support from westerners with a scheme of Senate reform, and from native people by constitutionalizing a right of aboriginal self-government. Many of Charlottetown's provisions were vague and incomplete, requiring further negotiation.

Soon the politicians had to acknowledge that a quiet constitutional revolution had already taken place in the country. Three provinces had committed themselves to holding referenda before ratifying any new deal. The other first ministers dared not try to proceed without popular consent. It was decided that the Charlottetown Accord would be put to the Canadian people in a referendum on October 26, 1992. In a five-year period, thanks to the first ministers' bungling, real constitutional power had moved from them to the people. The initial polls showed that Canadians overwhelmingly favoured the accord.

The referendum campaign was hugely one-sided. The nation's political and business elites closed ranks, spent millions, and threatened disaster if Charlottetown did not go through. The Prime Minister, who had never regained credibility or popularity, resorted initially to the old Tory tactic of trying to brand opponents as disloyal, arguing that only "the enemies of Canada" would oppose Charlottetown (the germ of truth, of course, was that Quebec's separatists strongly opposed it). Possibly the silliest comment was made by Joe Clark, in suggesting that Canada could

---

* The quickest way to restore a sense of the moral legitimacy of the federal government would have been for the Prime Minister to resign. While Canadian politicians loudly fretted about the nation being in peril during the constitutional wars, none ever offered to sacrifice more than his liver or his sleep in the national interest.

see civil strife similar to the ravages of Beirut, Lebanon. The most seasoned manipulators in Canadian politics—a "Dream Team" of backroom hucksters—collaborated on a massive advertising campaign to sell Charlottetown and obtain a national "Yes."

Pierre Trudeau, a one-man elite, slammed Charlottetown as "a mess that deserves a big NO" in an instantly famous speech to friends at the Maison Egg Roll in Montreal. His intervention had a noticeable impact, reinforcing English-speaking Canada's growing dislike of the Charlottetown deal as another decentralizing, Quebec-oriented leap in the dark. In Quebec the accord was sliced to pieces by federalists who felt it went too far and nationalists who thought it inadequate tokenism. On October 26 the Charlottetown Accord was rejected nationally by a vote of 54.4 per cent to 44.6 per cent. To carry, it would also have had to be approved in every province; it was defeated in Nova Scotia, Quebec, Manitoba, Saskatchewan, Alberta, British Columbia and among the native peoples. The country did not collapse.

*   *   *

The failure of constitutional engineering in the Mulroney years ended a weak prime minister's attempts to appease nationalist sentiment in Quebec and constitutionalize a sense of Canada as a league of provinces. It also destroyed the belief that in constitutional matters it was possible for informed elites to remake a country. First ministers' deal-making would no longer sell in the political marketplace, no matter how hard the salesmen pushed the product. Meech and Charlottetown had been constitutional analogues of the National Energy Program—attempts to change Canada from the top down that had foundered on the complex shoals of the real world. In both cases politicians and bureaucrats and intellectuals learned rough lessons about the limitations of their wisdom and power, while the public paid the bills.

Would a more astute or a more popular prime minister have made a difference? Mulroney's primary mistake was to have reopened Pandora's box in 1987, setting off a chain of events he and his friends could not control. There was no real consensus in Canada to change the constitution between 1987 and 1992. Mulroney failed to realize this, partly because he had acquiesced in a provincialist, government-centred view of Canada that failed to take into account both the new sense of popular sovereignty and the underlying nationalism of most Canadians. As well, he had not understood the complexities of constitution-making after the Trudeau revolution had created a sacrosanct charter and a cumbersome amending formula.

Without realizing the obstacles in his way, the Prime Minister had thrown caution to the winds to try to turn nationalist Quebec into a Tory fiefdom. Or, to be positive, he had determined to wrench the Progressive Conservative Party out of its old identification with one of Canada's charter ethnic groups, the British—only to make it a prisoner of the other ethnic group, the French.* Mulroney's naive constitutional activism distinguished him from most of his predecessors, including the other specialist in negotiations, Mackenzie King. It is impossible to believe that the canny King, who so well understood that prevention of mistakes was in itself a great accomplishment, would have pressed ahead at Meech Lake or the Langevin Block. King was too smart and too psychologically well-adjusted to have felt any need to prove himself a better man than Trudeau.

*   *   *

There was no sense of triumph or purpose, or even energy, in the final months of the Mulroney prime-ministership. The boom years were over and the opportunities to reform public finances had been squandered. Ministers now had to wrestle with persistent recession and immovable deficits. The sense of bankruptcy in high places, economic, intellectual, and often moral, was palpable. The government's important legislative achievements—pressing ahead with NAFTA, finally bringing an end to universality in most social programs, continuing to privatize and deregulate business—commanded support only from pockets of thoughtful conservatives. Much outsiders' speculation about the contest to succeed Mulroney centred on calculations of who could most quickly cleanse the party of his tarnished image.

To the very end the Conservative caucus remained publicly united and loyal. One of the Prime Minister's most remarkable achievements had been as a leader of his parliamentary band. Behind the closed doors of

---

* In 1991 the Progressive Conservative Party of Canada officially recognized a right of self-determination for Quebec, for which there is no basis whatever in Canadian constitutional law or practice.

caucus, he was said to be masterful at rousing the troops for battle, explaining himself, reminding the MPs of how and why they had had such wonderful success under his leadership. In the Mulroney years the Progressive Conservative Party of Canada had been more united and purposeful and flush with money and the other fruits of power than at any time since Macdonald's day. Whatever its short-term ailments, whatever the polls said, Mulroney thought he was leaving the party in good health.

The Prime Minister had many more friends abroad than inside Canada. His policy of harmonious relations with the United States had been consistent and effective, in part because of what Lawrence Martin calls Mulroney's "pals diplomacy" with presidents Reagan and Bush. Canada finally joined the Organization of American States, was a dutiful soldier in the Gulf War against Iraq, seldom criticized other American interventions, and in certain cases, such as Mulroney's desire to intervene in Haiti, outhawked even the Yankees.

The Trudeau government had persuaded the great powers to grant Canada membership in the Group of Seven industrialized nations. Brian Mulroney made a point of making friends and being a good listener and helpful fixer at international meetings. The government tried to avoid being a U.S. satellite by working to strengthen the United Nations. Support for U.N. peacekeeping operations became the bedrock of Canadian foreign policy, not least because of the impact that the blue-beret tradition seemed to have in supporting domestic unity.

Canadians were always at the meetings and in the photographs, but otherwise did little to influence evolving events on the world stage. The collapse of Communism in the late 1980s was one of the great events in the history of the world. A vast empire crumbled to pieces virtually overnight; tens of millions of oppressed people won their freedom. The Americans had done a great deal to bring about that liberation. The Canadians were surprised bystanders.

Mulroney never had Trudeau's international "star" status or flamboyance. Possibly he was more respected on the world conference circuit for his lack of pushiness. In 1992 he apparently seriously considered becoming a candidate for the secretary-generalship of the United Nations. As an outgoing prime minister in the spring of 1993 he enjoyed a farewell tour of world capitals, saying goodbye to other heads of state. There were no farewell appearances to say goodbye to the Canadian people, only a fiasco about selling the Mulroneys' used furniture to the government.

* * *

Mulroney's parting message to the new American president, Bill Clinton, was to "wear unpopularity as a badge of honour." It was odd advice to give to any politician aiming at re-election, virtually a recipe for political suicide. The comment made sense only as a rationalization by the most unpopular Canadian prime minister since R.B. Bennett. The leader was to take comfort in having aimed in the right directions, even if the people were too stupid or stubborn to follow. Elites knew best, and history would vindicate them.

History will more likely ask why they did not do a better job of persuading people to follow their lead. Soldiers will follow an unpopular officer into battle, so long as they respect him. Pierre Trudeau was the most effective political warrior in Canada during the Mulroney years, not because he was loved or popular, but because he was respected. "This time that son-of-a-bitch is right," people said of Trudeau during the constitutional battles. Brian Mulroney knew how to lead elites—how to get premiers on his side, business groups in his pocket, and unity in his caucus—but when he urged Canadians to go over the top with him, they shot him in the back.

His image problem had more than "roll-of-the-dice" dimensions, more than the rap against "Lyin' Brian" and "Imelda" and all their shoes. With the free-trade agreement, deregulation, privatization, and other aspects of its commitment to a market economy, the Mulroney government was eroding some of the more visible institutional differences between Canada and the United States. CPR/Via Rail nationalism was running on empty. Canada would no longer be defined as a country whose economy was nurtured and protected by Crown corporations, regulatory agencies, and grants from Ottawa. At the same time, many of the qualities that made its parliamentary political system different from that of the United States, especially its elitist, authoritarian traditions, were starting to be seen as drawbacks rather than assets. Certainly the monarchy had become an absurd anachronism, and Great Britain, the motherland, was for most Canadians just another foreign country, and a weak one at that.

Forty years' effort to build a distinctive Canadian culture by subsidizing writers, dancers, filmmakers, and the CBC had not had much impact on the masses of Canadians. An official policy of multiculturalism, adopted during the Trudeau years, seemed to be an example of the state working at cross-purposes with itself. There was little sense that Canada possessed an obvious cultural identity to make the border a reality once the economic barriers came down. How could distinctively Canadian values be articulated?

These circumstances created an unprecedented need for the national leadership to be seen to uphold values that Canadians identified as the essence of their country. Brian Mulroney and his friends could not rise to that challenge. The party of John A. Macdonald and John Diefenbaker had failed miserably to articulate a public philosophy of one Canada, opting instead for what many Canadians saw as balkanization and special favours to Quebec.

Despite his stable marriage and loving family, the Prime Minister was unable to stand for personal values in tune with Canadians' aspirations for themselves and their children. Climbing the success ladder to the top of the mountain and then revelling in the good things of life, Palm Beach style, was very much part of the American dream and perhaps the dream of Tory partisans who saw politics as an escalator to power and privilege. It was not a lifestyle with more than a superficial appeal to most ordinarily nationalistic Canadians.

If Canada was to be defined as a quieter, gentler United States, it needed a Laurier, a King, or a Pearson. If it was going to evolve a distinctive system of government in the age of new democracy, it needed a Trudeau. Instead, it was governed by a gladhanding, ambitious throwback to the political world of the nineteenth century—a man who was, in Ron Graham's phrase, one part John A. Macdonald, one part Duddy Kravitz.

He left office exuding a sense of bafflement at the ingratitude of Canadians for having scorned and rejected his honest efforts. He had given his best, but it had been leadership without substance, like trying to make bricks without straw. Canada's best prime ministers, Mackenzie King and Pierre Trudeau, were men who knew who they were. For Mulroney, a better-developed sense of class, akin to a sense of self, tempered by a sense of history, might have given him a better foundation. Nation-building in a democratic age was a job for men and women with more in mind than reaching out to snatch the brass ring.

Epilogue

The Party's Over

After nine years in power as a majority government under Brian Mulroney, the Progressive Conservative Party collapsed in the October 1993 general election. Novice prime minister Kim Campbell led the Conservatives to one of the most total disasters in the history of politics. The party fell from forty-three per cent of the popular vote and 169 seats in the House of Commons in 1988 to sixteen per cent and 2 seats. Heavily indebted and all but leaderless, the party of Macdonald, Cartier, Thompson, Borden, Meighen, Bennett, Diefenbaker, Stanfield, Clark, and Mulroney lay in ruins.

A revived Liberal Party under Jean Chrétien took power with a majority government. Opposition in the House of Commons fell into the hands of Lucien Bouchard's Bloc Québécois and Preston Manning's Reform Party. The 1993 election was a watershed in Canadian political history for several reasons—not least being the near certainty that a semi-bankrupt country whose people still had high expectations would be harder to govern than in the past. A new political and economic age seemed at hand. The Conservative Party was its first casualty, and the national New Democratic Party was also mortally wounded. The future seemed to belong to political parties in tune with the new populism.

The Conservatives had begun losing their hold on conservative Canadians by the middle of the Mulroney government's first term. A 1986 decision to favour Quebec over Manitoba in granting a major defence contract had pushed angry westerners into creating a new party, Reform, under the leadership of Preston Manning, son of a former Social Credit premier of Alberta. The Mannings had long advocated a political realignment along more clearly ideological lines. Their political credo combined free-market small-c conservatism with midwestern, vaguely Diefenbakerish populism, with a dollop of western alienation. Reform grew fitfully, as Conservatives who had become disillusioned by the Mulroney government's spending and sleaziness and obsession with Quebec quietly drifted away from the party. The free-trade issue in 1988 brought many of them scurrying back, but only temporarily.

Mulroney's Quebec supporters never had deep roots in the Progressive Conservative Party. Many were conditional Conservatives, in Ottawa to advance the interests of Quebec, and particularly to rewrite the 1981–82 constitutional settlement. As it became clear that the pay-off for their loyalties, the Meech Lake Accord, was headed for trouble, the most mercurial of the Prime Minister's Quebec protégés, Lucien Bouchard, betrayed his leader by resigning from Cabinet and caucus. Only a handful of Tory MPs followed Bouchard into the wilderness, but with the defeat of Meech and then Charlottetown thousands more Québécois changed their allegiance to the Bloc Québécois.

Having stumbled into the tar-pit of the constitution, the Mulroney government exhausted vital energies thrashing around with Meech and Charlottetown. If the Charlottetown constitutional accord had been accepted in the national referendum, the victory might have pulled the Conservatives out of the slough with momentum towards renewal. The defeat of Charlottetown, engineered in part by *bloquistes* in Quebec and Reformers in the west, left the government exhausted and dispirited. A severe recession and an uncertain recovery added to its woes.

Mulroney had no standing, no credibility in the country. His unpopularity vied with Bennett's or Meighen's in their darkest hours (polling only began in 1942, so dissatisfaction indices were imprecise). Many observers noticed a visceral contempt in the country for the Prime Minister, intense personal hatred of a man most Canadians had never met.

From the top down, Tories avoided accepting responsibility for the constitutional fiasco. The political elite had done the right thing, they argued, but had been undercut by an ignorant, fractious, cranky populace which had been misled by demagogues such as Manning, Bouchard, and Trudeau. Who should face the music for the disaster? If a government's major policies had been rejected by Parliament, it would have had to resign and be reconstituted. When the Mulroney government's major policy was rejected by Canadians, nothing happened. No heads rolled. Politicians and backroom professionals who had committed some of the worst miscalculations in the political history of the country now applied their talents to saving the Conservative Party—with the same result.

The Conservative tradition had not stressed the development of ties to the grassroots. Except in the later Diefenbaker years, the party had always been stronger on money and manipulation and the ideal of the powerful leader than on mass involvement. As Conservatives considered a successor to Mulroney, they relied on polling rather than political instinct to predict "winnability." When early polls suggested that one minister, Kim Campbell, was a possible winner in the country, the "experts" and the fundraisers flocked to her so quickly that more senior, more seasoned veteran ministers, such as Barbara McDougall and Perrin Beatty and Michael Wilson, bowed out of the leadership race before it had started. Only one junior minister from Quebec, Jean Charest, allowed himself to be persuaded to toss his hat in the ring to make a contest.

Kim Campbell, a Vancouver lawyer, a former school trustee and member of the British Columbia legislature, was first elected to parliament in 1988, and was advanced rapidly by Mulroney into senior portfolios. She seemed to be smart, a bit sassy, and bound to garner attention and probably extra support as the first female prime minister. She stumbled repeatedly in the leadership race, however, and it was realized that both her linguistic and her educational attainments had somehow been exaggerated in various biographical profiles. The Conservatives had made a serious error in assuming that the image she projected in pre-race polls could be maintained. The coronation the Tories had expected to attend in June 1993 turned into a desperate struggle between a faltering Campbell and a fast-closing Charest. After hanging on to win by the skin of her teeth, Campbell had only a few weeks to try to establish an image in the country before plunging into a general election.

By the end of the 1993 election campaign, it was evident to even the most partisan Conservatives that Kim Campbell was the inadequate head of a spent organization. She had talked vaguely about a new "politics of inclusion," but when the campaign officially began she had little to offer in the way of either a new political style or concrete policy proposals. She dared not run on the record of the despised Mulroney government, but could not disguise her own past support for the policies she could not defend. She was an inexperienced campaigner who, under pressure, tended to talk quickly and about herself. She was as classless in her mobility as Mulroney had been, with fewer roots in region and family, and neither the charm nor the political smarts. She wore out her welcome in the country very quickly.

Afterwards, Mulroneyites and Campbellites fell instantly to blaming each other. In fact they had all been cut from the same cloth. Most of the Conservative strategists were unchanged from one administration to the other. Some of the threadbare attitudes that led to the party's final rejection by the voters could be traced back to Macdonald's time.

Campbell had wanted to present herself as being in tune with the new populism, for example. But she had also said she was a Burkean Conservative, and she repeatedly proved it in her attitudes towards the voters. From Macdonald's day the dominant Burkean tradition in Canadian politics had emphasized a member of Parliament's prerogative to make decisions on behalf of the electorate. Ordinary Canadians elected representatives who would master the complex business of government, govern, and then present themselves every four or five years for re-election. In the later Mulroney years the Conservatives, including Campbell, had come to believe that their troubles stemmed largely from their courage in taking necessary but unpopular decisions. Let the democracy have its say on specific issues, and it was likely to be wrong. Kim Campbell's response to the rejection of the Charlottetown constitutional accord (which she had stoutly defended as Minister of Justice) had been to tell an audience at an elite American institution how ignorant the Canadian voters had been.

During the leadership campaign Campbell made a striking verbal slip when she referred to those who disagreed with the Conservative Party as "enemies of Canadians." Shades of Macdonald's old loyalty cry. Shades of the old expectation that Canadians would trust their leaders, as the party tried to campaign on image and credibility alone. An election campaign was the "worst possible time" to debate complex issues like social policy, Campbell stated during the election campaign. While it was possible to understand what she was trying to say, this was close to the worst possible misstatement a modern politician could utter. It was evident that she was a new face but not a new figure on the political stage. She had limited political talents. Her gender proved no advantage. The new leader did not appear to have anything new to offer, possibly not even the competence of the despised Mulroney.

To win the support of apathetic, ignorant, or otherwise uncivic-minded voters, political parties in Macdonald's day had sometimes resorted to naked bribery. By the mid-twentieth century the handouts of ready cash had given way to advertising campaigns appealing to irrational fears and instincts. Motivational research aimed to teach the manipulatively minded how to push the right buttons, cultivate the right image, to "sell" any candidate, regardless of merit, to even the apathetic and gullible.

When a massive fear-based television advertising campaign failed to sway voters in the 1992 constitutional referendum, some strategists realized that the electorate was now too well-educated and too cynical to be easily manipulated. But the Conservatives were prepared to try it one more time. First they tried a summer of image-building, parading the Prime Minister at barbecues and barn dances. Then, when the going got rough in the last days of the campaign, they reached to the bottom of their bag of tricks and came up with television commercials that seemed to mock Jean Chrétien's physical deformity (immobile facial muscles from a childhood illness).

Decent-minded Conservative candidates led an instant public protest against ads as improper in their way as bribery had been in the nineteenth century, and just as anachronistic. The commercials were withdrawn. A party with nothing else to offer, all credibility and credit exhausted, slid to electoral oblivion. In all of Canada there were only two ridings, Jean Charest's and one in New Brunswick, whose voters preferred a Progressive Conservative member of Parliament. As Chrétien had wryly predicted, Canada's first female prime minister had held the office only as a summer job.

While the Conservatives were hoist on a petard of their own making (and the national New Democrats drowned in their irrelevant ideology), the other parties had begun to come to terms with the new realities. Reform, which won 52 seats in 1993 and finished second in the national popular vote, proved itself more in touch than the Mulroney/Campbell party with the concerns of conservative Canadians about government debt, moral standards, and political accountability. Preston Manning was too transparently political to be entirely credible as a down-home populist, but he and his followers obviously had listened to people in ways that Conservatives had scorned. Reform defied all the conventional wisdom about political saleability when it talked bluntly about the need for drastic cuts in social programs, including health care. Reform broke all the rules. It attacked the sacred cows, advocated the unpopular policies, promised short-term pain, and went up in voters' esteem.

The born-again Liberal Party knew it would be suicidal to ask voters for a trust that no politician after Trudeau could hope to obtain. So the party based its campaign on a detailed, published platform, the 112-page "red book." The Liberals offered a kind of contract with the people. They offered a few traditional goodies in the form of a limited public-works program, but knew the time called for backing away from tax-and-spend welfare Liberalism. Jean Chrétien presented himself as a statesmanlike prime minister in the making. The days of offering to bribe voters with their own money and frightening them with the power of television appeared to be over. With the death of the old politics, the old Conservative Party passed into history.

*   *   *

Canada's twentieth prime minister, Jean Chrétien, was a veteran politician, a child of the Pearson–Trudeau years whose extensive Cabinet experience began in the 1960s. In the 1990s he had to lead a country far less sure of itself and its destiny than it had been thirty years earlier.

Laurier was wrong. The twentieth century never really belonged to Canada (the Americans won again in the century sweepstakes). But Canadians enjoyed a splendid moral and intellectual heritage from Western European culture, and they owned half the North American continent. Most decades since Confederation had been reasonably kind to Canada. In the golden years after World War II, the future seemed particularly unlimited, as the possibilities of wealth-creation in a fabulously rich northern giant of a land seemed endless. Expo 67, the Montreal World's Fair during Canada's Centennial year, was possibly the happiest, most successful major event in Canadian history.

When the great resource boom of the 1970s petered out in collapsing prices and a ruined National Energy Program, the Government of Canada began living in the past. To maintain the elaborate structure of welfare liberalism, now fully accepted by the Conservatives, it resorted to deficit-financing on a massive scale. The regime of grants, subsidies, and entitlements, in the context of a very high general standard of living, was kept going on borrowed money and borrowed time.

The Mulroney Conservatives promised to face up to reality, but did not. The Trudeau government left office with the annual budget deficit at $34.5 billion; the Mulroney/Campbell government went out at more than $40 billion. The total national debt by 1994 was over $500 billion, increasing by more than $110 million a day. All previous generations of Canadian politicians would have been utterly appalled at the irresponsibility of this magnitude of borrowing in peacetime. Responsible people in the present generation, especially those who thought about the prospects for their children, knew the party must come to an end.

Unless developments in Asia or from some other unforeseen quarter sparked another prolonged resource boom, there was little prospect of Canadian politics in the 1990s falling back into the old patterns. Governments had no more money to spend, and everyone knew it. The social safety net could not be maintained without drastic reforms. The massive networks of subsidies to culture and business and special-interest groups would have to be contracted, perhaps folded up altogether. Hitherto privileged sectors of the economy could no longer be sheltered from technological change and the other pressures of global competition. Austerity was bound to cause an increase in social pain and tension.

The Quebec question promised to supply more tension, not least because most Canadians outside of Quebec thought the matter had been put to rest by the rejection of the Charlottetown Accord. Canadians had voted for the constitutional status quo in 1992. Very few of them had the slightest interest in changing it at the behest of the province whose demands had been at the top of the national agenda for most of the past thirty years. If the ethnic, tribal politics of the Bloc and Parti Québécois resulted in another revival of the separatist option, the rest of Canada would stand aloof and unbending.

Quebec would have to make up its mind to stay in Canada or get out. There would be no more tolerance for further negotiations, further decentralization, or French Canadians' desire to be a fully sovereign people enjoying Canadian pensions and passports. In the matter of English–French relations, the politics of elite accommodation had achieved a final settlement, with important concessions to nascent populism, in the 1981–82 constitutional changes. If Canadians, especially the Québécois, were truly determined to turn their backs on the Trudeau compromise and reopen Pandora's Box, the furies unleashed would be wilder and more savage, and the politics of national dismemberment would be unprecedented and frightening. The self-immolation of a 400-year-old French cultural tradition in North America might be at hand.

*   *   *

Canada has become a far more complex, factious country to govern than even great juggling men like Macdonald or King could have imagined. Habits of deference and acceptance of marginalization have long since faded in a population that is better educated, more individualistic, more assertive than ever. The Trudeau Charter of Rights at once recognized, legitimized, and stimulated this aggressive thrust for the rights and other entitlements of citizenship. Native peoples, women, immigrants, the aged, gays, and other organized interest groups now insist that their voices be heard.

So does everyone else. The era when a comfortable political elite and a chummy media could run the country from Parliament Hill, checking in with the voters every few years to change the seating around, ended in the 1980s. The habit of authority, planted distant generations ago as a British population made monarchy and hierarchy work in the New World, has gone the way of the British connection itself, and been replaced by the maturing spirit of North American democracy. Even in Britain itself, there is mounting interest in constitutionalizing rights and getting rid of the royal anachronisms.

In Canada the dawning of the new democracy, the new populism, calls the parliamentary system itself into question. The Senate has become a more absurd collection of political fossils and barnacles than ever. The House of Commons has tarnished itself with extreme partisanship, suffocating party discipline, and fat, fat lists of pensions and perquisites available to its members. In the 1970s and 1980s lobbyists settled on the institutions of Canadian government like fat geese in a waterfront park, spreading their excrement everywhere.

The 1993 election surely taught the politicians that the old revels have finally ended. When the political elite told us that we had the right to pass judgement at election time, they never dreamed the accounting could be so severe. If the Chrétien government does not find new, more open ways of doing the public's business, if it does not become a reform government, it will surely go the way of the Conservatives. One way or another, reform is going to be in Canadians' future.

Can the stern voices of the new democracy be trusted to make the right decisions? Perhaps as trusted as the whisky-soaked voices of old male elites corroded by the comforts of power and their Burkean belief in their superiority. The ultimate logic of democracy—one person, one vote—is egalitarian. In a real democracy there are not leaders and followers, only citizens. The best leader hurries to help the other citizens make their way in the directions they choose.

From Macdonald to Mulroney, the central Canadian political tradition has been benevolently suspicious of the country's broadening democracy. Only Canada's two greatest prime ministers, Mackenzie King and Pierre Trudeau, began to think through the fact that they had no power except that which derived from the people. In the hands of a few other skilled and sensitive leaders—Macdonald, Laurier, Borden, Pearson—institutions driven by top-down, accommodating leadership have been reasonably responsive. The careers of lesser prime ministers, the Meighens, Bennetts, and Mulroneys, exposed the deep flaws in a system concentrating so much power in a single office. The hope for the twenty-first century is that Canadians will develop new and better ways of governing themselves, and a community of free and equal citizens will bring forth the leaders it needs.

Sources

Like most Canadian historians, I have occasionally consulted the personal papers of Macdonald, Laurier, King, and other prime ministers and politicians. The main collections are in the National Archives in Ottawa. Some of the general impressions and a few specific arguments developed in this book derive from that archival work, just as some of my observations have been shaped in off-the-record interviews with politicians and politics-watchers. For the most part, though, these essays rely on a wealth of secondary literature—the biographies and memoirs generated by Canadian historians, journalists, and politicians.

The golden age of Canadian political biography may have ended some time ago, but even in the lean years we produce a steady stream of important political writing and scholarship. We have a richer national library of political history than we realize. My main debts for this book are to those who have invested many years of their lives in creating the good books about Canadian politics that I have studied and enjoyed—academics such as Donald Creighton, F.H. Underhill, P.B. Waite, Gordon Stewart, S.J.R. Noel, R.M. Dawson, Blair Neatby, Roger Graham, C.P. Stacey, R.C. Brown, J.L. Granatstein, Robert Bothwell, David Bercuson, and John English; political journalists such as Joseph Schull, Peter C. Newman, Knowlton Nash, Richard Gwyn, Jeffrey Simpson, John Sawatsky, Andrew Cohen, and Ron Graham; and all the politicians from Sir Richard Cartwright to Pierre Elliott Trudeau who wrote or commissioned the writing of their memoirs.

Many more sources were consulted than can or should be mentioned here. It was decided to omit footnotes from the final text, but a footnoted earlier version of the manuscript will be deposited in the University of Toronto archives. Specific questions about my sources can be addressed to me at the university.

Here are the good or the important works that have directly influenced the shaping of these chapters. Most of the books are discussed apropos of the chapter for which they first become relevant, but often they contain material used in other chapters. Unless otherwise noted in the following entries the place of publication is Toronto.

GENERAL

There are many textbook histories of Canada, of varying quality (the older ones are better written, the newer ones contain the latest scholarship), and political scientists have produced many introductions to most facets of Canadian politics. But there are no useful general histories of Canadian politics or collective biographies of the prime ministers. The older journalists' anthologies, such as Bruce Hutchison's *Mr. Prime Minister, 1867–1964* (Longmans, 1964), are occasionally insightful, but for the most part thin and dated. The splendid *Dictionary of Canadian Biography* as yet only covers the lives of people who died before 1910, thus excluding most post-Confederation politicians. Most of the essays in Marcel Hamelin, ed., *Les idées politiques des premiers ministres du Canada/ The Political Ideas of the Prime Ministers of Canada* (Les Éditions de l'Université d'Ottawa, 1969) are still worth reading, but the book ends with St. Laurent. Heather Robertson's *More Than a Rose: Prime Ministers, Wives, and Other Women* (Seal, 1991) is gossipy and trivial, fun in places, wildly distorting in others.

Putting political historians to shame, the scholarly journalist Jeffrey Simpson has written the most useful overview of the evolution of a major sector of the Canadian political system, *Spoils of Power: The Politics of Patronage* (Collins, 1988). Simpson has been influenced, as I have too, by a seminal historical work full of insight about the framework of nineteenth-century politics, Gordon T. Stewart's *The Origins of Canadian Politics: A Comparative Approach* (University of British Columbia Press, 1986). Another very suggestive application of political scientists' concepts to the early evolution of the system can be found in S.J.R. Noel, *Patrons, Clients, Brokers: Ontario Society and Politics 1791–1896* (University of Toronto Press, 1990). Quite a bit of useful information is packed into Allan Levine's *Scrum Wars: The Prime Ministers and the Media* (Dundurn, 1993) and into Lawrence Martin's *The Presidents and the Prime Ministers* (Doubleday, 1982). My Creighton lecture, "Privatizing the Mind: The Sundering of Canadian History, the Sundering of Canada," is published in the *Journal of Canadian Studies*, 26, 4, 1991–92, pp. 5–17.

MACDONALD

If you are going to read only one other piece of writing about Canada's first prime minister it should be the twenty-one-page biography of him by J.K. Johnson and P.B. Waite in the *Dictionary of Canadian Biography,* v. XII (University of Toronto Press, 1990). It's a balanced, affectionate portrait that incorporates the scholarly insights of the past forty years. However, if you like reading major works of political biography, Donald Creighton's classic two-volume study, *John A. Macdonald* (Macmillan, 1952, 1955) takes you more deeply and elegantly into Macdonald and his Canada than anything written since. Some modern readers are beginning to find Creighton's prose style a bit contrived and his sympathies sometimes transparent and distorting. There are two good short biographies, Donald Swainson, *John A. Macdonald: The Man and the Politician* (Quarry Press, 2nd ed., 1989), and Peter B. Waite, *Macdonald: His Life and World* (McGraw-Hill Ryerson, 1975). J.K. Johnson's several articles on Macdonald's personal life, most notably "John A. Macdonald, the young non-politician" (Canadian Historical Association, *Historical Papers*, 1971, 138–53), have had a noticeable influence on Macdonald scholars, but, as I suggest, go too far in trying to de-emphasize his commitment to politics.

My essay draws heavily on several collections of Macdonald's correspondence. These include various older volumes, such as Joseph Pope's misnamed *Memoirs of the Right Honourable Sir John Alexander Macdonald* (Ottawa, 2 vols., 1894), and his edition of the

Correspondence of Sir John Macdonald (Oxford University Press, 1921), as well as the more recent collection of family papers edited by J.K. Johnson, *Affectionately Yours: The Letters of Sir John A. Macdonald and His Family* (Macmillan, 1969). As a centennial project, the Public Archives of Canada began a series of publications entitled "The Papers of the Prime Ministers of Canada." Two volumes of *The Letters of Sir John A. Macdonald* were published (Ottawa, Public Archives, 1968–1969) before the money ran out and the series, which would have run to hundreds of volumes, abruptly ended. The other essential Macdonald documents are his contributions to the Confederation movement, which can be sampled in the various editions of *The Confederation Debates*, as well as G.P. Browne, ed., *Documents on the Confederation of British North America* (McClelland & Stewart, 1969). The best of several books on the Confederation era is still P.B. Waite, *The Life and Times of Confederation* (University of Toronto Press, 1962).

Creighton's biography was almost matched in the magisterial *magnum opus* competition by J.M.S. Careless's two-volume treatment of Macdonald's great opponent, *Brown of the Globe* (Macmillan, 1959, 1963), and it, too, remains essential reading. Brown's protégé and Canada's first Liberal prime minister, Alexander Mackenzie, was given adequate biographical treatment by Dale Thomson in *Alexander Mackenzie: Clear Grit* (Macmillan, 1960), and more recently Peter B. Waite has written a definitive, revealing study of "Sir John the Lesser" in *The Man from Halifax: Sir John Thompson, Prime Minister* (University of Toronto Press, 1985).

We know little about the Macdonald–Cartier relationship, partly because Cartier's papers were destroyed, partly during the Pacific Scandal. The only useful biography of him is Brian Young, *George-Étienne Cartier: Montreal Bourgeois* (McGill-Queen's, 1981). The best personal memoir stretching back to the Macdonald years is Maurice Pope, ed., *Public Servant: The Memoirs of Sir Joseph Pope* (Oxford University Press, 1970). A very different and hostile portrait of the old chieftain is to be found in Sir Richard Cartwright's *Reminiscences* (Briggs, 1912).

Macdonald's private life during his prime-ministerial years is best portrayed in Louise Reynolds, *Agnes: The Biography of Lady Macdonald* (Carleton University Press, 1990), and the social history of his and Laurier's time has been brilliantly captured by Sandra Gwyn in *The Private Capital: Ambition and Love in the Age of Macdonald and Laurier* (McClelland & Stewart, 1984).

Scholars have produced a vast profusion of articles about the intellectual roots of Canadian political ideas (the best guide to early Conservative political thought is the writing of the historian S.F. Wise), and to many other aspects of Macdonald's life and times. The most useful to me have been Peter J. Smith's "The Ideological Origins of Canadian Confederation," *Canadian Journal of Political Science*, 20, 1987; Gordon Stewart, "John A. Macdonald's Greatest Triumph" [the Franchise Act of 1885], *Canadian Historical Review*, LXIII, March 1982, 3–33; and Ben Forster *et al.*, "The Franchise, Personators, and Dead Men: An Inquiry into the Voters' Lists and the Election of 1891," *Canadian Historical Review*, 67, 1986. An important study of relations between the political parties and rising business interests in Macdonald's years is Ben Forster's *A Conjunction of Interests: Business, Politics, and Tariffs 1825–1879* (University of Toronto Press, 1986).

LAURIER

There is no history of the Liberal Party of Canada. The best essays on early Canadian Liberalism, and Laurier's place in it, are found in F.H. Underhill, *In Search of Canadian Liberalism* (Macmillan, 1961). The Laurier (and Borden) years are discussed particularly well in Robert Craig Brown and Ramsay Cook, *Canada 1896–1921: A Nation Transformed* (McClelland &

Stewart, 1974). The best insider history of Liberal politics, from Laurier to St. Laurent, is Norman Ward, ed., *A Party Politician: The Memoirs of Chubby Power* (Macmillan, 1966).

The most accessible and in many ways the best Laurier biography, *Laurier: The First Canadian* (Macmillan, 1965), was written more than a quarter of a century ago by Joseph Schull. One year later, Paul D. Stevens finished an important doctoral thesis on Laurier at the University of Toronto, "Laurier and the Liberal Party in Ontario, 1887–1911," and began work on a Laurier biography which has yet to appear. There are useful insights in the thesis. Stevens did for Laurier and Ontario what H. Blair Neatby had earlier done in his widely read doctoral thesis, which was finally published in 1973 as *Laurier and a Liberal Quebec: A Study in Political Management* (Carleton Library). These works eclipsed the two-volume "official" Laurier biography, O.D. Skelton's *Life and Letters of Sir Wilfrid Laurier* (Oxford University Press), originally published in 1921, but Skelton still contains material not available anywhere else in print. His omissions and his tendency to whitewash Laurier provoked John W. Dafoe to write the shortest and possibly the most insightful of all the biographies, *Laurier: A Study in Canadian Politics* (Thomas Allen, 1922). Other accessible biographies include Réal Bélanger, *Wilfrid Laurier: Quand la politique devient passion* (Les Presses de l'Université Laval, 1986), and Richard Clippingdale, *Laurier: His Life and World* (McGraw-Hill Ryerson, 1979).

Several old collections of Laurier's speeches can be consulted. His most intimate correspondence, as sampled in Charles Fisher, ed., *Dearest Emilie: The Love-Letters of Sir Wilfrid Laurier to Madame Emilie Lavergne* (NC Press, 1989), is guarded and unrevealing.

David J. Hall's two-volume biography, *Clifford Sifton* (University of British Columbia Press, 1981, 1985), is the most detailed history of how the Laurier government actually worked, showing the many continuities with the Macdonald era. Various inside views are also found in Paul Stevens and John T. Saywell, eds., *Lord Minto's Canadian Papers* (Champlain Society, 1981, 1983), as well as the memoirs of a disillusioned Liberal insider, Sir John Willison's *Reminiscences, Political and Personal* (McClelland & Stewart, 1919). For the beginnings of Canadian external affairs in the Laurier years, C.P. Stacey's *Canada and the Age of Conflict: A History of Canadian External Policies*, v. I: 1867–1921 (Macmillan, 1977), is authoritative. My views of both Laurier and Borden have also been substantially influenced by studying their governments through the records of a thoughtful business leader of the era; see my book *A Canadian Millionaire: The Life and Business Times of Sir Joseph Flavelle* (Macmillan, 1978).

BORDEN

Sir Robert Borden was the first Canadian prime minister to write real memoirs. *Robert Laird Borden: His Memoirs* (2 vols., Macmillan, 1938) edited by Henry Borden, is usually dismissed as stupefyingly dull, not unlike its author. Carefully studied, however, both the memoirs and their author project layers of insight, irony, and dry wit. Borden's retirement reflections, also edited by Henry Borden, were published many years after his death as *Letters to Limbo by the Right Honourable Sir Robert Laird Borden* (University of Toronto Press, 1971), and these nicely round out the picture of a gentleman and a scholar one would have particularly liked to meet. After many years of neglect, Borden was also very well served in having his life fall into the hands of a fair-minded scholarly biographer, Robert Craig Brown. Along with the memoirs, Brown's two-volume *Robert Laird Borden: A Biography* (Macmillan, 1975, 1980) is the key work shaping my understanding of Borden.

John English wrote a short, useful biography, *Borden: His Life and World* (McGraw-Hill Ryerson, 1977). But English's more important contribution to the history of this period is the published version of his doctoral thesis, *The Decline of Politics: The*

Conservatives and the Party System, 1901–1920 (University of Toronto Press, 1977). English overstates his argument, I think, and then loses track of it, but sparkles all the while. Aspects of Borden are also approached through the biographies of several of the other PMs, my Flavelle biography, and articles written by R.C. Brown while the biography was in progress.

MEIGHEN AND BENNETT

Roger Graham's massive *Arthur Meighen: A Biography* (3 vols., Clarke Irwin, 1960–65) is a remarkable exercise in prolonged special pleading on Meighen's behalf which at the same time strings out the rope that figuratively hangs Meighen. Grattan O'Leary and Eugene Forsey, the other two members of the Meighen fan club, also put the most favourable possible "spin" on his disastrous career in, respectively, *Recollections of People, Press, and Politics* (Macmillan, 1977), and *A Life on the Fringe: The Memoirs of Eugene Forsey* (Oxford University Press, 1990). Meighen speaks for himself, tediously, in *Unrevised and Unrepented: Debating Speeches and Others* (Clarke Irwin, 1949). We also see him, thrashing and floundering, through the eyes of King's biographers and in Peter Oliver's study of a truly successful, smart, and slippery Conservative politician, *Howard Ferguson: Ontario Tory* (University of Toronto Press, 1977).

Poor R.B. Bennett didn't even have the luxury of a few friends who would say nice things about him. When your only "intimate" biography is by Max Aitken (Lord Beaverbrook), whose writings were dedicated to grinding one axe only, you are not going to appear as the heroic personality you imagined yourself to be. Nonetheless, Beaverbrook's *Friends: Sixty Years of Intimate Personal Relations with Richard Bedford Bennett* (Heinemann, 1959) contains important material available nowhere else. Western Canada's leading raconteur and social historian, James H. Gray, has recently filled in a great deal about Bennett's pre-leadership career in *R.B. Bennett: The Calgary Years* (University of Toronto Press, 1991). While Peter B. Waite was preparing a thorough biography of Bennett's prime-ministerial years, he tantalized us with *The Loner: Three Sketches of the Personal Life and Ideas of R.B. Bennett, 1870–1947* (University of Toronto Press, 1992). The sketches are sympathetic without being sycophantic.

There were several slim, earlier biographies of Bennett, none of them either flattering or very good. We now also have a significant history of Bennett's leadership and his government in Larry A. Glassford, *Reaction and Reform: The Politics of the Conservative Party under R.B. Bennett, 1927–1938* (University of Toronto Press, 1992), which is discussed in the text.

The economic problems of Canada in the Great Depression, and Bennett's approach to trying to solve them, are still not particularly well understood in our historical literature. My treatment here is based on a more detailed consideration in my book *Northern Enterprise: Five Centuries of Canadian Business* (McClelland & Stewart, 1987). My overall sense of Meighen's and Bennett's problems as party leaders was strongly reinforced by reading the good doctoral thesis done at the University of Toronto in 1991 by Ann M. Capling, "Political Leadership in Opposition: The Conservative Party of Canada, 1920–1948."

KING

Mackenzie King's diary is now fully open to students of history. The original is in the National Archives of Canada, and the text was published on microfiche by the University of Toronto Press in 1973. Earlier, four volumes of edited excerpts from the diary, covering the years 1939 to 1948, were published as *The Mackenzie King Record* (University of Toronto Press, 1960–1970). J.W. Pickersgill edited the first volume, D.F. Forster the next three.

C.P. Stacey's attempt at an intimate personal biography of King, *A Very Double Life: The Private World of Mackenzie King* (Macmillan, 1976), is discussed and criticized in the text. Two other works that try to probe King's psyche based on his diaries are Joy Esberey's *Knight of the Holy Spirit: A Study of William Lyon Mackenzie King* (University of Toronto Press, 1980), and an as-yet-unpublished manuscript, "Canada's King: An Essay in Political Psychology," by the distinguished political scientist and historian of psychiatry Paul Roazen. I have read King's summary of his views on international relations and much else, *Industry and Humanity* (1919, new ed. University of Toronto Press 1972), but it is a book best read about.

The single best book about Mackenzie King is R.M. Dawson's *William Lyon Mackenzie King: A Political Biography, 1874–1923* (University of Toronto Press, 1958). The first volume published in the official biography of King, it is judicious and surprisingly frank for its time, and demonstrates King's tremendous intellectual promise and web of contacts. The next two volumes in the official series, both by H. Blair Neatby, take the story to 1939 and are also distinguished by rigorous scholarship, sharp insights, and fairmindedness. These three books stand up as models of scholarly biography long after the "weird Willie" industry has had its day.

For the intellectual background of King's spiritualist beliefs, the best Canadian source is Ramsay Cook, "Spiritualism, Science of the Earthly Paradise," *Canadian Historical Review*, LXV, I, March 1984, pp. 4–27. The best insider account of King's personal habits is by a former secretary, F.A. McGregor, *The Fall and Rise of Mackenzie King: 1911–1919* (Macmillan, 1962). As the text indicates, I also made considerable use of H.S. Ferns's memoirs, *Reading from Left to Right: One Man's Political History* (University of Toronto Press, 1983), which largely disavows the mostly useless quickie book *The Age of Mackenzie King: The Rise of the Leader* (Heinemann, 1955) that Ferns wrote with Bernard Ostry. Yet another former secretary, Arnold Heeney, recorded his and his father's recollections of King in *The things that are Caesar's: The Memoirs of a Canadian public servant* (University of Toronto Press, 1972). And journalist Bruce Hutchison wrote from considerable first-hand and off-the-record acquaintance with King in *The Incredible Canadian: A Candid Portrait of Mackenzie King: His works, his times, and his nation* (Longmans, 1952). C.P. Stacey describes his own personal contacts with King as well as the writing of *A Very Double Life* in *A Date with History: Memoirs of a Canadian Historian* (Deneau, n.d.).

The amazingly prolific historian J.L. Granatstein has written a good short biography, *Mackenzie King: His Life and World* (McGraw-Hill, 1977); the standard history of his government's war policies, *Canada's War: The Politics of the Mackenzie King Government* (Oxford University Press, 1975); the standard history of the rise of the great civil servants, *The Ottawa Men: The Civil Service Mandarins, 1935–1957* (Oxford University Press, 1982), and supplementary works too numerous to mention. His comment that King brought prime-ministership near to tactical perfection is contained in his essay in the generally useful collection *Mackenzie King: Widening the Debate* (Macmillan, 1978), edited by John English and J.O. Stubbs. King's early career is described, in somewhat tortured prose, in Paul Craven, *"An Impartial Umpire": Industrial Relations and the Canadian State, 1900–1911* (University of Toronto Press, 1980).

The Liberal Party that King built and St. Laurent presided over has been brilliantly described in one of the best works written by a Canadian political scientist, Reginald Whitaker's *The Governing Party: Organizing and Financing the Liberal Party of Canada, 1930–1958* (University of Toronto Press, 1977). Dale Thomson's *Louis St. Laurent: Canadian* (Macmillan, 1967) is a dull, semi-official biography that reveals little, while J.W. Pickersgill's *My Years with Louis St. Laurent: A Political Memoir* (University of

Toronto Press, 1975) is so clever a piece of partisanship and self-promotion that it can only be labelled "pickersgillian." Aside from the Pearson literature, discussed below, the best biographies of leading King–St. Laurent ministers are *True Patriot: The Life of Brooke Claxton, 1898–1960* (University of Toronto Press, 1993), by David Jay Bercuson, and *C.D. Howe: A Biography* (McClelland & Stewart, 1979), by Robert Bothwell and William Kilbourn. The Chubby Power memoirs, volume one of Paul Martin's memoirs, *A Very Public Life* (Deneau, 1983), and *Jimmy Gardiner: Relentless Liberal* (University of Toronto Press, 1990), by Norman Ward and David Smith, were also useful. Ramsay Cook's *The Politics of John W. Dafoe and the Free Press* (University of Toronto Press, 1963) is a good intellectual biography of another Liberal who relented of his early distrust of WLMK and became a true believer.

The awakening of the "sleeping dogs of provincial power" is described in Robert Bothwell *et al.*, *Canada since 1945: Power, Politics, and Provincialism* (University of Toronto Press, rev. ed. 1989), which is the best political and economic history of the postwar period. T.D. Regehr's *The Beauharnois Scandal: A Story of Canadian Entrepreneurship and Politics* (University of Toronto Press, 1990) is a gem of a monograph on a fascinating subject. The relationship between the government and its journalist friends is authoritatively explored in Patrick H. Brennan, *Reporting the Nation's Business: Press–Government Relations during the Liberal Years, 1935–1957* (University of Toronto Press, 1994).

DIEFENBAKER

John Diefenbaker cashed in on his prominence and struck back at all his opponents in the three volumes of *One Canada: Memoirs of the Right Honourable John G. Diefenbaker* (Macmillan, 1975–77). For the most part heavily ghosted and dull, they are sometimes enlivened by his story-telling and they are laced with his paranoia. Because of defective glue used by his publisher in those years, the books literally do not stand the test of time. The only other available entrée into Diefenbaker's mind is Thad McIlroy, ed., *Personal Letters of a Public Man: The Family Letters of John G. Diefenbaker* (Doubleday, 1985). It reveals little.

At the time of writing there were no biographies of John Diefenbaker, although a major work by political scientist Denis Smith was said to be nearing completion. The most widely consulted book about his prime-ministership may still be Peter C. Newman's first record-breaking bestseller, *Renegade in Power: The Diefenbaker Years* (McClelland & Stewart, 1963). Newman's special distinction was to be the first to break the aura of gentlemanly clubbiness and self-censorship in the Ottawa press gallery and to publish no-holds-barred profiles and insider accounts of life on Parliament Hill. *Renegade* had an enormous impact, not least on its subject, who loathed its author. The passage of thirty years has considerably dulled the book's immediacy and thrown many of its interpretations into question, but *Renegade* is still worth reading for some of its inside stories and clever turns of phrase. A similar book by a lesser-known Ottawa journalist who had better connections with Diefenbaker and his friends, Patrick Nicholson's *Vision and Indecision: Diefenbaker and Pearson* (Longmans, 1968), is still often the best account of the final crisis of the Diefenbaker government. In 1965 philosopher George Grant published a meditation on the collapse of the Diefenbaker government, *Lament for a Nation: The Defeat of Canadian Nationalism* (McClelland & Stewart), which became something of a cult classic of the emerging nationalist movement. It has much more to do with 1960s Red Tory nationalism than with the real world of Diefenbaker and his Canada.

Oral history projects had just come into vogue by the 1970s and Peter Stursberg carried out a good one, interviewing many former ministers and prominent Conservatives and publishing excerpts in *Diefenbaker: Leadership Gained, 1956–62* and *Diefenbaker: Leadership Lost, 1962–1967* (University of Toronto Press, 1975–76). The tension between authoritarian individualism and traditions of loyalty in the Conservative Party generally means that Conservatives write more revealing memoirs than Liberals do, because they dislike one another so heartily. Edwin A. Goodman, *Life of the Party: The Memoirs of Eddie Goodman* (Key Porter, 1988) is easily the best of this genre. Donald Fleming's two-volume autobiography, *So Very Near: The Political Memoirs of the Honourable Donald M. Fleming* (McClelland & Stewart, 1985), easily outclasses all prime-ministerial memoirs in the dullness and pomposity competition, while revealing that this Toronto establishment politician could be nearly as paranoiac and vituperative and egocentric as his Saskatchewan chief. By contrast, there is a suitably jaunty tone to Pierre Sévigny's *This Game of Politics* (McClelland & Stewart, 1965), published before the author was implicated in the Munsinger affair. Mellow amiability and the occasional sharp barb also characterize *Red Tory Blues: A Political Memoir* (University of Toronto Press, 1992), by (Senator) Heath MacQuarrie, which describes personal and party fortunes well into the 1980s. The most elegantly written of the Tory memoirs, almost a classic in the literature, is Dalton Camp's *Gentlemen, players and politicians* (McClelland & Stewart, 1970). It deftly savages Diefenbaker without discussing Camp's campaign to oust him from the leadership. The book is also a fascinating portrait of the rise of admen in postwar politics.

Particularly after the ouster, Diefenbaker loyalists struck back with their own books, mostly studies in the psychopathology of loyalty. Easily the most honest and most revealing of these are the memoirs of the ill-fated Sean O'Sullivan, *Both My Houses: From Politics to Priesthood* (Key Porter, 1986), written with Rod McQueen. Jack Horner's *My Own Brand* (Hurtig, 1980) tells the story of his progression from Diefenbaker loyalist to the Trudeau cabinet, and Erik Nielsen's *The House Is Not a Home* (Macmillan, 1989) is another sad story of a disillusioned Tory. There are also useful snippets in Thomas Van Dusen, *The Chief* (McGraw-Hill, 1968); James Johnston, *The Party's Over* (Longman, 1971); and Robert C. Coates, *The Night of the Knives* (Brunswick Press, 1969).

The best insights into the working of Diefenbaker's mind, and his government, as well as the best study of foreign policy in the Diefenbaker years, is H. Basil Robinson, *Diefenbaker's World: A Populist in Foreign Affairs* (University of Toronto Press, 1989). As well, the noted journalist and anchorman Knowlton Nash has proven himself no mean historian. His *Kennedy & Diefenbaker: The Feud That Helped Topple a Government* (McClelland & Stewart, 1990) is solidly researched as well as enlivened by the author having been there, and his *History on the Run: The Trenchcoat Memoirs of a Foreign Correspondent* (McClelland & Stewart, 1984) is a readable earlier run-through. It was the political scientist George C. Perlin who coined a famous term in *The Tory Syndrome: Leadership Politics in the Progressive Conservative Party* (McGill-Queen's, 1980). Peter Regenstreif offered a pioneering work of psephological analysis in *The Diefenbaker Interlude: Parties and Voting in Canada* (Longmans, 1965), which unwittingly forecast how little that line of research would contribute to our understanding of politics. The best general history of the Diefenbaker and Pearson years is *Canada 1957–1967: The Years of Uncertainty and Confusion* (McClelland & Stewart, 1986), by the ubiquitous J.L. Granatstein.

Finally, there are two revealing portraits of aspects of Diefenbaker's personal life. His early law career is discussed, somewhat anecdotally, in Garrett and Kevin Wilson, *Diefenbaker for the Defence* (Lorimer, 1988). And journalist Simma Holt almost managed to recreate a lost world of romance and spiritual collapse in *The Other Mrs. Diefenbaker: A Biography of Edna May Brower* (Doubleday, 1982).

PEARSON

Lester Pearson also had the help of ghost writers for his three-volume *Mike: The Memoirs of the Right Honourable Lester B. Pearson* (University of Toronto Press, 1972–75), but he liberally salted the first two volumes (the third was posthumous) with his special blend of self-deprecation and disarmingly sharp wit. So while he lost most of his debates in the House to Diefenbaker, he won the battle of the memoirs.

His semi-official biographer, John English, has also set a high standard of grace and excellence in modern prime-ministerial biographies. *Shadow of Heaven: The Life of Lester Pearson, Volume One, 1897–1948* (Lester & Orpen Dennys, 1989) and *The Worldly Years: The Life of Lester Pearson, Volume II, 1949–1972* (Knopf, 1992) have been deservedly praised as the best in the genre since Creighton on Macdonald. Just possibly, then-professor English (he is now a Liberal MP) was not tough-minded enough in forcing himself to wrestle with the ambiguities and extravagances of the Pearson achievement in domestic policy. For a short, serviceable biography, see Robert Bothwell, *Pearson: His Life and World* (McGraw-Hill Ryerson, 1978), and for a special study of Pearson the diplomat, enriched by filial insight, see Geoffrey A.H. Pearson, *Seize the Day: Lester B. Pearson and Crisis Diplomacy* (Carleton University Press, 1993).

Peter Stursberg's two volumes of oral history of the Pearson years, *Lester Pearson and the American Dilemma* and *Lester Pearson and the Dream of Unity* (Doubleday, 1978, 1980), lack the sizzle of the Diefenbaker project. Similarly, Peter C. Newman's *The Distemper of Our Times: Canadian Politics in Transition, 1963–1968* (McClelland & Stewart, 1968), while containing a wealth of detail and insider gossip, is less focused and slashing than *Renegade in Power*.

The indispensable memoir of the early Pearson years is Tom Kent, *A Public Purpose* (McGill-Queen's, 1988). It's heavy going but reveals an immense amount about the mindset of those Liberals who ushered Canada into the age of neo-socialism. It's arguable that Judy LaMarsh's *Memoirs of a Bird in a Gilded Cage* (McClelland & Stewart, 1969) is the best portrait of the Pearson government in action; certainly it's the most passionate and most critical of the Prime Minister. The joke about Paul Martin's *A Very Public Life: Volume II, So Many Worlds* (Deneau, 1985) is that it should have been titled "so many words," though anyone who compares Martin with, say, Donald Fleming will understand why Canada prefers to be governed by egocentric Liberals. Don't bother with J.W. Pickersgill, *The Road Back, by a Liberal in Opposition* (University of Toronto Press, 1986), which must have been written after Pickersgill lost most of his cleverness and good judgement. Unfortunately Mitchell Sharp fully retained his sense of discretion in *Which Reminds Me: A Memoir* (University of Toronto Press, 1993), which is hard not to put down.

The Pearson–Gordon relationship has been described from Gordon's point of view in Denis Smith's hagiographic *Gentle Patriot: A Political Biography of Walter Gordon* (Hurtig, 1973) and Gordon's own *A Political Memoir* (McClelland & Stewart, 1977). But much the best portrait of Gordon and a host of other Liberal insiders is to be found in what may be the single best work of political journalism yet done in Canada, Christina McCall-Newman's *Grits: An Intimate Portrait of the Liberal Party* (Macmillan, 1982). Another intimate and still readable profile of the seamier side of the party is Richard Gwyn's *The Shape of Scandal: A Study of a Government in Crisis* (Clarke Irwin, 1965).

There is a massive literature on the coming of the Quiet Revolution in Quebec and the beginnings of the movement for constitutional change, but Richard Simeon's revealingly titled *Federal–Provincial Diplomacy: The Making of Recent Policy in Canada* (University of Toronto Press, 1972) is still the best starting-point.

TRUDEAU

Both Pierre and Margaret dictated memoirs to ghost writers, and the resulting volumes were widely criticized as trivial. Still, Trudeau is such a private, elusive figure that the self-revelations and justifications in his *Memoirs* (McClelland & Stewart, 1993) may be the best basic reading in beginning to understand him. Paradoxically, he was also the most visual, televisable of all Canadian politicians, so that the television version of the "Memoirs" is a must-see. Then, to introduce oneself to his intellect, the 1968 collection of his essays, *Federalism and the French Canadians* (Macmillan), is a must-read.

While Margaret Trudeau's self-absorbed meanderings, *Beyond Reason* (New York, Paddington Press, 1979) and *Consequences* (McClelland & Stewart, 1982), are trashy and pathetic, she could not help but relate insights and anecdotes only a spouse could experience—and, it should be said, no other Canadian prime-ministerial wife has published a single competing word about her husband.

The Trudeau marriage broke up in the years when Patrick Gossage, who was married to the Liberal cause, saw a lot of Trudeau and wrote it down to good effect in *Close to the Charisma: My Years Between the Press and Pierre Elliott Trudeau* (McClelland & Stewart, 1986). Don Jamieson, who was briefly in the Trudeau Cabinet, wrote down quite a bit in diaries that have been published as *The Political Memoirs of Don Jamieson* (2 vols.; Breakwater, 1989, 1991), but they must be read carefully and critically for the October 1970 crisis because Jamieson was away for much of it. Both Jean Chrétien, in *Straight from the Heart* (Key Porter, 1985, rev. ed., 1994), and Mitchell Sharp in *Which Reminds Me* have described what it was like to serve in Trudeau's Cabinet. Senator Keith Davey's *The Rainmaker: A Passion for Politics* (Stoddart, 1986) is another fine insider's memoir, stretching back to the Pearson years. Trudeau's perpetual, powerful, and loyal Minister of Agriculture, Eugene Whelan, offered a slightly quirky but not uninteresting perspective in *The Man in the Green Stetson* (Irwin, 1986). Trudeau himself and several of his former ministers, apparatchiks, and civil servants attempt, with varying degrees of success, to explain and justify the policies of that era in Thomas S. Axworthy and Pierre Elliott Trudeau, eds., *Towards a Just Society: The Trudeau Years* (Penguin, 1990, rev. ed. 1992).

Christina McCall-Newman's *Grits* is packed with inside material on the early Trudeau years, and then, writing as Christina McCall, she co-authored with Stephen Clarkson the much-lauded *Trudeau and Our Times: Volume 1: The Magnificent Obsession* (McClelland & Stewart, 1990). There were some problems co-ordinating that book with *Grits*, however, and the very detailed story of the battle to change the constitution had already been well told in Robert Sheppard and Michael Valpy's *The National Deal: The Fight for a Canadian Constitution* (Fleet, 1982). Volume 2 of the McCall–Clarkson collaboration is eagerly awaited.

There had been several earlier biographical studies of Trudeau, most of them forgettable quickies. Two of the first wave that still repay reading are Martin Sullivan, *Mandate '68* (Doubleday, 1968), and Donald Peacock, *Journey to Power, The Story of a Canadian Election* (Ryerson, 1968). George Radwanski was given special access to interview Trudeau at length for his semi-authorized profile, *Trudeau* (Macmillan, 1978). Richard Gwyn did not have access to Trudeau, but substituted high intelligence, good contacts, and vast Ottawa experience to good effect in *The Northern Magus: Pierre Trudeau and Canadians* (McClelland & Stewart, 1980). The decline and fall of the Trudeau Liberals in the 1980s, along with the emergence of the Mulroney Conservative regime, is beautifully told in Ron Graham's *One-Eyed Kings: Promise and Illusion in Canadian Politics* (Collins, 1986).

Historians, for the most part, have yet to begin to come to terms with the Trudeau years. The shining exception, a model of scholarship by the prolific veterans J.L. Granatstein and Robert Bothwell, is *Pirouette: Pierre Trudeau and Canadian Foreign Policy* (University of Toronto Press, 1990).

MULRONEY

Neither Mulroney memoirs nor an official biography (Peter C. Newman was the chosen biographer) has as yet appeared. The only "book" by Mulroney is a potted collection of his speeches, *Where I Stand* (McClelland & Stewart, 1983).

There is one massively researched biographical study, John Sawatsky's *Mulroney: The Politics of Ambition* (Macfarlane, Walter & Ross, 1991), which portrays the rise of a man with overwhelming aspirations and an unquenchable ego. Sawatsky did not have Mulroney's co-operation. L. Ian MacDonald did, for a friendly, campaign-style biography in 1984, *Mulroney: The Making of the Prime Minister* (McClelland & Stewart), which nonetheless has some revealing comments. The slightest of the Mulroney biographies, though not without value (the biographers all tend to agree on several facets of his character), is Rae Murphy *et al.*, *Mulroney: The Boy from Baie-Comeau* (Lorimer, 1984).

Jeffrey Simpson's prize-winning *Discipline of Power: The Conservative Interlude and the Liberal Restoration* (Personal Library, 1980) is about the Clark government of 1979. In some ways not relevant at all to the Mulroney years, it is in other ways the most important book written about the Conservative Party in modern times, not least because so many Conservatives read and thought about it. *Contenders: The Tory Quest for Power* (Prentice-Hall, 1983), by Patrick Martin, Allan Gregg, and George Perlin, is a fruitful collaboration that explains much about the party and its choice of Mulroney over Clark. Graham's *One-Eyed Kings* and Norman Snider's *The Changing of the Guard: How the Liberals Fell from Grace and the Tories Rose to Power* (Lester & Orpen Dennys, 1985) cover the change of government.

The one "kiss-and-tell" (unfortunately for him, in more than one sense) memoir by a former Mulroney press secretary is Michel Gratton's *"So, What Are the Boys Saying?": An Inside Look at Brian Mulroney in Power* (McGraw-Hill Ryerson, 1987). Ottawa journalists wrote damaging, scandal-mongering exposés of Mulroneyite extravagances and missteps in Stevie Cameron's *Ottawa Inside Out: Power, prestige & scandal in the nation's capital* (Key Porter, 1989) and Claire Hoy's *Friends in High Places: Politics and Patronage in the Mulroney Government* (Key Porter, 1987). Professional historians attempted an unusual exercise in instant mid-term history in *Sacred Trust? Brian Mulroney and the Conservative Party in Power* (Doubleday, 1986), by David Bercuson, J.L. Granatstein, and W.R. Young.

A team of political scientists headed by Richard Johnston spent large amounts of taxpayers' money, supplied by the Social Sciences and Humanities Research Council, on an ambitious 1988 election study written up in a book whose conclusions range from the trivial to the incomprehensible, *Letting the People Decide: Dynamics of a Canadian Election* (McGill-Queen's, 1992). You learn more about the dynamics of that election from Graham Fraser's *Playing for Keeps: The Making of the Prime Minister, 1988* (McClelland & Stewart, 1989), which was written by a single journalist without cost to the public purse.

We await studies of foreign policy after 1984. Lawrence Martin's *Pledge of Allegiance: The Americanization of Canada in the Mulroney Years* (McClelland & Stewart, 1993) is a readable though strongly nationalist beginning. The free-trade and constitutional struggles generated vast amounts of literature, ranging from sleep-inducing parliamentary studies to incoherent nationalist rants. The one excellent and objective history of the coming of free trade is G. Bruce Doern and Brian W. Tomlin, *Faith & Fear: The Free Trade Story* (Stoddart, 1991). A similarly indispensable work on the Meech Lake Accord is Andrew Cohen's *A Deal Undone: The Making and Breaking of the Meech Lake Accord* (Douglas & McIntyre, 1990). It can be usefully supplemented with Patrick J. Monahan's *Meech Lake: The Inside Story* (University of Toronto Press, 1991), and the progress towards Charlottetown and the constitutional referendum is described, somewhat unevenly, in Susan Delacourt, *United We Fall: The Crisis of Democracy in Canada* (Viking, 1993). The wisest member of the constitutional-comment fraternity, by a considerable measure, is the distinguished political scientist Alan C. Cairns. See, especially, his *Disruptions: Constitutional Struggles, from the Charter to Meech Lake* (McClelland & Stewart, 1991). Pierre Trudeau's various interventions in the debate were also published: *With a Bang, Not a Whimper: Pierre Trudeau Speaks Out* (Stoddart, 1988) and *Trudeau: "A mess that deserves a big NO"* (Robert Davies, 1992). No one thought any of Mulroney's speeches on the constitution were worth publishing.

Kim Campbell was no sooner a candidate for the Conservative leadership than book-length biographies of her began to appear. Like their subject, they proved to be ephemeral.

Index

Manning, Preston, xiv, 186, 307–8, 311
Manufacturers Life Insurance Company, 20
Marchand, Jean, 234, 249, 252
"Maritime Rights", 160
Martin, Lawrence, 295, 304
Martin, Paul (senior), 140, 173, 221, 222, 233–34
Massey, Vincent, 139, 219
Mazankowski, Don, 290
McCall, Christina, 267, 269, 275
McCarthy, Senator Joseph, 196, 201, 239
McCormick, Colonel Robert, 292
McCrae, John, 63
McCully, Jonathan, 16
McDougald, Senator W.L., 156
McDougall, Barbara, 311
McGregor, F.A., 139–40, 142
McKim Advertising, 171, 189
McNaughton, General A.G.L., 149–50
Meech Lake Accord, xiv, xv, xvi, 3, 292–303, 308
Meighen, Arthur, **93–107**; *also:* 89, 108–21 *passim*, 138–45 *passim*; 155, 188, 192, 251, 269, 315; on Macdonald, 120n
Menzies, Merril, 190
Mercier, Honoré, 23, 38
Minto, Earl of, 58
Monahan, Patrick, 293
monarchy, 9, 28, 237; absurd anachronism, 305, 314
Monk, Frederick, 73
Mowat, Sir Oliver, 23, 33, 36, 38, 40
Mulock, Sir William, 53, 55, 68, 130
Mulroney, Brian, **277–306**; *also*, xii, xiii, xvi, 3, 52, 65, 91, 107, 113, 148, 189, 257n, 264n, 307–15 *passim*.
Mulroney, Mila, 292, 295, 305, 306
multiculturalism, 305–6
Munsinger affair, 239
Murphy, Rae, 299
Murray, Lowell, 300

N

Nash, Knowlton, 206n, 209n, 210
National Energy Program (NEP), 269–70, 288, 312
National Policy, 10, 18–20, 22, 35–36, 40, 47–48, 73, 99. *See also:* free trade
native peoples, 26, 252, 255, 301–2, 314

naval debates, 71–76, 110
Neatby, Blair, 124, 127
New Democratic Party (NDP), xi, 200, 225, 260, 293
Newman, Peter C., 230, 241, 250
Nicholson, Patrick, 210
Nixon, Richard, 272
North American Air Defense Agreement (NORAD), 192, 198, 209–10
North American Free Trade Agreement (NAFTA), 296
North Atlantic Treaty Organization (NATO), 197–99
"North Atlantic triangle", 87, 101, 176, 197
Northwest Rebellion, 22. *See also:* Riel
nuclear arms issue, 198–200, 210–11, 225

O

O'Leary, Grattan, 113
O'Sullivan, Sean, 202n, 203, 214
October crisis, 245, 258, 298
Official Languages Act, 1969, 252
Ontario Hydro, 68
Ottawa Imperial Economic Conference, 1932, 114

P

Papineau, Louis-Joseph, 34
Paris Peace Conference, 80, 86
Parti Québécois, 261–64, 281, 288, 313
Patenaude, E.L., 103
patronage, *passim*; attempted abolition, 89
Patteson, Joan, 142–43
Pattullo, Duff, 161, 163
Pearson, Annie, 219
Pearson, Geoffrey, 218n, 221
Pearson, Lester Bowles, **217–43**; *also:* 54, 155n, 166, 175–83, 196–97, 203, 210, 245, 249–57, 274, 315; comp. with WLMK, 129
Pearson, Maryon, 220, 221, 224, 237
Pearson, Rev. Edwin A., 219
"Pearsonalities", 203
Peckford, Brian, 289, 298
Pelletier, Gérard, 234, 249
Pelletier, Louis-Philippe, 76
pensions, old age, 106–7, 111, 159, 256, 289; auctioned for votes, 179, 192, 228